SCARNE
on dice

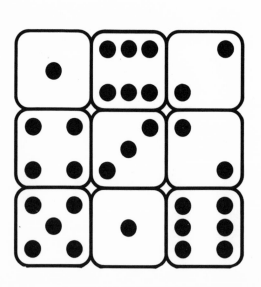

SCARNE
on dice

John Scarne

PHOTOS BY GEORGE KARGER

Stackpole Books

SCARNE ON DICE
Copyright © 1974 by
John Scarne Games, Inc.

Published by
STACKPOLE BOOKS
Cameron and Kelker Streets
Harrisburg, Pa. 17105

© 1945 by John Scarne and Clayton Rawson, published by The Telegraph Press, Harrisburg, Pa.
© 1946, 1949, 1952 and 1957 by John Scarne and Clayton Rawson; published by Military Service Publishing Co., Harrisburg, Pa.
© 1962 by John Scarne and Clayton Rawson; published by The Stackpole Co., Harrisburg, Pa.

A revised and updated edition.

Printed in the U.S.A.

Library of Congress Cataloging in Publication Data

Scarne, John.
    Scarne on dice.

    Includes bibliographical references.
    1. Craps (Game) 2. Dice. I. Title.
GV1303.S4 1974   795'.1   73-22019
ISBN 0-8117-1516-7

Dedicated to my good friend
the late John H. Winn, the
father of Modern Craps.

Other Books by John Scarne

Scarne's Encyclopedia of Games
Scarney Dice—40 New Kinds of Dice Games
The Woman's Guide to Gambling
The Odds Against Me
Scarney—25 New Kinds of Skill Games
Scarne's Complete Guide to Gambling
The Amazing World of John Scarne
Skarney—30 New Card Games
Scarne On Teeko
Scarne On Magic Tricks
Scarne On Card Tricks
Scarne On Cards

———————————————

Games by John Scarne

Scarney Dice®   Skarney Gin®
Scarney 3000®   Scarney Baccarat®
Skarney®

The designs and names are trade-marked and their contents copyrighted;
no part of these games can be reproduced in any form without written
permission from their owner: John Scarne Games, Inc., 4319 Meadowview Avenue, North Bergen, New Jersey 07047.

STACKPOLE BOOKS is the exclusive distributor of all boxed games invented by
John Scarne and copyrighted by John Scarne Games, Inc. These include TEEKO,
SCARNEY, SKARNEY, SKARNEY GIN, SCARNEY DICE, FOLLOW THE
ARROW, and SCARNEY 3000. Requests for information or orders should be
directed to Stackpole Books, Cameron & Kelker Streets, Harrisburg, Pa. 17105.

Contents

John Scarne at the offices of John Scarne Games, Inc., of North Bergen, N.J. with his wife, Steffie, and his son, John Teeko, who is holding a Teeko game, one of the 200-odd games invented by the author.

Foreword

John Scarne has been a very busy man since the first publication of *Scarne On Dice* during World War II. We could write a book about the things he has done since then, except that John Scarne has already written it in his autobiography, not once but twice: *The Amazing World of John Scarne* and *The Odds Against Me*. All we can do here is hit a few of the high spots of his fantastic career.

Scarne On Dice was hailed on its first publication as the definitive work on the subject. Later, the reviewers, gaming experts, mathematicians, gamblers, and the millions of ordinary game enthusiasts said the same thing of *Scarne on Cards, Scarne's Complete Guide to Gambling,* and *Scarne's Encyclopedia of Games*. These four best selling books without a doubt proved Scarne to be the world's foremost gaming authority.

Scarne's books are the only ones that leading makers of professional gaming equipment such as Ewing Manufacturing Company of Las Vegas, Nevada, B.C. Wills & Company, Reno, Nevada, and others list in their catalogs, which, in essence, says that no casino employee or operator should be without any of Scarne's books. Carl Cohen, Executive Casino Director of M.G.M.'s Grand Hotel Casino in Las Vegas, like most other Nevada casino bosses insists that his casino employees read Scarne's books as a post-graduate course in gambling. Famed magazine writer and editor, Sidney Carroll, aptly wrote about John Scarne, "To call Scarne an outstanding expert on games and gambling is to praise him with a faint damn. He is by all odds the world's greatest."

The once universal phrase, "According to Hoyle" has been replaced among millions of game fans throughout the world with the phrase, "According to Scarne." Such a change could only be achieved by a man who has spent a lifetime in constant study and research into every phase of games and gambling.

John Scarne's fame as the world's foremost gaming authority dates from World War II when he was officially appointed as gaming advisor to the United States Armed Forces. During the war he wrote countless gambling articles for *Yank Magazine, The Army Weekly,* and gave hundreds of gambling lecture demonstrations here and abroad before thousands of members of the Armed Forces to teach them how to avoid being cheated by crooked gamblers operating both in and out of the services.

During these lecture gambling demonstrations, John distributed more than one million printed cards to attending servicemen. These cards listed the correct odds on Craps and illustrated a method of cutting a deck of cards called the Scarne Cut. Top Army brass told Scarne that this cut alone saved servicemen millions of dollars during World War II. The Scarne Cut was invented by John Scarne as a defensive weapon for men in the armed forces. It protected servicemen and it will protect you, too, against all private card cheats. Here's how it is accomplished.

1. Pull a block of cards from the center of the pack (deck).
2. Place them on top of the pack and square it up.
3. Pull a block of cards from the bottom of the pack, place them on top.
4. Repeat steps 1, 2 and 3 again, several times if you wish.
5. Finally square up the pack and cut it in the regular manner.

The drawings on page 15 picture the Scarne Cut in action. Use it and you won't need to worry about nearly all bottom deals, stacked decks, false shuffles and false cuts. At the very least, it will give any card cheat enough headaches to cut his cheating down close to the vanishing

1 Pull a block of cards from the center of the pack.

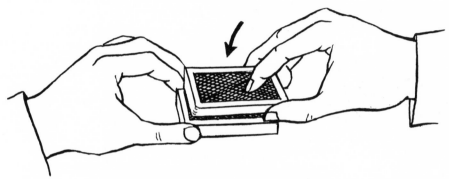

2 Place them on top of the pack and square it up.

3 Pull a block of cards from the bottom of the pack, place them on top.

4 Repeat steps 1, 2 and 3 again, several times if you like.

5 Finally, square up the pack and cut it in the regular manner.

point. It may frighten him out of the game entirely or even into playing honestly.

During the World War II years, John made a series of overseas short-wave broadcast records for the Army's Morale Division Armed Forces Radio Broadcast in which he lectured and answered the gaming questions posed by thousands of letters from servicemen.

At the end of World War II, General Hap Arnold, Commanding General of the U.S. Army Air Forces, said, "John Scarne's one-man crusade against crooked gambling in the Armed Forces during World War II saved servicemen hundreds of millions of dollars a month in potential gambling losses when he practically cleaned up crooked gambling in the Armed Forces single-handed." Five-star Admiral Ernest J. King, then chief of United States naval operations, told John, "You have done a great service both to your country and to the members of the Armed Forces."

Scarne has been called into consultation as an expert on games and gambling by the United States Senate, the Federal Bureau of Investigation, the British Home Office, the Puerto Rican Government, the Government of Panama, the Government of the Netherlands Antilles, the Hilton International hotel chain and numerous other government and hotel agencies throughout the world. He is also game consultant to the Encyclopaedia Britannica and to the World Book Encyclopedia. In addition to the books already mentioned, he has authored hundreds of magazine articles and more than twenty books on magic, games, and gambling. Scarne has appeared on more than 600 national television shows during his lifetime and has made numerous television commercials displaying his magical dexterity. He has appeared as a magician at the White House numerous times for Presidents Franklin D. Roosevelt, Harry S. Truman, and Dwight D. Eisenhower.

How does one get to be the world's foremost authority on games and gambling? The answer is simple: you need to be a magician. It helps even more, of course, if you are also a magician's magician, a reputation John Scarne acquired when he first appeared on the magic scene at the age of seventeen. Nate Leipzig, who was starred for many years in vaudeville as the International King of Cards, saw an exhibition of the young Scarne's skill and said, "He is the most expert exponent of wonderful card effects and table work that I have ever seen in my life." John Northern Hilliard, the author of *Greater Magic*, a classic treatise on conjuring and manager of Thurston the Magician wrote the following when John was only nineteen:

John Scarne as gambling advisor to the United States Armed Forces is seen dealing himself a four aces poker hand at an Army camp demonstration during World War II.

"To those who do not know magic, John Scarne's card effects must seem to be little short of true sorcery. To those who do magic, his card tricks and table effects are equally bewildering. I have seen all kinds and conditions of magicians in all parts of the world, but I have yet to see anyone who surpasses him in originality and sheer skill of hand; his skill is unbelievable."

By the age of twenty-one, Scarne had baffled all of America's top magicians including such immortals as Houdini, Blackstone, and Thurston, as well as the infamous racket bosses of the prohibition era which included Al Capone, Arnold Rothstein, Lucky Luciano, and Dutch Schultz, amazing them all with his fantastic ability with a deck of cards. Fooling magicians and professional gamblers with his fantastic card dexterity today is still Scarne's hobby.

But proficiency in sleight of hand is not the whole answer. Scarne is also a natural mathematical genius, and since all games of chance have a mathematical basis, this helps. Early in his career, not knowing that mathematicians Daniel Bernoulli, Laplace, Gauss, and others had worked out the probability formulas that are used to figure odds and percentages—about a hundred and fifty years earlier—Scarne started from scratch, worked out his own methods and, in effect, redid the work for himself.

Since 1949, Scarne has been retained by the Hilton International hotel chain to oversee their global casino operations. In this capacity he screens prospective casino administrators, helps install new casino operations, selects and buys the proper gaming equipment, helps set up and supervises training programs and croupier schools to teach new employees, and makes frequent inspections of these casinos to insure that both management and patrons continue to get an honest deal.

Making certain that everyone gets an honest deal is John's main business. The casinos hire him for this purpose and he carries on the work in his books, magazine articles, lectures and nation-wide television demonstrations which expose crooked gambling and explain how to detect crooks at work. Law enforcement agencies, gaming operators, players, and gamblers have praised him, and countless cheats have damned him for having done more to combat dishonesty in private and casino gambling than all the other efforts made toward this end combined.

No card or dice cheat anywhere can perform as many different cheating moves as can John Scarne. There's a reason. A skilled card mechanic or bust-out man can make a good living if he is expert at one method of executing a smooth and undetectible second deal or dice switch. That's all he needs to know and all he bothers with. But there are many different methods, and everytime John spots a new one, he isn't satisfied merely to know how it is done. He doesn't sleep until he has practiced it so that he can do the move as well or better than the cheat he caught using it. This comprehensive knowledge enables him to detect cheaters quickly and surely.

John's knowledge of playing strategy equals his skill. In fact, he knows so much that he is barred from playing in casinos in Las Vegas and Reno. He was first barred from playing Black Jack in late 1946 by Benjamin (Bugsy) Siegel, then the owner of the Flamingo Hotel Casino in Las Vegas.

Guesses in games of chance and skill never satisfy Scarne. He is, by far, the foremost authority on odds, percentages, and the mathematical structure of gambling games. He has, time after time, calculated the precise mathematics of many games and gambling problems where other game book authors, professional gamblers, operators, and even top-notch mathematicians have failed.

John Scarne is also on the alert to expose the many so-called sure-fire winning systems that constantly keep popping up in books, magazines and newspapers due to the fact that each year thousands of unsuspecting casino players fall for these so-called sure-fire winning systems. In addition to the purchase price of the book or pamphlet, they lose their hard-earned cash at the casino tables before they realize the system is worthless. Scarne claims it is his duty as the world's foremost gaming authority to expose every one of these ridiculous get-rich-quick casino gambling systems as they appear.

Example: Shortly after the publication of *Scarne's Complete Guide to Gambling*, the book which carried the first mathematical breakdown on Black Jack, more than five hundred books and articles were published on the subject: "How to beat the black jack tables in Las Vegas!" Each author told how he was barred from playing in Las Vegas because his system was sure to beat the house. Several of these book authors, notably mathematicians Edward O. Thorp, author of *Beat the Dealer*, and Allen N. Wilson, author of *The Casino Gambler's Guide*, told their readers in effect that their black jack systems of play permitted even an amateur to beat the Las Vegas black jack tables consistently over the long run. Rubbish! Need we say more?

In 1964, in order to prove Thorp's black jack system was lot of hokum, Scarne challenged him to a $100,000 contest to be staged at the Sands Hotel Casino in Las Vegas. As Scarne expected, Thorp's reply was a big, "No!" Later Scarne issued the same challenge to Allen N. Wilson. Scarne is still waiting for his reply.

Since *Scarne On Dice* was first published, John has invented more than two hundred games, among them the skill board games of Teeko, Scarney and Follow the Arrow, the card games of Skarney, Skarney Gin, Scarney Baccarat, and the dice games of Scarney Craps, Scarney Dice and Scarney 3000. He has his own game company, John Scarne Games Inc., 4319 Meadowview Avenue, North Bergen, New Jersey, 07047, to market them.

Scarney Baccarat is the first really new casino banking game in the past century. It combines the principles of Baccarat, Chemin de Fer, Bank Craps and black jack. This fantastic new banking card game is featured in dozens of casinos the world over and seems destined to become the number one casino banking card game in the near future.

Skarney, based on several entirely new game principles, is the most bizarre, exciting and charmingly exasperating card game in history. It has the bluff as in poker, scores like canasta and is played like no other card game. Skarney Gin is the game that is rapidly displacing regular gin rummy as America's favorite two-handed card game.

Teeko, a two-handed board game which makes use of only four pieces to a side, surpasses checkers as a skill game. It can be played in more than twenty different ways with or without point scoring. Teeko's scope is so great that John wrote a 257-page book, *Scarne On Teeko*, explaining its playing strategy.

Scarne once challenged ten of the nation's top ranking chess, checkers, and bridge masters that he could beat them all at Teeko in simultaneous play, and he offered to pay $1,000 for each game he lost. This match took place on March 14, 1955 at New York's 21 Club and the ten contestants whom John played simultaneously included the U.S. Open Chess Champion, Larry Evans; the World's Checker Champion, Tom Wiswell, and Contract Bridge Master, John Crawford. There were three rounds of play, a total of thirty games. Scarne won all thirty games and did not have to pay a nickel.

John's other great skill board creation is Scarney, which by the way is how "Scarne" is pronounced. It is so simple that a child can learn it in a few minutes and at the same time so complex in its possibilities that its scope surpasses chess. Scarney can be played in many different ways. It is not only a true checkers-style solitaire game, but a true singles game that can be played by two, three, four or more players, each playing for himself. It has an inner world and logic of its own, taxing the capacity of the most skilled gamester. There is almost no chance that you will ever play two games alike because the starting positions alone number nearly 21 trillion; to be precise, exactly 20,-922,789,800,000!

Scarne has also developed an entirely new set of dice called "Scarney Dice." There are more than forty new home, club and casino-style games including Scarney 3000 that can be played with these dice.

We tell you this about these games so you will understand why the famed sports columnist, the last John Lardner, once wrote: "Scarne is to games what Dr. Einstein is to advanced physics."

And now, having updated you on John Scarne, let's go on to *Scarne On Dice*. In this new revised up-to-date edition of *Scarne On*

Scarne watches World's Checker Champion, Tom Wiswell, make a move in Teeko match in which Scarne played ten players simultaneously and won all games. Other players shown are movie stars Judy Holliday, Patti McCormick and former Heavyweight Champion, James J. Braddock.

Dice, you will find considerable dice material that has never appeared in print before, such as all the old and latest secrets of dice cheating explained, the exact house percentages for all the latest up-to-date casino craps layouts including the Las Vegas, Bahamas, New York Craps layout and the Scarney Craps layout which the author especially developed for the Curacao Hilton Hotel Casino in Curacao, Netherlands Antilles and which has since been copied and installed by dozens of casinos in the Carribbean area and elsewhere. Also included are the up-to-date rules for dozens of private dice games and many home, club and banking games which appear here for the first time. In addition you will find the best bets at each and every banking dice game that are sure to save you money. This new revised edition of *Scarne On Dice* is the most all inclusive, comprehensive and authoritative book on dice and dice games ever written. It is a book that only John Scarne could have written.

The Publisher

1

Modern Dice and Their History

Dice have been fascinating people and deciding fates for over 2,000 years. Even the language of dice echoes history. When Caesar made the critical decision to take his victorious army across the Rubicon against the edict of Rome, he took his retort from the lexicon of the dice player: "Tacta alea est." *The die is cast.* However, before we continue with the history of dice, let's discuss today's modern dice.

MODERN DICE

Modern dice are almost all made of a cellulose or other plastic material. The standard die is marked with a number of small dots (called spots) from one to six. The spots are arranged in conventional patterns and placed in conventional relative locations. Thus, the spots on the opposite sides must always total seven, one opposite six, two opposite five, three opposite four. When the visible vertical sides are two and three and the top side is one, then the six must be the bottom-most number and five and four must be on the opposite vertical sides. The combinations of the six spots plus the number of dice in play determine the mathematical probabilities.

In most games played with dice, the dice are thrown (rolled, flipped, shot, tossed or cast) from the hand or from a receptacle called a dice cup, in such a way that they will turn at random. The spots that face skyward when the dice come to rest are the deciding spots. The combination of the topmost surfaces of the dice decides, according to the rules of the game being played, whether the thrower (called the shooter) wins, loses, continues to throw, or loses possession of the dice.

There are two kinds of dice, Perfect dice—known as gambling house or casino dice—which are made by hand and true to a tolerance of 1/5,000 of an inch and commonly used to play Bank Craps, Money Craps, Scarney Craps, and New York Craps; and round cornered or imperfect dice called "drugstore" or "candystore" dice, which are fabricated automatically, have recessed spots and are generally used as implements to play social and board games. Makers of perfect dice advertise their dice as being true to a tolerance of 1/10,000 of an inch. Of the thousands of perfect dice I have examined during my lifetime none have measured to a tolerance of 1/10,000 of an inch. Perfect dice come in flush spot, bird's eye spot and concave spot (see illustration). Modern flush spot and bird's eye spot dice are sawed from extruded rods of cellulose. The spots are drilled into the faces of the die approximately 17/1,000 of an inch. Then all recessions are filled with a paint equal in weight to that of the cellulose drilled out. The dice are then buffed and polished and since no recessions remain, are known as "flush spots" or "bird's eye spot" dice.

CONCAVE SPOT   BIRD'S EYE SPOT   FLUSH SPOT

The three most popular kinds of spot work put on casino or perfect transparent dice.

Concave perfect dice have slightly recessed spots. Most casinos use red flush spot dice which are transparent and come in sets of five. The standard size used in Nevada, the Carribean, and most casinos the world over is .750 of an inch. The dice edges come in various styles, the most popular are as follows: square, feather turned edge, slightly turned edge, and light round edge and corner (see illustration). The most popular dice edges are square and known as razor edge. Casino or gambling house dice usually carry their own special monogram and coded serial number as a means of thwarting dice cheats. Perfect dice

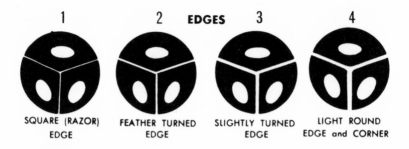

1	2 EDGES	3	4
SQUARE (RAZOR) EDGE	FEATHER TURNED EDGE	SLIGHTLY TURNED EDGE	LIGHT ROUND EDGE and CORNER

used in various other banking dice games range from a .250 inch cellulose or bone "pee wee" die to an extra large size .770 inch. Perfect concave spot dice are rarely seen in topnotch casinos.

Dice in various forms are the oldest gambling instruments known to man, and countless games are and have been played with them. Craps, the most popular gambling house game, is played with two dice. In more social play there are Poker Dice and Scarney 3000, each of which is played with a special set of five dice, and various counter and bar games such as Twenty-Six played with ten standard dice. In Backgammon and hundreds of board games, two or more dice are thrown to determine the moves. With this updating on modern dice, let's consider some interesting history on the use of dice.

Sophocles reported that dice were invented by one Palamedes, a Greek, who taught the game to the G. I. Joes at the siege of Troy three thousand years ago, and Herodotus went to press with a claim that the galloping ivories were invented by the Lydians as a means of diverting themselves from a great famine in the days of King Atys. Both dates are several thousand years shy of the mark. Dice were old before Troy was founded and before the Lydians had a king.

Man's very earliest written records not only mention dice and dice games, but crooked dice as well. Dice of one sort or another have been found in the tombs of ancient Egypt and the Orient and in the prehistoric graves of both North and South America. It is probable that in the long nights when Neanderthal man rested from the day's hunt and the sabre-tooth tiger prowled outside, guttural cries issued from the cave that meant something very similar to "Seven, come eleven!" and "Baby needs new moccasins!"

Primitive tribes all over the globe—the American Indian, the Aztec and Maya, the South Sea islander, the Eskimo, the African— have gambled with dice of many curious shapes and markings—dice made of plum and peach stones, of seeds, of buffalo, caribou and moose bone, of deer horn, pebbles, pottery, walnut shells, of beaver and woodchuck teeth. In later Greek and Roman times although the majority were made of bone and ivory, others were of bronze, agate, rock crystal, onyx, jet, alabaster, marble, amber, porcelain, etc.

DICE AND THE WITCH DOCTOR

Their probable inventor was that same man who first presided at the birth of the sciences of medicine and chemistry—the witch doctor. Dice, before they became gambling implements, were magical devices which primeval man used to divine the future. Not only dice, but most of our other gaming implements have been traced back to man's still earlier practice of divination by arrows.*

All these primitive devices had to do with good and bad luck. When the prehistoric priest or witch-doctor, with many incantations and much mumbo-jumbo, threw the sacred arrows, or the sticks, reeds and straws which were also used, upon the ground, he read the future and foretold what good or bad fortune would attend the tribe. Even today small boys sometimes follow his age-old example when they toss a twig in the air and then follow the direction in which it points in hope that it will lead them to a lost toy.

Marco Polo, who overlooked very little, described a variation of the process.

---

* Notably by Stewart Culin, formerly director of the Brooklyn Museum. See his *Chess and Playing Cards*, 1897.

... when the two great hosts were pitched on the plains of Tanduc ... Chinghis Kaan one day summoned before him his astrologers ... and desired them to let him know which of the two hosts would gain the battle—his own or Prester John's ... they got a cane and split it lengthwise, and laid one-half on this side and one-half on that, allowing no one to touch the pieces. And one piece of cane they called Chinghis Kaan and the other piece, Prester John. And then they said, "Now, mark; and you shall see the event of the battle and who shall have the best of it ..." And lo! whilst all were beholding the cane that bore the name of Chinghis Kaan, without being touched by anybody, advanced to the other ... and got on top of it.

As a magician, I also note that this suggests that the astrologers were well acquainted with the uses of the magician's invisible black silk thread, or its probable equivalent—a length of yak hair!

The divinatory throwing of sticks is the casting of the lots of Biblical mention, and many ancient writers refer to the bundles of sacred tamarisk twigs used by the Magi of Chaldea and Babylonia, the divining rods of Assyria and the similar *baresma* of the Parsis of India.

The game of Jackstraws can be traced back to this divination by throwing sticks, and the fact that *kwai*, the name of the jade sceptres carried by the nobles of ancient China, is written with a character which, combined with the radical for "hand", stands for *kwa* meaning "to divine with straws", hints at the divining rod origin of the king's sceptre. The magician's wand would also be a blood brother.

THE GRANDPARENTS OF DICE

In other cultures the divining sticks were shorter and thicker and bore a greater resemblance to dice. Bent describes their use among the African tribes of Mashonaland. "They are common among all the Abantu races and closely bound up with their occult belief in witchcraft ... On the evening of the new moon the village witch-doctor will go around, tossing each man a set of *dollasses* in the air, and by the way they turn up he will divine the fortune of the individual for the month to come." The Livingstones who noted similar customs among the Zambesi referred to the diviner as a *dice doctor*. He also functioned as a detective since another use for his dice was that of discovering thieves.

Gradually these primitive fortune telling devices began to be used as fortune gaining devices. The mystical significance of the numbers

African Dollasses (Divining Staves)

was lost and the throw determined winning scores and decided the outcome of wagers. The liturgical rites became games.

As the arrow used in divination began, instead, to be used in gambling, three general types of games evolved—guessing games, games of chance and games of skill. In the guessing games, the arrow shaft became an ornamented gambling stick marked to denote rank which, in Korea, evolved into a deck of slim strips of oiled paper cards whose backs still bore an arrow feather design that indicates their origin. Later Chinese cards of the same shape, called "stick cards", bear figures whose resemblance to those on our present court cards is remarkable. The world's oldest known playing card found in Chinese Turkestan is of this type and is dated at the eleventh century. They were introduced into Europe from China in the thirteenth century. "Even the ancestry of the book in Eastern Asia", Culin says, "may be traced to the bundle of engraved or painted arrow-derived slips used in divination."

In many of the early games such as the Korean Nyout, the Egyptian Tab and the ancient Pachisi (Parcheesi) of India, the throw of the dice controlled the moves of counters upon a marked playing surface as in the Backgammon of today. Later, when the dice and the element of chance was omitted, the game of pure skill developed and the counters became the men of Checkers, Chess, the Chinese Wei-Kei and the Japanese Go.

But before any of these developments, the dice were tossed alone in games that were pure gambling. If we can judge by the American Indian, primitive man and woman (she was often even more addicted to the practice than he) was an inveterate gambler. The close association of gambling and the military man is also noted even that early. Edwin T. Denig in a report on the Indian tribes of the Upper Missouri said that, "Most of the leisure time, either by night or by day, among all these nations is devoted to gambling . . . every day and night in the soldier's lodge not occupied by business matters presents gambling in various ways all the time; also in many private lodges the song of hand gambling and the rattle of the bowl dice are heard. Women are as much

Chinese Playing Cards

addicted to the practice as men, though . . . not being in possession of much property their losses are not so distressing."

The most common method of play among the Indians was to toss the gaming disks of fruit stone, animal bone, wood or shell in a basket. The basket was raised a little, the stones tossed, and the basket brought smartly down to the ground. The combinations of sides which lie uppermost after the throw determined the count. In the Cheyenne basket game five plum stones were used marked on one side only, three with crosses and the other two with a symbol representing the foot of a bear.

1. Cheyenne gambling basket. 2. Cheyenne plum stone dice. 3. Seneca bone gaming disk. 4. Beaver teeth dice from Washington and British Columbia. 5. Mohave gambling block.

Two blanks, two bears and one cross counted nothing; one blank, two bears, and two crosses counted one point, etc. The thrower who tossed two bears and three crosses had the equivalent of the slot machine's three bars since it won the game and the jackpot.*

INDIAN SLEIGHT OF HAND

The dice shark's sleight of hand is no recent invention either. In a game played with dice of beaver teeth by the Twana tribe of Washington, one die with a string around its middle counted as high score when this die was up and the others down. "They sometimes learn very expertly to throw the one with the string differently from the others, by arranging them in the hand so they can hold this one, which they know by feeling, a trifle longer than the others."†

Most of these dice were flat two-sided objects but the knucklebone with its four sides, probably the oldest of them all, seems to have been the direct ancestor of our present day dotted cubical die. Marked and showing the polish that comes from long use, specimens have been found in American prehistoric Indian mounds—one unearthed in Florida was the knucklebone of a fossil llama. The knucklebone is found among primitive remains throughout the world and is still, according to Culin, "in common use in the Mohammedan East, in southern Europe

---

* Many slot machine players, for some strange reason, think that three lemons is the highest slot machine combination and the operator will tell you, "Sure that gets you a jack-pot; if you hit three lemons you can take the machine home with you!" He knows that two lemons is the most any slot machine carries.

† Rev. M. Ello in U. S. Geological and Geographical Survey Bulletin, III, No. 1.

and Spanish America." In Arabic the word for the knucklebones is the same as that for dice.

GREEK AND ROMAN GAMBLERS

The Greeks and Romans used the anklebones of a sheep and called them Astragali or Tali. The Greek word Astragalomancy meaning divination by the astragalus, shows that they were also still being used as fortune telling devices. In Rome gaming tables have been found engraved or scratched on the marble or stone slabs of the Forum, in the

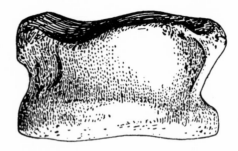

Astragalus of bison used as die by Papago Indians of Arizona

corridors of the Coliseum, on the steps of the temple of Venus and even in the house of the Vestals.

Ashton says, "Gaming tables were especially abundant in barracks, such as those of the seventh battalion of *vigiles* . . . and of the police of Ostia and Porto. Sometimes, when camp was moved from place to place, or else from Italy to the frontiers of the empire, the men would not hesitate to carry the heavy tables with their luggage . . ."*

Augustus, Nero and Caligula, who cheated at the game, were passionate dice players. Claudius had dicing tables in his carriages and Seneca describes him as condemned to hell and made to play at dice forever with a bottomless box. Their dice were cast from conical beakers of carved ivory and the dice were sometimes of crystal inlaid with gold. Professional gamblers were common and although severe laws were enacted forbidding dicing except during the Saturnalia, they were apparently not very strictly enforced; the *fix*, as today's gambler would say, was in. Loaded dice were not uncommon and one mis-

---

* *The History of Gambling in England*, John Ashton, London, 1898.

spotted die bearing two fours suggests that the sleight of hand necessary to switch in a die was known and practiced by Roman cheats.

In addition to the anklebone the Greeks and Romans also used the *tesserae* or cubical six-sided dice, both sometimes being employed in the

Early Egyptian six-sided die and two Roman dice

same game. And "they were thrown from dicing cups which contained crossbars to prevent the cheater from sliding the die out upon the board in a predetermined position." In Egypt Sir William Matthew Flinders Petrie found a very modern appearing six-sided die—a limestone cube with drilled holes for pips and dated it at 600 B.C.

MAGIC DICE OF THE ORIENT

But the first home of the modern die is probably the Orient. The Korean dice used in the Buddhist game of Promotion bear both a magical formula and directions for the next move, and the game sheet with which it was played bears directions in Sanskrit which suggests India as the origin. There we find that the custom of fortune-telling with a die is practiced as a science under the name *Ramala* and the dice used are of a very familiar pattern. They are cubical and marked with the "birds-eye" spots that some of our dice also have. They are strung upon a central axis about which they are spun to determine the magical numbers, reference then being had to the pages of a book of fortunes numbered to correspond. It is in India also that the first written records of dice (and loaded ones at that!) are found in the ancient Sanskrit epic, the *Mahabharata*, in which "Doorjooden, having made a false set of dice, challenged Judishter, the commander of troops he was fighting, to play, which being accepted by him, he, in a short time, lost all his wealth and kingdoms." This was written about 2,000 years ago—which shows that gambling with dice is certainly "the old Army game."

Hindu fortune telling die (Ramala Pásá)

Korean magic die

Dicing was a favorite pastime of the Middle Ages and both dicing schools and guilds existed. One of the earliest references in English is that in which Ordericus Vitalis (1075–1143) reports that "clergymen and bishops are fond of dice-playing." In 1190 an army regulation prohibited the Crusaders under the command of Richard the First of England and Philip of France from playing at any sort of game for money. But this blanket restriction applied only to the G. I. yeomen-at-arms. Knights and clergymen might play for money, but were penalized 100 shillings, payable to the archbishops of the army, if they were caught losing more than 20 shillings in one day and night. The two brass hats, Richard and Philip, were completely exempted and had the privilege of playing for whatever sum they pleased, apparently on the theory that they were better able to afford the losses.

References from this time on are increasingly abundant, especially in the court records of the day. Elmer de Multone, for instance, was indicted in 1311 "for being a common night walker; and, in the day, is wont to entice strangers and persons unknown, to a tavern, and there deceive them by using false dice." He pleaded not guilty, but the jury thought otherwise and he did a stretch in the clink.

THE ENGLISH HAZARD

One of the games that Elmer played was Hazard, the direct ancestor of craps. William of Tyre who died in 1190 claimed that it was invented during the Crusades in the twelfth century by English soldiers at the siege of the Arabian castle of Hazart, or Asart. The English soldier may well have learned the game in Arabia, but its invention during a siege sounds suspiciously like that earlier, but erroneous, report bearing Sophocles' by-line which claimed that dice were invented at the siege of Troy. Hazard, perhaps under some other name, was very probably played long before that date.

Writing in 1674 Charles Cotton in his *Compleat Gamester* remarks: "Certainly Hazard is the most bewitching game that is played on the Dice; for when a man begins to play he knows not when to leave off;

Wooden die and teetotum used in Korean Game of Dignitaries and (right) American ivory rolling log, gaffed to roll either high or low.

and, having once accustomed himself to play at Hazard, he hardly, ever after, minds anything else."

Cotton also gives a description of cheating methods which shows that loaded dice, the pivot test for loads, *High* and *Low Fullams* (misspotted dice bearing only high or low numbers, later called *Dispatchers* and today *Tops*), filed and rounded dice, and Bristle dice (The Pin Gaff) were known as well as some of the most highly prized sleight of hand secrets of today's dice sharks. He decribes Palming and Topping (methods of cheating when using a cup, known today as "holding it up"), Slurring (The Whip Shot), Knapping (The Drop Shot) and Stabbing (the use of a gaffed cup).

From this time on, during the 17th, 18th and 19th centuries gambling at Hazard, Faro and Macao in England and at Trente Et Un and Roulette in France, to mention only a few of the major games, was carried on at a fast and furious pace. At the famous gambling clubs of White's, Brookes' and Crockford's the play was frequented by the lords and ladies and the accounts of enormous losses are numerous.

Crockford's, with a nightly bankroll of £5,000 is said to have netted about £300,000 during the first two seasons, and expenses for dice alone, three new pair each night and more as called for by the players at about a guinea a pair, ran to £2,000 per year.

THE GAMBLING HELL A CENTURY AGO

The Act of 1822 outlawed gambling with a penalty of imprisonment at hard labor for the proprietor but, as Ashton says, ". . . all this legislation was of no use, the gaming-tables continued to flourish." They went underground and a description of the English gaming *hell* of 1833 would serve almost as well for one of today's gaming establishments; only the minor details are changed.

"The game of hazard is the principal one played . . . The inferior houses of play are always situated in obscure courts, or other places of retirement, and, most frequently, are kept shut up during the day as well as at night, as if unoccupied, or some appearance of trade is carried on as a blind. A back room is selected for all operations, if one can be procured sufficiently capacious for the accommodation of forty or fifty persons at one time. In the center of the room is fixed a substantial circular table. A man, designated the Groom Porter, is mounted on a stool, with a stick in his hand, having a transverse piece of wood affixed to its end, which is used by him to rake in the dice after having been thrown out of the box by the caster.

". . . the noise occasioned by proposing and accepting wagers is most uproarious and deafening . . . To prevent the noise being heard in the streets, shutters, closely fitted to the window frames are affixed, which are padded and covered with green baize; there is invariably, an inner door placed in the passage, having an aperture in it, through which all who enter from the street may be viewed; this precaution answers two purposes, it deadens the sound of noisy voices at the table and prevents surprise by the officers of justice."*

A number of writers seemed to have assumed that Hazard was first introduced into the United States by the French who settled New Orleans. Edward Larocque Tinker in an article, *The Palingenesis of Craps* (1933) says that Bernard de Marigny who had a reputation for high-stake gambling introduced Hazard and that it gained the name Craps because the Americans called De Marigny, as they did other Frenchmen and Creoles, Johnny Crapaud (frogeater) and then called his favorite game Crapaud, Crapo and finally Craps.

THE ORIGIN OF THE WORD CRAPS

This theory is full of holes. There is, first, no reason to assume that the French first introduced Hazard. It probably came over on the May-

---

* *Fraser's Magazine*, August, 1833.

A dice game of the 17th Century. From Cotton's "Compleat Gamester."

flower or very shortly thereafter because four years later in 1624 the Virginia Assembly passed a law that "Mynisters shall not give themselves to excess in drinking or yette spend their tyme idelie by day or by night, playing at dice, cards or any unlawful game." If the English settlers played at dice they would hardly have overlooked the most popular of all English dice games, Hazard.

As for the name Craps, Herbert Asbury* points out that De Marigny named a New Orleans street Rue de Craps about 1804, something which, since he hated all Americans, he would hardly have done if they had coined the name. He also showed that the word Craps has an earlier and European origin. At some time prior to 1792 when an article about the game appeared in the *Encyclopédia Méthodique*, Hazard emigrated to France and became known there as *Krabs*, after the English term, crabs, used in the game to denote a throw of 2 or 3.

The word was later corrupted to Creps and Craps, the latter appearing in the *Bibliothèque Historique* (1818) which gave a list of the tables in operation in nine Parisian gambling houses that included one

---

* *Sucker's Progress*, Dodd, Mead & Co., 1938.

of Hazard and one of Craps. I have found no evidence, however, to show this game had anything but the name in common with Craps as we know it and suspect that one of the games was the English two-dice Hazard, the other the three-dice Grand Hazard, a banking game.

The game De Marigny played in New Orleans was, according to Tinker's own statement, Hazard. Furthermore, when Craps first began to appear in the American Hoyles (1887), it was referred to as "Hazard or Craps" and the rules given were copied from the second Hoyle to appear in this country, the 1845 edition, and were those of Hazard.

HAZARD AS IT WAS AND WAS NOT PLAYED

Craps as we know it today may have taken its name and a few of its basic rules of play from the English Hazard which the French were calling Craps when it became popular in New Orleans around 1800, but the American Craps can hardly be said to be the same game as the 1845 rules show:

"If anyone choose to lay some money with the thrower or caster, he must place his cash upon the table within a circle destined for that purpose; when he has done this, if the caster agrees to it, he knocks the box upon the table at the person's money with whom he intends to bet, or mentions at whose money he throws . . ." Modern crap players will note that this is just the opposite of what now is done in Craps.

"The player, who takes the box and dice, throws a main—i.e., a chance for the company, which must exceed four, and not be more than nine, otherwise it is no main; he consequently must keep throwing till he produce five, six, seven, eight or nine; this done, he must throw his own chance, which may be any above three, and not exceeding ten; if he should throw two aces or trois ace (commonly termed crabs) he loses his stakes, let the company's chance, which we call the main, be what it may. If the main should be seven, and seven or eleven is thrown immediately after, it is called a nick, and the caster (the present player) wins out his stakes. If eight be the main, and eight or twelve be thrown immediately after, it is also termed a nick, and the caster wins his stakes. The caster throwing any other number for the main, such as are admitted, and brings the same number immediately afterward, it is a nick, and he gains whatever stakes he has made. Every three successive mains the caster wins he pays to the box, or furnisher of the dice, the usual fee."

Translated into crap terms, those rules mean that the shooter had to begin by throwing one of the numbers 5, 6, 7, 8 or 9. If he failed to do so on the first throw, he had to continue throwing until it did appear, often a tedious process since he might have to throw nine or ten times before one of those numbers came up and the game could get under way. Having finally thrown one of those numbers, it became the faders' point. Then the shooter had to try to throw a point for himself which could be any of the numbers, 4, 5, 6, 7, 8, 9 or 10.

If, when trying to throw a point for himself the shooter threw a 2 or 3, it was a crab and he was said to have crabbed, losing his stakes. If the faders' point was 7 and the shooter threw either 7 or 11, it was a nick and the shooter won. If the faders' point was 8 and the shooter threw either 8 or 12, it was a nick and he won.

If he threw any other number from 4 to 10 inclusive, including 7 and 8 when neither was the fader's point, he had thrown a point for himself.

Hoyle fails entirely to state what happens if the shooter throws the fader's point (and it is not a nick) when trying for his own. For all he says to the contrary the shooter and fader might both get the same point! This gets us no place fast.

After completely overlooking the fact that the game would come to a dead end right there, Hoyle goes on to say that the shooter continues to throw and, if he repeats his point on the next throw, wins. Then Hoyle comes to a sudden stop. What happens if the shooter does not repeat his point on this next throw? Hoyle, apparently hasn't the slightest idea. He stops right there leaving the players and all his readers suspended in midair and pretty completely confused.

This is probably as incomplete and curious a set of rules as any ever devised. According to Hoyle the *only* decisions that lose for the shooter are the crabs (2 and 3) made when the shooter is trying for his point. All other decisions win for the shooter.

If anyone ever played the game according to Hoyle's instructions and faded the shooter with real dough, he should have had his head examined.*

Actually, of course, the game never was played in any such way; it couldn't have been because only half the rules are given. If we go back before Hoyle was born and see what Charles Cotton in his *The Compleat Gamester*, published in 1674, had to say we find an authority who at least gave all the rules.

---

* Edmond Hoyle himself should not be blamed for these errors; he died in 1769, seventy-two years before the first American game book bearing his name was published.

We discover that when the shooter was trying for his own point and he threw the fader's point, it was a nick (what today we call a *natural*) and the shooter won; if the fader's point was 6 or 8 and the shooter threw a 12, it was also a nick and the shooter won.

The losing decisions when the shooter was trying for his point were called *Outs* (later called *crabs* and today called *craps*), they were: a throw of 2 or 3 no matter what the fader's point was; a throw of 11 when the fader's point was 5, 6, 8 or 9; and a throw of 12 when the fader's point was 5, 7 or 9.

If none of the above decisions occurred, if, when trying to make his point, the shooter did not throw either a nick or an Out (natural or crap) the number thrown became the shooter's point. The shooter then continued to throw until he either threw his own point which won for him or until he threw the fader's point when the shooter lost.

These rules make sense and are complete but the 1845 Hoyle left half of them out and when the later authorities, if they can be termed that, came to describe Craps they not only made the error of using the rules for Hazard instead but copied them as is without even looking at them closely enough to find out if they were complete and if the game could be played that way—a practise followed by later day authorities and which was remedied with the publication of this book.

WHAT HOYLE FORGOT

The 1845 Hoyle also forgot to mention the fact that the players placed side bets among themselves, laying and taking the odds as to whether the caster's or fader's point would be thrown first. Because the odds against a 6 coming before a 5 are different from those of a 5 coming before a 7, or a 9 before a 10, etc., etc., the expert Hazard player had to have a remarkable memory and a very clear head. This fact along with the action of the game, which may have been fast enough for the English players of the 17th and 18th centuries but was far too slow for the American gambler, is the reason that Hazard never acquired any great popularity in this country.* Although it is mentioned in the 1845 edition, probably not because it was popular in this country but because that Hoyle was simply a reprint of the English editions, the later game books omitted it completely. Then in 1887 when the compiler of Hoyle for that year heard that a game called

---

* The reader must not confuse this two-dice ancestor of Craps with the three-dice Hazard played today. Rules for the latter game are given on page 341.

Craps was popular, he took a very quick look at it, made a bad guess that it was Hazard and promptly copied down the 1845 rules for that game and called it Hazard or Craps. Even as late as 1914, when he should have known better, Foster's rules for what he calls "Crapshooting" are a curious mixture of rules from both games.

John Philip Quinn, a sharp who hit the sawdust trail in 1886 to spend his later years exposing gamblers' cheating tricks and lecturing and writing on the evils of gambling, relates his first contact with the new game of Craps in *Fools of Fortune* published in 1890. He first saw it played on the Mississippi steamboat *City of Chester* when, after he and his partner had fleeced a soft mark of $800 at poker in a cabin, he went on deck and heard a Negro exhorting, "Come 7 or 11" and "Chill'en cryin' fo' bread." Quinn investigated and lost $15 to the "Crap roller." His partner, whom Quinn called to see the new game, dropped $10. Quinn alibis the loss by saying that he thinks he was cheated either with loaded dice or mis-spots, but neglects to assist the historian by giving any date for the incident. In 1890 when he wrote, however, he said that "the game is an especial favorite among Negroes and deck-hands . . . and is frequently played by 'high-toned' gamblers and for large stakes."

THE REAL INVENTORS

Because the Negro played the game for a long time before the white man took any particular notice of it; because even when Quinn wrote, it was still called a Negroes' game; because the colorful slang that is still associated with the game is of obvious Negro origin, and because dice are still called "African dominoes," the placing of the credit for the invention of the game is obvious.

Around New Orleans sometime after 1800, the Negro tried his hand at the English Hazard which the French sometimes called Craps. But because the rules and betting odds were so intricate, he didn't play it according to the English and French rules. He simplified the whole procedure and began to play the game in his own way, at first probably in a number of different variations. As the game spread and the variations settled down into one standard method of play, a new and American game which the Negro called Craps after the French fashion came into being—a much faster and more streamlined game than its immediate ancestor, Hazard.

Craps spread up the Mississippi and then out across the country, its habitat the steamboats, the river wharfs and docks, the cotton fields and the saloons. But it did not appear in the clubs and gambling houses much before 1890. The big game there was Faro which, originally known as Pharao or Pharaon (the backs of the early French cards bore the picture of an Egyptian ruler) had been played in France since before the middle of the 17th century and had vied with Hazard for popularity in the English clubs during their heyday. Faro entered this country through New Orleans early in the 18th century and, shortly after the Louisiana Purchase, became the most widely played banking game in the United States and held that position until the close of the 19th century.

THE TAKE-OFF GAME

The gaming house operators paid little attention to Craps even when the white gambler began to play it because it was a private and not a banking game. But as its popularity increased, the gamblers noticed that, in preference to bucking the Tiger, many of their customers stayed outside playing the faster game, Craps—a situation that worried them. Their first step toward remedying the matter was to introduce

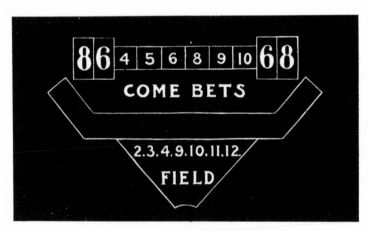

Early Pre-Winn Bank Crap Layout.

crap tables into the casinos and levy a charge, usually five, ten, or twenty-five cents whenever the shooter made two or more passes, as was done in Hazard. This became known as a Take-off game.

The operators, however, didn't feel that the income derived from this was sufficient and so they tried to make Craps a banking game by drawing a simple layout bearing the 6 and 8, the Field, the Win and the Come bets. The players all had to bet the dice to win against the house which took its cut not as a direct charge but indirectly and less noticeably by offering short odds so that it gained a percentage.

From the casino's viewpoint, this was a step in the right direction but it didn't go far enough. The players continued to get more action in the street game where they could bet either way, right or wrong, and could make a greater variety of bets.

WINN, THE FIRST CRAPS BOOKMAKER

This was the situation in 1887 when the players in the Two Johns crap game back of the Union Depot in St. Louis may have noticed a young man 20 years of age who was a dice-maker by trade and who had a head on his shoulders. His name, John H. Winn, has since become famous among gamblers although the gamebook compilers who still confuse Hazard and Craps apparently have never heard of it. It has been many years since he was a professional gambler, but I finally located him in New York City and heard his own first hand version of how he made Bank Craps a successful casino game, how he became the first crap bookmaker, and how he invented his famous "quarter charge" that made the game of Open Craps possible.

His first innovation, in New York in 1907, was when he began to book the Take-off game and allowed the players to bet against him either way, right or wrong. In addition to taking a cut whenever the shooter made two or more passes, he charged both right and wrong bettors a quarter for a $5 bet and fifty cents for a $10 bet. This charge was made on all except the flat bets (bets made before the come-out that the dice win) on which Winn knew, and most players didn't know, that the percentage was in his favor. This improvement gave Winn plenty of action and other operators, noticing it, began to follow suit. This was the origin of the present day game of Open Craps and New York Craps.

Shortly afterward Winn improved the banking layout in much the same way. He drew a space on the layout, "just a little piece off on one side" as he says, and lettered in the words: *Don't Pass*. This was done in Philadelphia where Winn used to go weekends and the layout became known as The Philadelphia Layout, the first bank crap layout to offer the players an opportunity to bet the dice to lose. He made the same charge for this bet as when booking the Take-off game, a quarter for a $5 bet and fifty cents for a $10 bet on the Don't Pass Line.

Later, other gamblers eliminated the direct charge and barred the Ace-deuce instead. And finally, when the wrong players' complaints that the Ace-deuce appeared too often on the come-out became insistent, the bar on two aces or on two sixes was substituted and became standard.

As Open Craps, New York Craps and the improved Bank Craps began to replace the vanishing Faro, other bets began to appear. One roll bets could be made, the 6 and 8 became known as Big 6 and Big 8, the hard way plays were added, and tables that took action on the points began to allow action on any number (Place or Box number betting).

Private Craps also gained many new players when, during the first World War in 1914, the American soldier, like the Crusaders and Roman legionnaires before him, took to gambling as a handy means of recreation. Afterward the habit persisted and Craps became the big game of the bootleg era. Like the liquor laws, those against gaming have always been distinguished by a lack of successful enforcement.

THE FASTEST AND BIGGEST GAMBLING GAME

In 1931 came the legalization of casino gambling in the state of Nevada and Craps was then on its way to becoming the biggest and fastest gambling game in history. The popularity of the American game of Bank Craps (Las Vegas style) has spread in the past four decades to the four corners of the globe. Today, Bank Craps tables can be found in the plush legal gambling casinos of Nevada, Monte Carlo, England, Puerto Rico, Turkey, North Africa, Asia, South America, Grand Bahamas, Curaçao, Aruba, Dominican Republic and many other Carribean islands that cater to American tourists. And wherever American servicemen are stationed, at home and overseas in Europe, Africa, and Asia, the galloping dominoes are in action.

Bank Craps and Open or New York Craps have not only replaced Faro as the favorite casino game of millions of Americans, but have also far outdistanced all other casino games in popularity. Private Craps is likewise the big favorite in the field of friendly or unorganized gambling.

The simplicity of the game and its fast action make it more exciting and, for the player who doesn't know his way around, far more dangerous than Hazard ever was. At Bank Craps the game is so simple to play that the players don't even need to know the rules; they simply place their money on a space on the layout, sometimes without even knowing what it is, and, if they win, the bank pays off. But this simplicity is deceptive. There is a greater variety of bets and the percentages are just as hard to figure as in Hazard.

The player who knows nothing of percentage nearly always finds himself playing and losing and wondering why he is so unlucky. Very few players seem to know that their losses often may not result from an adverse run of luck at all, but from the fact that they are trying to buck an impossibly high P. C. They don't know which bets have the least percentage against them. Most players not only don't know how much the percentage against them amounts to, but, in most dice games, don't even know whether it is an even-up proposition or if they have the worst of it.

This book is an attempt to correct that situation, to explain the proper way of playing Craps and the other currently popular dice games, the chance the player has to win, and the methods by which he can both avoid cheating himself and detect the wily stranger who tries to cheat him.

It also contains considerable evidence to show that gaming tables do *not* provide one of the more trustworthy methods for reaching and staying on Easy Street.

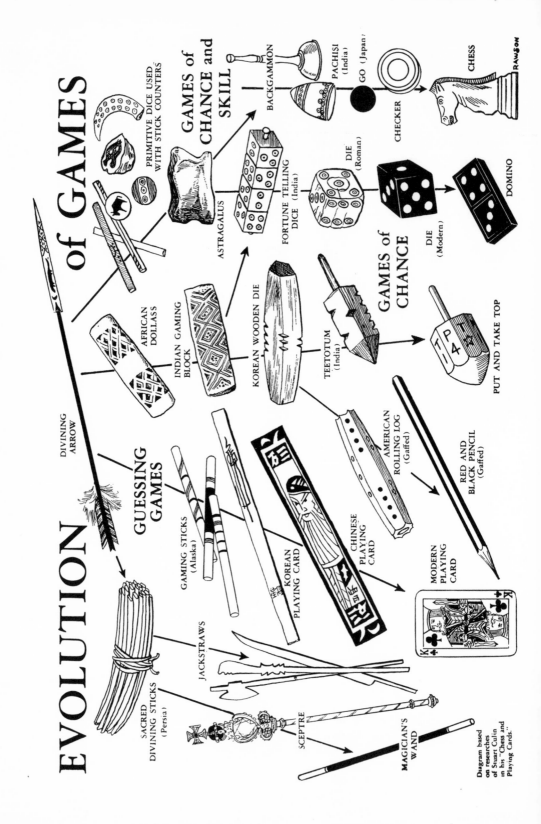

EVOLUTION of GAMES

RAWSON

GAMES of CHANCE and SKILL

BACKGAMMON

PACHISI (India)

GO (Japan)

CHECKER

CHESS

PRIMITIVE DICE USED WITH STICK COUNTERS

ASTRAGALUS

FORTUNE TELLING DICE (India)

DIE (Roman)

DIE (Modern)

DOMINO

GAMES of CHANCE

AFRICAN DOLLASS

INDIAN GAMING BLOCK

KOREAN WOODEN DIE

TEETOTUM (India)

PUT AND TAKE TOP

DIVINING ARROW

GUESSING GAMES

GAMING STICKS (Alaska)

KOREAN PLAYING CARD

CHINESE PLAYING CARD

AMERICAN ROLLING LOG (Gaffed)

RED AND BLACK PENCIL (Gaffed)

MODERN PLAYING CARD

SACRED DIVINING STICKS (Persia)

JACKSTRAWS

SCEPTRE

MAGICIAN'S WAND

Diagram based on researches of Stuart Culin in his "Chess and Playing Cards."

2

The Mathematics and Science of Gambling

If you are one of the countless millions of Americans who gamble at professional dice tables, casinos, racetracks, Bingo halls, poker rooms, play the numbers game, buy lottery tickets, bet with race and sports bookies, remember you must pay for your pleasure.

That is not unreasonable. You expect to pay for a Broadway show, so why not for your gambling pleasure? Moreover, someone has to pay the gambling operators' expenses. The gambling operator charges a commission for every bet he accepts. It is a business like any other; and if the operators did not wind up with a handsome yearly net profit, you would not have a place in which to gamble.

How much you pay for this entertainment is entirely up to you. If you are one of the millions of dice players who know little or nothing about the mathematics of dice and dice games, I guarantee the price you are paying for your gambling pleasure is much more than you ever imagined. My gambling survey revealed that the amateurish betting habits of most dice players greatly reduce their winning chances. Few players consider the percentage they are bucking in the dice game they are playing; only one in a thousand consistently takes advantage of the best dice odds. It is rare that you will find a dice player who places his bets in such a manner that when he wins he will receive the maximum possible amount on the smallest possible bet.

45

I can't tell you how to beat the casino dice table over the long run, but if you are an occasional gambler and you frequent gambling casinos in Nevada and the Carribbean now and then, I can tell you how to bet your money at the Craps table and make you as gambling-wise as the top professional gamblers in Las Vegas and elsewhere. However, I must warn you that the casino's dice table is not a game of skill. Dice tables make money for the house because at no time can your skill be of any real help to you. Knowledge of the odds can be a real help, but that is not skill, it is knowledge. When you come to the dice table with a good knowledge of the percentage you are bucking, you're one step ahead of the player who bets without that knowledge. But shooting dice is not a mechanical process wherein the expected always occurs. If it were, it would not have the thrills and the excitement it has for so many millions of dice shooters. So, let's try to define our terms. Let's see what we're talking about.

WHAT IS GAMBLING?

Gambling consists of wagering money upon the outcome of any event or game of chance or skill or game that combines both chance and skill. A game of skill is a game from which the element of chance has been utterly eliminated. Examples are Chess, Checkers, and three skill games that I invented myself: Teeko, Follow-the-Arrow, and Scarney.

In private dice games such as Backgammon, Scarney 3000, or Acey Deucey that combine skill and chance, the more skilled player enjoys an advantage over the player with less skill.

A game of chance is a game from which the element of skill has been utterly eliminated. These include games played with dice such as Bank Craps, Money Craps, Poker Dice, Buck Dice and others. As mentioned earlier, knowing the odds or operator's percentage in any banking dice game is not skill. It is knowledge.

The verb "gamble" and the noun "gambler" first appeared in print in the English language around the 1750's. From that period until 1931, with the legalization of casino games in the state of Nevada, both terms had an unsavory meaning. At best, a gambler was regarded as an undesirable, a cheat, and/or a criminal. These names sure fit most professional gamblers or operators of that era.

Prior to the first publication of *Scarne On Dice*, more than ninety percent of all illegally operated gambling casinos in resort areas that I visited were crooked and known in gambling circles as "bust-out joints."

Prior to 1945 I scouted one hundred gambling casinos in the Miami area and all but two of these were bust-out joints. In Saratoga Springs, New York, I scouted twenty plush casinos during the August racing season and found nineteen were bust-out joints. The same situation prevailed in all the big cities and hamlets throughout the country.

The honest dice games were honest not because the operators wanted to run honest dice games, but because their clientele was comprised of professional gamblers and card and dice cheats. Therefore, the games had to be honest.

Today, with government supervision of legalized casinos throughout the world, dice games are usually honest. However, there are still hundreds of illegal crooked dice games as well as some crooked legalized casinos which fleece unsuspecting dice players out of tens of millions of dollars yearly by the use of crooked dice.

Modern dictionaries define a gambler as one who makes a practice of wagering money on a game or event and does not carry any connotation of evil. However, millions of Americans and various law enforcement agencies still consider any known gambler as a potential lawbreaker. For the purpose of clarity, in the following pages, I shall define gambling as the wagering of money upon an uncertain event, a gambler as a player or one who gambles, and a professional gambler as the operator of a gambling joint or dice games that exist for the sole purpose of allowing the public to gamble.

TYPES OF DICE PLAYERS

There are five different kinds of dice players. Which category are you in?

1. The occasional dice player who knows little or nothing about the hard mathematical facts of the dice game or games on which he now and then wagers some money.

2. The degenerate or habitual dice player who knows considerably more about dice playing but is not smart enough to know that he cannot beat adverse odds. He craves action and lives in a dream world in which he hopes someday to make a big winning and then quit gambling forever. When he does win a bit, he almost always gambles it all back and like most gamblers winds up broke.

3. The dice hustler who knows a little more about dice gambling

than the occasional or habitual gambler. He favors private dice games where he offers other players bets that are less than the correct odds.

4. The dice crook, a cheat who makes money by cheating at dice. The cheat's gamble is not so much in winning or losing as in whether or not he will get away with it. To the average dice player, the person who makes his living by switching crooked dice into a game is simply a cheat. But, to the seasoned gamblers, he is known as a "dice mechanic." Dice mechanics spend years practicing to perfect their dice moves. They know no game but their own. They spend their spare time telling other cheats all the big swindles they perpetrated, usually exaggerated ten-fold.

5. The professional gambler or operator who gets his living or the greater part of it from operating dice games or a gambling joint.

GAMBLERS AND SCIENTISTS

Dice are the oldest of all gambling devices. Man's earliest written records not only mention dice and dice games but crooked dice as well. Dice of one sort or another have been found in the tombs of ancient Egypt and the Orient, and in the prehistoric graves of both North and South America.

The earliest gamblers thought that the fall of the dice was controlled by the gods, and, although a few of them tried to outwit divinity by loading the cubes, most of them probably considered that any prying into the matter was sacrilegious.

In the 16th century at least one gambler began to wonder if the scientists who were beginning to make valid predictions about other matters might not also be able to foretell how the dice would fall. An Italian nobleman asked Galileo why the combination 10 showed up more often than 9 when three dice were thrown. The great astronomer became interested in dice problems and wrote a short treatise which set forth some of the first probability theorems. His reply to the gambler was that $6 \times 6 \times 6$ for a total of 216 combinations can be made with three dice, of which twenty-seven form the number 10 and twenty-five the number 9.

In France, in 1654, the philosopher, mathematician and physicist, Blaise Pascal, was asked a similar dice question by one of the first gambler-hustlers on record. The Chevalier de Méré had been winning consistently by betting even money that a six would come up at least once in four rolls with a single die. He reasoned from this that he would also have an advantage when he bet even money that a double-six would come up at least once in 24 rolls with two dice. But he had been losing money on this proposition, and he wanted to know why.

Pascal worked on the problem and found that the Chevalier had the best of it by 3.549% with his one-die proposition. Throwing a double-six with two dice, however, would theoretically require 24.6+ rolls to make it an even-money proposition. In practice it can't ever be an even-money bet, because you can't roll a pair of dice a fractional number of times: it has to be either 24 or 25 rolls. Here is a calculation I have never seen in print before: The exact chances of rolling two sixes in 24 rolls are: 11,033,126,465,283,976,852,912,127,963,392,284,-191 successes in 22,452,257,707,354,557,240,087,211,123,792,674,-816 rolls.

This means that dice hustler De Méré had been taking a beating of 1.27+% on the bet. If he had bet that two sixes would come up at least once in 25 rolls he would have enjoyed a favorable edge of .85%.

Pascal corresponded with mathematician Pierre Fermat about this and similar gambling problems, and these two men formulated much of the basic mathematics on the theory of probability.

History doesn't state how many francs Chevalier de Méré lost on his double-six betting proposition before Pascal explained why he was getting the worst of it, but I do know that nearly 300 years later, in 1952, a New York City gambler known as "Fat the Butch" lost $49,000 by betting that he could throw a double-six in 21 rolls.

Fat the Butch, although a smart gambling-house operator who has made millions booking dice games, went wrong on the bet because he figured it this way: There are 36 possible combinations with two dice, and a double-six can be made only one way—so there should be an even chance to throw a double-six in 18 rolls. Consequently, when "The Brain," a well-known bigtime gambler, offered to bet $1,000 that a double-six would not turn up in 21 rolls, Fat the Butch thought he had the best of it and jumped at the opportunity.

After twelve hours of dice rolling, Fat the Butch found himself a $49,000 loser, and he quit because he finally realized something must be wrong with his logic. He was, later, part owner of the Casino de Capri in Havana, and when I told him it would need 24.6 rolls to make the double-six bet an even-up proposition, and that he had taken 20.45% the worst of it on every one of those bets, he shrugged his massive shoulders and said, "Scarne, in gambling you got to pay to learn, but $49,000 was a lot of dough to pay just to learn that." "That is for sure," I agreed.

Although most of the odds and percentage problems you will encounter in this book can be calculated simply, a few, like the double-six problem above, are more complex. Here is the formula for figuring problems of this type. To find out when the chances are approximately equal in any single event, multiply the "odds to one" by .693, the co-log of the hyperbolic log of 2. This will give the approximate number of chances, trials, rolls, guesses, etc., needed to make any event an even, or fifty-fifty proposition.

For example: the odds are 35 to 1 against throwing double-sixes with two dice in one roll. Multiply 35 × .693 and you find that a double-six can be expected to appear in the long run once in approximately 24.255 rolls. (The figure of 24.6+given earlier is more exact.) To calculate the approximate number required for a double event such as throwing double-sixes twice, multiply the "odds to one" by 1.678. For a triple event multiply by 2.675; a quad event, by 3.672; and a quint event, by 4.670.

The theory of probability is essentially a method of getting an approximate answer when part of the factors are unknown. It is used to calculate what can be expected to happen when some of the factors are not at hand or when the information is too complex to be easily broken down.

The modern physicist uses the theory of probability in studying the behavior of the atom, and the secrets of energy and matter; the biologist and bacteriologist use it in their studies of heredity; the whole insurance business depends on the mortality tables that are based on the theory of probability; and any business man who uses statistics or combinational analysis owes a debt to the gamblers who first asked Galileo to consider their problems.

Paradoxically, however, the gamblers who are the godfathers of a whole branch of mathematical science today know little about it. They got lost by the wayside when the professors began answering their questions in an argot even stranger than the gamblers' own—the language of mathematical symbols. As a consequence, although modern man has tossed the superstition that dice can divine the future into the discard, many gamblers still believe that the fall of the dice or the turn of the wheel is still controlled by some supernatural force.

The proof of this lies in the fact that many carry good luck charms; some of them ask to have the dice changed or call for a new stickman when they begin to lose; some won't bet at all unless they stand at a certain spot at the table; some walk around the table to change their luck; others avoid betting on Friday. One gambler I know must always go to the game by exactly the same route and the cab driver catches hell if he misses a single turn. Another won't allow the barber to cut one particular hair on his head because if it is clipped, he always loses—or that's what he thinks.

I'm superstitious about gambling, too. I won't gamble during any week that has a Friday in it!

Many gamblers don't seem to realize that the correct answers can all be obtained with figures—and that the mystic symbols having to do with black cats and four leaf clovers can be thrown out the window. As a class gamblers are superstitious for the usual reason—ignorance. They don't understand how chance operates or know what luck really is.

WHAT IS LUCK?

The dictionary defines luck as a person's *apparent* tendency to be fortunate or unfortunate. Most people who use the word, however, forget that this tendency is not real but only apparent. When they say that someone who has had good fortune in the past is lucky or will be lucky in the future, they don't seem to realize that they are making exactly the same sort of prediction that the prehistoric witchdoctor did when he threw his divining sticks upon the ground.

Anyone who believes that one player has a better chance of winning a bet because he is luckier than another is no smarter than the sorceror and witch of the Middle Ages, the African voodoo doctor and the gypsy fortune teller who reads tea leaves.

If you gambled and won yesterday, you may correctly say that you *were* lucky because you are merely stating that you placed your bets in such a way that they agreed with the fall of the dice or the turn of the wheel. But the fact that you were lucky or that you have always been consistently lucky in your affairs does not guarantee you a better break than the next guy tomorrow. The odds on dice are not different for different people at different times. If your past luck has any effect on your future luck then the law of gravitation that pulls the dice to a stop must be throwing curves just because you carry a rabbit's foot.

The supernatural will continue to try to get a foot in at the door just as long as we try to investigate chance as it applies to a single person. But if we consider chance as it applies to large groups of players and long series of throws, then we begin to make sense, and superstition gets a quick brush-off.

LUCK ISN'T AS STRANGE AS IT SEEMS

One of the first things we shall discover is that the marvelous run of luck you had yesterday or last week isn't always as astonishing as it seemed. At Bank Craps the gambler who puts his money on two aces and takes 30 to 1 that they will appear on the next roll feels that he is a very lucky egg indeed when the two aces are thrown four times in a row and he bets on each roll, especially if he happens to know that the odds against such a thing happening are 1,679,615 to 1. He is amazed that some mysterious Fate has singled him out for such a favor. And the guy who was placing big bets on the pass line or shooting a large amount in the center at Private Craps when those two aces appeared four times in succession would consider himself as being the champion hard-luck guy of the world.

Both players forget that the statement that the odds are 1,679,615 to 1 against such an event also means that the event can be expected to happen on an average once in every 1,679,616 times. They forgot that on the night when that succession of double-aces appeared there were thousands of other crap games in progress and several millions of throws were made. It would have been even more amazing if someone somewhere had *not* thrown double-aces four times in a row. The fact that it may have happened to you merely means that you happened to be around at the time. If you had stayed at home with a good book or a blonde, the run of double-aces would have happened just the same somewhere or other and made someone else exclaim over his remarkable luck, or if he was betting the dice to win, his bad luck.

The reason the scientist cannot predict the result of the throw of a pair of dice is that the varying physical forces that operate on the cubes during the throw are so hard to measure and so fantastically complex.

He might have more success predicting the result of tossing a coin provided he knew in advance the exact amount of force that would be applied and the exact point on the coin at which it would be applied. He could calculate the trajectory, the amount of spin and the drop, and predict: "Heads!" A machine might even be constructed which would toss a coin, apply exactly the same amount of force in the same place each time, and always throw either heads or tails as desired. Such a gadget would eliminate chance and would be worthless as a gambling device. Unless, of course, some smart guy disguised it as a slot machine!

But when a player tosses a coin, none of those factors are known. That does not, however, mean that nothing is known. A coin has two sides and, as long as there is no data which says that one side must come any more often than another, in a series of several thousand throws all the minute variations in the force of the throw and the manner of throwing eventually tend to cancel each other. We can say that heads can be expected to be thrown approximately as often as tails and that the greater the number of throws, the more closely the number of heads will equal the number of tails.*

WHAT ARE ODDS?

We cannot predict whether heads or tails will be thrown on the next toss but, since heads can be expected to come 1/2 the time, we can say that its chance of being thrown or its probability is 1/2. With a perfectly symmetrical die of six sides, since any side has an equal chance with any of the others, any one side can be expected to be thrown an average of once in 6 times. Its probability for the next throw is 1/6. And with two dice, each of the six sides of one die may be combined with each of the six sides of the other to form 6 × 6 or 36 combinations. The chance that the same number will appear on the two dice is, therefore, 1 in 36 or 1/36.

When the probability is 0, the event is impossible; when it is 1, the event is certain. All other probabilities are expressed by fractions falling between those two numbers. When the probability is 1/2, we say that the chances are fifty-fifty or that they are even. But a probability of 1/6 or of 1/36 is less than an even chance and, for betting purposes, is usually expressed in terms of the advantage that the unfavorable events have over the favorable events, that is, in terms of the *odds* against the event.

With a single die any one side has a probability of 1/6 and the odds against that side being thrown on the next roll are the 5 ways that the other sides can be thrown against the 1 way that the specified side can be thrown. The odds are 5 to 1 that that side will not appear. When the probability is 1/36, the odds are 35 to 1. When the probability is 2/36, the odds are 34 to 2 or 17 to 1, etc.

In placing bets, if I bet $35 to your $1 that a double-ace will not be thrown on the next roll, the betting odds are fair because they are the same as the correct odds. In the long run I can expect to win at the rate of 35 out of every 36 bets and you can expect to win at the rate of 1 out

---

* Various experimenters have tested this conclusion by tossing coins and throwing dice and found that the experimental results agree with the theory. The operation of a gambling house is, in fact, proof in itself since its income depends directly upon the predictions of the theory of probability.

of every 36 bets. The odds are fair odds because, in the long run, neither of us will have won or lost but will be even. Gamblers call such a bet an *even-up* proposition.

MEET OLD MAN PERCENTAGE

The professional gambler who makes a living at gambling cannot offer even-up bets. As he says, "There's no percentage in that." He must, in some way, gain an advantage or an *edge* on the law of averages; he must have a slightly better chance to win than the next guy. The crooked professional obtains this by cheating. The reputable house operator obtains it either by making a direct charge or by *percentage*, usually called the P.C.

Most players know that the house takes a percentage, but because they can't calculate it, they never know how strong it is, and because it works so quietly, they forget most of the time that it is even there.

Let us take a simple example and suppose that you walk up to a bank crap table with $36 in your pocket. Before each throw of the dice you make a $1 bet that double-aces will be thrown on the next roll. If the dice act the way probability says you can expect them to fall in the long run, you can expect to lose 35 of those bets and win 1.

Suppose you lose the first 35 bets. You are out $35 and have one buck left. Now you bet that and win. If the house paid off at correct odds of 35 to 1, they would pay you $35 which with the $1 you put up gives you $36 altogether, or just what you had at the start.

But no house ever pays off that way. They pay 30 to 1 or less. After losing $35 on the first 35 bets, you put down that last $1, win, and are paid $30. This with your $1 stake leaves you $31 which is $5 less than you had at the start. That $5 is the house percentage.

Today all gamblers and even the greenest players know that this P.C. exists, but the chumps always think it is less than it really is and few professionals know precisely how much it amounts to in spite of the fact that the method for figuring it is neither complicated nor difficult. Briefly, the rule is simply this: *The house percentage (or the player's disadvantage) is the amount the player is short divided by the total amount he should have collected if paid off at correct odds.*

In the example above, the player is $5 short and should have collected $36 if paid off at correct odds. Five divided by 36 is .13-8/9 or *13-8/9%*.

If you make 100 such $1 bets, the probability is that you will end by losing $13.89-8/9. But don't make the common mistake of supposing that if you start with a $100 bankroll and place $1 bets on this proposition all evening for a total of 100 bets that you will end up losing only $13.89-8/9. The 13-8/9% is not your loss for the evening but your *rate* of loss. Old Man Percentage is in there grinding away on every bet made. You are losing at the rate of $5 on every 36 bets of one dollar made and, at the end of 720 such rolls the bank will have earned an amount equal to the $100 with which you started.

GAMBLING HOUSES DON'T GAMBLE

This favorable percentage is what enables the house to pay its expenses and make a profit. If it is paid off at correct odds, the house would be gambling, something that it avoids like a plague. It would win some evenings, lose others and, in the long run, come out with the same bankroll it had at the start.

When expenses were deducted, the remainder on the profit and loss sheet would have to be written in red ink, a shade of writing fluid that the gambling house operator seldom uses.

The house P.C. is the price you pay to make use of its gambling facilities. In the military or private game when the hustler collects a percentage with his sucker bets, it is the price you pay for your ignorance of the game's mathematics. Most players, because they can't figure percentage, play without ever knowing how much they are paying and without ever suspecting that the price is a lot higher than they think.

Most players don't even know that the P.C. is not the same on all bets. They place their money at random and make all sorts of bets, unaware that they are paying far more for the opportunity to gamble than the smart player who knows enough to avoid bets having a strong P.C. The player who falls for the sucker bets often bucks such stiff percentages that even when he hits a lucky streak, he ends a loser. His chance to win is chopped down to next to nothing, simply because he knows so little about the game.

YOU DON'T HAVE TO BE A CHUMP

The crap player who wants to find out how to bet with the least chance of losing can find all the answers—all the correct odds and percentages on all bets in Bank Craps, Money Craps, New York Craps,

Scarney Craps and Private Craps in our later chapters where for the first time all the correct information is put together in one handy reference book. From here on, if you play the sucker bets and let a strong P.C. reduce your chance to win to next to nothing—don't say you had no way of knowing any better. That excuse may have gotten by up until now, but it won't serve any longer.

If you think that the picture just presented is too gloomy and if you wonder why, when the house or hustler has a better chance to win on every bet, it is ever possible for anyone to win, the answer is that dice, cards, and wheels do not and are not expected to act *exactly* according to their probabilities.

If you will toss a coin a hundred times, you should find that you have made several runs of 5 or 6 or even more successive heads or tails. Shooting dice, you may at some time find yourself making pass after pass. When this happens, the player who is betting the dice to lose often growls and wants to know "what the hell happened to the law of averages; was it repealed along with Prohibition?" And when they go cold for a spell and make nothing but missouts, the right bettor can't understand it either.

The answer is that the theory of probability does not pretend to make precise statements about what can be expected to happen in a small number of throws. Its statements are only an approximation of what can be expected to happen in the long run. Although heads will eventually be thrown very nearly the same number of times as tails, coins do not turn up heads and tails alternately. And dice do not throw each of the 36 possible combinations every 36 rolls although they average that eventually.

HOT AND COLD SPELLS

Any limited sequence of rolls is likely to be full of surprises. It may be filled with what the gamblers call "hot and cold spells" or "storms in the law of averages." The dice may go all around the table without any player making a pass. I have often seen cold spells where ten or more successive missouts were thrown, then one pass, then another long run of missouts. I have seen hot spells in which the shooter has thrown ten or more passes before missing out with the next shooter following through with four or five more passes.

Without allowing for the 1-41/99 P.C. that favors the fader, probability says that there is only one chance in 1024 that ten passes will be

thrown in succession. But there are so many thousands of players rolling dice every day in the year that such hot and cold spells are to be
expected. If they were not, there would be no games of chance. The
expectation of hot and cold spells is what makes hope spring eternal in
the gambler's breast.

The house insures itself against the risk inherent in these storms by
placing a *limit* on the size of the bets that can be made. The limit
prevents the players from winning too much in too short a space of
time. It means that, in order to make the big killing they all hope for,
they must play longer. And the longer they play, the less chance they
have of making a big win because the law of averages gets more opportunity to work and balance the hot and cold spells. The house is also
partial to long sessions because they produce a greater number of bets
and a larger total take in percentage.

In addition, the limit prevents the progressive system player from
doubling up his bets indefinitely each time he loses until he finally wins
one bet, recoups all his losses plus a profit and eventually breaks the
bank. It also prevents the big bettor doing the same thing in short order.
Without a limit he could walk in, ask how big a bankroll the house had
and bet the full amount. The house would then stand to double its
money if the big bettor lost and would go broke at once if he won, a
situation that has altogether too many "ifs" in it. The house doesn't
operate on any if basis; it is in business not to *win* money if possible but
to *earn* money all the time by taking a percentage on the bets made.

Amateur game operators who rent gambling apparatus for use at
outings and bazaars, not knowing what a limit is for, sometimes make it
higher than their bankroll can stand or neglect to have one at all. The
first question the smart boys ask when when they find such a game is,
"How much can I bet, buddy?" And if the amateur operator who thinks
that his Chuck-a-Luck cage will bring him in a steady 7-47/54% profit
under any and all conditions says, "Why, anything you like, boys," his
goose is already cooked!

As further proof that the house doesn't like to gamble and that
some operators don't like storms even when they are favorable, take the
case of one operator I know who found that he had won about $50,000
over and above the earning power of his P.C. As the money continued
to come in, he got gloomier and gloomier until, as the game started on
the sixth night, one of the other bosses asked, "What's biting *you?* Why
all the gloom?"

"And why shouldn't I be worried?" he replied. "We've had too
damned much of a good thing. No winning streak ever lasts and, when

we begin to lose, how do I know we won't lose more than we've won? I don't like it. That kind of money never stays with you." He gave the tables a sour look. "Tonight'll be the night," he predicted glumly.

He was wrong. It wasn't. But the losing spell he expected did set in shortly afterward and a few weeks later the pessimistic operator's face had lost its worried look. "We've lost thirty grand back to the players," he said with a pleased grin. "Now I can sleep nights."

THE GAMBLER'S FALLACY

This story not only illustrates the gambler's attitude toward storms, but also his tendency to believe that a run of good luck must always be followed by a run of bad luck so that in the long run the two will even up. This idea, known as the doctrine of the *maturity of chances,* has caused many a gambler to lose a fortune in folding money. In spite of the fact that mathematicians have for years referred to the belief as "the gamblers' fallacy" there are still many otherwise well educated persons who argue heatedly in its favor.

They are the players who, after heads have appeared on several successive tosses of a coin always bet that tails will appear next because they think the odds favor it. In a crap game they bet the dice to lose after the shooter has thrown a series of passes. "He can't make another one," they say. "The law of averages states that there has got to be more missouts than passes in the long run."

Their first error consists in their habit of referring to the theory of probability as the *law of averages* and in forgetting that the important part of that phrase is not the word law but the word average. The theory of probability does *not* state that tails *must* come more often than usual after a series of heads has been thrown. There is no such law. If tails began to appear more often for any such reason, it would mean that the coin could remember what had happened and had the ability to base its future actions upon its past performance.

Given a long enough run of heads, the odds against tails on the next throw, according to the maturity of chances, would gradually be reduced until the appearance of tails was a near certainty. And if there is ever anything certain about the next toss of a coin, it would mean that our old friend the supernatural bogieman was back again pushing the coin this way and that, and defying gravitation so that the coin will fall as it should!

The theory of probability does not say that there is a law that heads must come half the time. It says that they will probably come an *average* of half the time in the long run, which is something considerably different. To illustrate, suppose that you tossed a coin 1,000 times and discovered at the finish that you had thrown fifty more heads than tails. The gambler who believes in the maturity of chances would say, "Hmm. Tails has got to come fifty more times than heads from here on so that they'll even up. I'll start betting on tails."

What he doesn't realize is that heads and tails can almost even up in the long run even if tails only appears from that point on exactly one half the time. An extra fifty throws of tails is not only not to be expected, but is entirely unnecessary. The extra fifty heads that amounted to 1/20 of the total in the series of 1,000 throws will, in a series of 100,000 throws, automatically be reduced to a mere 1/2000. And the more throws that are made the more minute this difference becomes.

If the gambler would consider, as he should, all the previous tosses of coins that preceded his 1,000 throws, the extra fifty heads amounts to a percentage so infinitely small that an electronic microscope couldn't find it.

The probability that either heads or tails will appear on the next throw is always one-half, no matter what may have happened before or who may be tossing the coin. The sole exception is when the coin has been so gaffed that it is not symmetrical or when the thrower is adept at sleight of hand.

THE "GUESSERS' DISADVANTAGE"

There is another curious belief held by many players including a lot of professional gamblers who have spent their lives around the gaming tables and who should know better. They say: "The guy who does the guessing has the worst of it. Even when you toss a coin and the chances are fifty-fifty, the guy who cries heads (or tails) is more likely to be wrong and will lose more bets than the guy who keeps his mouth shut and just covers the bet."

This "guesser's disadvantage" theory originated back in the days when the players had no clear notion of why it was that operators of games always showed a profit. They noticed that the operators never expressed any opinion as to the result of the next throw of the dice or turn of the wheel but merely covered the players' bets and let the latter do all the guessing. They jumped to the conclusion that this explained the operator's advantage.

The theory was repeated so often and gained such wide acceptance among gamblers that even today players who know the odds and have some knowledge of the operation of percentage still insist "there is something in it."

If anyone ever tries to give you such an argument, here's the way to stop him. Just reply, "Okay, suppose we bet on the toss of a coin and suppose I do all the guessing. And suppose I always guess heads. Are you trying to tell me that the coin is going to land tails oftener than the law of averages says it can be expected to just because I have a stubborn habit of guessing heads?

"And how does the coin know what I'm guessing? Does it have ears? And suppose it's a Chinese coin and I make my guesses in English; would the coin be hep to what I am saying or would it have to send out a hurry call for a translator? And even if it did know, how does it manage to make that extra half turn part of the time so it will land tails more often and cross me up? Maybe it's part jumping bean and part acrobat? Or maybe it's haunted?"

If the guy still wants to argue that his "guessers have the worst of it" theory is right, you should phone the nearest newspaper and tell them you have discovered a freak who believes that a fifty-cent piece is so smart it should have the right to vote!

GAMBLING DICE SYSTEMS

In the gambling casinos where I am a consultant, players often come up to me and say, "Hey, Scarne, give me a system so I can beat the dice table." They all get the same answer: "If I knew any system that would overcome the house percentage, I would keep it strictly to myself. If you had a sure-fire winning system you would do the same." There is nothing more futile than the attempt to cook up betting systems that will overcome adverse odds.

The oldest and commonest betting system is the Martingale or "doubling up" system, in which bets are doubled progressively. This probably dates back to the invention of dice, but every day of the week some gambler somewhere re-invents it, or some variation of it, and believes he has something new. Over the years hundreds of "sure-fire" winning systems have been dreamed up, and not one of them is worth the price of yesterday's newspaper.

The reason is simple. When you make a bet at less than the correct odds, which you always do in any casino dice game, you are paying the operator a percentage charge for the privilege of making the bet. Your chance of winning has what mathematicians call a "minus expectation." When you use a dice system you make a series of bets, each of which has a minus expectation. There is no way of adding minuses to get a plus, or adding losses to show a profit.

Add to this the fact that all dice table operators place a minimum and maximum betting limit on their tables so that it is impossible to double-up bets indefinitely. This and the table's house percentage make all gambling dice percentage worthless.

The system player believes his system will overcome the dice table's favorable house edge. He couldn't be more wrong. All dice systems actually work against the player and for the house because they are all based on a combination or series of bets, and the more bets the system player makes, the more he increases the operator's percentage take.

If a casino player with $100 wants merely to double it, the soundest plan is to risk it all in one bet on the "Don't pass" line on the crap table. When he splits his $100 into smaller bets, as he would have to do playing most systems, he merely reduces his chance of doubling his money; the smaller the bets, the less chance he has.

3

Psychic or
Educated Dice

The newest craps betting system to hit Las Vegas casinos is the Psychic or P.K. Betting System, and it is for my money the most ridiculous form of craps betting in history. It results from the many magazine and newspaper articles describing the dice rolling experiments of a number of psychic researchers who claim that their P.K. (psychokinesis) experiments with dice have proved that the mind can influence and control the action of rolling dice. These psychic researchers say that some people have a mysterious supernormal, possibly psychic power, which enables them occasionally to make desired numbers come up on dice just by wishing much more often than probability predicts.

Many crapshooters decide that if some people can emit thought waves and make the dice behave as desired, they can, too. So they head for the nearest crap table, hoping that these mystic powers will bring them a fortune. Hundreds of E.S.P. and PK believers lose thousands of dollars each year at the Las Vegas Bank Craps tables.

The question of supernormal forces and the effect they don't have on the throw of a pair of dice was all started by Dr. Joseph Banks Rhine and the curious crap game he once operated in his parapsychology laboratory at Duke University in Durham, North Carolina. After rolling the Memphis dominoes for ten years under all sorts of conditions, he comes up with a claim that is even more astonishing and harder to believe than his famous Extra Sensory Perception. He submits that his evidence proves the existence of what he calls Psychokinesis, or, for short, the PK effect.

He defines PK as "the direct influence exerted on a physical system by a *subject* without any known intermediate energy or instrumentation." In other words, he means that some people can concentrate hard enough on certain numbers or groups of numbers to make those numbers come up when the dice are thrown more often than their chance expectation. More briefly, PK is the influence of mind over matter.

Dr. Rhine reports that his choice of dice as the experimental procedure for PK research was suggested to him by a man whom he describes in one report as a "young amateur gambler" and in another as a young "experienced gambler." This man claimed that he was able to influence dice by the "mind over matter" principle and demonstrated by rolling a pair in Dr. Rhine's office and throwing high dice (8 or above) more often than could be expected by chance.

I should like to know more about the subsequent history of this young, but experienced amateur gambler and whether or not he has since made a fortune at the gaming tables, and if not, why not. He reminds me a little of a gambler I know who was grousing about his luck to a bank crap dealer. "I'm the greatest hard luck guy in the world," he said. "Why when I shoot the dice, I *never* make a pass."

"You call that hard luck, buddy?" the dealer said. "Why you should be a millionaire."

"Millionaire?" the gambler said blinking. "What do you mean?"

"The layout has a Don't Pass line on it, doesn't it? If you never make a pass, how come you haven't been betting the dice to lose? Didn't you ever think of that?"

If Dr. Rhine is right and the mind can influence matter in this way, then the present betting odds in all games of chance are shot to hell. All the customary odds will have to be figured all over again from scratch every time that a new player with a different mental rating enters the game!

But before we let ourselves in for this I would like to ask Dr. Rhine a few questions. He admits that, as in his ESP tests, when a subject's score is not above chance expectation or when it drops to that level, he eliminates that person on the ground that it is not worth experimenting with subjects who have no psychophysical abilities or who have lost interest. And he publishes only the significant reports in which high scores have been made and leaves out those which are at or below the chance level. He says that, if he were studying those mathematical freaks known as "lightning calculators," it would be only common sense not to bother with any subjects who had not made high scores on their math exams. On the other hand, if I were to select from among the gamblers I know only those who have had more than their share of luck at even-up bets, I could also make out an impressive case for the existence of some supernormal sixth-sense ability to predict the future and tell what the dice were going to do next. But I certainly wouldn't consider that I had made a fair test.

ARE RHINE'S DICE EVERYTHING THEY SHOULD BE?

There is one thing I am positive that Dr. Rhine should do and that is to exercise considerably more care in selecting the dice he uses. His reports state that "the common commercial variety" are used in the experiments. This description covers far too much territory and includes a lot of very queer dice. Dr. Rhine uses the chance expectation of the dice as a yardstick in measuring his results and yet no casino operator who depends upon exactly the same thing to bring him a profit would ever think of using dice that answer to any such vague description. They certainly would not use the opaque white dice that a photo published in the June 1944 issue of the *Journal of Parapsychology* shows were used in certain experiments.

These cubes were bounced around in a wooden and wire mesh cage for 35,784 throws and the experimenter adds the further note that they were the same three dice that had been used in an earlier experiment two years before in which they were thrown some 1,056 times. Whether the dice were kept in cotton wool in the interim or whether the experimenter's children played with them on a concrete sidewalk is not stated.

In another experiment* six dice were thrown more than 150,000 times and nothing is said as to whether the dice used were new or whether they were family heirlooms. Any die not made of an indestructible material, and the common commercial variety are anything but that, will gradually become more and more imperfect as its edges, corners and surfaces become chipped and worn from use.

Furthermore, the manufacture of the "common, commercial variety" Rhine admits using is definitely not a precision operation. I have known for years that dicemakers, professional gamblers and casino operators insist that store dice are imperfect and not to be trusted to

---

* The Gibson-Rhine series reported in the *Journal of Parapsychology*, Dec. 1943.

supply the percentage that the law of averages says can be expected. But just to check up I recently spent an afternoon examining 12 boxes of store dice, each box containing 60 dice. There were 12 different varieties in different sizes, colors, and materials (both transparent plastic and opaque plastic, and bone) and with different types of edges (light and heavy trims) and corners (more or less rounded).

With 720 dice before me, I began testing samples from each box using a dicemaker's right-angle square with a knife edge. (I did not bother with many micrometer readings because a die can caliper the same diameter in all directions and still be out of square.) I did not find a single die which did not show some light under the knife-edge on one or more sides. Some surfaces showed slight *bevels* (convex), some were concave, others were high in some places, low in others, others were not at right angles to the adjacent sides. In addition, the rounded edges and corners were not equally rounded on all edges and corners.

After testing more than one hundred dice, the dicemaker who was watching me said, "Johnny, you're wasting your time. I've been buying and selling store dice and making perfect dice for forty years. Once in a blue moon you might find a single store die that classes as a *perfect,* but the chance of finding two of them in the same box of 60 and the chance that they would both be sold to the same purchaser as a pair is so small you can forget about it. It never happened. Store dice, also known as "drugstore" or "candystore" dice, are imperfect because they are machine-made. Perfect dice, true to a tolerance of 1/5000 of an inch, can only be made by hand.

MATHEMATICAL MONKEY WRENCHES

Each individual store die has small imperfections which make it deviate in the long run from the normal chance expectation. Each die has an individual chance expectation all its own which depends upon its own individual, slightly lopsided characteristics. And worse, as the dice are rolled their chance expectation changes. They may begin by favoring some sides more than others, wear a bit and favor another set of sides, wear some more and favor still another combination of surfaces.

Throws made with such dice are bound to show deviations from what chance says can be expected—deviations which are not constant but which shift. To use admittedly imperfect dice and then conclude that the deviations found must be due to a mysterious psychic PK factor which, if it is ever proved to exist, will upset the whole scientific applecart, is in my opinion scientific applesauce.

In addition there is always the ever present possibility that the hot and cold spells which can be expected to appear once in a million times may very well show up during the few thousand throws of the experiment and throw a big mathematical monkey wrench into the results.

Furthermore, it must always be remembered that the predictions of the theory of probability are only nearly true for an infinite number of throws, not exactly true for a short number. If the number of throws is too short, the probability theorems have no meaning at all. The theory of probability is a very tricky yardstick to use because the law of averages is not a law but only a mathematical guess at what may happen.

Also, I have so far found no evidence in the Rhine reports that the experimenters decide upon a specified number of throws *before* each experiment is begun. Unless that technique can be adopted, the suspicion keeps popping up that the subjects may be terminating a series of throws when they are ahead of the game just as the smart gambler stops when he has won.

If, instead of placing all his eggs in the statistical basket, Dr. Rhine would also buy a professional brand of dice and discard them after a reasonable number of throws, it would help to eliminate the possibility that his results might be due to imperfect dice. He should take at least the same amount of pains in selecting his dice that the operator of a gambling house does. He should purchase them from a manufacturer who does not deal in cheating devices and should insist that they be true to a tolerance of 1/5,000 of an inch with all surfaces perfectly flat.

These dice come wrapped in metal foil so that the "hi-tempered" plastic material of which they are made is protected against shrinkage or expansion due to extremes of temperature or moisture. The manufacturer has checked and double checked them with a micrometer and a square-edge and Dr. Rhine, when he receives them should, as the house operator does, check them again in the same way.

At the crap table 15 to 20 of these professional dice are used each evening and each pair is rolled during the session on an average of 100 to 150 times. After *one night's* use, they are discarded. Since his tests have such vastly important implications, and since such small deviations are important, Dr. Rhine should also, as most casino operators do, always insist upon flush spot dice whose spots are not countersunk. If he does not have the name and address of such a manufacturer in his files, I shall be glad to supply one.

THE QUESTION BEFORE THE HOUSE

Dr. Rhine's theory, if proven, will also cause some unusual changes in gambling house operation. For years the casino operators have gone merrily ahead assuming that the theory of probabilities insured them a certain percentage of the play. But if Rhine's PK really works, whenever a high-domed-individual walks in who looks as though he might be able to make the dice behave merely by thinking about it, they may have to have a house concentrator handy whose mental gymnastics will protect the bank from going broke.

To date no gambling house has yet hired such an employee. The operators I have questioned all want to ask Dr. Rhine one question. "Why is it," they want to know, "that we have never noticed the presence of any unsuspected PK factor upsetting the operation of the percentage we depend upon?"

And I have a question too. "When twenty or thirty players at a bank crap table with one-way action (having a Pass but not a Don't Pass line) bet the dice to win by putting their money on the Pass line, they all begin wishing that the dice pass with much more voltage than any lone, calm and dispassionate scientific experimenter who has not wagered any money on the outcome would ever do. Why then, if the PK effect is a fact, doesn't the bank lose that bet more often than it does?"

The combined mental efforts of the players are certainly not offset by any concentrating the dealer may do; he has no interest at all in the outcome of the roll because he places his trust in Old Man Percentage and, in any case, is far too busy to give any thought to the matter.

If the PK effect produces a favorable percentage as high as 1.414%, a bet on the win line is an even-up proposition and the house take on that bet is reduced to zero. If the PK effect produces a higher percentage, then the house has the worst of it. In either case, they would have noticed long ago that something was haywire in Denmark. The pass line would have disappeared from the layouts quicker than you can say Duke University. There has been no noticeable trend in this direction; all bank crap layouts still carry the pass line space.

If Dr. Rhine can get an okay from the cops to operate a bank crap layout at Duke University, and if he would like to send a team of his best subjects up against a bank crap layout to find out how much their concentrated will power can whittle down the P.C., I'll be glad to take a layout down there and deal the game. And although I apparently do not have the PK faculty, having made a few tests at influencing the dice by will power without any success, I will nevertheless promise not to do any anti-concentrating of my own. I should, however, warn the doctor that the cost of such an experiment may be more than he suspects!*

As an example of how tricky statistics, and probability mathematics in particular, are to handle let's take an article Dr. Rhine published in the September 1944 *American Magazine*. He tells about one of his subjects who consistently gets an above-chance score in ESP tests and relates an instance in which the young man first called 5 ESP cards wrong and then, when Dr. Rhine bet him one hundred dollars that he couldn't call the next one right, hit it on the nose. Spurred on by additional $100 bets, he continued to call them correctly, getting 25 cards without a miss!

Then Dr. Rhine says, "The odds against that young man's calls having been due to pure and undiluted chance are 1 in 298,023,223,-876,953,125."

There are several things wrong with that one small sentence. First, the term *odds* is incorrectly used. You don't say, "the odds against an event are 1 chance in 10." You either say "there is 1 chance in 10" or "the odds are 9 to 1 against the event."

Secondly, the figure he gives refers only to the 25 hits and leaves out of account the 5 misses. The tendency to ignore the misses is hardly scientific cricket.

But those criticisms are minor. It is very difficult to know just what Dr. Rhine and his subject were doing from his report of the procedure he employed. It is worded much more vaguely than any laboratory report ever should be even when paraphrased for a popular magazine. He says, that after shuffling a deck he drew off a card and the subject called it wrong. "He called five wrong in succession . . . got the next three right . . . each time I cut the deck. He got it right. He got the next one . . . In an unbroken sequence he called 25 cards correctly."

---

* Dr. Rhine says he hasn't the slightest idea as to how to explain the PK effect. He doesn't know what it is that makes the dice fall the way the person concentrating wants them to. It would seem, however, since the dice are normally acted upon by two main forces—the momentum of the throw and the pull of gravity that brings them to a stop, that any interfering, mysterious PK influence must be an opposing *force* of some sort. The dice must be given a small extra push or pull in one direction or another. If this is the case, there would seem to be a far simpler method of isolating that force for study. Why not balance a small arrow on the point of a needle? Place it in a vacuum under a bell jar and on a large concrete block in a place where there is a minimum of vibration. The arrow would need to be made of material that would not be attracted by magnetic substances and should be grounded so that it does not pick up electrical charges. Then if Rhine's subjects can concentrate their will power and generate the same amount of steam needed to influence a moving die whose inertia and gravitational attraction is considerable, the needle should spin around like mad. If it only moves slightly, that would still be much better proof than the complicated statistics which Rhine compares with a very tricky theory or probability. The movement could be seen and measured and it would not have to be measured against the theory of probability whose statements of what can be expected are only approximate for an infinite number of throws.

At first glance this would seem to mean that Dr. Rhine has dealt out 30 cards from an ESP deck which contains only 25 cards, a good trick if you can do it. He may, of course, have returned those first five cards to the deck, but he nowhere gives any hint of having done so. What is more important is that the only way in which the odds could be as stated are in the event that Dr. Rhine did *not* tell the subject either what card was drawn each time or even whether or not his guess was correct. And yet Rhine says nothing whatsoever about his procedure on this point. On the contrary he speaks of the tension growing as the test continued and, after the 25th card had been called correctly, he says, "Then the tension broke." And the subject cried, "You'll never get me to do that again." This would seem to indicate that the subject knew what had been happening. If so the odds given are completely incorrect.

And then, making matters even worse, Rhine proceeds to draw an analogy. To help the reader understand what an astounding feat his subject had performed he says, "Can you imagine anybody standing beside a poker table, not kibitzing, and calling in sequence every card in 5 hands of draw?" He very plainly infers that this is comparable to calling 25 ESP cards in sequence. He seems to forget that the ESP deck, which he invented, consists of only five different cards five times repeated, whereas a poker deck contains 52 cards that are all different.

The chance of calling 25 ESP cards in sequence, when the caller is not told the result after each call, is, as the doctor says, 1 in 298,023,-223,876,953,125. But the chance of calling 5 hands of draw (25 cards) in sequence from a poker deck are just a little bit different. Figured by logarithms they are 1 chance in 74071 followed by 35 zeros. Computed by the more laborious but more accurate method of simple arithmetic they are 1 chance in 7,407,396,657,496,428,903,767,538,970,656,-768,000,000.

If you care to check that figure all you need to do is multiply $52 \times 51 \times 50 \times 49$ and continue the operation all the way down to the number 28.

Dr. J.B. Rhine and his psychic experiments first came to my attention when I read a copy of the Journal of Abonormal and Social Psychology, Volume 23 (1929) and on pages 449–466 was an article entitled *An Investigation of a Mindreading Horse* by J.B. Rhine and Louisa E. Rhine, Ph.D., of Duke University. The article states in part:

"The animal subject of the experiments herein described is a three-year-old filly, Lady, (later named Lady Wonder), owned by Mrs. C.D. Fonda of Richmond, Virginia.

"According to reports which led to our inquiry, the horse could make predictions, solve simple arithmetical problems, answer questions aptly and intelligently and do all this without verbal commands. All that was needed was that the question be written down and shown to Mrs. Fonda. In Mrs. Fonda's opinion these accomplishments were due to a combination in the horse of unusual intelligence and the capacity for mind-reading.

"Our experiments were begun December 3, 1927, and ended January 15, 1928, covering in this period a total of six days. The tests were made at the residence of Mrs. Fonda in a demonstration-tent about 9 × 12 feet.

"Professor William McDougall was present and participated in the experiments on two days and Assistant Superintendent John F. Thomas of the Detroit schools on one day. Others present were Mrs. C.D. Fonda, J.B. Rhine, and Louisa E. Rhine."

So Dr. J.B. Rhine, after employing his great telepathic testing techniques on the horse named Lady for six full days, aided by a number of his colleagues including his superior at Duke University, Professor William McDougall, and after taking one year's time to think over his experiments with the horse named Lady and to discuss them with his colleagues at Duke University, wrote the following:

"There is left then, only the telepathic explanation, the transference of mental influence by an unknown process. Nothing was discovered that failed to accord with it, and no other hypothesis proposed seems tenable in view of the results."

In plain everyday language the above simply means that Dr. J.B. Rhine, after an extensive investigation aided by Professor William Mc-Dougall, the head of the department of psychology at Duke University, states in print that Mrs. Fonda's horse, Lady, can read a person's mind.

Shortly after I read the above article I decided to investigate Lady, the mind-reading horse, personally. The day I arrived at the farm of Mrs. Fonda, the owner of the mind-reading horse, I had to wait until a crowd of people—who were having their minds read by the horse—thinned out, before I could enter the tent harboring Mrs. Fonda and Lady.

Lady was standing in front of an old wooden table on which were arranged several rows of children's small, lettered wooden blocks, each block showing one letter of the alphabet.

Mrs. Fonda readily advised me that Lady would read my mind and answer any question I thought of. I then asked Mrs. Fonda, "Does Lady also talk?"

Mrs. Fonda smiled a bit and then explained to me that Lady, after reading my mind, would answer my question simply by spelling out the answer. She went on to explain that the horse's nose would touch one letter at a time and thereby spell out the answer to my question.

I didn't say a word but just tried to look interested. She then told me to ask Lady any question I wished. "How do I do that?" I asked.

Mrs. Fonda replied, "Just say, Lady, please tell me: how did I get out here?"

I repeated the question. "Lady, please tell me: how did I get out here?"

Lady moved her head a bit, then dropped her head close to the lettered blocks resting on the table. After a few seconds hesitation Lady's nose pushed the lettered block marked C. Lady brought her head upward again, then down again and her nose pushed the letter A. Next Lady with her nose pushed the lettered block marked R. The three letters spelled out CAR.

After this demonstration of mindreading on Lady's part, I turned to Mrs. Fonda and said, "That's wonderful, but I have a question I'm thinking of that I would like Lady to answer. How do I ask her without telling her what the question is?"

Mrs. Fonda seemed stumped for a moment, then handed me a pad and pencil. "Write your question on this pad and don't let Lady see it."

I was prompted at this moment to say, "Mrs. Fonda, don't tell me Lady can also read? And how did the Duke researchers miss that?" But I thought better of it and just wrote my question on the paper, but did so without Mrs. Fonda seeing it.

She looked a little disappointed but turned to Lady and said, "Lady, answer Mr. Scarne's question." Lady didn't move her head and the reason was obvious to me. Mrs. Fonda had not seen the question I had written on the pad. So after about five minutes' wait I realized that if Mrs. Fonda did not see my question, Lady wasn't going to push those children's blocks around with her nose. So I decided to let her get a glimpse of the question without my apparently knowing that she did. As I turned to talk to a man next to me, I surreptitiously turned over the pad so that Mrs. Fonda could read the question which read, "Where do I live?"

I turned around again after being convinced that Mrs. Fonda had read the message and immediately Lady started to push the children's blocks around with her nose. The lettered blocks that Lady pushed with her nose spelled N-E-W Y-O-R-K.

I acted surprised and said, "That's wonderful! How did Lady know I live in New York?" (Although I actually then lived in Fairview, New Jersey, I decided to go along with the gag.) I handed Mrs. Fonda five dollars and left.

As I think back through the years, the only clever thing about Mrs. Fonda and her mind-reading horse, Lady, (later named Lady Wonder), was Mrs. Fonda's salesmanship in duping the professors from Duke University. The simple feat of having Lady push the proper lettered block with her nose at the proper time is easily explained.

Mrs. Fonda carried a small whip when I saw her and she cued the horse by waving the whip. I had caught Mrs. Fonda cueing Lady when Lady moved the first block with her nose. This method of doing the trick might have puzzled me for a few minutes if I hadn't known that the placement of a horse's eyes on the sides of the head gives it a wide backward range of peripheral vision. Therefore, it was no problem to detect. It was done as follws:

When cueing Lady, Mrs. Fonda stood about two-and-a-half feet behind and at approximately a 60-degree angle to Lady's head. She cued Lady by shaking a small whip carried in her right hand. The shaking of the whip the first time was the cue for Lady to bend her head within a couple of inches of the lettered blocks. The second shake of the whip was the cue for Lady to move her head continuously in a bent position back and forth over the blocks. When Lady's head was above the desired block, Mrs. Fonda cued Lady to drop her head onto the desired block by again shaking the whip. It was as simple as all that.

Why some people still believe in such nonsense as mindreading and psychokinesis, is due in part to the television exposure of the many so-called mindreaders, including Kreskin. Kreskin, in addition to making false claims of reading minds, also claims to be barred from gambling in Nevada casinos because he knows too much, and this with his supernormal extrasensory perception powers makes black jack a cinch of a game to beat. I have $100,000 to wager that says Kreskin can't read minds, $100,000 to wager that says he can't beat black jack and $100,000 to wager that says he's not barred from gambling in Nevada casinos. Another $100,000 wager says that all self-styled psychics are imposters. This includes Uri Geller, the guy who claims that he can bend nails or keys with his psychokinesis powers. As a rule I seldom expose these trick store magicians such as Kreskin and Geller, even when they deceive the public by claiming that they possess psychic powers. But, when I see women and men who believe this rot lose their hard earned cash at the gaming tables, which many of them can ill afford, because they believe there are such thing as psychic betting systems to beat the tables, it is my duty as a gambling expert to expose such humbug.

Kreskin's forte, his so-called audience mindreading feat on television, is accomplished as follows. He fakes his so-called mindreading or extra-sensory experiments by using confederates or by passing out slips of paper on which the audience are requested to write their questions and answers before a television show goes on the air. Then Kreskin or his confederates collects or steals several of these slips while pretending to seal them in envelopes. These stolen slips are brought backstage where Kreskin reads them and copies them on a hidden sheet which he conceals when on stage. Then when the show goes on the air, he secretly reads the written answers and pretends to be reading the minds of people in the audience. The rest of his phony mindreading tricks can be purchased in any magic store for a couple of bucks. How the television networks stand for such out and out deception is beyond my comprehension.

In concluding this chapter, I would like to repeat what I have been saying for years and that which the Great Houdini had said earlier, namely that hypnotism, extra-sensory perception, psychokinesis, mindreading, thought reading, telepathy, and clairvoyance are all humbug. To back up the above statements, I am prepared to wager $100,000 against an equal amount that I can prove that all so-called psychic feats are simply magic tricks and I haven't seen one of these tricks done that I cannot duplicate or surpass. Modest? No, just telling the truth.

4

Various Craps and Scarne's Rules

Very few men have not played a game of Craps at some time or other. Women, however, seldom played Craps until it appeared in Nevada casinos in the form of Bank Craps.

Let us look at the differences among the five modern variations of Craps: Private Craps, Bank Craps, Money or Open Craps, New York Craps, and Scarney Craps, all of which are usually referred to as "crap-shooting" or "shooting crap."

Private Craps is a friendly social game that does not use a casino, Craps table, or banker. The only requisites for Private Craps are two or more persons with cash in their pockets and a pair of dice. It can be played on a street corner, in a back alley, private club, army barracks, living room—anywhere the players have room in which to roll the dice.

Bank Craps is the version of the game found in all Nevada Casinos and in most legalized establishments throughout the world. Bank Craps is played on a specially constructed dice table of size and form similar to a billiard table. (For a description, see: Bank Craps, page 100.) Three dealers and two house employees known as *boxmen* stand at the side of the table. One of the dealers, known as a *stickman*, handles the dice and stands opposite the boxmen. Although there are other different-shaped layouts, the actual difference is small. Players are not permitted to gamble against each other; all bets are made against the house. Chips or checks are used instead of cash when wagers are placed on the layout. The layout is fixed so that the house has a mathematical advantage on every bet.

Money Craps, Open Craps, or Fading Craps is a game played with cash in which players are permitted to bet on point numbers among themselves. A houseman, called a banker or bookie, is present to accept any bet within the house limit on all other bets and to point numbers that a player is unable to place with another player. For this privilege, the player must pay the banker a charge, usually 5 percent of the amount wagered.

New York Craps is a version of Bank Craps found in gambling houses in the eastern part of the United States, the Bahamas, and in England. The game is played on a specially constructed dice table that is similar to a Las Vegas or Bank Craps table. However, the table and layout are somewhat different and the house employees (dealers) are posted at each end of the table. A stickman stands at the center of the table and two boxmen sit opposite the stickman. The table is known as a *double-end dealer* and the dealers take a charge of 5 percent of the amount wagered on the point numbers (4, 5, 6, 8, 9, 10).

Scarney Craps, a recent creation of the author, is a version of Bank Craps and New York Craps combined. Scarney Craps, like New York Craps, lacks a Come and Don't Come space. However, like Bank Craps, it makes use of place betting instead of the 5% charge. The game is found in casinos in Europe, Curacao, Aruba, St. Maarten, Turkey and South America. It is played on a Las Vegas type of Bank Craps table.

SCARNE'S RULES FOR PRIVATE CRAPS

Equipment

1. Two dice each numbered from one to six in such a way that the spots on opposite sides add to seven.

2. A wall or backboard against which the dice are thrown.

Players

1. Any number may play.

2. The player throwing the dice is the *shooter*. Any player, by consent of the others, may start the game by becoming the shooter.

3. A new player may enter the game at any time provided there is an opening in the circle. If no player objects at the time he takes his position, he becomes the shooter at his proper turn even though he may take a position directly at the left of the shooter.

4. The dice pass around the circle of players to the left—clockwise.

5. Players may leave the game at any time (without regard to their wins or losses).

The Play

1. The dice are thrown and the two numbers that face skyward when the dice come to rest, added together, are the deciding numbers.

2. If on the first roll, called the *come-out*, the shooter throws—
a *natural* (7 or 11) it is a winning decision called a *Pass*.
a *crap* (2, 3 or 12) it is a losing decision called a *Missout*.
4, 5, 6, 8, 9, or 10, that number becomes the shooter's *point* and he continues throwing until he either
  (a) throws his point again which effects a winning decision or *Pass*
or (b) throws a seven which effects a losing decision or *Missout*

3. The shooter's first roll and each roll after a decision has been effected is a *come-out*.

4. When the shooter misses out on the point, the dice pass to the next player on his left and it becomes his turn to shoot.

5. The shooter may pass the dice to the next player on completion of any decision without waiting to missout on the point if he wishes.

6. Any player may, if he likes, refuse to shoot in his turn, and pass the dice to the next player.

7. When more than one pair of dice are employed, players may call for a *box-up* or change of dice at any time, the change taking place immediately after the next decision.

The Throw or Roll

1. The shooter shakes the dice in his closed hand and must try to throw them so that both dice hit and rebound from the backboard.

2. If only one die hits the board, the roll counts but the players may reprimand the shooter.

3. If this occurs a second time, the other players may designate someone else to complete the shooter's turn at throwing. If they wish, they may also bar him from shooting for the duration of the game.

4. If neither die hits the board, or if, when playing on a table or elevated surface, one or both dice fall off the playing surface, the roll is *no-dice*. It does not count and the dice must be thrown again.

5. If the dice hit any object or person after hitting the board, the roll counts. It is not *no-dice*.

6. If a die comes to rest cocked at an angle on a coin or any irregularity on the playing surface, and there is a difference of opinion as to which number faces skyward, a neutral player, or any player designated by common consent, or a bystander shall stand at the shooter's position and decide which number counts by stating which top surface of the die appears to be the skyward surface from that position.*

7. If, after hitting the backboard, a die rolls out of sight under a bill or any other object on the playing surface, either a neutral player, a player designated by common consent, or a bystander shall take extreme care in trying to ascertain the skyward number.

8. The practice of knocking or kicking the dice aside on the roll and calling "Gate!" or "No dice!" (known as *gating*) is not permitted.

Betting

1. RIGHT BET. A wager that the dice will *pass* (win either by making a natural on the come-out or by throwing a point on the come-out and then repeating it before throwing a seven). Players making right bets are *right bettors.*

2. WRONG BET. A wager that the dice *don't pass.* Players making wrong bets are *wrong bettors.*

3. PROPOSITION BET. This term is applied in Private Craps to any bet not a Point or Off Number bet or a Flat bet.

---

* Foster and others state that when a die comes to rest at an angle it is a cocked die, is no-dice and does not count. This is never adhered to in any of the top casinos and is not advisable even in the private game. It causes too many arguments because some players will cry "no dice" when the die is only slightly cocked and others, to whom the number showing is important, will disagree. When playing on an irregular surface there is no satisfactory way of deciding how much of an angle constitutes a cocked die.

4. All bets must be made before the dice are thrown and cannot be made while they are rolling.

5. Any Point or Off Number bet may be called off by the bettors concerned before a decision is effected.

6. CENTER BET. Before the come-out the shooter may (but is not required to) bet that he will *pass*. Players who cover this wager by betting an equal amount against the shooter *fade* the shooter and are known as *faders*. These wagers, placed in the center of the playing surface, are *center bets*.*

7. If only a part of the shooter's center bet is covered, the shooter may shoot for that amount or he may call the bet off by saying "no bet."

8. SIDE BET. Any bet not a center bet is placed at one side of the playing surface and is known as a *side bet*. The shooter may make any side bet including the flat bet.

9. FLAT BET. A side bet made before the come-out that the dice pass or don't pass. Same as the center bet except that the shooter is not being faded and the bet is placed at the side.

10. POINT BETS. After the shooter has thrown a point on the come-out, a bet made by a right bettor that the shooter makes his point is a *right point bet*. A bet by a wrong bettor that the shooter misses his point is a *wrong point bet*. The right bettor *takes the odds* on that point; the wrong bettor *lays the odds* on that point.

11. COME BET. A bet that the dice will *pass* (win), the next roll to be considered as a come-out roll.

Example: Suppose the shooter's point is 4 and he bets that he *comes*. If he throws a 7, he loses any bet he has made on the 4 but wins the come bet because, on this bet the roll is considered to be a come-out, and the 7 is a natural and wins.

If he throws an 11 the point bet is still undecided but he wins the come bet.

If he throws a crap the point bet is still undecided and he loses the come bet.

If he throws a 4, he wins the original point bet, but must continue throwing and make another 4 before throwing a 7 in order to win the come bet. If he then throws any other number (such as 6), it counts as a second point and he continues throwing in an attempt to make either or both points before throwing a 7.

---

* Although not a rule, the player who has just lost a center bet to the shooter is usually given first opportunity to fade the shooter on the next come-out.

12. DON'T COME BET. A bet that the dice *don't pass* (lose), the next roll to be considered as a come-out.

13. THE HARD WAY or GAG BET. A bet that a specified even number (which may be either the shooter's point or an off number) will or will not be thrown the hard way with two like numbers, that is, a 4 with double-two, 6 with double-three, 8 with double-four, 10 with double-five. If the number is thrown any other way, or a 7 is thrown, the bettor loses the Hard Way bet.

14. ONE ROLL or COME-OUT BET. A bet that the shooter does or does not throw (a) a certain number any way, (b) a certain number a certain way, or (c) any one of a group of numbers *on the next roll.*

For example: (a) A bet that the shooter will or won't throw a 7 with any of the combinations 1-6, 2-5, 3-4. (b) A bet that the shooter will or won't throw a 7 with one specific combination such as 3-4. (c) A bet that the shooter will or won't throw any of the numbers in the group 2, 3 and 12 (craps); or in the group 4 and 10, or the group 11 and 3; etc.

15. ONE NUMBER BET. A bet that a certain number or group of numbers will or will not be thrown before another number.

16. OFF NUMBER BET. A bet made at odds that the shooter will or will not throw a specified number other than his point (any of the numbers 4, 5, 6, 8, 9 or 10) before throwing 7.

17. TWO NUMBER BET. A bet that one of a certain two (sometimes more) numbers will or will not be thrown before a 7.

18. TWO or THREE ROLL BET. A bet that a certain number or group of numbers will or will not be thrown in a specified number of rolls.

LET'S SHOOT CRAPS!

For the benefit of any readers whose first contact with the game is the rules just given, the following play by play description of a private crap game may be of interest.

The first player tosses a coin on to the center of the playing surface. "Shoot a quarter," he says. He has placed a *center bet* that he will pass.

Another quarter bounces on to the playing surface and the man who threw it calls, "Shoot. You're faded!" He has placed a *center bet* that the shooter will not pass and has covered the shooter's money.

The shooter shakes the dice and throws them out against the board. He snaps his fingers and calls, "Come seven eleven!" or "Baby needs new shoes." If either 7 or 11 appear, the shooter calls, "Natural!" and either picks up the 50¢ or says, "Let it ride," which means that he is wagering the whole amount on the next come-out.

Another fader tosses out a quarter. "I've got two-bits," he says. The shooter continues to shake the dice in his hand, saying, "A quarter open." Then another player throws out another quarter. "Shoot. You're faded."

This time a pair of Aces may appear. "Craps!" one player calls. "Snake-eyes!" says another. The shooter has lost that one and each of the faders takes down 50¢.

Then the shooter throws down a dollar calling, "A dollar open." "Go ahead, I've got you," someone else says, throwing down another dollar.

Before long the size of the bets begins to increase and the sound of the rolling cubes and the cries of the bettors attract more players until ten or twenty or more have gathered around. Then the shooter throws a 4 on the come-out and someone calls out, "Little Joe!" The shooter has thrown a point number and must, in order to win the two bucks in the center, try to throw it again before throwing a 7.

Other players can be heard shouting, "I'll lay two bucks" or "I'll lay ten. Who'll take it?" These are the wrong bettors offering to wager that the shooter does not throw a 4 before a 7. The right bettors can be heard saying, "You got a bet." A right bettor who takes a $2 bet on the 4 places $1 (since the odds are 2 to 1) at the side of the playing surface near or on the two bucks the wrong bettor has put down. These bettors are making *side bets*. The wrong bettors are making *wrong point bets* and *laying the odds*, the right bettors are making *right point bets* and *taking the odds*.

Then the shooter rolls again. He throws a 5. He rolls again and throws a 10. Then he throws a 4 and has made his point. The right bettors scramble to pick up their winnings and the wrong bettors growl a bit. The shooter either lets the money in the center ride for the next come-out, or pulls down part of it and bets the rest, or pulls it all down.

If he lets it ride and the faders only cover part of the amount, he may either shoot for that amount or pull down all his money and call the bet off, saying, "No bet." He can continue to shoot whether a center bet is made or not.

When he is shaking the dice before the come-out roll and the faders are covering his money, other players may also be making side bets among themselves that the shooter will or will not pass—*flat bets* which are the same as the bet between shooter and fader except that they are made between other players; the money is put on the side of the playing surface.

This time he may throw a point number and then, before repeating it again, throw a seven. In this case the wrong bettors collect their side bets, the faders collect the money in the center, and the shooter passes the dice to the next player on his left.

This new shooter may be a consistent wrong bettor or someone who knows that the shooter has a slight disadvantage on the come-out and may shout, "Pass them," to indicate that he does not desire to shoot. The dice then go to the next player.

This shooter picks the dice up, bets an amount in the center and throws a 6 on the come-out for his point. All the wrong bettors jump at this one. "A dollar he don't" they cry, or "Five he don't." They get down as many bets as the right bettors will accept because in all too many games, this bet is made at even money and the right bettors eventually take a licking. Why? Stick with us and you'll find out.

Sometimes a bettor will call, "A dollar he don't six" when the shooter is trying to make some point other than 6, such as 5 or 10. This player is offering to bet that the shooter will not throw a 6 before a 7. Because his bet concerns a number that is not the shooter's point, it is an *Off Number bet*.

And in some parts of the country when a player is trying to make his point, a wrong bettor may shout, "A dollar he don't come," and a right bettor accepts it, answering, "A dollar he does come." These *Come* and *Don't Come bets* are the same as flat center bets except that they are made while the shooter is trying to make his point. The next roll after the bet is made is considered by the Come and Don't Come bettors to be the same as a come-out, the right bettor winning if a 7 or 11 appears and losing if a crap is thrown.

There is one player you want to watch out for. Before any roll of the dice, you'll hear him offering *One-Roll* or *Come-out bets* that sound like this: "Four to one he don't seven on the next roll," "Fifteen to one he don't seven with a three-four," or "Seven to one he don't crap." Unless you know a lot more than the average player does about odds, you'll probably accept these bets and then wonder why you have such hard luck.

This is the same guy who, when the shooter throws a 10 will shout, "I'll lay it the hard way," or "Who wants 5 to 1 on the gag?" He is offering to bet that the shooter won't make his 10 the hard way—with two 5s. Betting one buck with a chance of getting five may sound okay, but on this proposition it's another sucker bet designed to clip you.

And if one sucker bet doesn't get you, he has others—plenty of them. When he takes the dice to shoot, he doesn't put up any money in the center; he offers you this one: "I'll bet a buck I six or seven in two rolls." Or perhaps, "I'll take it on the point but bar the first roll," or "A dollar I don't six or eight in two rolls." At the even money he offers, these are all sucker bets and, if you bite, don't be surprised if you lose and don't blame it on hard luck.

If you can't tell when a bet is loaded with dynamite, if you can't recognize a sucker bet when you hear it, you need to turn to Chapter 9 of this book where the secrets and dangers of the sucker bets are exposed—but quick! And don't get into any more crap games until you have read it.

5

Scarne's Correct Odds on Craps

In his book *Sucker's Progress*, Herbert Asbury makes a very curious statement. "Hazard," he says, "especially in its earlier forms, was a complicated business, and for successful play the caster required a thorough knowledge of the odds and probabilities . . . Craps puts no such strain upon the mind . . . Assuming that the dice are honest, an imbecile has as much chance to win at Craps as the most intelligent of men; he is required only to roll the dice away from him, grunt heavily, and utter one or more of the magic phrases, such as 'Baby needs new shoes!' and 'An eighter from Decatur! . . .'"

We are sorry to have to contradict Mr. Asbury but the fact remains that if he would like to bet a little money on Craps there are several thousand smart-money players and hustlers in the country who would jump at the chance to cover it and would be delighted to show him that his chance of winning without any knowledge of the odds and probabilities is exactly zero!

The notion that Craps as a game is mentally on a par with Tic-Tac-

Toe is held by a lot of people including many crap players. Very few of them realize that Craps is primarily a mathematical game of numbers. In spite of the fact that the big difference between the dub and the expert is a knowledge of the correct odds, only one or two players out of a hundred, and perhaps less, have more than the vaguest idea of what the correct odds are.

WHAT YOU DON'T KNOW HURTS YOU

Craps is a battle between the right and wrong bettors, and the man who gets into this fight knowing nothing about the game beyond the rules is sure to find himself taking wrong odds and getting the worst of it. Due to the extremely fast action of the game, even the smallest percentage against the player becomes a major obstacle to winning, and the percentage increases in direct proportion to the player's ignorance of the odds. In Craps it is what you don't know that *does* hurt you!

Dice hustlers call the player who doesn't know the odds a sucker, a monkey, a soft or easy mark with plenty of reason. Anyone who accepts 91 cents when he wins and pays out $1.00 on the same bet when he loses, which is exactly what the man who doesn't know the correct odds often does, can hardly be said to be hep to the game.

No crap player in his right mind is going to stand on a street corner and pass out dollar bills to anyone who comes along and asks for one. But the player who bets even money on an event that happens only 5 out of 11 times and wins only $5 for every $6 that he loses does exactly that every time he plays. He does it and doesn't know it.

Those players ascribe their losses to the fact that they are unlucky. Actually they aren't giving their luck a chance to operate. They may even be lucky, but because of the sucker bets they accept, they lose anyway! They are being cheated, not by crooks, but by themselves and their own ignorance.

If *you* want to find out whether your losses are due to a lack of luck or a lack of knowledge, this chapter will tip you off to the answer.

WHAT ODDS ARE

Since most players know so little about correct odds that it sometimes seems as if they didn't even know what odds are, perhaps we'd better start by defining odds. When a coin is tossed once, each side has an equal chance of being thrown. The bet is at even money. But when a die having six sides is thrown, each side has only 1 chance in 6 of being thrown. There is one chance that it will be thrown and five chances that some other side will come up. At even money and in the long run, the player who bets that a particular side won't come up will win five times as many wagers as the man who bets that it will appear.

Betting at odds instead of even money will give both players an equal chance to win the same amount of money in the long run. If, because there are five unfavorable chances against one favorable chance, the wrong bettor must bet $5 to the right bettor's $1, the fact that he will win five times as often only even things up. In the long run, if the die is tossed several thousand times, each player will win the same amount.

In Craps if a player bets $1 at *even money* on each point to pass and each point appeared equally often, he would find himself losing $9.40 for every $6 he won. He would be fighting a percentage of 22.077 plus percent. But if he bets at the correct odds on each of those numbers, in the long run he can expect to come out even. Proper betting at proper odds gives each bettor an equal chance. The outcome is decided by Lady Luck and not Old Man Percentage.

The bridge and poker player can study the fine points of his game by reading one or more of the numerous books that have been written on the subject. But the crap player, until now at least, has had no such manual, and he has had to pick up what knowledge he has of the odds as he went along. The only school in which the subject has ever been taught is the School of Hard Knocks.

That is not a very good place to learn the odds for the simple reason that since the other players don't know the correct odds either, the beginner learns wrong ones—usually gambling house odds which are carefully calculated to pay the house a neat profit in percentage. Any player who accepts such odds in the military or private game is cheating himself because he is paying the man who lays the odds the same percentage.

The simplest way of discovering what the correct odds are is to refer to the Odds Tables given later in this chapter.

But so that you can understand how those odds are obtained and can figure them for yourself, and so that you won't snow the authors under with letters announcing that you have done some figuring and come up with a different answer, here's the method by which they are computed.

HOW TO FIGURE ODDS

Our first step is to discover what chance each number on a single die has of being thrown. If the die is a perfect cube and nothing acts to favor any one side more than another, each side has as much chance of being thrown as any other. Since the die has six sides, each side has a 1/6 chance of being thrown in one roll. And since it can, therefore, be expected to come up once in every six rolls, its probability is 1/6.

But Craps uses two dice, each of which has six sides bearing the digits 1, 2, 3, 4, 5 and 6. Both dice are thrown together and the two digits on the skyward surfaces are added together to form a number. Taken two at a time the six digits can form eleven different combinations, the numbers: 2, 3, 4, 5, 6, 7, 8, 9, 10, 11 and 12.

But there are more than eleven ways of making these numbers. The FIVE for instance can be made in four different ways by throwing the combinations 1–4, 2–3, 3–2 and 4–1. Our next step is to find out in how many different ways (permutations) each individual number can be formed, and then in how many ways altogether the twelve digits can form the eleven numbers.

The number TWO can be made only by throwing an Ace on each die or in just one way.

THREE, however, can not only be made with an Ace on the first die and a 2 on the second, but also with the 2 on the first die and the Ace on the second. It can, therefore, be made in 2 ways.

And FOUR can be formed with 1–3, 3–1 and 2–2, or in 3 ways.

Continuing this operation, we find that the twelve digits on two dice can combine in 6 times 6 or in 36 different ways, all of which are shown in the table below.

Table No. 1
COMBINATIONS AND WAYS

2 can be made in 1 way   1-1
3 can be made in 2 ways 1-2 2-1
4 can be made in 3 ways 1-3 3-1 2-2
5 can be made in 4 ways 1-4 4-1 2-3 3-2
6 can be made in 5 ways 1-5 5-1 2-4 4-2 3-3
7 can be made in 6 ways 1-6 6-1 2-5 5-2 3-4 4-3
8 can be made in 5 ways 2-6 6-2 3-5 5-3 4-4
9 can be made in 4 ways 3-6 6-3 4-5 5-4
10 can be made in 3 ways 4-6 6-4 5-5
11 can be made in 2 ways 5-6 6-5
12 can be made in 1 way   6-6

Since we now know that there are 36 ways of making the eleven numbers and since we know in how many ways each individual number can be made, we can now calculate what chance each number has of being thrown in one roll as well as the chances against it being thrown. Then, by taking the ratio of the unfavorable chances against the favorable chances, we will have the *odds* against each number being thrown in one roll, and will know what odds to take or lay when making come-out or one roll bets.

These odds are computed from the information given in the *Combination and Ways Table* as follows:

Since Two can only be made in one way (Ace-Ace) out of 36 possible ways we can expect that some other number will be thrown 35 times for every once that Two is thrown. Two's unfavorable chances are, therefore, 35 and its favorable chances are 1. Since odds are the unfavorable chances against the favorable chances, the odds against Two being thrown in one roll are 35 to 1.

Since the same reasoning holds true for all pairs or double numbers (2–2, 3–3, 4–4, 5–5, 6–6) the odds against throwing *Any Pair* are also *35 to 1*.

ELEVEN can be made in 2 ways. Its probability is, therefore, 2 in 36 times or 2/36. There are 34 chances that some other number will be thrown and the odds against throwing ELEVEN in one roll are *34 to 2, or 17 to 1*.

SEVEN can be made in 6 ways. Since 6 from 36 is 30, the unfavorable chances are 30 and the odds against SEVEN are 30 to 6, or *5 to 1*.

One Roll or Come-out bets that SEVEN will or will not be made with a particular combination of numbers are common. For instance the bet may be that SEVEN will or will not be made by throwing 3-4. There are two ways that this combination may be thrown—with a 3 on the first die and a 4 on the other, and with a 4 on the first die and a 3 on the other. The odds, therefore, are 34 to 2, or *17 to 1*. And, by the same reasoning, the same one roll or come-out odds apply to any combination of two numbers.

Since the wager that Craps will or will not be thrown is a common bet, we must also obtain the odds on the numbers 2, 3 and 12 considered as a group. Two can be made in 1 way, THREE in 2 ways and TWELVE in 1 way. Craps then can be made altogether in 4 ways. Four from 36 leaves 32 unfavorable chances and the odds against crap are 32 to 4, or *8 to 1*.

The odds against throwing any other number in one roll can be found in the same manner. Simply refer to the *Combination and Ways Table,* find out in how many ways the number or group of numbers whose odds you want can be made. Then subtract this number of ways or favorable chances from the total of 36 ways which gives you the unfavorable chances. *The unfavorable chances against the favorable chances are the odds against the number.*

All the one roll odds are listed in Table 2 and each odds figure is, in addition, translated into corresponding terms of dollars and cents.

Table No. 2
ODDS ON ONE ROLL OR COME-OUT BETS

Numbers	Correct Odds	Odds in Terms of $ and ¢ Bets	
Any Pair	35 to 1	$1.75 to .05	$35.00 to $1.00
11	17 to 1	.85 to .05	17.00 to 1.00
Any Crap	8 to 1		
5	8 to 1	.40 to .05	8.00 to 1.00
9	8 to 1		
4	11 to 1	.55 to .05	11.00 to 1.00
10	11 to 1		
6	6 1/5 to 1	.31 to .05	6.20 to 1.00
8	6 1/5 to 1		
Any 7	5 to 1	.25 to .05	5.00 to 1.00
1-2 (3)	17 to 1		
3-4 (7)	17 to 1	.85 to .05	17.00 to 1.00
5-2 (7)	17 to 1		
6-1 (7)	17 to 1		

Even more common than One-Roll bets are the Pass and Don't Pass bets on the point. The ODDS AGAINST PASSING on the point can also be determined by using the information in the *Combination and Ways Table.* Reference to it shows that the points 4, 5, 6, 8, 9 and 10 can be made altogether in 24 ways out of the total of 36. Since we may expect 24 points to be thrown in 36 come-out rolls, the probability is 24/36 or 2/3, and the shooter has a 2/3 chance of throwing a point on the come-out.

But after the shooter has thrown a point, he must throw it again before throwing a 7 to win. Since the odds are the unfavorable chances against the favorable chances, the odds against any point being made can be found by taking the 6 ways *seven* can be made (unfavorable because *seven* now loses) against the number of ways the point can be made.

In the case of the point FOUR, since *seven* can be made in 6 ways and *four* in only 3 ways, *seven* will be thrown 6 times for every 3 that *four* is thrown. The odds against passing when *four* is the point are therefore 6 to 3, or *2 to 1*.

Since TEN can also be made in 3 ways, the odds against passing when ten is the point are also *2 to 1*.

FIVE can be made in 4 ways as against the 6 ways seven can be made, giving odds of 6 to 4 or *3 to 2* against passing when five is the point.

NINE can also be made in 4 ways and the odds are, therefore, the same as five—*3 to 2*.

SIX can be made 5 ways as against the 6 ways seven can be made and the odds are consequently *6 to 5*.

EIGHT can also be made in 5 ways and the odds are, therefore, also *6 to 5*.

For ready reference, and as an aid to memorizing these odds, they are also given below in tabular form along with a translation into terms of dollars and cents bets.

Table No. 3
ODDS AGAINST PASSING ON THE POINTS

The Points	Correct Odds	Odds in $ and ¢ Bets	
4 can be made in 3 ways; 7 in 6 ways	2 to 1	$.20 to .10	$2.00 to $1.00
5 can be made in 4 ways; 7 in 6 ways	3 to 2	.30 to .20	1.50 to 1.00
6 can be made in 5 ways; 7 in 6 ways	6 to 5	.60 to .50	1.20 to 1.00
8 can be made in 5 ways; 7 in 6 ways	6 to 5	.60 to .50	1.20 to 1.00
9 can be made in 4 ways; 7 in 6 ways	3 to 2	.30 to .20	1.50 to 1.00
10 can be made in 3 ways; 7 in 6 ways	2 to 1	.20 to .10	2.00 to 1.00

Since another common wager is to bet that one of the even numbers (4, 6, 8, 10) will or will not be made the *hard way* or with the *gag*, we also need to find the odds against passing on the points or off numbers the hard way.

Table No. 4
ODDS AGAINST PASSING THE HARD WAY

The Points	Correct Odds	Odds in $ and ¢ Bets	
4 can be made with 2-2 in 1 way	8 to 1	$.40 to .05	$8.00 to $1.00
10 can be made with 5-5 in 1 way	8 to 1	.40 to .05	8.00 to 1.00
6 can be made with 3-3 in 1 way	10 to 1	.50 to .05	10.00 to 1.00
8 can be made with 4-4 in 1 way	10 to 1	.50 to .05	10.00 to 1.00

You are probably all set to give us an argument on this one. Why, since 4 can be made in only 1 way with 2–2, and since 6 can be made in only 1 way with 3–3, are the odds 8 to 1 on 4, and 10 to 1 on 6?

Most players believe that it is just as easy to throw a double-two as it is a double-three and that the odds should therefore be the same against making either 4 or 6 the hard way. They see no reason why, if the odds are 8 to 1 against throwing a double-two, it shouldn't also be 8 to 1 against throwing a double-three.

Why do we give odds of 10 to 1 against making a 6 with a double-three? Well, as a matter of fact, when you are betting on the hard way, it is *not* as easy to throw a double-three as it is a double-two!

Some players even figure that since double numbers can only be thrown in 1 way and SEVEN can be thrown in 6 ways that the odds are neither 8 to 1 nor 10 to 1 but *6 to 1*.

Are we crazy? Every time these hard way odds have appeared in print in one of my articles, letters begin arriving by the next mail, pointing out the printer's typographical error. And the printers invariably think that I am off the beam. The night this chapter giving these odds went to press, the printer phoned me at 3 A.M. My publishers had assured him that, silly as it looked, those odds were correct. But he wanted to be sure; they didn't look right to him at all. And when *Time* magazine's New York editorial office sent the same copy to their Chicago printer, a teletyped reply came right back: "PLEASE CHECK HARD WAY ODDS. COPY AS RECEIVED DOESN'T MAKE SENSE."

And yet the odds are as given in the table. Can you figure out for yourself why it is easier to throw a double-two than a double-three in Craps, and why the correct odds are 8 to 1 and 10 to 1 and not 6 to 1? Now that you know how odds are computed it should be easy. But, if you run into trouble, or if you don't like puzzles and feel that the price you paid for this book entitles you to the answer without any wear and tear on the brain cells, read on.

HOW TO FIGURE HARD-WAY ODDS

The fallacy in the average player's reasoning is that when he makes the statement that it is just as easy to throw double-threes and double-fours as it is double-twos and double-fives, he seems to forget that he is talking about the Hard Way. The odds against throwing 3–3, 4–4, 2–2 or 5–5 on the come-out roll are the same—35 to 1. But the odds against making a point with those combinations is something else again.

Suppose your point is FOUR and you bet that you can make it the hard way, with 2–2. There are, according to our *Table of Combinations and Ways*, 3 ways to make a FOUR, with 2–2, 1–3 and 3–1. If either 1–3 or 3–1 is thrown, you have made your point, but, since you didn't make it the hard way, you lose the bet. You have 1 way to win and 2 ways to lose. In addition, you can also lose if you seven out, and since there are 6 ways to make SEVEN, there are altogether 8 ways you can lose as against 1 way in which you can win. Consequently, the odds are *8 to 1*. The same reasoning also applies to making the point TEN with 5–5.

Let's try the same process with the points SIX and EIGHT. SIX, according to the *Combination and Ways Table*, can be made in 5 ways. Betting on the SIX the hard way means that only 1 of these ways (3–3) wins and the other 4 lose. Add to those the 6 losing ways that SEVEN can be made and you have 10 ways to lose against 1 way to win. The odds, therefore, strange as it may seem to players who don't think logically, are 10 to 1. The same reasoning applies to making EIGHT with 4–4.

An additional bit of evidence is the fact that some bank crap layouts offer 8 for 1 on FOUR or TEN the hard way and 10 for 1 on SIX and EIGHT.

DON'T TRY TO BUCK OLD MAN P.C.

If all wrong bettors lay the odds shown in the foregoing tables, and all right bettors take those odds, each player will have an equal chance of winning the same amount of money in the long run. Over a short period Lady Luck may smile on one player more than another, but in the long run she will, provided bets are placed at the correct odds, cast her favors equally on all players.

If bets are not made according to the correct odds, Old Man Percentage rears his ugly head and, in the long run, the guy who takes the wrong odds is going to find he has been to the cleaners. Old Man P.C. doesn't stand for any nonsense; his insidious operations are every bit as certain as Death and Taxes. The player who tries to buck him is battling an irresistible force and must eventually go down for the count just as surely as if he tried to tangle with my lifelong friend, James J. Braddock, the ex-heavyweight champion of the world.

If you know that SEVEN will be thrown 6 times for every 5 times that a SIX or an EIGHT is thrown, and you thumb your nose at Old Man P.C. and accept even-money bets on those points, you can't beef if you overhear someone call you a sucker. At even-money you can expect to lose six $1 bets for every five $1 bets that you win. If you wager real folding money in that manner, it doesn't take a fortune teller to predict your financial future. A baby can do it. You'll go home in a barrel.

6

One Reason
Private Game
Right Bettors Die Broke

There is one bet that has not been analyzed and which is not listed in the *Odds Against Passing* table—The Center or Flat wagers to win or lose. Since it is customary to make these bets at even money, most players assume that the shooter and fader have the same chance of winning, and that the correct odds are 1 to 1 or fifty-fifty. But in this man's game, one thing you should never do is take something for granted. If you don't have a good mathematical reason for every statement you make, your best bet is to keep your mouth tightly closed.

Are the center and flat wagers even money bets? Are the right and wrong bettors' chances of winning before the come-out equal? And if not, why not, and why are the bets placed at even money? Many crap players have put in a good many man hours of heavy thinking trying to dope answers to those questions and most of them have come up with a mixed and very odd lot of wrong answers. The author has received many letters disagreeing with the results about to be given. The only thing that all the letters had in common is the fact that almost all their writers disagreed with each other.

HOW TO FIGURE CENTER AND FLAT BED ODDS

We hope that the following explanation of the method of computing the center and flat bet odds will settle the arguments. It should because there's really nothing very difficult about it. There's no algebra, geometry, trigonometry or differential calculus involved—nothing but simple grade school arithmetic plus the very important ingredient: straight thinking.

All we need to do is find out how many of the throws made by the shooter will, in the long run, be winning throws and how many will be losing throws. If there are an equal number of each, it's an even-money bet. And if not—well, let's see.

We're not going to calculate how many rolls out of 36 will win and how many will lose because we'll run into fractions. We shall instead avoid the fractions by multiplying 36 rolls by 55 to get the lowest common multiple or 1980 rolls.

Suppose that Joe or Pete throws the galloping dominoes 1980 times. And suppose he considers that each roll is a new come-out and that it effects a decision. Suppose, too, that the law of averages is strictly enforced and that each number is thrown exactly as often as the theory of probability indicates that it will be thrown in the long run.

Since SEVEN (*natural*) can be made in 6 ways out of the total of 36, it will be thrown 6/36 of the 1980 rolls and Joe will win 330 times.

ELEVEN (*natural*) can be made in 2 ways out of 36 and will be thrown 2/36 of the 1980 rolls, winning 110 times.

The *point* FOUR can be made in 3 ways out of 36 and will be thrown 3/36 of 1980 or 165 times. But, since SEVEN which now loses will be thrown 6 times, Joe will miss the point twice for every once that he makes it. Since he only passes 1 out of 3 times, he will win only 1/3 of the 165 rolls or 55 rolls.

Since TEN can also be made 3 ways, it will also win *55* times.

The *point* FIVE can be made 4 ways out of 36 and will be thrown 4/36 of 1980 rolls or 220 times. Since SEVEN will be thrown 6 times for every 4 times that FIVE is thrown, Joe will win only 4/10 of the 220 times, or *88* times.

Since NINE can also be made 4 ways, it will also win *88* times.

SIX can be made 5 ways and will be thown 5/36 of 1980 or 275 times. Since SEVEN will be thrown 6 times for every 5 times that SIX is thrown, SIX will win only 5/11 of the 275 times or *125* times.

Since EIGHT is also made 5 ways, it will also win *125* times.

Now if we put these figures in a column and add up the winning rolls, we get this:

Table No. 5
FIGURING CENTER AND FLAT BETS

		Times Thrown	Winning Rolls
Natural	7	330	330
"	11	110	110
Craps 2, 3, 12		220	——
Point	4	165	55
"	10	165	55
"	5	220	88
"	9	220	88
"	6	275	125
"	8	275	125
Totals		1980	976

And then Joe subtracts his 976 winning rolls from his total of 1980 rolls and finds that he has lost *1004* rolls! Surprised? If the center and flat bets before the come-out were really even-money bets, Joe should have come up with 990 winning rolls and 990 losing rolls. But Joe, having only won 976 times, has 14 fewer winning rolls than he should to make it an even money bet.

It's even worse than that in a way because Joe not only loses 14 rolls too many, but the fader wins 14 rolls more than he should. Altogether the fader or wrong bettor has an advantage of 1004 minus 976 or *28 rolls*. That is his *advantage* or *edge,* and it is Joe's disadvantage.

THE RIGHT BETTOR'S P.C.

Figured as percentage, the shooter or right bettor before the come-out has a 49-29/99% chance of winning against the fader's or wrong bettor's 50-70/99% chance. The shooter or right bettor's disadvantage is the difference, or 1-41/99%, which, expressed decimally, is a percentage of 1.414 plus.*

Remember that 1.414 per cent because it is one of the commonest disadvantages in Craps. It is one of the reasons behind the gamblers' saying that "all right bettors die broke."

To give it more meaning, let us see what it means in terms of cash.

---

* No exact expression decimally is possible since if you carry the decimals out, you get 1.41414141414 etc., etc.

Suppose that Joe rolls the dice just 36 times, that all the combinations appear strictly according to their probabilities, that each roll is considered as a come-out and as effecting a decision, and that Joe as the shooter wagers $1 on each combination to win. Mr. Wrong Bettor fades him each time by covering Joe's dollar bet with another dollar. They each wager $36, a total sum of $72. Here's what happens.

Natural 7 can be made 6 ways and shooter wins 6 two-dollar bets or $12.

Natural 11 can be made 2 ways and shooter wins 2 two-dollar bets or $4.

Crap 2 can be made 1 way and shooter loses 1 two-dollar bet or $2.

Crap 3 can be made 2 ways and shooter loses 2 two-dollar bets or $4.

Crap 12 can be made 1 way and shooter loses 1 two-dollar bet or $2.

Point 4 can be made 3 ways. $6 is wagered altogether, but since *seven* can be made 6 ways, the shooter will win 1/3 of the amount wagered and lose 2/3. He wins $2 and loses $4.

Point 10 can be made 3 ways. (See above.) Will win $2 and lost $4.

Point 5 can be made 4 ways. $8 is bet altogether but since *seven* can be made 6 ways, the shooter will win 2/5 of the amount wagered and lose 3/5. He wins $3.20 and loses $4.80.

Point 9 can be made 4 ways. (See above.) Wins $3.20 and loses $4.80.

Point 6 can be made 5 ways. $10 is bet altogether but since *seven* can be made 6 ways, the shooter will win 5/11 of the amount wagered and lose 6/11. He wins $4.54-6/11¢ and loses $5.45-5/11¢.

Point 8 can be made 5 ways. (See above.) Wins $4.54-6/11¢ and loses $5.45-5/11¢.

Putting this information into a profit and loss table, we have:

Table No. 6
PROFIT AND LOSS ON CENTER AND FLAT BETS

Numbers		No. of Ways	Amount Wagered	Amount Won by Shooter	Amount Won by Fader
Natural	7	6	$12.00	$12.00	——
"	11	2	4.00	4.00	——
Craps	2, 3, 12	4	8.00	——	$8.00
Points	4	3	6.00	2.00	4.00
"	10	3	6.00	2.00	4.00
"	5	4	8.00	3.20	4.80
"	9	4	8.00	3.20	4.80
"	6	5	10.00	4.54-6/11	5.45-5/11
	8	5	10.00	4.54-6/11	5.45-5/11
Totals 11		36	$72.00	$35.49-1/11	$36.50-10/11

The difference between the $35.49-1/11 which Joe collected and the $36.50-10/11 which the fader collected is $1.01-9/11 which is 1.414 percent of the total of $72 wagered.

Since Joe started with a $36 bankroll and finished with $35.49-1/11, he has lost .50-10/11 cents. And if he were to continue to place $1 win bets in the same manner with the dice acting according to the probabilities (which is just what they eventually will do if Joe keeps on betting), he will lose at the rate of .50-10/11 cents every 36 come-out rolls.

There isn't much that can be done about equalizing the center and flat bets so that the right and wrong bettors' chances are exactly fifty-fifty instead of 49-29/99 to 50-70/99. To do that the right bettor would have to take odds of 1004 to 976 or $1.0286 to $1.

Since this would require 1/100 cent pieces and since the U. S. Treasury is not likely to go to the trouble of minting those just to even up the right and wrong bettors' chances before the come-out, getting rid of that 1.414% disadvantage is a rather remote possibility. It would, in any case, make betting far too complicated a business and would slow the game down so much that it would be about as full of action as chess!

WHAT THE 1.414% DOES TO YOU

Most players look at that 1.414 percent disadvantage and decide that it is so small they can forget about it. They think that paying 1 and 414/1000 cents on every dollar, or 14¢ on every $10, is a small charge for the enjoyment they get out of playing. It would be if that were all they paid. But is it?

Would you believe me if I told you that by actual clocking it has been found that on center or flat bets the right bettor often pays the wrong bettors not a mere 14¢ on $10, but sometimes as much as *five* or *six times* $10! Impossible? Let's have Joe place a few $1 center bets and see what happens to him.

Suppose he shoots the dice and bets $1 in the center that he's right. He passes, lets the center bet (both the original wager and the money won) ride, shoots the dice and passes again. It is, in fact, Joe's lucky day. Before he's through, he makes five consecutive passes, letting his money ride each time. His $1 grows to $2, then $4, then $8, then $16 and finally $32. At that point Joe decides that he had better pull out before the law of averages catches up with his luck and makes him throw a missout. He takes down the $32 and passes the dice. He has a net profit of $31.

If Joe ever thinks about the unfavorable percentage he has been bucking, which he seldom does, he figures that the fader took a $31 beating trying to pick up 1.414 percent of the $1 that Joe started with or about 1-2/5 cents.

We hate to throw cold water on Joe's happiness at winning thirty-one bucks by telling him that his logic is full of holes big enough to drive a ten-ton truck through, but that is exactly its condition.

In the first place Joe risked a lot more than one lone dollar. He made five different bets. He risked $1 and won another dollar. Both dollars are his own money. Then he risked his $2 and collected $4. He risked his $4, collected $8, risked that, collected $16 and risked that. Altogether he has risked not $1 but $31, *all his own money.*

If the Treasury had minted 1/100 cent pieces and if the fader had covered each of those thirty-one bucks with the correct amount of $1.0286+, then Joe would have won $31.8866. That 1.414 percent has gypped him out of not 1-41/99 cents but out of 88-66/100 cents.

But that's not the worst of it. Joe, you remember, was letting his winnings ride. Figuring percentage on percentage, if Joe had collected at the correct odds, he would, after the first pass, have had $2.0286 to bet, and the fader would have had to cover that with $2.08661796. When Joe passed a second time and won that amount as well, his stake would be $4.11521. Carrying this through five passes, we find that instead of winning $31, Joe should have won $33.45.

JOE IS SHORT $2.45

He's happy because his $1 got him $31, but he doesn't realize that it should have paid off $33.45. He thinks that that insignificant 1.414 percent has nicked him for only 1-2/5 cents when it has actually cost him $2.45, an amount that is nearly *two and one half times* the one dollar he bet at the start!

Of course, if everyone would shoot the dice at his turn, each player has a disadvantage when he shoots and has the advantage when he fades. This would just about even matters up provided flat bets were not allowed. The hitch is that there are many players who pass the dice and do not shoot but instead fade the center and make flat bets that the dice don't pass.

Perhaps, at this point, you are thinking, "Hmm. No more right bets for me. From here on in I'm strictly a wrong bettor."

It's not a bad system, but there's one little difficulty. If all the crap players in the country buy this book (we hope), read it, and then decide to go and do likewise, there wouldn't be any right bettors left, and center and flat bets wouldn't be made.

You can, however, keep your right flat bets small and few. As for shooting money in the center, that's a decision you'll have to make yourself. Most players get a kick out of shooting the center and letting it ride, and, in spite of the slight disadvantage, many games have been broken by shooters who have done just that.

But what you should *always* do is take and lay the correct odds on all points. If you do that Old Man Percentage will have to stay away from your door. At least he won't walk off with your shirt when you aren't looking. You may have bad luck and lose your shirt, but you won't be giving it away.

If you don't know the correct odds by heart and can't rattle them off just as quickly as your own telephone number or your best girl's name, then you should either swear off Craps and play marbles instead, or you should take time out right now and start memorizing the odds.

If you can't memorize them all in one sitting, then place only those bets whose odds you do know, and turn a deaf ear to all others until you have learned them. You will also find the ODDS tables printed in the Appendix for quick and easy reference and so that you can, if necessary, cut them out and paste them in your hat.

And remember that as long as you are even you are ahead!

7

Bank Craps
Las Vegas Style

Bank Craps not only replaced Faro as the great American banking game in this country but also outdistanced all the other casino games in popularity. One reason was that it offers the players a greater chance of participation. In Roulette and Chuck-a-Luck, the croupier spins the wheel or the cage; in Chemin-de-Fer and Blackjack the dealer turns up the cards. But in Craps the player has the opportunity of trying to change his luck by throwing the dice himself. The thrill he gets when he matches his luck against that of the others is of a more personal kind than the one he gets when he simply waits and hopes that the ball will drop into his number or that the card he wants will turn up.

Bank Craps' popularity was also due to its two-way action. In most casino games the player can bet only that a certain event will happen. He can't bet that it won't; the house does that. But in bank crap games the player may bet either with the dice or against them. He can be a right or wrong bettor as he likes. This plus the fact that many different types of bets can be made gives Bank Craps an unequalled rapid action and a thrill and excitement that no other banking game has ever offered. The real gambler is impatient and when he has once tasted the fast action of Craps, other games seem too slow.

Gamblers who have a knowledge of odds and percentages also prefer Bank Craps to other casino games because they have a better chance of winning since the P. C. in favor of the bank is not nearly as strong. The American brand of Roulette, for instance, with its 0 and double 0, has a P. C. against the player of 5-5/19% which is almost four times as strong as the 1.414% against the right player's win bet in Craps. In Poker the house takes a 5% cut of the winnings on each pot and in Chuck-a-Luck, whose layout looks particularly inviting to the non-thinker, the house has an advantage of 7-47/54%. Habitual gamblers stay away from Chuck-a-Luck because they know how little chance they have against such a high P. C. They call Chuck-a-Luck "the champ chump's game."

A word of caution is necessary, however. The P. C. operating against the player in Bank Craps can be as low as 1.414 or less *only* if the player knows what bets to make and which to avoid. If he doesn't even Roulette can be a better P. C. gamble because some Bank Crap wagers have a P. C. as high as 16-2/3 against the player! Once again it is what you *don't* know that hurts you in Craps.

BETTING LIMITS AT BANK CRAPS

The maximum betting limits at Bank Craps vary throughout the world. The usual top limits in Nevada casinos are $500 on the Pass and Don't Pass line, and $500 on the Place numbers. Some Nevada casinos have a bank-crap maximum limit as low as $25. The most popular bank-crap limits in legally and illegally operated casinos in America may be $20, $25, $50, $100, $200, $300 or $500, and there are a few illegally operated bank-crap tables catering to seasoned gamblers and racketeers which have $1,000 and $2,000 maximum limits. Many top Nevada casinos will, however, up their $500 maximum to as high as $2,000 at the request of an outstanding bigtime crap player.

Betting limits on proposition bets such as the come-out bets and hardways are usually about 1/3 of the table's maximum betting limit. *Example:* At a $500 limit table the betting limit on each proposition bet (the Two Aces, Two Sixes, Eleven, All Craps, All Sevens or the hardway bets) usually range from $50 to $200. At a $300 limit game the proposition bet limits range from $25 to $100. Occasionally a bank-crap operator will permit a player to bet the usual maximum betting limit on each of the come-out or hardway bets. A player placing a $500 bet on the Two Sixes coming out and winning would receive a return of $15,000, a figure no casino manager likes to lose on a one-roll bet.

There is little difference between Bank Craps and Private Craps as far as the rules of the game are concerned. The big difference lies in the fact that bank-crap players cannot bet amongst themselves; all bets must be placed on the spaces of the crap layout and made against the bank. Hence, the name Bank Craps. Another major difference between Bank Craps and Private Craps is that each bet made at Bank Craps has a percentage in favor of the bank. Bank Craps also has many additional bets on the layout which are not often made in Private Craps.

Bank Craps is usually played with crap checks or chips instead of cash, although the Nevada casinos use silver dollars instead of dollar-valued checks. Crap checks in most luxury casinos range in value as follows: $1, $5, $25 and $100 checks. Some sawdust joints deal in dime and quarter chips.

Chips have been used instead of cash in European casinos for centuries. The reasons are obvious: (1) Since each casino gaming table is supplied with thousands of dollars worth of redeemable chips, the casino needs a much smaller bankroll to operate. I know of one casino in the Caribbean which uses $1 million worth of chips nightly, yet its cash bankroll is only about $50,000. (2) Chips in their varied colors make a fine background and make the dealer's job much easier and faster. The possibilities of theft by both dealers and players are minimized because chips are worthless unless they can be cashed.

BANK CRAPS TABLE

The basis of Bank Craps, from the shooter's point of view, is the same as the private game. That is, the shooter makes a bet that he'll pass or win. The shooter wins immediately if on the come-out he rolls a 7 or 11; he loses immediately if on the come-out he rolls a 2, 3, or 12. If on the come-out he doesn't roll a natural or a crap, and instead rolls either 4, 5, 6, 8, 9, or 10—whichever of these he rolls now becomes his "point" and he continues rolling until he either wins by rolling his point once again, or loses by rolling a 7. Remember that the shooter retains the dice as long as he continues to roll naturals and craps and *make points*. When he rolls a 7 while trying for a point, he loses the dice, and

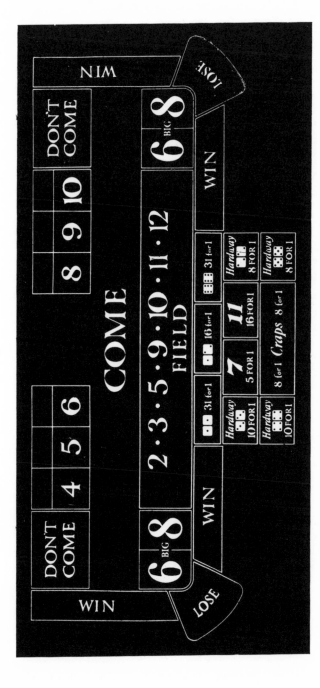

Single Dealer Bank Crap Layout. Note use of the word "for" in the odds offered and the small space allowed for placing of Lose (Don't Pass) bets. The numbers barred are not specified, but are announced by the dealer.

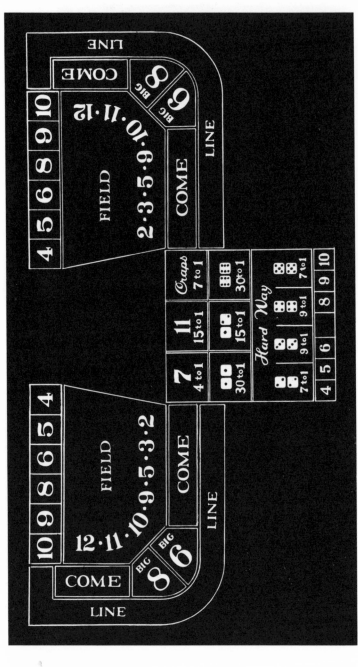

Double Side Dealer Bank Crap Layout. This is a one-way action layout; the players must bet they win and cannot bet they lose.

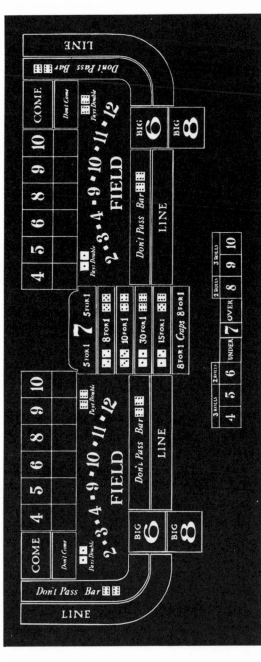

California Double Side Dealer. Here the Don't Pass line runs the length of the layout and the two sixes are barred. Note the addition of the Under and Over 7 and the Two and Three Roll bets.

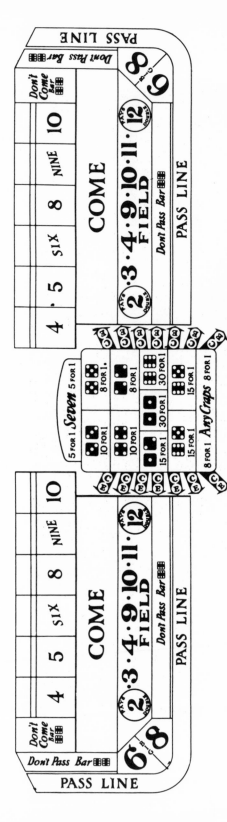

A modern Las Vegas Bank Craps layout. The center portion shows the letters C - E. They stand for Crap and Eleven. Note the center pay-off odds pay one unit less than the Scarney Bank Craps layout shown on page 129.

the shooter to his left becomes the next shooter. This person may decline to shoot the dice; then the person to his left becomes the next shooter, and so on. But, before you can consider yourself a Bank Craps player, you must know the different wagers and payoff odds that may be made at the dice table. And so let's take a look at the dice table itself.

The table is about the size of a standard pool or billiard table, with a ten-inch upright wooden rail running around the table's outside edges, forming a rectangular enclosure. The rail serves as a backboard, and also helps to prevent the rolling dice from falling off the table. The rail opposite to the boxmen's seating position is fitted with a nine-inch by six-foot mirror. This is a protection device to help spot misspotted dice that a cheat may have introduced into the game. The mirror permits the boxmen to see five sides of each die while it is resting on the table layout.

Modern dice tables have grooves running around the top edges of the rail. The grooves are for the players to place their chips so that they do not clutter up the table's playing surface. The inside of the four-sided rail is lined with sponge rubber, embossed in various patterns to ensure that the dice rebound in a random manner.

The five men required to run a dice table include three dealers and two boxmen. The boxmen, the men who sit in-between the two dealers at the table's center, are the bosses. Their duty is to keep their eyes on everything—dice, money, chips, players, dealers, and so on. Two of the dealers stand on each side of them. After each dice decision, the dealers take in the losses and pay off the winnings. The third dealer, who stands opposite the boxmen, has charge of the dice. He calls out the dice numbers as they are made and helps with the proposition bets when placed. He is often referred to as the "stickman" because he retrieves the dice after each roll with a curved stick and holds them until such time as all previous bets have been settled and new bets are made. Whereupon, with the stick, he pushes the dice toward the shooter.

BANK CRAPS LAYOUTS

The table's surface is covered with a tight-fitting green baize cloth on which are printed two exact large-sized designs separated at the table's center by another large design allocated for various side bets. The purpose of the duplicate designs is to accommodate more players and to permit them to make their bets without leaning forward too far or leaving their places at the table. Because of these duplicate layout designs, the Craps table itself is called a *double-side dealer*. Each of these designs is divided into spaces, of different shapes and sizes, representing the various bets that can be placed against the house. This green baize table covering is known as a *Craps layout*. Although there are numerous differently shaped layouts, the actual difference is small. Some layouts may carry one or two wagers that others don't have; some may differ more or less in the odds offered. This last variation depends directly upon the players who patronize that particular casino—how much they know about dice odds and how much of a house percentage they will stand to buck. The smarter the patronage, the better the odds approach the correct ones; the less they know, the greater the house percentages.

All Craps layouts are clever exercises in mathematics, designed to give the player an exciting run for his money—and at the same time to give the house a mathematical edge on every bet shown on the layout. Unfortunately, the majority of Craps players know little or nothing about the house percentages they are fighting, and this lack of knowledge puts them in the chump, or sucker, category. The following odds and percentages will tell you how to stop being a chump and become as gambling-wise as the most seasoned dice gambler found in Las Vegas or anywhere else.

Although it may seem to some people as though the bank were gambling, that is one thing a bank rarely does. The amount of risk involved in the financial operation of an average Bank Crap table is ordinarily much less than that in the average legitimate business venture. A Bank Crap table is seldom a venture. If the operators can get a steady volume of play, it is very close to a gilt-edge sure thing.

THE BANK HAS THE BEST OF IT

There is little difference between Bank Craps and Private Craps as far as the rules of play are concerned. The big difference consists in the fact that players may not make side bets among themselves. All bets, right or wrong, must be placed on the layout and wagered against the Bank. This prevents the player making an *even-up bet* in which there is no favorable P. C. either way. The bank always has the best of it on every bet made. If you were a manufacturer and designed a layout that gave the players an even chance the only guy who would buy one would be an antique collector.

Since the bank is well aware that there are nimble-fingered players

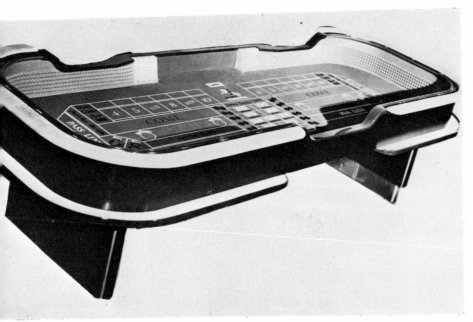

Las Vegas and Reno Bank Craps table. The two dealers stand on the farthest side of the table in the two cut-out spaces and the two boxmen sit in between. The stickman stands at the cut-out space opposite the dealers.

who have spent many hours mastering the fine art of making fair dice roll in a predetermined manner, the cubes in all casinos must hit the boards, except on those tables where this is impractical because there are two layouts and two dealers working at opposite ends of the table. In this case a string is stretched across the table's center at a height a little less than that of the dice used and the shooter must throw the dice out over the string and so that they roll. Since, in most controlled shots, it is necessary for the dice to hit the table soon after leaving the hand, throwing them over the string serves as protection against the practice. Some spin and slide roll experts can bounce the dice over and still control the roll often enough to pay off, but if you persist in making *bounce shots*, it won't be long before you find yourself having a heart to heart talk with the house bouncer.

Since layouts vary as to bets and the odds offered, the following analysis will cover all the common Bank Crap bets without regard to any particular layout.

Before we begin our analysis of Bank Craps odds and percentages, you must remember that if you become a habitual crap shooter, you will lose, no matter how smart you bet. It makes no difference in the long run whether you make bets having less than 1 percent against you or whether you place bets that have a big 16-2/3 percent going against you. Over a long period of play, the house's percentage is bound to take both the smart dice player and the chump. The only difference is that the chump doesn't have even a fighting chance—he gives his money to the house.

Line Bets

There are two different types of line bets: the *pass line bet* and the *don't pass line bet*. Each bet can be made only before a come-out roll. After the come-out, they cannot be withdrawn. First to be discussed is the pass line bet.

Pass Line, Pass, Line, Win or Do

The player who wants to bet the house that the shooter will win— that the dice will pass—places his chip or chips, before the come-out, on the long narrow space of the layout printed with any of the following words: *Pass Line, Pass, Line, Win,* or *Do*.

This bet is without a doubt the most popular bet made by dice players in the Craps table, because it's the bet they first learned when shooting Private Craps. The house pays this bet off at even money (1 to 1) and enjoys a favorable edge of 1.414 percent, or about 7 cents on a $5 wager. Owing to the house's low percentage take, this is one of the wisest casino bets a player can make. But most Craps players are attracted by other bets that pay off at bigger odds; and because they don't know odds, they don't know they are fighting greater house percentages. Like all bets placed on the Craps layout, this wager can be made by any player whether he is the shooter or not; however, it cannot be withdrawn; it remains until it's won or lost.

Don't Pass Line, Don't or Lose

A player who wants to bet that the shooter will lose—that the dice will not pass—places his chip or chips, before the come-out, on the small corner layout space marked with the words *Don't Pass, Don't,* or *Lose*. The house pays off at even money (1 to 1). If you were to make this bet in a private or noncommercial crap game, you'd have an advantage for, as I told you above, the shooter has a 1.414 percent disadvantage. Remember, however, that you are not playing in a private crap game—you're playing in a gambling casino. And casinos wouldn't stay in business long if they took a beating of 1.414 percent. The casino resorts, therefore, to a simple tactical maneuver: It bars either the double sixes (or the double aces) on the come-out roll. This means that if, on the come-out, the shooter throws a double six (6–6) or a double ace (1–1), as the case may be, your bet is a standoff; there is no action for the player or players who have placed bets on the spaces of the layout marked *Don't Pass, Don't,* or *Lose.* In a private or noncommercial game of Craps, the fader or wrong bettor would have won the bet; but at the Bank Craps table, it is no decision or "standoff" for the don't bettor. By barring the two sixes or the two aces and counting a standoff as a neutral roll in this bet, the house is taking away the 1.414 percent edge you would have had, and has replaced it with a house advantage of 1.402 percent or about 7 cents on a $5 wager. If a standoff is counted as a roll the house advantage becomes 1.364 percent. So, for all practical reasons, it doesn't matter whether you bet the pass line or don't pass line; the house percentage remains about the same. However, because this wager has a standoff, players think erroneously that it has a much higher house percentage than it actually does—hence you'll seldom find many players betting the don't pass line. If the house bars the double aces instead of double sixes, as some do, it gets the same results as if it were barring two sixes.

In order to see what this means to the bank, suppose we place five $1 bets on the Win line and five $1 bets on the Lose line. The shooter can be expected to throw two Sixes an average of once out of every thirty-six come-out throws, and whenever this happens, the bank sweeps the $5 off the Win line while the $5 on the Lose line must remain there until a new decision is effected. If the bank had not barred the two Sixes, it would have broken even. Barring the two Sixes has earned it $5. The same, of course, holds true for the bar on the two Aces.

How much does this cut down that 1.414% advantage? Reference to the *Rolls Table* (page 95) reminds us that the right bettor can expect to win 976 rolls and lose 1004 out of a total of 1980. One thirty-sixth of those 1004 losing rolls or 55 rolls are double-sixes. (The same is true of double-Aces). When the bank counts those 55 rolls as stand-off or neutral rolls, it reduces the 1004 losing rolls by 55 and stands to win 976 times and lose only 949.

The bank thus has a 50-54/77% chance of winning as against the wrong player's 49-23/77% chance. Of the 1925 deciding rolls, there are 27 more rolls that win for the bank than for the wrong player, an advantage of 1-31/77% or a P.C. of *1.402, which is about 7¢ on a $5* wager.

The stand-off on the two Sixes has not only wiped out the 1.414% advantage which the wrong bettor ordinarily has, but has replaced it with a 1.402% disadvantage! This is so nearly the same that for all practical purposes the bank has just as much edge in its favor no matter whether the players bet they win or lose.

The Ace-Deuce Stand-Off

The first Bank Crap games barred Ace-Deuce instead of double-Sixes or double-Aces, and some banks still do. Some players think it doesn't make too much difference. And those who do try to figure it out usually decide, since Ace-Deuce can be made in 2 ways and a double-Six in 1 way, that Ace-Deuce must be twice as strong. This may sound good, but the logic is bad and the answer is wrong. The bank won't argue the matter with you, however. It's the customers with the wrong answers who make their business a profitable one.

The correct computation is made as follows. One thousand four losing rolls for the bank which is acting as a right bettor minus 110 stand-off rolls leaves 894 rolls that lose for the bank as against 976 that win for the bank. The player consequently has a 47-151/187% chance as against a 52-36/187% chance for the bank. The bank's edge is 82 rolls or 4-72/187%. Decimally this is *4.385% or about 22¢ on a $5 wager.*

Consequently when the bank bars Ace-Deuce, instead of double-Six or double-Ace, the P.C. in its favor is not merely doubled as so many players think; it has more than tripled!

And when the Ace-Deuce is barred it is a tip-off that the bank is either not patronized by smart-money wrong bettors or doesn't care for that kind of action and is trying to discourage it.

Come and Don't Come

The player who wishes to bet on the come or don't come places his bet on the spaces of the layout marked *Come* or *Don't Come*. These bets are put there to help speed up the line action because, even if a shooter is trying for a point number, a bettor can put his money on the layout and bet as he would on the come-out. The come bet is essentially the same as the pass line bet, and the don't come bet mimics the don't pass bet, except that the come and don't come bets are made after the come-out. Both are paid off at even money, and the house percentages on these wagers are the same as on pass line bets and don't pass line bets. The house edge is 1.414 percent, or about 7 cents on a $5 wager, on the come; and 1.402 percent, or about 7 cents on a $5 wager, on the don't come.

If you put a chip on the space of the layout marked *Come*, then the first roll of the dice is the point number as far as you're concerned. For example, the shooter is trying to make his point, which happens to be 8. You make a come bet, and on the next roll the shooter throws a 5, your point number is 5. In every subsequent roll of the dice, your come bet stands until either a 5 is made and you win, or a 7 is made and you lose. This also holds true for the don't come bet and the don't pass bet—even to the bar on the two sixes or the two aces. Come or don't come bets, like line bets, cannot be withdrawn; they remain until they are won or lost.

FREE SINGLE ODDS BETS

The smart dice player ("do bettor") can slice down the house's edge of 1.414 percent on the pass line bets and come bets to less than 1 percent by taking the odds that the shooter will make his point number. When you have made a pass line bet or come bet, and the shooter already has come out on a point or a new number, you're allowed to make a free second bet, limited to the amount of your wager on the pass line or come, that the shooter will make his point number. This is called "taking the free odds," meaning that the house will give you the true odds that the shooter won't make the point. To repeat, the true or correct odds on each point number are as follows:

ODDS AGAINST MAKING THE POINT NUMBERS

The Point Numbers	Correct Odds	Correct Payoff Odds in Dollars
4 or 10	2 to 1	$2.00 to $1.00
5 or 9	3 to 2	$1.50 to $1.00
6 or 8	6 to 5	$1.20 to $1.00

Let's say that you have a $10 bet riding on the pass line, and on the come-out the shooter rolls a 4; the above chart reveals that the correct odds against the shooter making this point are 2 to 1. If you want to "take the odds," you place an additional $10 on the layout directly behind your $10 pass line wager. If the shooter makes the 4, the house pays you $20 for the second bet plus $10 for your original pass line bet.

When you have a bet riding on the pass line, it's always advantageous to take the free odds on the point, since this reduces the 1.414 percent the house originally had on the pass line bet to less than 1 percent (to be exact, .848 percent). However, if you are one of the few players who do bet the don't pass line, remember that the house will allow you to "lay the odds" on the point equal to your don't pass line bet or don't come bet. Suppose the point is 4 again and you have $10 riding on the don't pass line. Also, you want to lay the odds that the shooter will not make it, and you can put down any even amount up to $20. When you take the odds, on a pass bet, you are limited to the amount of your line bet. But when you lay the odds on a don't pass bet, you are limited to the amount that could give you winnings of not higher than your original bet. If the shooter fails to make the point, the house pays you $10 for each of your two winning bets. The house advantage on both these wagers also runs to less than 1 percent (to be exact, .832 percent).

The free odds bets made on the pass line, don't pass line, come, or don't come, may be taken down (removed) at any time before the bet is decided. One thing should be remembered, however: The lowest-valued chip in a luxury casino is a $1 chip and, for that reason, dealers cannot pay off on any part of a dollar. Therefore, when you're taking the free odds, make sure that your bet doesn't pay off in cents. For example, if your pass line bet is $1 and the point is 5, taking the free odds for $1 would hurt you rather than benefit you. The dice dealer would not pay you the $1.50 your bet should bring; rather, you would be paid one lone $1 chip—that's all. To receive the correct odds of 3 to 2, your pass line bet should be $2.

The only way to take full advantage of the free odds is to make your bet a minimum (or multiple) of ten ($10). Since the average pass line bettor usually bets only a buck or two, he cannot take full advantage of the free odds. Here's why: When you make your pass line bet, you don't know what the come-out number will be. If you bet $1, and the come-out is 4 or 10, you're all right because you can get the full 2-to-1 odds. If the come-out is 5, 6, 8, or 9, you're in trouble. You'd get $1 to $1, instead of $1.50 to $1, on the 5 or 9. You'd get even money, instead of $1.20 to $1, on the 6 or 8. Similarly, on every bet up to $10, you'd be blocked from getting full odds on one or another number. But, on a $10 bet, you can get 2 to 1, 3 to 2, or 6 to 5, depending on the come-out number. This is true of any multiple of ten, but not of any other number or multiple. You can figure it yourself. This does not mean that you have to bet $10. With a smaller bet you can still find free odds on some numbers, though not all.

If you happen to be in a situation like that just described and the Craps dealer tries to induce you to increase the amount of your pass line bet after the come-out by telling you that it is to your best advantage, since it will permit you to take full advantage of the free odds offered, *don't*. Acceptance is to take even money instead of odds that the shooter will make his point and the free odds bet is no longer free. Although "betting the line" and taking or laying the free odds as described is the smartest way of gambling at casino dice tables, it is strange how very, very few gamblers take full advantage of such a play. I have found that many players are just as unpredictable as the dice. During the thrill, action, and excitement of the game, they bet as their emotions, rather than their minds, dictate. They follow their intuition rather than their knowledge of the game, and seldom do the right thing at the right time.

FREE DOUBLE ODDS BETS

Several Las Vegas Casinos Craps tables where the action is highly competitive allow players taking or laying free odds bets to wager double the original amount made to win or lose before the come-out. The bank's percentage in the above instances is .606+% on right action and .591+% on the wrong action. Banks that permit such action would not stay in business long if all the players made only that type of bet because a casino operation doing fair business requires, on the average, a greater percentage than that on all bets in order to pay its operating expenses before showing a profit.

PLACE OR BOX NUMBER BETS

Now we come to two spaces of the layout exactly similar in design, and with each situated nearest the dealer. Each design depicts six large boxed numbers that read *4, 5, 6, 8, 9, 10*. These are called *place* or *box numbers*, and are similar to the free odds bets previously discussed, such as taking or laying the odds that the shooter will or will not throw a given number or numbers before making a 7. Most gamblers don't bet the place numbers until after a come-out. However, place bets can be made at any time, and withdrawn whenever desired.

The two major differences between a free odds bet and a place number bet are that, when you bet a place number, you don't have to make a line bet first; and, unlike the free odds bet, you may bet one or all six place numbers at any time before the next roll of the dice. But, for this privilege, the house charges you a percentage fee for each and every place bet you make.

The house extracts its percentage by paying off place bets at less than the correct odds, instead of charging a fee.

Place betting accounts for a great deal of the action on most Bank Craps layouts. Since the bank cannot pay off the place bets at correct odds and stay in business, it resorts to a simple tactical gimmick to make place betting profitable. It insists that the right bettor accept less than the correct odds on each right place bet, and that the wrong bettor lay greater odds than the correct odds when placing a bet to lose. Place bets may be removed, if so desired, at any time during play. Here is a detailed description of place betting odds and the bank's favorable percentages.

PLACE OR BOX NUMBER BETS TO WIN

FOUR or TEN. The correct odds are 10 to 5 (2 to 1). The right player wagers $5 on Four or Ten, the bank pays off winning bets at odds of 9 to 5. This gives the bank an advantage of *6-2/3% or 6.666% which is about 33¢ on a $5 wager.*

FIVE or NINE. The true odds are 7-1/2 to 5, the bank pays off winning right bets at odds of 7 to 5 and takes an advantage of *4% which is 20¢ on a $5 wager.*

SIX or EIGHT. The correct odds are 6 to 5. The bank pays off winning right bets at odds of 7 to 6. This means that the bank has an advantage of *1-17/33% or 1.515% which is about 8¢ on a $5 wager.*

Some banks pay off this right wager at even money or 5 to 5. This means that the bank has an advantage of *9-1/11% or 9.090% which is 45¢ on a $5 wager.*

These percentages prove that the so-called smart dice player who places a right bet on the Four or Ten is a bigger sucker than the average field player whom most so-called smart dice players ridicule as being novices and suckers.

Obviously the best place bet is the Six or Eight when the bank pays 7 to 6 odds.

Most Las Vegas dice tables also permit a player to *buy* the above bets by paying a 5% charge. In such instances it is to a player's advantage to buy the 4 and 10 and place the 5, 9, 6 and 8. For detailed information about the 5% charge see New York Craps, page 127.

PLACE OR BOX NUMBER BETS TO LOSE

These wagers are not as popular as Win Place bets since eight out of ten dice players are born right bettors and don't like the idea of laying the odds (putting up more money than they can win). Here are the bank's percentages the player must buck when he lays a place bet.

FOUR or TEN. The correct odds are 10 to 5. The player must lay odds of 11 to 5. This gives the bank an advantage of *3-1/33% or 3.030% or about 15¢ on a $5 wager.*

FIVE or NINE. The correct odds are 7-1/2 to 5, the player must lay odds of 8 to 5, which gives the bank an advantage of *2-1/2% or 2.500% or about 12¢ on a $5 wager.*

SIX or EIGHT. The correct odds are 6 to 5, the player must lay odds of 5 to 4, which gives the bank an advantage of *1-9/11% or 1.818% or about 9¢ on a $5 wager.*

The bank's favorable percentage on the most popular bets discussed in the preceding pages, placed in tabular form for easy reference, gives us this.

THE BANK'S P.C. ON THE MOST POPULAR LAS VEGAS BANK CRAPS BETS

Bet	P.C. in Bank's Favor	Bank's P.C. on $5 Bet
Win (pass)	1.414%	$.07*
Come	1.414	.07
Lose (don't pass) Bar 6–6 or 1–1	1.402	.07
Don't Come, Bar 6–6 or 1–1	1.402	.07
Lose (don't pass) Bar 1–2	4.385	.22
Don't Come, Bar 1–2	4.385	.22
Place Bets to Win		
Bank lays 9 to 5 on 4 or 10	6.666	.33
Bank lays 7 to 5 on 5 or 9	4.000	.20
Bank lays 7 to 6 on 6 or 8	1.515	.08

* The bank's edge on a $5 wager given in cents has, in each case (except for the place win bet on numbers 5 or 9) a plus fraction which we have omitted.

THE BANK'S P.C. ON THE MOST POPULAR LAS VEGAS BANK CRAPS BETS (cont.)

Bet	P.C. in Bank's Favor	Bank's P.C. on $5 Bet
Place Bets to Lose		
Bank takes 11 to 5 on 4 or 10	3.030	.15
Bank takes 8 to 5 on 5 or 9	2.500	.12
Bank takes 5 to 4 on 6 or 8	1.818	.09
Win Bet (pass) Line plus free single point odds bet to win	.848	.04
Lose (don't pass) plus free single point odds bet to lose	.832	.04
Win Bet (pass) Line plus free double point odds bet to win	.606	.03
Lose (don't pass) plus free double point odds bet to lose	.591	.03

PROPOSITION BETS

It soon becomes clear that once you've learned the basic rules of Bank Craps, the bets that may be made on the Craps layout aren't at all difficult to understand. The trouble with the average player lies not in not knowing how to play the game, but in knowing little or nothing about odds and the house percentages he is out to beat. As a result, in a game where he has an opportunity to slice the house edge down to less than 1 percent, as explained in the foregoing, he insists on making all sorts of ridiculous side bets where at times he's bucking a house edge as high as 16-2/3 percent. Side bets are called "proposition bets" by casino operators. I call them by their right name: "sucker bets."

Let's analyze some of these ridiculous bets favored by many dice players, starting with field bets.

THE BIG 6 AND BIG 8

The player who bets the Big 6 or Big 8 is wagering that the number will be thrown before a 7. He can put his money on that space at any time. The bank pays even money and most players labor under the impression that it actually is an even-money bet. Why they think the bank would give so much space on the layout to a bet that would give it no percentage at all I don't know; but they do. Even people who should know better believe this. A famous syndicated sports columnist once offered to bet the author that sixes and eights are thrown just as often as sevens. His argument was the common one that each number can be made in 3 ways (the SIX with 1–5, 2–4, 3–3 and the EIGHT with 2–6, 3–5, 4–4) and SEVEN can also be made in 3 ways (1–6, 2–5, 3–4). He deduced from this that each number has the same chance of being thrown as does SEVEN and that the correct odds must therefore be 1 to 1, or even money.

What he persisted in overlooking was the fact that the smart-money players who never bet the Big 6 and Big 8 would, if his theory were correct, concentrate entirely on those bets. Eventually other players would follow suit and, in the long run, instead of showing a profit, the bank would merely break even on the betting and have nothing in the cash drawer with which to pay operating, maintenance and other costs. Since the bank is a business proposition and the operator is not running it for the thrill of gambling, this just doesn't make sense. The very fact that the 6 and 8 spaces are made large to entice bets should be sufficient proof that the 6 and 8 can't possibly be even-money bets.

We know from our *Combination and Ways* and our *Odds* tables that since either SIX or EIGHT can be made 5 ways and SEVEN in 6 ways that the correct odds are 6 to 5 and that the bank should pay off $1.20 to each $1 wagered. The bank's advantage is *9-1/11% and amounts to about 45¢ on a $5 bet.*

The SIX and EIGHT spaces on the layout have grown large and come to be known as the Big 6 and Big 8 not because they are the best bets on the layout, but because the bank has such a big edge. They are strictly sucker bets.

Take a quick look, for instance, at what happens to the man who puts $1 on one of these spaces and wins five times letting his money ride. His $1 grows and becomes $2, $4, $8, $6 and finally $32. He takes this down and is more than pleased with his $31 profit.

But what has actually happened is even worse than what happened to Joe when he rode through five passes with his center bet! On the Big 6 at correct odds of 6 to 5 the bank should have paid off with $1.20 for that first $1 wager. Then, when the bettor let the whole $2.20 ride, he would, at odds of 6 to 5, have won $2.64 on the second pass and so on. Placed in chart form, what happened to him looks like this.

Table No. 7

At the Even Money Odds Offered	But If the Bank Paid Correct Odds
He bets $1 and wins $1	He bets $1 and wins $1.20
He bets 2 and wins 2	He bets 2.20 and wins 2.64
He bets 4 and wins 4	He bets 4.84 and wins 5.808
He bets 8 and wins 8	He bets 10.648 and wins 12.7776
He bets 16 and wins 16	He bets 23.4264 and wins 28.11168
He takes down $32	He takes down $51.53808
His net profit: $31	His net profit: $50.53808

The player won $31 from the bank but the bank paid him $19.53808 less than it would have had to pay at correct odds. In fact, although he thinks he has obtained $31 by risking $1, he is shy nearly $19.54!

If you think that that $19.54 is merely a paper saving and has not actually earned the bank anything in hard cash, look at it this way. The correct odds are 6 to 5 and the bank that pays even money will, in the long run collect 6 units for every 5 units that it pays out. The player who continues to place bets of the same amount on the Big 6 or Big 8 can consequently, expect to lose the amount of his bet to the bank every 11 bets.

With these facts staring him in the face, a consistent player of the Big 6 and Big 8 should not need a crystal ball to dope out whether he will wind up a winner or loser in the long run. If on some particular evening he should as much as break even, he should realize that he has been enjoying an exceptional run of luck—luck that given half a chance would have won him money.

FIELD BETS

The *Field* usually bears the numbers 2, 3, 4, 9, 10, 11 and 12. When the player puts his money on the Field space, he is betting that one of the group of numbers listed there will be thrown on the next roll. The bank pays off at even money. Since the Field shows seven numbers and there are only four (5, 6, 7 and 8) which can make him lose, the non-thinker figures that his chances are excellent. He may even think that he has the best of it or at the very least an even chance. But appearances are nearly always deceptive, especially in casino games.

If we add together all the ways in which the winning and losing numbers can be thrown, we find that the above field numbers can be made in only 16 ways as against 20 ways for the losing numbers. The bank, consequently has an advantage of 4 rolls out of 36 which in percentage is 4/36 of 100 or *11-1/9% or about 56¢ on a $5 bet.*

When the bank pays double on the 2 and 12 as many of them do, the bank's advantage is reduced to *5-5/19%.* And here one of the strangest percentage problems in bank craps pops up. Some dealers will tell you that the bank's advantage is 5-5/19% and others that the player's disadvantage is 5-5/9%. Some of them argue for hours over their difference of opinion, but the curious thing is that the argument is unnecessary because both of them are right!

The discrepancy is explained by the fact that they are arguing not about the same problem but about two slightly different problems with two different answers! This fact, which no writer or bookmaker to my knowledge has ever before realized, and the analysis of both problems given below should clear up the matter and settle the arguments at last.

Suppose that the player and bank each cover the 36 possible Field combinations with dollar bets. The player's wagers will total $36, but the bank's wagers, because it puts an extra dollar on the 2 and 12 that are circled for a double payoff, will total $38.

If the dice fall exactly according to probabilities—all 36 different combinations being thrown in 36 successive rolls, the bank wins 20 bets for a total of $40 and makes a profit of $2. The player wins 16 bets, 14 which have $2 riding and the 2 and 12 which pay $3 each. He therefore takes down $34 and is short $2.

Since the bank wagered $38 and made a profit of $2, its favorable percentage is 2 divided by 38 or 5-5/19%.

The player, on the other hand, wagered $36 and lost $2. His percentage of loss or his disadvantage is 2 divided by 36 or 5-5/9%.

We have two problems rather than one because the bank and player are wagering different amounts.

Some banks pay 3 to 1 on double aces which supplies the same P.C. as paying double on both 2 and 12.

Other layouts are made with a 5 in place of the 4 so that the Field bears the numbers 2, 3, 5, 9, 10, 11 and 12. This gives the bank 19 chances against the player's 17 and the bank's edge is 5-5/9%. Some banks pay double on two aces, others pay 3 to 2 on double aces and double sixes. In each case the bank's advantage is *2-26/37%* and the player's disadvantage is *2-7/9%*.

The lure of Craps is its fast action but, because wagers on the Field are either won or lost *every time* the dice are rolled, the action is so fast and furious that most players can't take it. With a 5-5/9% or 5-5/19% depending which way you prefer to figure it, grinding away and taking 1/18 of every bet the player makes, the bank can expect to eat up the amount of the player's wager in 18 rolls.

THE DOUBLE PAY OFF

As proof of the fact that most gamblers and some dealers know almost nothing about figuring percentages, let me tell you the story of the Bank Craps table that did carry an even-up proposition. A few years ago I went into a casino that had two tables in operation on one of which I was amazed to see the field numbers 2, 3, 5, 9, 10, 11 and 12 with the 2 and 12 marked for a double pay-off.

I had some difficulty believing my eyes. It was the only even-up proposition I had ever seen or heard of on a Bank Crap table. The logical deduction was that the game must be crooked, but after observing the action for awhile, I was convinced that the game was on the level and that the mystery must have some other answer.

I also noticed that the other table, carrying the field numbers 2, 3, 4, 9, 10, 11, 12 with a double pay-off on the 2 and 12 and with a 5-5/19% in favor of the bank, had a bigger crowd of players around it and was getting *more* action than the field that had *no* percentage in the bank's favor. Those players, because they knew nothing about figuring P.C. were passing up the best proposition that ever appeared on a Bank Craps layout or any other for that matter.

Completely mystified now, I talked with some of the dealers and then with the boss only to discover that they didn't know what was going on either. The layout made money and that's about all they knew about it. But when I told the boss that he was offering his customers an even-up gamble, he gulped and turned a bit green around the gills.

"I'll be damned!" he said weakly. "And I've been using that layout for a month!"

When he had calmed down a bit and recovered his balance, he told me how it had happened. "I lost so much here and there around the country at Bank Craps that I decided to set up a game myself. I ordered two layouts from a catalog house and when they were being put on the tables, I noticed that one had the 'Pays Double' wording on the two and twelve and the other didn't. I figured the supply house had forgotten to put the 'Double' marking on the other, so I had it done."

He also added that he had no idea that such a difference could be obtained just because one layout differed from another by having a 5 on the field instead of a 4. And he knew too that he was damned lucky that none of the players knew any more about percentage than he did. If they had, they would have given the even-up field a heavy play, the boss would have been gambling with the players, and on the long run his overhead would eat up his bankroll. I hardly need add that the layout was changed before the house opened the next night.

HARD-WAY OR GAG BETS

These wagers can be found on all layouts and here again some players think that the odds offered by the bank are fair enough. Some even think they are getting correct odds, a form of logic that almost classes as not thinking at all!

The layout not only does not offer correct odds on any of these bets, but in many cases offers even less than it appears to. This *misdirection*, as gamblers call it, is accomplished by wording the proposition so as to mislead the player who doesn't remember that there is a distinction between the meanings of the two little words *for* and *to*. The way in which this deception operates can be seen in the following analysis of the Hard Way wagers.

On the Hard Way wagers the players bet that a specified number will be thrown the hard way (with double numbers) before it is made any other way or before 7 appears.

4 THE HARD WAY. There are 3 ways to make a FOUR and 6 ways to make a SEVEN. But, since the player wins only 1 way (by a throw of 2–2) and loses 8 ways, the correct odds are 8 to 1.

Most banks offer 7 to 1 on this bet. Its probability is 1 over the total number of ways that FOUR can win or lose, in this case 1/9. Its probability times 100 gives the percentage on one way. 1/9 of 100 is 11-1/9%. The bank that pays off at 7 to 1 when the correct odds are 8 to 1 thus gains the percentage on one way which is *11-1/9% or 56¢ on a $5 wager*. If it paid off at 6 to 1, it would gain the percentage on two ways or *22-2/9%*.

Some banks do pay only 6 to 1 on this, although it doesn't look that way. They simply offer to pay 7 *for* 1, and most players take that to mean 7 *to* 1 and never give it another thought. The difference is this: When paying off at 7 to 1 the bank gives you $7 *and* the $1 you bet. When paying off at 7 *for* $1, the bank pays you $7 but keeps the $1 you bet. It pays $7 *for your* $1. The bank is, consequently, actually giving you odds of only 6 to 1 on what is really an 8 to 1 proposition!

10 THE HARD WAY. Since there are also 3 ways to make TEN, the bank's P.C. is the same as on the FOUR and for the same reasons.

6 THE HARD WAY. A SIX can be made 5 ways. 1 Way only (33) wins; the other 4 ways lose as also do the 6 ways SEVEN can be made. Correct odds are therefore 10 to 1. Most banks pay off at 9 to 1 and thereby have an advantage of 9-1/11% or 45¢ on a $5 wager. Other

banks, without blinking, pay off 9 for 1 and have an advantage of 18-2/11% or 91¢ on a $5 wager.

8 THE HARD WAY. An EIGHT can also be made 5 ways and the bank's percentage is therefore the same as on the SIX, 9-1/11% or 18-2/11%.

These percentages, placed in tabular form for easy reference, give us this:

HARD WAY BETS

The Bet	Bank Pays	Correct Odds	Bank's Percentage	Bank's P.C. on $5 Bet
4 with 2-2 10 with 5-5	7 to 1	8 to 1	11 1/9%	$ .56+
6 with 3-3* 8 with 4-4*	9 to 1	10 to 1	9 1/11%	.45+
4 with 2-2 10 with 5-5	7 for 1	8 to 1	22 2/9%	1.11+
6 with 3-3 8 with 4-4	9 for 1	10 to 1	18 2/11%	.91+

* Some banks pay only 7 to 1 on the hardway SIX or EIGHT and have an advantage of 27³/₁₁%, or $1.36 on a $5 wager.

ONE ROLL OR COME-OUT BETS

On these proposition bets, the player puts his money on a specified number or numbers, betting that it will appear on the next roll. He can make the bet before any roll.

DOUBLE SIX IN ONE ROLL. This can be found on nearly every layout. Since the correct odds are 35 to 1 (see One Roll table p. 88), and since the bank lays 30 to 1, the bank has an edge of *13-8/9% about 69¢ on a $5 wager.*

DOUBLE ACE IN ONE ROLL. Pay-offs odds and P.C. same as the double-Six. See above.

OTHER DOUBLE NUMBERS IN ONE ROLL. Although not always shown on the layout, some banks will allow you to place come-out bets on other pairs of numbers. The pay-off odds and P.C. are the same as on the two-Sixes.

ELEVEN IN ONE ROLL. Correct odds are 17 to 1. Bank pays off 15 to 1 and has an edge of *11-1/9% or about 56¢ on a $5 wager.*

THREE IN ONE ROLL. Odds are 17 to 1, pay-off 15 to 1, and the bank's P.C. is the same as on the ELEVEN.

SEVEN IN ONE ROLL. Odds are 5 to 1. Bank lays 4 to 1 and has an edge of *16-2/3% or about 83-1/3¢ on a $5 wager.*

ANY CRAP (2, 3, 12) IN ONE ROLL. Odds are 8 to 1. Bank lays 7 to 1 and has an edge of *11-1/9% or about 56¢ on a $5 wager.*

3-4, 5-2, 6-1 IN ONE ROLL. Here number 7 must be thrown with the particular combination of numbers on which you place your money. Correct odds in each instance are 17 to 1. Bank pays off 15 to 1 and has an edge of *11-1/9% or about 56¢ on a $5 wager.*

BANK'S PERCENTAGE ON THE STANDARD ONE-ROLL OR COME-OUT BETS

The Bet	Bank Pays	Correct Odds	Bank's P.C.	Bank's P.C. on $5 Wager
Two Sixes (6–6)) Two Aces (1–1))	30 to 1	35 to 1	13 8/9%	$.69
Eleven (6–5) Three (1–2)	15 to 1	17 to 1	11 1/9%	.56
All Sevens (7)	4 to 1	5 to 1	16 2/3%	.83
Any Crap (2, 3 or 12)	7 to 1	8 to 1	11 1/9%	.56
7 with 3–4 7 with 2–5 7 with 6–1	15 to 1	17 to 1	11 1/9%	.56

Las Vegas and Reno layouts increase their percentage take by listing their odds payoff with the word *for* instead of *to.* Their percentages placed in tabular form are as follows:

The Bet	Bank Pays	Correct Odds	Bank's P.C.	Bank's P.C. on $5 Wager
Two Sixes (6–6)) Two Aces (1–1))	30 for 1	35 to 1	16 2/3%	$.83
Eleven (6–5) Three (1–2)	15 for 1	17 to 1	16 2/3%	.83
All Sevens (7)	5 for 1	5 to 1	16 2/3%	.83
Any Crap (2, 3, 12)	8 for 1	8 to 1	11 1/9%	.56
7 with 3–4 7 with 2–5 7 with 6–1	15 for 1	17 to 1	16 2/3%	.83

The following one-roll action bets are listed because some smaller banks carry proposition bets on their layouts and include all possible one-roll bets:

The Bet	Bank Pays	Correct Odds	Bank's P.C.	Bank's P.C. on $5 Wager
4 in one roll 10 in one roll	9 to 1	11 to 1	16 2/3%	$.83
6 in one roll 8 in one roll	5 to 1	6 1/5 to 1	16 2/3%	.83
5 in one roll 9 in one roll	7 to 1	8 to 1	11 1/9%	.56

UNDER AND OVER SEVEN

Some banks carry spaces on the layout marked Under 7 and Over 7. Money placed on the Under 7 space is a bet that the shooter will throw less than 7 and on the Over 7 space that he will throw more than 7. Both bets are paid off at even money. The player has 15 chances to win against 21 for the bank giving the bank an advantage of *16-2/3%* *or about 83¢ on a $5 wager.*

INSURANCE BETS

Many Bank Craps players have a habit of making two wagers simultaneously in an attempt to insure one or the other. For example, a player places a bet on the win line and tries to protect it against a crap on the first roll by making a come-out bet on All Craps.

He thinks that if he loses one bet he may win the other, thus cutting down or canceling out his loss when actually he stands to lose at least one of the bets and maybe both. Or he may attempt to insure a lose bet after the come-out by taking odds on the point. Since every wager in Bank Craps must be considered as a separate and distinct wager, the only effect of insurance betting is simply to give the bank a P.C. on two bets rather than one. Instead of insuring himself against loss, the player has merely increased the P.C. against himself.

Since insurance bets class as system plays, they will be discussed in more detail in the chapter on Systems, page 292.

HORN, SANTRUCE, MIAMI, OR CURAÇAO ONE-ROLL BETS

Some casino layouts permit the player to make four one-roll bets (2–3–12–11) at the same time. The layout space that permits these one-roll bets is marked differently in various casinos. At the Caribe Hilton Casino in Puerto Rico, it is marked *Santurce*; in the casinos of

Curaçao, it is marked *Miami* or *Curaçao*, while in some Nevada Casinos it is known as the *horn bet*. For instance, in Puerto Rico, when you wish to place a one-roll Santurce bet, you hand the stickman a $5 chip (or a multiple bet of $5) and call *Santurce*—which means you are betting one unit on the number 2, one unit on 3, one unit on 12, and two units on 11. The one-roll pay-offs odds are the same as one-roll come bets: 15 to 1 or 15 for 1 on the 3 and 11, and 30 to 1 or 30 for 1 on the 2 or 12. This house gimmick forces a player to make four different one-roll bets at the same time, thereby giving the house a favorable edge of 13-8/9% on the double aces and double sixes and 11-1/9% on the three and eleven.

NEW YORK CRAPS

New York Craps is a version of Bank Craps found in most illegal gambling houses in the eastern part of the United States and legal casinos in the Bahamas, England, Yugoslavia and wherever gamblers from eastern United States operate dice games. The big differences between Bank Craps and New York Craps is that the New York dice layout does not possess a *Come and Don't Come* betting space and that *place betting is not permitted*. Players are compelled to buy the box numbers (4, 5, 6, 8, 9, 10). In buying the boxes, the player is paid off at correct odds, such as 6 to 5 on Six or Eight, 3 to 2 on Five or Nine, and 2 to 1 on Four or Ten. However, for such services, the bank levies a direct charge of 5% on the total sum of right money wagered; this amounts to a charge of 25¢ on each $5 bet. For example, if you take or lay $10 to $5 on a Four, the bank charges 25¢ for either bet.

New York Craps is played on a specially constructed dice table that is similar to a Las Vegas or Bank Craps table. However, the table is shaped somewhat different and the dealers are posted at each end of the table. A stickman stands at the center of the table and the two boxmen sit opposite the stickman. A Lookout, known as a ladderman, sits on a stand high above the table.

Each dealer is supplied with a hundred or more quarters (twenty-five cent pieces) which are spread out on the table in front of him. These quarters are used to help the dealer in taking his 5% charge of a player's box number bet or bets. There is one very peculiar fact about the direct 5% vigorish charge: in most games, the bank's favorable percentage is greater than most players think, but the 5% vigorish charge at New York Craps is less than nearly all crap players and most casino operators suspect. Here are the correct percentages in favor of the bank when the operators levy a 5% vigorish charge:

RIGHT BETTOR PAYS   4.761+%, or about 25¢, when taking $5 worth of odds on any point or box number.

WRONG BETTOR PAYS   2.439+%, or about 12¢, when laying odds of $10 to $5 on point or box number 4 or 10.

3.225+%, or about 15¢ when laying odds of $7.50 to $5 on point or box number 5 or 9.

4.000+%, or about 20¢, when laying odds of $6 to $5 on point or box number 6 or 8.

SCARNEY CRAPS

New York Craps always appeared to me as an undignified way to play Craps. The dealer's constant handling of quarters used to make change seemed a cheap way of running a modern dice table. Often, while

John Scarne seen teaching the casino personnel at the Hilton Hotel casino, in Curaçao, Netherlands Antilles, how to detect a crooked dice switch. A Scarney Bank Craps layout covers the table surface.

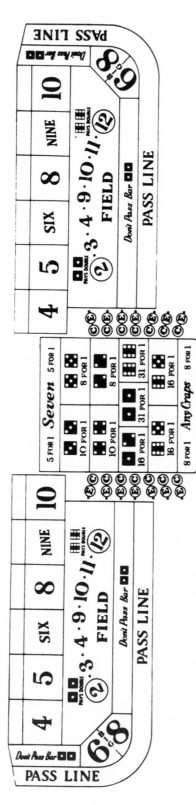

The Scarney Bank Craps layout created by the author and first introduced in the Curaçao Hilton Hotel casino in the Netherlands Antilles. The layout is minus a Come and Don't Come space. The proposition bets pay one unit more than the Las Vegas layout shown on page 106. The center portions shows the letters C and E. They stand for Crap and Eleven and help the stickmen remember the person who made each particular bet.

scouting the casinos of the Bahamas and England, I have observed dice players a $5 bet on a box number (4, 5, 6, 8, 9, 10). The dealer then shouts, "25¢, please." The players usual answer is, "What for?" "The 5% house charge," cries the dealer, to the bewilderment of the players.

The reason why some casino operators prefer New York Craps to Bank Craps is that New York Craps has a greater house percentage than Bank Craps. Any casino that opens only in the evening and caters only to gambling junkets—with little or no walk-in business—cannot run a profitable Bank Craps or Las Vegas style of dice game. Many casino operators in an area where the action is limited to a few hours a day, have tried unsuccessfully to operate by dealing Las Vegas odds. The result, they went broke in the attempt, and either went out of business or resorted to running a bust-out joint.

Several years ago, the Administrator of the Hilton Hotel Casino in Curaçao, Netherlands Antilles, informed me that casinos in the area—because of the lack of walk-in business (where natives are not permitted to gamble)—were going broke. Gambling junkets proved to be unprofitable. So then and there I decided to develop a craps layout that would permit casinos such as these a chance to survive and at the same time give the junket player a run for his money. I also took into consideration the fact that for years everything was increasing in cost, casino rent, salaries, entertainment, drinks, cigarettes as well as paying for hotel accommodations and plane transportation for junket players. Strangely enough, the only thing that had not gone up was the house percentage at casino tables.

Shortly thereafter, a new craps layout which I invented appeared for the first time at the Curaçao Hilton Hotel Casino. I have taken the creator's liberty of naming this *Scarney Craps*. In other words, I simply dignified New York Craps by eliminating the 5% charge and made use of place betting. Scarney Craps, like New York Craps, lacks a Come and Don't Come space, but the proposition bets at Scarney Craps pay an extra unit more than most Bank Craps tables throughout the world. Scarney Craps is played on a standard bank craps table. As stated earlier, Scarney Craps is being played in many Carribean casinos as well as in Europe and South America.

So that the reader can see at a glance the bank's favorable percentages on all forms of bank craps bets such as Bank Craps Las Vegas Style, New York Craps, and Scarney Craps, they have been placed together in the following tables.

THE CASINO'S P.C. ON MOST BANK CRAP BETS

Bet	P.C. in Bank's Favor	Bank's P.C. on $5 Bet
Win (pass)	1.414%	$ .07*
Come	1.414	.07
Lose (don't pass) Bar 6-6 or 1-1	1.402	.07
Don't Come, Bar 6-6 or 1-1	1.402	.07
Lose (don't pass) Bar 1-2	4.385	.22
Don't Come, Bar 1-2	4.385	.22
PLACE BETS TO WIN		
Bank lays 9 to 5 or 4 or 10	6.666	.33
Bank lays 7 to 5 on 5 or 9	4.000	.20
Bank lays 7 to 6 on 6 or 8	1.515	.08
BOX NUMBER BETS TO WIN (5% CHARGE)		
Bank lays 10 to 5 on 4 or 10	4.761	.25
Bank lays 7½ to 5 on 5 or 9	4.761	.25
Bank lays 6 to 5 on 6 or 8	4.761	.25
PLACE BETS TO LOSE		
Bank takes 11 to 5 on 4 or 10	3.030	.15
Bank takes 8 to 5 on 5 or 9	2.500	.12
Bank takes 5 to 4 on 6 or 8	1.818	.09
BOX NUMBER BETS TO LOSE (5% CHARGE)		
Bank takes 10 to 5 on 4 or 10	2.439	.12
Bank takes 7½ to 5 on 5 or 9	3.225	.16
Bank takes 6 to 5 on 6 or 8	4.000	.20
FIELD BETS		
Field (2, 3, 4, 9, 10, 11, 12)	11.111	.56
Field (2, 3, 4, 9, 10, 11, 12) with double payoff on 2 and 12	5.263	.26
Field (2, 3, 5, 9, 10, 11, 12)	5.555	.27
Big Six	9.090	.45
Big Eight	9.090	.45
Win Bet (pass) Line plus free single point bet to win	.848	.04
Lose (don't pass) plus free point odds bet to lose	.832	.04
Win Bet (pass) Line plus free single point odds bet to win	.848	.04
Lose (don't pass) plus free single point odds bet to lose	.832	.04
Win Bet (pass) line plus free doubel point odds bet to lose	.606	.03
Lose (don't pass) plus free double point odds bet to lose	.591	.03

---

* The bank's edge on a $5 wager given in cents has, in each case (except for the Place win bet on numbers 5 or 9 and in the box numbers 6 or 8 to lose) a plus fraction which we have omitted.

For the bank's favorable percentages on Hardway and One-Roll bets, see tables on pages 124 and 125.

HOW TO GAMBLE SENSIBLY AT BANK CRAPS

As in any banking game, the house earns a percentage on every bet made at Bank Craps Las Vegas Style, New York Craps and Scarney Craps. This is not unreasonable because somebody has to pay for the casino rent, equipment, employees' salaries, etc. But just how much you pay for the privilege of shooting Craps in a casino is entirely up to you.

Nobody can tell you how to win at Bank Craps because, if you gamble long enough and often enough, the house P. C. will take its toll. But if you still insist on taking a fling at the dice tables, here are several rules to follow which can save you money.

1. Whenever you gamble at Bank Craps, set aside in advance the amount of money you are willing to lose. If you lose that amount, quit the game for the evening. And do not borrow money, write a check or obtain credit to continue gambling.

2. Also set for yourself a reasonable amount that you might expect to win, and if you succeed in winning that much, quit the game, no matter how lucky you happen to feel. If you follow this rule, you will retain your winnings more often, and you will have more winning plays because you are trying to win smaller amounts.

3. If you lost yesterday, do not gamble today with the object of recouping yesterday's losses. That is the most dangerous course any gambler can follow. Trying to get even has sent more players to the poorhouse than anything else. Write off yesterday's losses and forget them.

4. Naturally, I expect the player, after reading this text on Bank Craps, to place his bets on the layout spaces which have the least percentage against him. If you follow this rule your chances of winning are greatly increased.

5. Try to win the amount you hoped to win in the fastest time possible. Making bets back and forth all night merely gives the law of averages a chance to perform as expected in the long run and helps Old Man Percentage slowly but surely eat up your chances of winning.

If the bank crap player follows the above rules, he will be gambling intelligently, his winnings may be greater, and when he does lose, his losses won't hurt him.

TIPS ON HOW TO SPOT A CROOKED CASINO

Is there any simple, sure-fire method by which you can be sure your favorite casino is on the level? No, it's not that easy. But it can be done. Your best protection is to have in your head the information on cheating at casino games which you will find in this book. In addition, ask yourself the following questions:

1. How long has the casino been operating? The fact that a casino is crooked leaks out faster than you think, and only the honest ones stay in business year after year.

2. Is the casino lavishly decorated or is it a makeshift affair? The bigger the casino's investment in its quarters and furnishings, the more likely it is to be honest. Crooked dice, roulette and card games are usually found in small casinos, hotel rooms, private homes, at charity balls and conventions behind closed doors.

3. Is the casino well patronized and doing good business, like the legal casinos in Nevada and Puerto Rico? If so, you can almost be sure the operators aren't out to take you for every nickel they can get. A crowded casino is the best proof that it is honest. Don't be the only player or one of a few players in a nearly empty casino whose operators have worried faces!

If you are a high roller and are betting as if you are trying to win the casino—pardner, you're on your own!

As in many other things, your best protection lies in knowing what you are doing. If you know the cheating methods explained in these pages, you have a chance of spotting crooked work. And then, give yourself the best possible chance of winning by sticking to those casino bets which have the smallest house percentage against you. You'll find all that information here, too.

LAS VEGAS CASINO OPERATION

Most of the bigtime illegal gambling establishments in the United States are controlled by gambling combines. In Nevada, although former illegal operators are responsible for opening most of the casinos on the Vegas Strip, many law-abiding businessmen have bought in. Few of the old-time professional gamblers that helped make Nevada the gambling mecca of the world are in the state today. Most have passed away or retired.

It is a tribute to Nevada's law-enforcement agencies that in spite of some underworld infiltration in the casinos, and despite the fact that gambling draws thousands of undesirables to the state each year, there is little crime in Las Vegas and Reno, and no gangland violence has occurred in Nevada for several years. Even when you add the 17 million tourists who visit Nevada annually to the state's population, it still has one of the lowest percentage crime rates in the United States.

You can find among Nevada casino employees a good many veteran dealers and croupiers who learned their trade in illegal joints and have police records to prove it, but this picture is changing. Dealer and croupier schools are turning out hundreds of formally trained dealers who are *clean* (without police records). It is probable that the next generation of casino employees will be indistinguishable from an equal number of bookkeepers or salesmen. It is also probable that the great majority of the owners and operators will eventually be businessmen without police records like those in Monte Carlo, France, Italy and other countries where legalized casinos have been in operation for half a century or more.

Most of the casinos on the Strip have no windows in their gaming rooms to remind a player whether it is day or night, and there are no clocks to indicate the hour. From the casino point of view, day or night means nothing—it is all gambling time. The wheels never stop, the cards are always being dealt and the dice continue to roll. Spectators have no place to sit, except at the black-jack and roulette tables, and anyone who sits there becomes a player because the chairs are reserved for that purpose.

The average Las Vegas casino has six bank-crap tables, nine black-jack tables, three roulette tables, and one side game such as the Big Six. Around the walls are scores of one-armed bandits ranging from nickel to dollar machines. Maximum betting limits at the tables run from $200 to $500, although the casino will raise this for high rollers.

A Las Vegas casino has the following employees who, except for the dealers, croupiers, and a few others, work a total of six hours of each eight-hour shift—each hour is divided into forty minutes on and twenty minutes off.

Casino Manager

He is in charge of the operation and supervises the shift bosses on the three working shifts. Salary: $40,000 to $75,000 or more per year, plus bonus.

Casino Host

He acts as a good-will ambassador to outstanding high rollers and their wives; he takes them to dinners, shows, makes their hotel and plane reservations and generally keeps them happy. He sends the women orchids and candy and even gives them money to play the slots when their husbands are high-rolling at the tables. Salary: $30,000 to $50,000 per year; he sometimes owns a couple of points in the casino.

Credit Manager

The next most important employee. He screens your credit cards and has the authority, if they prove satisfactory, to extend whatever credit you require—$500, $1,000, $5,000, or more. Salary: about $30,000 to $50,000 per year.

Since few people carry thousands of dollars in cash around with them, high rollers pay big losses by check. But don't just walk into a Nevada casino and ask to have a check cashed. None of them will do it unless you have filled out a casino credit form and have been issued a casino credit card. The credit manager, whose responsibility this is, checks on you by telephoning your bank; don't expect him to okay you for credit unless you ask during banking hours. If you already have a credit card from another casino it's simpler; the manager makes a phone check with them, and casinos are always open. Ordinary credit cards to most credit managers don't even rate $50 in credit.

Casino operators have considerable patience with broke credit players. They will make a deal with a loser who has lost more than his checking account holds, allowing him to pay off on the installment plan. But they don't like welshers. If, after returning home, you put a stop on checks signed in Nevada because you believe that gambling debts are by law uncollectible in your state, you will first get a firm letter demanding payment, then a phone call, and finally a couple of tough-looking visitors. At this point or shortly thereafter, the would-be welsher pays up. One casino manager told me: "We had a character here last year who took $5,000 worth of credit, won $10,000 at Craps the last night, walked out without picking up his 'hold checks,' and later when we put the checks through he stopped them. Some character, eh? But he changed his mind later."

Shift Boss

He acts as casino manager during his working shift. Salary: $100 per day plus bonuses.

Cashier

He counts the casino bankroll and makes a chip inventory before and after each work shift. He supplies each gaming table with the necessary number of chips at the beginning of the game and more when required. Some casinos allow players to cash their chips at the main cashier's cage. In others, the pit boss pays off winners at the table where the money was won, and, in this case, the pit boss makes three copies of a cash-out slip. A runner takes two of these to the cashier, who initials the slips and exchanges one of them for the cash amount. The cashier is the employee who does all the casino's bookkeeping. Larger casinos have a main cashier's office and a pit cashier at a small desk in the ring formed by the circle of roulette and black-jack tables. There are usually three cashiers to each working shift. Salary: $350 per week each.

Pit Boss

He acts as a floorman or inspector over a black-jack or roulette table, makes out and signs cash-out and fill slips, and watches constantly for any errors the dealer or croupiers may make and for any cheating on players' or dealers' part. Salary: $80 to $100 per day.

Spotter or Lookout

An employee who observes the play secretly when the house wants to check on the honesty of the dealer. He does this either from behind a one-way mirror glass, usually located in the ceiling, or by acting as a player at the table. Salary: $60 per day.

Black Jack Dealer

He deals at the black-jack table, collects losing bets and pays off winning bets. Salary: $26 per day plus *tokens* (tips) which may total considerably more than his salary.

Croupier

He deals the game of Roulette, collects losing bets and pays off winning bets. Salary: $26 per day, plus tokens.

Crap Dealer

He collects and pays off bets at the crap tables, and alternates with other crap dealers as a *stickman* (one who calls the numbers thrown). Salary: $26 per day plus tokens.

Shill

A male or female employee who poses as a player in order to stimulate the action. Salary $12.50 to $15 per day.

Runner

He runs errands between the cashier's cage and the pit bosses or box men, carrying cash-out and fill slips and money. Salary: $17.50 per day.

Box Man

He has charge of a dice table and handles all cash and chip transactions between the table and the cashier's office. Salary: $60 per day. When a player gives the crap dealer money in exchange for chips, the dealer passes the paper money to the box man seated at the center of the table. He is called a box man because, using a paddle, he pushes the paper money into a slot in the table and it falls into a locked *drop box* underneath. *Cash-out slips* and *fill slips* which he writes and signs go into the same box. Fill slips indicate how many additional chips have been brought to the table from the cashier's cage.

At black-jack and roulette tables, money and duplicate slips are pushed into the drop box by the dealer, but the slips must be written out by the cashier or pit boss and signed by the pit boss and the dealer and a copy returned to the cashier. At the end of each eight-hour shift, the locked boxes are taken from each table to the *count room*, where they are unlocked and the contents counted by three or four casino part owners or their representatives.

Ladder Man

He sits on a high stand overlooking the dice table just above the dealers and box man, corrects any mistakes the dealers may make that go unobserved by the box man, and watches for dice cheats. He usually alternates as a box man. Salary: $60 per day.

Side Game Dealer

He deals one of the following games: Big Six, Money Wheel, Race Horse Wheel, Hazard, Chuck-a-Luck, and sometimes others. Salary: $26 per day plus tokens.

In addition to the above employees there are also floorwalkers, house spotters, slot-machine attendants and mechanics, waitresses, keno runners, bus boys, bartenders, porters, doormen, bouncers, publicity agents, lawyers, tax experts and accountants. The busy swing shift requires about 60 employees to keep the action rolling and about half that number during the slower day and graveyard shifts.

The casino payroll is small compared to the tens of thousands of dollars spent weekly for the live entertainment in the casino's night club as a lure to bring in the customers. These shows have made Las Vegas a capital of live entertainment. More television, motion-picture, and night-club stars perform there nightly than in Hollywood and New York City combined. The top-notch casino night-club shows cost hundreds of thousands of dollars to produce and feature stars sometimes receive as much as $250,000 per week. All of this is paid by the casino management, and when you add in state taxes, employees' salaries, rent, free drinks for customers and other incidental expenses, the annual cost runs into the millions.

GAMBLING JUNKETS

A group of gamblers solicited to travel to a casino for the sole purpose of gambling is called a "gambling junket." The organizer of such a group is known as the "junket leader," or "junketeer," and the gamblers are called, "junketors." To the best of my knowledge, the first gambling junket came to Benjamin (Bugsy) Siegel's Flamingo in Las Vegas in early 1947. It came from Hollywood, California and was comprised of mainly movie moguls and their wives. The gambling junkets for the next decade or so were, as a rule, put together by the casinos themselves. They involved a host of certified gamblers who loved to gamble and had the cash to do so. In return for their business, these invited guests received everything free—room, food, drinks, plane transportation. The only charges were tips and phone calls. Therefore, Bugsy Siegel not only was the "father of the Las Vegas Strip," he also fathered the gambling junket.

With the building of more strip hotel casinos, the bigtime gambler became the casino's invited guest and to this day, he still is "comped" any time he visits his favorite casino. That is, providing he does not owe the casino money. However, in the late '60's, many small travel agents and gamblers, who were once on junkets, became junketeers. They knew little or nothing about the gambling business and most of the people they put on junkets as gamblers had never been in a casino before. By 1969, there were over 2,000 junketeers in the United States and most of the so-called "gamblers" on their junkets were vacation seekers and free loaders. To discourage this practice, some casino operators now insist that "front money" of $1,000 had to be put up for each man on the juket—wives had to pay their plane fare, usually $250 or more as front money. Out of the $1,000 front money, the male gambler received $750 in non-negotiable chips . . . upon arrival at the casino. In addition, each gambler in advance had to fill out a credit form, and had to state the full amount of credit he wished to be granted by the casino.

Most junketeers rarely, if ever, collected all the monies due the casino and if they did, they held out a considerable sum and swore on a stack of Bibles that the player never paid them. In all my casino experience, I have still to meet one junketeer who is honest and does not owe one or another casino thousands of dollars. The operation of many junketeers is first to load a casino with stiffs and then to cop a plea that the players they put on the junket failed to pay their markers. In the old days, the airlines and the junketeers were the only ones who made money with the junkets. The airline sold plane tickets. The junketeer gets $50 or $75 a head from the casino for each male gambler on his junket, plane commissions from the airline, and at times receives 10% of all monies lost by gamblers on his junket. In addition, the junketeer and his wife, or mistress, received room and board as guests of the hotel casino.

I must point out to the reader that when a casino fails to collect their gambling debts, they lose not only what is owed to them—but monies that these same gamblers received from the casino—so for every $10,000 owed the casino, it is a sure bet that $5,000 in cash was lost by the casino. These characters give chips to their friends and wives to cash in and at times sell their chips to other players at a reduced price. For example, they'll take $400 for $500 worth of chips.

Today most casinos in Nevada, to avoid such skullduggery, insist the junketeer must put up $2,500 in cash for each gambler and his wife, and all gamblers must pay their markers on leaving. This sort of thing helps a bit, but does not completely eliminate stiffs (non-gamblers). Believe me, junkets are not the bonanza many people believe them to be. Several casino operators in the Caribbean Islands remarked to me that they do not know if a junket they have okayed will be loaded with stiffs or not, but since they have little business otherwise, they have to take that chance. "Our only hope is to beat one or two high-rollers on the junket real big—that will pay our hotel expenses, plane fares, junket commission, etc., and all the small amounts lost by the stiffs will be profit. If we don't beat one or more gamblers big, we are sure to have a losing junket."

Recently one gambling operator returning from Europe said, "Scarne, you know we ran dozens of junkets to *blank blank* and we cheated every person on the junket—and you know what? We still couldn't meet our plane and hotel expenses! We went broke simply because most of these junkets carried too many non-gamblers and free loaders."

I predict that organized junkets will be a thing of the past in the top casinos in the near future. Individual high-rollers, of course, will always be welcomed by the casino and receive everything free except for tips and phone calls. However, I doubt if there will be enough high-rollers around to satisfy the countless number of casinos springing up throughout the world. Thus, then a toast, "To the millions of small time gamblers who are the kings of gambling."

CASINO EARNING POWER

As a gambling consultant, casino figures are very important to me. When I visit a casino where I'm employed, my first duty is to check the hold (win) percentages at each table. A table's hold percentage is the percentage expected to be earned by each table. This comprises the difference of the cash and credit slips dropped into the cash box situated beneath each table against the payout slips (money paid to winning players). The cash box is situated under the slot opening into which the dealer pushes the player's money upon the sale of chips. If the win percentage equals or exceeds the expected hold percentage, I have have had an easy visit, but if it falls far below, I have to check out the reason. If the winning payouts are greater than the money and credit slips in the box, the table is a loser. If the money and credit slips total a greater amount than the winner's payouts, the table has won money.

There is no mathematical formula that can be used to compute the overall earning power for a given period at any casino game. This is especially true for Bank Craps Nevada-style simply because of the dozens of different craps bets made at the dice table, each having a different favorable house percentage. Also players are very unpredictable as to the type bets they make. However, I have standardized a percentage that each bank craps table is expected to earn over a month's period. This earned percentage is based on my study of daily, weekly, monthly and yearly financial records of bank craps tables in a number of major casinos in Nevada and the Caribbean for over 25 years. The study of these reports shows that the expected earned percentage at Bank Craps over a month's period amounts to about 20% of the gross amount of chips purchased. This means that when a player hands a boxman at a bank craps table $100 to purchase chips, the house is expected to earn $20 of the $100. Even though some players will win, some will lose, and some will break even, the table's expected earning power over a month's time will average about 20%.

At times, for days and even for weeks, a bank craps table may lose. At other times, the table may win heavily and hold a much higher percentage, but in the long run, the 20 percent figure is the approximate hold percentage of each and every craps table that is run honestly both from the inside and the outside.

My study of the casino records of the black jack over the past twenty-five years shows that under conditions just described, the black jack tables hold about 26% over the month's period. Roulette's hold percentage under the same conditions is about 30%. Baccarat's hold percentage amounts to about 10 percent over a month's period. For any of the casino side games, such as the Big Six or the Money Wheel where the house's advantage is 20% or more, the month's hold percentage will total about 80%.

These percentages on a casino's earning power should convince the reader that the house's overall percentages will knock out even the best player in the long run.

8

Open or Money Craps

Bank Craps succeeded and replaced the great banking game of the last century, Faro, because Bank Craps supplied more action by allowing the players to bet both ways. But today the big professional gamblers, the players who sometimes win and lose fifty and a hundred grand in one session at craps don't do it at Bank Craps. Such heavy gambling occurs very rarely in a private game and, with the usual limits, is impossible in Bank Craps. But the game in which it does happen and with considerable frequency is that king of all the house games—the one the professional gamblers call Money, Fading or Open Craps.

Fortunes are won and lost nightly at the open crap tables because it is here that the professional gambler, the smart gambler, the hustler, the dice mechanic and the underworld big-shot play along with those other big money gamblers: the millionaire play boys, the politicians and the big business man.

These people prefer Open Craps for one major reason. It offers them their biggest chance to win, and no matter how much dough they have salted away or what other excuses they give, they all play primarily because they want to win. Some, like the wealthy contractor who gets a kick out of life by being able to lay down such large bets that the biggest gamblers in the country often have to shake their heads and admit they don't want to cover the bet, also play because it satisfies their urge to be known as a fast gambler among other gamblers.

The cafe society crowd sometimes alibis a big loss by saying that they expected to lose and that they only played for the thrill. Maybe so, but the thrill derives from just one thing, the possibility of winning. No one, no matter what they tell you, ever enjoyed losing. The gambling fever is a money fever.

THE BARN

The most successful of all Open or Money Craps games, one which played a prominent part in the Senate crime probe in the Fifties, was located in Bergen County, New Jersey, and was called the Barn. It started in 1937 about eight blocks from my home in Fairview, in the cellar of a local gambler. It housed one money-crap game, and the gambler booking the game was known as the Baron. The game grew in size so fast that the Bergen County racket boys pushed the Baron out and took control. The joint moved from Fairview to Cliffside Park, back to Fairview, to Little Ferry, to Fort Lee and to Lodi, where it was when it folded as a result of the United States Senate probe back in 1950.

Lodi is only a few miles from where I live, but when I visited the Barn there in 1945 I first had to go to New York City; local patronage was discouraged. A Cadillac limousine picked me up outside the swank Sherry-Netherland Hotel (a service that extended to all the first-rate New York hotels) and took me to a used-car lot in Little Ferry, N.J., where I met other men with the same destination. Another car took us to the Barn.

We entered a large rectangular building, formerly a taxi-repair garage, and found ourselves in a small anteroom just about big enough to contain four men. A sliding panel in an inner door moved aside and a pair of eyes gave us the once-over through the small glass window. Then this opened and we passed into another small room, where we were searched for weapons. This was not just a formality; I saw that several pistols and revolvers had already been checked in the "frisk room" by their carriers. It was done to minimize the possibility of the casino's being held up by gunmen.

Leaving the frisk room, we entered the Barn itself. There were six dice tables, four black-jack tables and a *shimmy* (Chemin de Fer) table. It was in this sawdust joint that I saw the biggest dice gambling of my career. Seven of the biggest gamblers and casino owners in the country were present: Bugsy Siegel, New York and West Coast gambler and racketeer; Willie Moretti, then racket boss of Bergen County; his brother, Sally Moretti; a wealthy shirt manufacturer, a celebrated New York lawyer, a well-known movie star, and a Chicago department store owner. The wagers made that night were all in the thousands of dollars and few bets were made with the bank. The biggest single bet was on the point 4. Willie Moretti took $120,000 to $60,000 from the other bigtime gamblers. P.S.: Willie missed the 4. At the end of the evening the shirt manufacturer, now long retired, had won $800,000—in cash, not chips or IOUs.

The Barn's annual gross during its fifteen years of operation was greater than that of any casino in the world. Its monthly gross profits averaged more than the annual gross profit of Monaco's Monte Carlo Casino during its best years. The largest single night's take by the Barn's operators was that of September 1, 1946, when the eleven gaming tables showed a gross profit of $1,250,251.

The largest number of gaming tables in a single illegal casino at one time in America were in operation during the early Forties at the Devon Club, a sawdust joint in Toledo, Ohio. It catered largely to Detroit horse bettors who were transported the intervening fifty-odd miles in Greyhound buses at the club's expense. The Devon Club had 20 money-crap tables, 25 black-jack tables and 8 casino side games—53 gaming tables in all.

OPEN OR MONEY CRAPS

Open or Money Craps was once the most popular form of Craps played in this country. However I expect it shortly to erupt and become the number one craps game. It is the favorite gambling game of the country's high rollers and big-money gamblers, but it is seldom, if ever, found in any luxury casino.

Money Craps, as the name implies, is almost always played with cash rather than chips. Some big-money crap operators, in order to speed up their game, use small denomination chips ($5 or $10), but all the big bets are made with currency. The two biggest money games I ever saw were at the 115 Club in Miami which closed in 1947, and at

The Barn in Bergen County, New Jersey, in 1949. The big-time gamblers in both these joints had a cute money gimmick which helped speed up the action, and which is now often used. Hundred dollar bills are made up into packets, each secured by a rubber band. One packet contains one hundred $100 bills ($10,000), another fifty $100 ($5,000), another twenty-five $100 ($2,500) and another ten $100 ($1,000). The original owner pencils his initials on the top bill so that if the eventual winner should find that it contains less than the stipulated amount, he can be reimbursed by the original owner.

This makes it possible to get big bets down quickly without having to take time to count hundreds of bills. A player laying $20,000 on the point numbers Four or Ten, simply throws down two $10,000 packets; if laying $7,500 to $5,000 on the points Five or Nine, a $5,000 and a $2,500 packet does the trick; and if the player lays $6,000 to $5,000 he simply uses one $5,000 and one $1,000. It is not uncommon to see fifty or more such packets being wagered on a single point decision in games presently operated in our big cities.

Money Craps in a gambling house uses a dice table similar to a bank crap table, except that the layout has no proposition bets, such as the Field, one roll come-out bets, and the Hard-way bets. The only betting spaces on the layout are the Lose Line, the Win Line, and the box numbers (4, 5, 6, 8, 9 and 10).

The Book's maximum betting limit at Money Craps ranges from a low $25 on up to $1,000 and $2,000, with even that limit lifted in special cases. Fortunes are won and lost nightly at Money Craps. Winnings and losses of $500,000 or more in one dice session are common at Money Craps. Such heavy gambling occurs very rarely at Private Craps and is impossible at Bank Craps, unless the usual betting limits are upped considerably.

It is in games operated in New York City, Chicago, Philadelphia, Detroit, etc. that the big-time gamblers, the horse bookies, the numbers operators, the thieves and dice and card hustlers of the private game and the underworld big-shots gamble with industry's business tycoons, millionaire playboys, stock brokers, politicians, and various other legitimate businessmen.

Again I must say these people prefer Money Craps because it offers them their biggest opportunity to win large sums of money. Money Craps permits players to take and lay odds on the point wagers among themselves, something that is not permitted at Bank Craps. Flat or center bets, one roll come-out bets and Hardway bets must be placed with the Book which pays off these wagers at the same odds the Bank does at Bank Craps.

The big action that the Book receives is on the Off Numbers. Players cannot make an off or box number wager with each other and the Book gets this action whenever players cannot get players to take or lay odds on the point.

Open Craps has undergone many betting changes in the past few years. Back in 1945, the Book permitted players to make all types of bets among themselves. As the game is played today, it should really be called Semi-Open Craps.

Open Craps is not restricted to gambling houses. Smaller games cover the country—in streets, back lots, hotel and pool rooms. Nearly every city of any size at all (say 125,000 population or more) has at least one game regularly operating. It may not always be in the same spot, but it's there.

Open Craps requires no layout, although in the gambling house the numbers 4, 5, 6, 8, 9 and 10 are usually painted on the table so that the operator can keep track of the Box Number wagers. When the players take the odds on the box numbers, most dealers place their money on the numbers, and when the players lay it, the dealer puts the money alongside the numbers. Some dealers ask the players to put their bills face up when they bet right, and face down when they bet wrong. Other operators remember that it is win-money by placing it in a horizontal position, lose-money by placing it vertically. With these few aids a single man can deal to a full table of about thirty players.

The book never covers the player's wager with his own money because it would waste too much time. Instead, without bothering to count or straighten the bills, he sweeps in all bets he has won after each decision and then, while the stickman holds up the dice, pays off on all bets lost. After new bets are placed and while the dice are rolling, the book straightens out his pile.

Since the smaller books and those out in the open get less action on the box numbers, they can operate without any visible layout although some dealers carry a mental image of it in their heads and place their bets in the same relative position as though a layout were being used.

Open Craps is distinguished from Bank Craps on several counts. Because in the smaller open crap games players can fade the shooter, which cannot be done in Bank Craps, the game is also known as *Fading Craps*.

But the main distinguishing feature and what originally gave Open Craps its present popularity is the fact that the players may not only bet either right or wrong, but may also make wagers among themselves. They are not required to place any bets against the house. This, plus the fact that the game is often played outdoors in the open, is what gives it the name of Open Craps. As in the private game, it is open for any player to bet with any other player as much and as often as he likes.

In other games under such circumstances, in Chemin de Fer and poker, for instance, the house gets its income by taking a cut out of the pot. Even bridge clubs make a per hour charge for the play. Some of the smaller open crap games also have a charge, a *cutter* taking twenty-five cents more or less out of the center bet whenever the shooter makes a specified number of passes, usually one or two. He also sometimes charges the wrong bettors whenever they pass the dice and refuse to shoot when it becomes their turn.

YOU CAN PLAY WITHOUT CHARGE

But in the Open Game center bets are not allowed because they tend to slow the game and because, in any case, the shooter or players who want to fade the shooter can get the same action if they want it by placing flat bets with the house. Since the players can bet among themselves without being charged, and since center bets are not made and there is no cutter, Open Craps stands alone as the only house game in the world in which the players do not have to take the wrong end of a percentage and can play without paying the house anything at all!

You can, in fact, walk into most houses, play Open Craps all evening, make use of all the house's facilities, and, although its operating expenses may be as much as $10 per player, you can leave without ever having paid a thin dime for your entertainment either in P.C. or as a charge. What's more, if you hit it lucky and make a big win, the house will, if you request it, furnish you with a car and chauffeur to make sure that you get safely home with the cash!

It is obvious, of course, there is a joker in all this somewhere. The situation as described would, from the house's standpoint, be economic suicide. But you know as well as I do that gambling houses are not philanthropic institutions; they are in business like anybody else to make money. If under these circumstances, you suspect that their only hope of showing a profit is to cheat, then you have another guess coming.

In the Open Game the house doesn't dare try to get the best of it by using *work* or *moves*.* For one thing anyone who attempted any dirty work would have to have nerves of steel, be a sleight-of-hand genius and willing to take a damned long chance. Cheating either by the house or players is nearly impossible because it would almost never get by the sharp, watchful and knowing eyes of the big-time gamblers, the accomplished dice mechanics and the smart-money players around the table.

A single crooked play, if detected, would ruin a steady profitable business that may have taken months or even years to build up and in which thousands of dollars have been invested. One hint that the house was cheating would lose all the important business quicker than you can say "Come seven!" The smart-money boys who are the big bettors would take their patronage elsewhere but fast. The politicians would chill, the heat would go on, and the fix would curdle.

Add all this to the fact that the house employees and the bosses who own the business gamble at their own tables and it becomes obvious that cheating is not only bad business policy, but simple lunacy. The so-called gambling authorities who write popular exposés and who tell you, as one did in a recent book, that "nine out of ten gambling houses are crooked" have apparently never visited anything but steer-joints where *all* visitors are suckers.

WHEN GAMBLERS FALL OUT

If the game is not crooked, if there is no hidden percentage operating in favor of the house, and if the players can bet with each other without charge, how does the house manage to make out a profit-and-loss sheet without using red ink? The answer lies in the fact that although the players may gamble among themselves, they seldom do so for long.

Many of them try, but when they do, here's what nearly always happens. Because the table is so large that the player can't reach across easily to bet with the players opposite, he usually bets *left and right*, that is, with the players on either side of him.

Bookie Joe, or maybe Nick the Greek, begins, let us say, by betting the man on his left, a friend with whom he came to the game. If Joe wants to lay it on the points, his friend may take it for awhile, but then, because he has a hunch that the number will be thrown or for a dozen other reasons, he says no to the bet. Joe has to look around for another

---

* *Work:* Crooked dice. *Moves:* Sleight of hand.

taker. But before he finds one, the shooter sevens out. Joe scowls and mentally counts up the amount he would have won on that decision if he had had his money down. He suddenly doesn't feel quite as friendly toward his friend.

While he is thinking this over, another missout or two occurs and Joe has lost another chance of winning. He gets impatient, decides to pay no attention at all to his ex-friend and turns and starts looking for business on his right. But this player also says no to Joe's bet because he's a wrong bettor too. Another missout is made. Joe growls and, anxious to get down a bet of one sort or another, switches over and starts betting they win.

But the dice still continue to miss and Joe finds himself in the red. He tries to recoup by increasing the size of his bets. But his opponent is satisfied with the bets the way they are and he says no to that idea. Joe is stopped again. Or the other player may bet the amount Joe wants and, if he continues to win, may *pack up* (quit the game entirely), taking Joe's dough with him.

Joe now tries to get action anywhere he can by shouting "I'll lay it" for three or four minutes. But the other players have business of their own and he doesn't get a tumble. So he changes his tune once more and says, "I'll take it. Who'll lay it?" This still doesn't get him any business for the same reason. Finally, fit to be tied because he has money in his hand and no place to put it, he shouts, "I'll take it or lay it, any way you want to bet!" Still busy with other bets, no one pays any attention.

Or maybe, instead of being unlucky in his first betting, Joe hit a winning streak. This time his friend lays off Joe because Joe is winning; he doesn't like to buck a lucky player. Either way both Joe and his friend find themselves without takers. If the game is active, they can't pull out and move around the table so as to get into different company because they might lose the places entirely. Even if they could, they are sure to run into further difficulties.

Sometimes other players won't bet when a certain man is shooting. Some players will quit after winning a small amount, some make two bets and walk out, some wait half an hour before making a bet, some bet two passes and off and won't bet the third, some wait until it becomes their turn to shoot because they think they are luckier when shooting.

Some fast players like to double their bets, some like to keep their bets to the same amount all the way through, some smart players won't make a flat win bet because that means bucking the 1.414 P. C., some players have favorite numbers and won't bet on others, some players like the gag bet and others don't like it at all.

Eventually, Joe, his friend and many of the other players find themselves making bets so seldom that they aren't players any longer but spectators. The operators of the game are naturally aware that this betting difficulty will develop. They are, in fact, counting heavily on it, and would not only be surprised but considerably put out if it didn't happen.

The fact that most players can't gamble for long among themselves without running into trouble is one of the reasons the practice is allowed. The other reason is that this open feature is the come-on which originally made Open Craps so popular and is one of the things that still draws the players.

The whole situation, unless you know what comes next, looks fairly hopeless at this point. The players don't need to buck a P. C. or have to pay a charge and they can gamble among themselves, only it won't work. Why is it possible to have a game at all?

HOW THE HOUSE GETS ITS MONEY

The answer is that there is one man present whom we haven't yet described—a very obliging gentleman who saves the whole situation. He stands at the center of the table behind the box numbers on the layout with crisp, crackling new bills of all denominations stacked high before him—enough folding money to make even a busy army paymaster blink and rub his eyes.

You will have to go a long way and do a lot of hunting before you meet a more agreeable gentleman. Practically anyone can get along with him. He never gets angry and gives no one (except for the few guys who get sore when they lose) any reason to feel unfriendly toward him. He is not superstitious about the bets he makes; he won't pack up if he wins; he'll bet right or wrong just as you say; he'll cover bets of any amount (within the limit) at any time. It doesn't seem to make the slightest difference to him whether you are winning or losing or whether you walk off with your profits. He just rolls right along like Old Man River, giving any player action win or lose at any time.

He is the house man or the *book*. Whenever the players can't get their money down on the outside, the book will oblige. When they are losing, they go to the book to recoup. When they are winning and crave a killing, the sight of the book's tall stacks of crisp new bills is more temptation than they can withstand and they go in for a stab. "Money goes where money is."

The smart gambler rarely goes to the Big Game intending to buck the book with his own dough. But the moment he gets ahead of the game and has some of the other players' money in hand, he figures that if he sends it in to the book he may hit that lucky streak he thinks he has coming. He goes to the book for the big kill hoping, if his luck holds out long enough, that he may win $100,000 with which he can quit and never return. He knows that few players who make such wins ever do quit but he is always sure that he will be the exception that disproves the rule.

The only man who almost never goes to the book, but makes all his bets on the outside is the hustler who is trying to grind out a day's pay and who, because he looks at the game from that angle, is satisfied with slow action and willing to play a waiting game. He doesn't like to gamble by taking the worst of it and he waits patiently until he can get a point lose bet at correct odds on the side. He also has a sharp eye for *sleepers*—bets left on the table by the busy player who has made more bets than he can keep track of.

And he stands next to the greenie and tries to *short** him, apologizing, when caught at it, for his carelessness. But the hustler's lot at Open Craps is a mean one and the management often tells him to take his business elsewhere. Among gamblers the term hustler is too polite for the guy who hustles the Open Game; they simply call him a chiseler.

So, although the players do not have to bet against the book, sooner or later, nearly all of them find themselves doing exactly that. It is then that the house earns the money that pays the overhead and turns in a profit.

And here's how it's done. The two most common bets at Open Craps are the Flat Bets and the Point Bets. When the player throws his money down near the book and says "They win" he is bucking the same P. C. as when he puts his money on the Pass Line in Bank Craps and the book has the same favorable advantage of 1.414%.

When the player bets they lose, the book, like the bank, bars either two-sixes or two-aces† and still has an edge of 1.402%.

---

* *Short:* To short change, also called the *short cake.*

† Players making flat bets are not permitted to take or lay free odds as in Bank Craps.

In some smaller games the ace-deuce is barred for a P.C. of 4.385%.

On the proposition bets which are not as common here as in Bank Craps because they are not on the layout the book pays bank crap odds and has the same percentages in its favor. The proposition bets usually made in Open Craps are the hard-way bets and the one-roll or come-out bets on two sixes, two aces, 11, 3, All Craps and 7.

But point and box or off-number bets get most of the action, and here the book pays off at the correct odds and has no percentage at all in its favor. Its willingness to accept these bets is not given away for free, however. There is a slight service charge.

THE HISTORY OF THE SERVICE CHARGE

The history of this charge and the way it came about explains why the game of Open Craps is played today. The man who invented that charge made Open Craps possible. Before 1907 bank crap layouts carried only five win bets and no lose bets. Because of this one-way and slow action, the houses that tried to popularize it as a banking game were unsuccessful. The Indian or Take-Off crap games got the play because, like the private game of today, the players could bet both ways—right or wrong.

The Indian game was called that because the stooping position of the players, crouched above the rolling bones, was reminiscent of a gathering of redskins hunched about a council fire. When a cutter was present who took off five or ten cents on each pass it was called a Take-Off game.

Then John Winn went to work on the game. He knew that most of the gamblers of that day had only a vague idea of the correct odds even on the most common bets. They knew the odds on 5 and 9 and on 4 and 10, but most of them thought that 6s and 8s were even-money bets. Even the smarter boys who had a hunch that this was wrong but couldn't figure it guessed that it might be 5 to 4. And, although most players thought, as the inexperienced players do today, that the center and flat bets were even-up wagers, a few began to suspect that the wrong bettor had an edge. They didn't know how much and they over-estimated badly. They guessed that the advantage, which we now know to be 1.414%, was as high as seven or eight percent.

Winn was well aware that the gambler who thinks he has the best of it is the player who bets the big money. He knew, if he could only find a way to allow these wrong bettors to bet against him and still retain an edge in his favor that he would do all right for himself. In New York City in the latter part of 1907 Winn solved the problem with a solution that resulted eventually in the Big Game. He invented his "quarter charge."

He told the boys, "You can bet any way you want, either right or wrong, taking or laying the odds, and I'll cover your bets, but if you want to bet $5 you throw me a quarter; if you want to bet $10 you throw me fifty cents."*

Since Winn was, in effect, furnishing the same sort of service the racetrack bookmaker does, he was called a *book*. Because Winn laid 6 to 5 on sixes and eights, the right bettor who only received even money at the Indian game made no objection to the charge. Quite the opposite; some of them even thought that Winn didn't know what he was doing and that this was their big chance to win some real money.

But the wrong bettors who had to lay the odds and risk larger amounts than they won naturally didn't go for Winn's idea with the same enthusiasm.

As Winn says, "I knew I was going to have to educate those boys to get them to like it. Besides you can't let a player out-talk you and when they beefed I told them 'if you pay a nickel carfare to ride up-town, how much does it cost to ride downtown? Well, it's the same here. You pay both ways.'

"With the quarter charge I could take any and all bets any time. And because I showed a lot of money, whenever the gamblers got stuck, they came for a stab at my book. That was exactly what I wanted. I didn't care how often they tried to best me. I knew that my quarter charge gave me enough edge that getting the money was only a matter of time.

"I saw another thing too. Most of the houses had been using six-ace flats† to protect their take, but with the players betting both ways, right and wrong, that was out. I not only had to be sure that the dice weren't crooked but also that they were perfects. The dicemakers hadn't bothered to turn out absolutely perfect cubes—anything that was approximately square had been good enough up until then. But if I was going to depend on P. C. to get the money, I had to have something better. The dice had to be perfect. My insistence on square cubes made the manufacturers pay some attention to turning out dice that, for the first time, really calipered square.

"The players had always stuck pretty much to $5 and $10 bets because there was too much cheating and the inside was always afraid the outside was beating them and vice versa. But now they began to

---

* There was one exception. He did not charge the right bettor who placed a win bet before the come-out because he knew he already had the best of it on that wager. In those days barring double-six, double-ace, or ace-deuce was unknown.

† *Six-ace flats:* Shaped percentage dice that tend to make more sevens and fewer points than fair dice and which, since the players could only bet to win, favored the house.

increase their bets. They discovered that when they could bet both ways, percentage dice were of little use either to themselves or the house.

"Consequently, when the size of the bets went up, my quarter charge was applied to the bigger bets in the same ratio of 25¢ to $5, or 5%."

THE VIGORISH

John Winn, therefore, invented the book, the quarter charge that developed into the 5% charge, and is responsible for the game of Open Craps. Eventually, because the 5% charge brought in the money so dependably and was so strong gamblers took the word *vigor*, added a syllable of jargon as they have a habit of doing when they would rather the laymen couldn't follow their conversation, and called it *The Vigorish*.

Today most books charge 5% of the amount of the right money wagered. If you take odds of 2 to 1 on the 4 and put down $20 against the book's $40, you lay down the $20 and throw the book an extra 5%, or $1. If you lose, you are out $21. If you win, you take down $60 (your twenty plus the book's wager of forty) and the book keeps the $1 vigorish. A bet of $50 against the book's $100 costs you $2.50, etc.

Winn's crack, however, about paying the carfare both ways never completely quieted the objections of the wrong bettors. Many of them still beefed and something eventually had to be done.

The house fixed in this way. In the wrong bettor's case the vigorish is still figured as 5% of the right money wagered (in this case the book's wager) but it rides with the player's bet and is picked up by the book only when the wrong bettor loses.*

The wrong player who lays $20 to the book's $10 must put down $20.50. If the player loses, he is out $20.50, but if he wins, he takes

---

* Point or Off-Number bets may be removed by the players at any time before a decision is effected, and when the shooter makes his point some right bettors want to take their Off-Number wagers down because they believe that sevens are thrown more often on the come-out roll. No gambler can prove that any such thing happens because seven is no more likely to be thrown then than at any other time, but many gamblers believe that it happens just the same.

When the right bettor wants to take his bet down the book lets him do so but retains the 5% vigorish he has paid. Or he may leave his bet stand and ask to have the first roll barred. The book says yes to this too but charges another 5% for the privilege.

These maneuvers gain the player exactly nothing. When he takes the bet down he has paid a 5% charge for no action and when the first roll is barred he pays the 5% charge twice. This is not a system; it's a gift toward the care and feeding of able-bodied gambling house operators, given so freely that it could be deducted by the player from his income tax returns as a charitable donation!

down $30.50 (the twenty he bet, and the ten wagered by the book and the 50¢ vigorish).

The right bettor has to pay the vigorish before the dice start rolling, but the wrong bettor's vigorish rides with the bet and the house picks it up only when the wrong bettor loses the decision. You may wonder, under these circumstances not only why two-thirds of all bettors are right bettors but why there are any right bettors at all. The answer is that the average player thinks he stands to win more by taking the odds than by laying them. He wants to risk a little and win a lot; he forgets or doesn't know that one of the basic rules of chance states that in the long run the expectation of winning is in direct proportion to the amount of risk taken.

Even if he does realize this fact, he still knows that he is putting up less money and that if he can make five or six passes in a row—which is not unusual—he stands to take down more than the wrong bettor, betting the same amounts, can win in SIX or SEVEN successive missouts. Right bettors have broken plenty of wrong bettors in one lucky shot because they stand to win and do win larger amounts. When he is lucky, the right bettor wins larger amounts than the wrong bettor, and when he is unlucky his bankroll doesn't melt away as fast. But his big wins come less frequently and the wrong bettor wins his smaller amounts more often.

There is one very peculiar believe-it-or-not fact about the vigorish. In Bank Craps the P. C. in the bank's favor is greater than most players think. But in Open Craps the 5% vigorish is, strangely enough, *less* than nearly all gamblers and even most of the bookmakers suspect.

They use their common sense and insist that a 5% charge has to be a 5% charge anyway you look at it. They say that if the book collects an extra 5% on the amount of the right bettor's wager in cold cash, the book must therefore be collecting 5% vigorish. When the right bettor bets $5 against the book's $10 and pays the book 25¢ for the privilege, it does look as though the book were collecting exactly 5%. But common sense is noted for coming up with wrong answers—and this is one of them.

CALCULATING THE VIGORISH

The 5% answer is not far off, but it's not right either. The joker lies in the fact that when the player pays a charge he is not actually betting $5 against $10 at all. When he puts down his $5 and throws the book a quarter, a nearly invisible monkey wrench has been tossed into the percentage machinery.

The player is actually betting $5.25 and if the book were to give him action on all of that amount at 2 to 1 on the 4 or 10, it would have to put up $10.50. But the book does no such thing. It doesn't even put up the $10 it appears to. When you consider the quarter it has collected, the book is actually only putting up $9.75.

Since the book puts up 75¢ less than it should, the percentage in favor of the book is figured by dividing 75¢ by $15.75 which is the total amount of the bet at the correct odds of $5.25 to $10.50.

Our answer is not 5%. It is *4-16/21%*. Decimally this is *4.761+%*. And this percentage is the same for all points.

Here's the way it works out using either of the points 5 or 9. At odds of 3 to 2 we take $7.50 to $5 from the book and pay the book 25¢ vigorish. When we win, we take down $12.50. But if we received action on the quarter vigorish, the book would have to lay 37-1/2¢ to the 25¢ and we would then receive 37-1/2¢ plus 25¢ plus $12.50 or a total of $13.12-1/2¢.

If we divide the 62-1/2¢ we are short by the $13.12-1/2¢ we should have received which is the way percentage is always figured, we again get 4-16/21% for our answer.

If you want to calculate it using the points 6 or 8 you will find that you get the same result once again.

Some bookmakers sniff at that figure because they say "4-16/21% of $5 is only 23-17/21¢ and I know damned well I collect a quarter on each five buck bet." They insist on forgetting that the right bettor is putting down $5.25 and that 4-16/21% of $5.25 *is* the quarter they collect.

When the book *takes the odds,* the 5% vigorish, figured correctly, dwindles even more. Most bookmakers figure that when the odds are 2 to 1 in the wrong bettor's favor (as on the points 4 or 10) the book will win the wager once and lose it twice and that the wrong bettor therefore pays the 5% vigorish 1/3 of the time. They believe that the book's favorable P. C. must be 1/3 of 5% or 1-2/3%. Figuring it on the other points by the same method, they get an answer of 2% vigorish on the points 5 or 9, and 2-3/11% on the points 6 or 8.

This is another flock of wrong answers. The bookmaker's method of calculation is good enough but is not applied properly. The P. C. is correctly figured as follows. When the player lays the book $10 to $5 on either the 4 or 10 plus 5% vigorish, he is actually laying $10.25 to $5.00. If he places three such bets and wins two and loses one as he can expect to do in the long run, he loses one bet of $10.25 and wins two bets of $5 each. He has risked $10.25 three times—a total of $30.75 and is short 25¢. His 25¢ loss divided by the total risked gives the correct percentage against the player and in favor of the book: *.813-1/123%*.

On 5 or 9 at odds of 3 to 2 the book takes $7.75 to $5. If the player received action on his 25¢, he would take down $12.91-2/3 when he wins. Since the book only pays off $12.75, the player is shy 16-2/3¢. The 16-2/3¢ loss divided by the $12.91-2/3 he should have taken down gives the P. C. in favor of the books as *1.290-10/31%*.

On 6 or 8 at odds of 6 to 5 the book takes $6.25 to $5. If the player received action on his 25¢, he would take down $11.45-5/6 when he wins. Since the book only pays off $11.25, the player is shy 20-5/6¢. Again dividing the 20-5/6¢ loss by the $11.45-5/6 he should have taken down, the P. C. in favor of the book is found to be *1.818-2/11%*.

Placed in tabular form, we have:

Table No. 10
CORRECT VIGORISH ON THE ODDS WAGERS WHEN THE BOOK PICKS UP THE 5% CHARGE ON RIGHT ACTION AND LETS IT RIDE ON WRONG ACTION

RIGHT BETTOR
Pays 4.761 19/21% or .25¢ on a $5.25 bet on all points
WRONG BETTOR
Pays .813 1/123% or .04¢ on a $5 bet on 4 or 10
Pays 1.290 10/31% or .06¢ on a $5 bet on 5 or 9
Pays 1.818 2/11% or .09¢ on a $5 bet on 6 or 8

Some books, however, do not give the wrong bettor such a good proposition; they pick up the 5% both ways. And other books charge only 3% and pick it up both ways giving the right bettor more of a break. The exact percentages in both cases are tabulated below:

Table No. 11
CORRECT VIGORISH WHEN THE BOOK PICKS UP THE 5% CHARGE BOTH WAYS

RIGHT BETTOR
Pays 4.761 19/21% or .25¢ on a $5.25 bet on all points
WRONG BETTOR
Pays 2.439 1/41% or .12¢ on a $5 bet on 4 or 10
Pays 3.225 25/31% or .16¢ on a $5 bet on 5 or 9
Pays 4.000% or .20¢ on a $5 bet on 6 or 8

Table No. 12

CORRECT VIGORISH WHEN THE BOOK PICKS UP THE 3% CHARGE BOTH WAYS

RIGHT BETTOR
Pays 2.912 64/103% or .15¢ on a $5.15 bet on all points
WRONG BETTOR
Pays 1.477 169/203% or .07¢ on a $5 bet on 4 or 10
Pays 1.960 40/51% or .10¢ on a $5 bet on 5 or 9
Pays 2.439 1/41% or .12¢ on a $5 bet on 6 or 8

In Chapter 10 *Illegal Craps is Big Business,* we shall see just how strong this sometimes apparently insignificant vigorish really is and how much profit it makes for the book.

My tip on the subject of Open Craps is this: don't touch it! It's a game for the big-money bettor, not for the guy who works for a living.

9

The Private or
Military Game of Craps

For every banking crap game found in gambling establishments there are dozens of private games which take place daily, weekly, monthly or annually in homes, convention sites, factories, office buildings, hotel rooms, saloons, clubs and military installations all over the country, no matter what the law may say.

Since the smart wrong bettor in the average private-crap game enjoys a favorable advantage of about 2% over the sucker right bettor, he has to win all the money in sight.

The great majority of right bettors are plain chumps who accept incorrect odds from the strictly wrong bettors, the *crap hustlers* (players who knowingly hustle a crap game by offering right bettors wagers at less than the correct odds). A crap hustler is half gambler and half cheat. He is the guy who won most of the millions of dollars lost by the millions of chumps in the private-crap games that take place in the country each year.

The casino extracts a house percentage by offering the players less than true odds on all crap bets, in exchange for supplying a place in which to gamble. In the private game the hustler collects the same or an even greater percentage and supplies, at the most, a pair of dice. More often than not, it is the chumps themselves who supply the dice and the place to gamble. It's as screwy as all that.

The tips, hints and information contained in this chapter are dedicated to the members of the Armed Forces, however, they also apply to all private craps games in civilian life. Gambling has immemorially been a favorite pastime for soldiers and sailors. During the training period in isolated camps, during troop movements by train and transport, and even on active duty there are off-duty hours when other forms of entertainment and relaxation are not accessible. The simple games that can be played anywhere at any time with a pair of dice or a deck of cards are obvious answers to the problem of what to do.

Large groups of men living together without women, without the cares and responsibilities of home life naturally fall back on games. When they have money in their pockets, no place to spend it, and the average man's ever-present desire to win, the games they choose are betting games. Craps, because of its simplicity and its fast action leads the field.

NOT AS INNOCENT AS IT LOOKS

To some people who look at it from a distance, the military game seems like a simple, harmless, and, because the players have low salaries, probably an inexpensive way of passing the time. But as anyone who has taken part in such a game knows, the two players who may begin by shooting a nickel eventually find themselves elbowed out by a crowd of players who are shooting dollars.

As the play continues the excitement grows, the game that began as a friendly one nearly always ends as a cut-throat affair with commando tactics being employed on all sides. The G. I. Joe who thought he was indulging in a harmless social pastime suddenly finds himself engaged in a hand-to-hand, no-holds-barred combat that eats up his month's pay, what he can borrow on next month's pay, and whatever extra money the folks back home may send him.

A curious thing about military craps is that most of the players seem to have consistent runs of bad luck. In each of the many games that spring up after pay day there always seems to be one or two guys who have a corner on the luck. They eventually wind up with nearly all the dough.

Then, as one player after another loses his shirt, the number of games decreases until finally there are only one or two big games whose players are the previous big winners. And here the dollar bet and even the five and ten dollar bets are piker bets. These boys are betting fifties and hundreds and more.

Even in these big games some of the players appear to be especially favored by Lady Luck. Some are such consistent winners that they regularly salt away amounts that make a five-star general's bank deposits look like something the cat brought in. These boys aren't always easy to pick out. They don't boast about their winnings; they try hard to conceal them instead. But stories of their prowess get around.

There is the famous World War I story of the ex-carnival worker doughboy who had no family and no home address. He won consistently throughout the war and, because he had no place to send it and, in any case, no practical means of doing so most of the time, he banked it in a money belt. As time went on the belt began to fill out like a barrage balloon. It held so much folding money that the doughboy didn't dare take it off even when he got a chance to take a bath. A friend of mine, in the same company, who met him after the war asked him if he had gotten the money safely home.

The doughboy nodded. "Yeah, all of it. And when I counted it up that old money belt held one hundred and ten grand and some loose change!"

A Vietnam War case, reported in the papers some time ago, concerned a guy who stands a good chance to equal that record. He won $20,000 at craps between the time his transport left this country and the day it docked in Saigon. He hired another soldier to keep an eye on him while he slept because he was afraid his pockets would be picked.

During World War II my mail brought me similar reports constantly. "I was in a crap game in my barracks where more than $4,000 turned over in two hours and one fellow left the game with $1,600." "Seventy percent of the boys in my barracks gamble and most of them are broke in no time at all after pay day." "There's one guy in our outfit who is luckier than all hell. He wins every time. It doesn't matter whose dice we use and we know he's not using controlled rolls because we won't let him shoot the dice. But he can't be *that* lucky. How does he do it? We are enclosing airmail, special delivery, self-addressed envelope. Please rush reply."

If you are in the services, I don't need to tell you more of these stories; you've heard them.

How do these consistent big winners do it? Are they using crooked dice and controlled shots? Or are they merely phenomenally lucky?

It can be deduced from the carnival background of the doughboy with the money belt that his consistent winning was very probably due in large part to cheating methods. I am glad to report, however, that in World War II cheating, although common in the beginning, was very greatly reduced. The information gathered on my camp tours and the mail I received back up this statement. Partly because of my lecture demonstrations, my overseas radio broadcasts and my articles in *Yank* and other magazines and newspapers the phony dice situation was gotten fairly well in hand. Many G. I.'s today won't play with any pair of dice that happen to turn up. They are more careful, more suspicious, and know more or less what to look for.

The dice cheat doesn't like that situation. He hesitates to put his work into the game because he is never sure just how much the chumps have been smartened up. He knows, if his gaff is rumbled, that he may not show up for reveille the next morning but will instead find himself surveying life from the inside of a plaster cast—a casualty without any Purple Heart to show for it.

WHY THE BIG WINNERS WIN

Today most of the consistent big winners in private or military games are not cheats in the customary sense of the word. Neither are they phenomenally lucky. The unfailing consistency of their winning streak explodes any such notion. Something more than luck has to be giving them an assist. Since Congress hasn't repealed the law of averages, it's obvious, or should be, that they have an edge on it somewhere.

I recently talked to a soldier in Germany who won $15,000 in a single session on a transport without doing anything crooked. His explanation of his success gives you the answer in a nutshell: "The guys just didn't know how to play the game."

He won simply because he knew more about the game than the other players. With this extra knowledge he didn't even have to care whether Lady Luck was playing on his side or not. He didn't really need her: he had an even more powerful partner—Old Man Percentage. And together they applied a Full Nelson to the law of averages, pinned it to the mat and made it cry uncle.

For decades I have been trying to show the boys that there is no reason why each one of them can't have exactly the same chance of winning as the big consistent winner and that, if they are content with anything less, they are only cheating themselves and taking the worst of it because they don't know enough to protect themselves.

In a gambling house where betting is permitted among players, as in Open Craps, the operators protect the greenie who doesn't know the correct odds. If someone offers him even money he don't six and he starts to take it, the dealer tells the man making the bet that he must lay odds of 6 to 5 on that bet. But in the private game every man is on his own; his only protection is the knowledge he carries under his hat.

Large "cold war" armed forces and frequent turnover of personnel have provided similar fertile fields for big games since World War II, Korea and Vietnam.

THE THREE KINDS OF PLAYERS

How does the smart crap player's extra knowledge pay off such handsome dividends? Well, in the first place, the whole situation is a set-up. In most military games the players fall into three classes. About two-thirds of them or 66 out of every 100 are right bettors. A little less than one-third, say 32, are right-and-wrong bettors who usually bet the dice to win when they are shooting and to lose on the other players' rolls. The remaining 2 out of 100 are strictly wrong bettors who always bet the dice to lose and pass them when it is their turn to shoot. These two wrong bettors are the lucky boys who eventually find themselves counting up all the other players' cash. Scratch a consistent winner and it's a 100 to 2 that you'll find a consistent wrong bettor.

THE RIGHT BETTOR USUALLY LOSES

The consistent right bettor almost always loses in the long run because—well, gamblers say it's because he is a chump. I'll be a bit more polite and simply say that he is making the bad mistake of thinking he can get an even break at a game about whose basic facts he knows next to nothing. He is playing a game of numbers without any knowledge of the game's mathematics. He thinks that all he needs to know are the rules, and because he doesn't know the correct odds, he not only bites on all the sucker bets, but swallows them hook, line and sinker.

Why is it that two-thirds of the players persist in being right bettors when the wrong bettor has the edge? Why is G. I. Joe so ignorant about his favorite game? Why is his knowledge of odds and percentages so slight?

The reason is that many servicemen were only occasional players and large numbers of the younger boys had never played at all before they were fitted for uniforms.

THE BEGINNER IS A RIGHT BETTOR

The beginner at the game is invariably a right bettor. He likes to shoot the dice because he thinks that by doing so he can favorably influence his luck. And if he should hesitate when it becomes his turn to shoot, a wrong bettor gives him a shove. He acts as though the beginner had no choice. "It's your shot, buddy," he says in an authoritative manner and tosses him the dice. The hustler carefully avoids any mention of the fact that the rules say that a player may avoid shooting at his turn by passing the dice.

Even when he is not shooting the beginner is still a right bettor for another reason. Since his knowledge of the odds is so hazy that a chemical unit could use it as a smokescreen, he naturally finds it easier to take the odds than lay them. If some other guy offers him 4 to 1 that the shooter won't seven on the come-out, Joe has no idea whether or not the proposition is a fair one. All he knows for sure is that if he wins, he'll get five bucks for his dollar. He notices too that other players are taking the same bet and he may even figure that, because his opponent knows enough to make such a proposition, he must know what he is doing. Joe may be right at that. The other guy may know what he is doing—but it is seldom what Joe thinks. All too often he's giving Joe the works!

The 32 out of a 100 players who bet right and wrong are a shade better off. They have one foot up out of the chump class. They have played craps before, often enough to have heard and believed the rumor that the wrong bettor has an advantage. But few of them know just how strong that edge is and they nearly always seem to forget that it works against them when they shoot. They are still as far from being expert crap players as is the guy who just graduated from boot camp from being a bomber pilot.

But the strictly wrong bettors—those two guys out of a hundred who walk off with all the dough—are the smart apples. Some of them were, in civilian life, bookmakers, dealers, gambling house employees, hustlers—men who, because their occupations led the parade on the non-essential list, got the office from their draft boards early. Others are merely experienced players who have played either Open or Bank Craps and have, at those tables, gained some knowledge of odds and the insidious operations of percentage. And some may simply know that if they lay the same odds as does the bank crap dealer they must eventually win the same way he does. In effect all these boys do the same thing—they set themselves up as the house and take a house commission in a game that is supposed to be a friendly one.

THE SUCKER BET

The out and out hustler goes even further. He tailors the bank crap odds a bit, offers the chumps even less for their money and gets a bigger edge for himself—an advantage often so great that it would make a bank crap dealer blush! The wrong bettor who uses hustlers' methods cleans up consistently not because he is lucky or because he uses work or moves, but because he uses an angle that in the Armed Services is more practical and gets just as good or better results—*the sucker bet.*

This is much the commonest way of relieving Joe of his dough and has taken far more money than all the crooked dice and sleight of hand moves combined. The hustler with his sucker bets doesn't need to cheat —he simply steps in, lets the guys who don't know any better cheat themselves, and walks off with their bankrolls.

In civilian life Harry the Hustler often had to do a bit of scouting around before he found a game whose players would go for his sucker bets. In the service he finds himself hip deep in such players all the time. He lives with them. In civilian life when Old Man Percentage didn't operate quite fast enough to take all of the chumps to the cleaners in one session, the hustler didn't always get a second chance. His victims didn't always come back for more—or perhaps some other hustler got to them in the meantime. But in the service the sucker and his bankroll are right there in the same barracks with the hustler and they stay there. Military life is the hustler's happy hunting ground where all is milk and honey, and where sawbucks multiply faster than rabbits or hard luck and transform themselves with very little effort into G-notes.

During WW II I lectured and gave hundreds of gambling demonstrations at Army camps, Navy and Marine bases, Coast Guard and Merchant Marine stations and in canteens. I would never have believed without seeing it that there were so many yard-birds who will snap at nearly any sucker bet offered quicker than a hungry robin will at a worm. The hard-working hustler sometimes even gets so much action he can't handle it all!

And yet some of the boys were apparently suspicious that something was haywire in Denmark. The questions they threw at me after my lectures and the scores of letters I got in every mail showed that. Ninety-five percent of those questions have answers that every G. I. Joe should know as well as he knows his own service number. Invariably the bets the boys want to know about are the hustler's favorite sucker bets.

The other five percent of the questions come from boys that I hope haven't been putting up any heavy money on the game. If they have, they've been getting the worst of it because they want to know how the hell I figure that the wrong bettor has an edge on the win bet before the come-out; they say they had always thought it was the other way around!

THE HUSTLERS CHANGE THEIR TACTICS

I broadcast the answers to these questions, tipped off as many of the boys as I could reach to the correct odds, and told them how to recognize sucker bets when they saw them. But as fast as they were educated the hustlers countered with other tactics some of which haven't been used since the days when Hazard was the big dice game. They are now offering different sucker bets—bets that are more complicated and whose correct odds they know G.I. Joe can't possibly figure out because he hasn't the foggiest notion how to go about it.

Even the slide-rule boys with college degrees who juggle algebraic formulae come up with a slightly dazed look and tongue-tied expressions when you ask them such nifties as: What advantage, if any, does a player have when he bets even money that the shooter will throw 6 or 7 in two rolls, or, even money that the shooter won't throw 6 or 8 in two rolls?

Let's begin by seeing what happens to G. I. Joe, a confirmed right bettor, when he plays the game at the usual Army odds and wagers one buck to win before the come-out and one buck to win on each point.

In Chapter 6 we discovered that the right bettor has a 1-41/99% disadvantage betting they win on the come-out. He takes a beating of 1-

41/99 cents, or nearly a cent and a half on each of those bets. It doesn't sound like much? Okay, stick around and watch it add up!

On the average, every 3.37 rolls effects a winning or losing decision (see Appendix A, page 483) and in a fast army game the dice are rolled very close to 337 times per hour. Since this means that there are 100 decisions per hour, Joe's 1-41/99% the worst of it will nick him for $1.41 per hour.

But that's less than half of it. There are those dollar bets that Joe makes on the points. The shooter throws a point on an average of 24 out of 36 times, or two-thirds of the time. On the points 4, 10, 5 and 9 Joe holds his own because the usual army odds of 2 to 1 on the 4 or 10 and 3 to 2 on the 5 and 9 are correct odds.* There is no hidden P. C. in the hustler's favor. But on that ace of all the sucker bets—even money they six and even money they eight—Joe gets clipped but good!

Two-thirds of those 100 decisions per hour or 66-2/3 decisions will be point decisions. And since 6 or 8 will be the point 5/12 of the time, we take 5/12 of 66-2/3 and find that Joe is betting on 27-7/9 sixes or eights in one hour's time.

Since the correct odds on either 6 or 8 are 6 to 5 the player who bets those points to win at even money takes 9-1/11% the worst of it, Joe with his dollar bets is out 9-1/11¢ on each decision. At 27-7/9 decisions per hour, he takes a beating of $2.52-52/99 or nearly $2.53 per hour.

G. I. JOE'S VANISHING PAY

Add this to the $1.41 he loses on come-out bets and we find that Old Man P. C. is clipping Joe at the rate of $3.94 per hour. If Joe consistently bets a buck, never doubling it or betting any greater amount—and dollar bets are piker bets in this man's Army—then it costs him $3.94 of hidden percentage which he never notices during the play and which the wrong bettor has picked up as commission. Joe pays Mr. Wrong Bettor $3.94 per hour just to enjoy what is supposed to be a friendly game of Craps.

If he sticks through several sessions totalling 12 hours of play, has the sort of luck the theory of probabilities says he can expect in the long

---

* There are spots where the players aren't even hep to those odds and where the hustlers consequently offer less. In some parts of the South I have actually seen players take even money on 4s, 10s, 5s and 9s!

run, and continues to place dollar bets in the same way, he donates the round sum of $47.28 to the wrong bettors! Out of fifty dollars that leaves him $2.72.

Craps may keep the boys from being bored when there is no other and better form of entertainment handy; it may be a morale building activity, but $47.28 for a few hours of the sport is certainly no bargain.

Actually it's even worse than that. In the example above Joe bought himself 12 hours of play for $47.28 because he stuck to dollar bets. He got himself a bargain. Most players don't have that much self-control especially on sixes and eights, the bet the hustlers press. The hustlers may offer a dollar he don't six at first, but before long they are shouting, "Five bucks he don't" and "Ten more he don't" and so on. Joe soon discovers that if he wants to get any action he has to use real folding money.

HUSTLERS ARE HARD OF HEARING

He also discovers when he asks for correct odds, $10 to $5 on the 4 for instance, that the hustler has suddenly developed a bum ear. He's so hard of hearing, in fact, that Joe wonders how he ever gets along without an earphone. If Joe persists and shouts so loud that there is some danger that an M. P. will investigate the commotion, the hustler may decide to take the bet—but not until he has chopped it down to size. "I'll lay you $2 to $1" he says without much enthusiasm.

Harry the Hustler never bets at correct odds if he can help it and he never bets big unless he has a strong edge. He can find more excuses not to bet at correct odds than you can shake a stick at. Anyone would think the medical unit had given him a shot that has made him immune to even-up wagers. G. I. Joe, consequently, discovers that those 27-7/9 bets per hour on sixes and eights constitute about 70% of his point bets and nearly all of his big bets. If he gets out of the game a loser to the tune of only $3.94 per hour, he has been luckier than all hell!

What's more, that $3.94 per hour was figured on the assumption that the dice fall exactly as the law of averages says you can expect them to fall in the long run. Of course, when Joe's luck is below par, he loses the $3.94 in less than an hour, sometimes much less.

And if it is Joe's lucky day, what then? Suppose he sticks to right bets at $1 each, takes even money on sixes and eights, and still comes out a $50 winner? It can happen. But the payoff is the same. Joe is still way behind the eight ball. *If* he had been betting at correct odds that kind of luck would have netted him not $50 but $97.27. At the usual Army odds Joe wins when his luck is out-of-this-world and even then he loses!

When Joe reads this, I can hear him saying, "Thanks for the tip, pal. From here on in I'm betting the dice to lose." Joe is beginning to use his think-tank now, but his answer is still way off the beam. Suppose the other yard-birds read this too, Joe? Even if they don't the rumor will get around. Then what? If they all decide to be wrong bettors, where's your game? You can't play ball when everyone wants to play on the same team.

The real answer, of course, is that Joe can bet either right or wrong provided he always bets at the correct odds. If he does that, the only commission he need ever pay the wrong bettor is the 1.414%, the worst of it he has when he is the shooter. The bet to win or lose on the come-out can't be evened up because, unless Joe is using Russian rubles paying correct odds of $1.0286 to $1 is highly impractical. Even then so much time would be lost in computing and making change that the players would all feel like overworked bank tellers.

If Joe and all his camp mates decide to try and duck this disadvantage by passing the dice, the game hits a dead end there too. Joe can, however, take a tip from the smart-money players at open craps and wager little or no money on the center and flat bets to win. He can, but he probably won't because this takes away the thrill for the shooter or bettor who enjoys letting the center or flat bet double up for pass after pass. And besides, shooters often break a game with one lucky shot. How much dough you put down on this one is something you will have to decide for yourself.

But there is one thing every player *can* do, and the guy who knows but neglects it deserves what he gets. You can memorize and insist on getting the correct odds. It is the only way you can avoid losing when you shouldn't—the only way you can have the same chance to win as the next guy.

The correct odds on most bets are given in Chapter 5, but there are some military and private craps bets not listed there—the *Proposition Bets*. These wagers are of two kinds, the fair propositions at correct odds and booby-trap propositions offered by Harry the Hustler. The following analysis lists all of Harry's favorite proposition bets together with the edge he has over the chump who is sucker enough to accept them.

DANGER! DON'T TOUCH! THESE BETS ARE MINED!

DON'T BET *on the One-Roll or the Come-Out numbers at bank crap odds*. The source of many of the hustler's one-roll or come-out bets is the bank crap table. He offers all the usual bank crap odds on two-sixes, two-aces, any seven, all craps and many other one-roll propositions. In each case he has the same favorable advantage that the bank has and he collects the same commission. I know of no good reason why anyone should pay a house percentage in any private game—do you? See the bank crap bets listed on page 125 and remember that all those bets are sucker bets when used in private games.

DON'T BET EVEN MONEY *that the shooter won't throw 5, 6, 7 or 8 in one roll*. In fact don't listen to any such proposition at all. If you take a close look at it, you'll see that it is our old friend the bank-crap Field bet in disguise. Since there is no layout in Military or Private Craps, the hustler can't very well bet that the shooter *won't* throw, 2, 3, 4, 9, 10, 11 or 12 in one roll, but he gets the same effect by turning the proposition inside out and betting that the shooter *will* throw 5, 6, 7 or 8 in one roll. His advantage over the chump is the same as the edge the bank has: 11-1/9%.

DON'T BET *on the one roll or the come-out numbers at LESS than bank crap odds!* This warning is not as unnecessary as it sounds. So many G. I. Joes know so little about odds that Harry the Hustler often chops the bank crap odds way down. He offers odds giving him favorable percentages that no bank crap dealer would ever think of trying to collect. He doesn't shave them just a little; he cuts them down as far as he possibly can and still gets takers. Often he cuts them in half!

On a 35 to 1 proposition, for instance, the bank offers 30 to 1 but the army hustler offers as low as 20 to 1. The bank's favorable P. C. is 13-8/9 but Harry the Hustler has the best of it by 41-2/3% which is $2.08-1/3 on each $5 bet!

Instead of offering correct odds of 5 to 1 that you don't seven, he'll offer 3 to 1 which gives him an edge of 33-1/3%. On throwing craps in one roll which should be 8 to 1, the bank offers 7 to 1 and has an edge of 11-1/9%; Harry offers 5 to 1 and has an edge of 33-1/3%. On 3 or 11 he sometimes cuts the correct odds of 17 to 1 down as low as 10 to 1 which gives him the best of it by 38-8/9% or about $1.94 on each $5 wager.

Are you hep now as to why some guys seem to be so "lucky"?

THE HUSTLER'S HARD-WAY BETS

DON'T BET *that the shooter will make 6 the hard way unless you get odds of 10 to 1.* The hustler always cuts this one down, sometimes as low as 5 to 1 which gives him the fantastic advantage of 45-5/11% in his favor! He finds takers too—yard-birds who, when they accept this hard-way proposition, are certainly learning the game the hard way!

The same holds true for 8 the hard way.

DON'T BET *that the shooter will make 4 the hard way unless you get odds of 8 to 1.* The hustler chops this down to 5 to 1 and has the best of it by 33-1/3%.

The same holds true for 10 the hard way.

DON'T TAKE EVEN MONEY *that the shooter WON'T throw an ace or deuce (or any other two numbers) in 1 roll.* A glance at the Combination and Ways table shows that there are 20 combinations containing an Ace or Deuce and only 16 that do not. The hustler therefore has 20 chances to win against 16 to lose and the true odds are 5 to 4. At even money the hustler's edge is 11-1/9% or 56¢ on a $5 wager.

THE HUSTLER'S TWO-ROLL BETS

Any time anyone offers you a two-roll proposition you'll know he's a hustler. These bets are strictly sucker bets from the word go.

You will note that I do not give the correct odds on these propositions, the reason being that it wouldn't do you any good. These propositions, like the Center and Flat Bets, can't be evened up because they are fractional and you would find yourself insisting that the hustler lay strange amounts like $1.0737 to your $1. This holds true for all two-roll bets whether listed below or not. Your answer to the egg that offers you any such bet should be simply, "Nothing doing, brother. What do you think I am, a chump?"

Figuring the correct odds and percentage on the two-roll bets is tough—unless you know how. That's why the hustler offers them. He knows that the guys who try to dope the odds seldom come up with anything but wrong answers and a headache. Harry the Hustler can't even figure the correct odds himself; he only knows that the odds he offers must be wrong because they give him the best of it and bring in the money. In case you want to check the percentages given below, you will find the method for figuring the odds on two and three-roll bets in Appendix B, page 485, and C, page 487.

DON'T BET EVEN MONEY *that the shooter WILL throw 6 or 8 in two rolls*. The hustler bets he won't and has an edge of 4.320% or about about 22¢ on each $5 wager.

DON'T BET EVEN MONEY *that the shooter WILL throw 5 or 7 in two rolls*. The hustler bets he won't and has an edge of 4.320% or about 22¢ on a $5 wager.

DON'T BET EVEN MONEY *that the shooter WILL throw 7 or 9 in two rolls*. The hustler bets he won't and has an edge of 4.320% or about 22¢ on a $5 wager.

DON'T BET EVEN MONEY *that the shooter WON'T throw 6 or 7 in two rolls*. The hustler bets he does and has an edge of 3.549% or about 18¢ on each $5 wager.

DON'T BET EVEN MONEY *that the shooter WON'T throw 7 or 8 in two rolls*. The hustler bets he does and has an edge of 3.549% or about 18¢ on each $5 wager.

DON'T BET EVEN MONEY *that the shooter WILL throw 6 or 9 in two rolls*. The hustler bets he won't and has an edge of 12.500% or about 63¢ on each $5 wager.

DON'T BET EVEN MONEY *that the shooter WILL throw 8 or 9 in two rolls*. The hustler bets he won't and has an edge of 12.500% or about 63¢ on each $5 wager.

DON'T BET EVEN MONEY *that the shooter WILL throw 5 or 6 in two rolls*. The hustler bets he won't and has an edge of 12.500% or about 63¢ on each $5 wager.

DON'T BET EVEN MONEY *that the shooter WILL throw 5 or 8 in two rolls*. The hustler bets he won't and has an edge of 12.500% or about 63¢ on each $5 wager.

DON'T BET EVEN MONEY *that the shooter WILL throw 4 or 7 in two rolls*. The hustler bets he won't and has an edge of 12.500% or about 63¢ on a $5 wager.

DON'T BET EVEN MONEY *that the shooter WILL throw 7 or 10 in two rolls*. The hustler bets he won't and has an edge of 12.500% or about 63¢ on a $5 wager.

THE HUSTLER'S THREE-ROLL BETS

DON'T BET EVEN MONEY *that the shooter WILL throw 2, 3, 11 or 12 in three rolls.* The hustler bets he won't and has an edge of 15.74% or about 79¢ on each $5 wager.

DON'T BET EVEN MONEY *that the shooter WILL throw 4 or 10 in three rolls.* The hustler bets he won't and has an edge of 15.74% or about 79¢ on each $5 wager.

DON'T BET EVEN MONEY *that the shooter WILL throw 4 or 5 in three rolls.* The hustler bets he won't and has an edge of 4.548% or about 23¢ on a $5 wager.

DON'T BET EVEN MONEY *that the shooter WILL throw 9 or 10 in three rolls.* The hustler bets he won't and has an edge of 4.548% or about 23¢ on a $5 wager.

DON'T BET EVEN MONEY *that the shooter WILL throw 5 or 10 in three rolls.* The hustler bets he won't and has an edge of 4.548% or about 23¢ on a $5 wager.

DON'T BET EVEN MONEY *that the shooter WILL throw 4 or 9 in three rolls.* The hustler bets he won't and has an edge of 4.548% or about 23¢ on a $5 wager.

DON'T BET EVEN MONEY *that the shooter WON'T throw 5 or 7 in three rolls.* The hustler bets he will and has an edge of 24.657% or about $1.23 on a $5 wager.

DON'T BET EVEN MONEY *that the shooter WON'T throw 7 or 9 in three rolls.* The hustler bets he will and has an edge of 24.657% or about $1.23 on a $5 wager.

DON'T BET EVEN MONEY *that the shooter WON'T throw 4 or 7 in three rolls.* The hustler bets he will and has an edge of 15.625% or about 78¢ on a $5 wager.

DON'T BET EVEN MONEY *that the shooter WON'T throw 7 or 10 in three rolls.* The hustler bets he will and has an edge of 15.625% or about 78¢ on a $5 wager.

These are the commonest three-roll bets. If you run into any others, you can figure the hustler's favorable P. C. by the method given on page 487, but whatever answer you get, you can be sure it will be too much. The simplest rule is to handle two or three-roll bets the same way you would a live grenade with the pin pulled out.

THE HUSTLER'S TWO NUMBER BETS BEFORE SEVEN

DON'T BET EVEN MONEY *that the shooter WON'T throw 5 or 9 before throwing 7.* Since 5 and 9 can be made in eight ways and 7 in six ways, the correct odds are 8 to 6 or 4 to 3 and the hustler's edge is 14.285% or about 71¢ on each $5 wager.

DON'T BET EVEN MONEY *that the shooter WILL throw 10 or 3 before throwing 7.* Since 10 and 3 can be made five ways and 7 in six ways, the correct odds are 6 to 5, and the hustler's edge is 9.09% or about 45¢ on a $5 wager.

DON'T BET EVEN MONEY *that the shooter WILL throw 4 or 3 before throwing 7.* Since 4 and 3 can be made in five ways and 7 in six ways the correct odds are 6 to 5, and the hustler's edge is 9.09% or about 45¢ on a $5 wager.

DON'T BET EVEN MONEY *that the shooter WILL throw 5 or 2 before throwing 7.* Since 5 or 2 can be made in five ways and 7 in six ways, the correct odds are 6 to 5 and the hustler's edge is 9.09% or about 45¢ on a $5 wager.

BARRING THE FIRST ROLL

Crap hustlers are ingenious characters who spend much of their time trying to dope out new angles, particularly when their usual methods of getting the best of it begin to wear a little thin and don't get the action they did before. One of the trickiest angles they have dreamed up is a method of acting as a bank or book in an army game without being called that and without the authorities getting hep to what is going on.

Because the biggest action is on the points or off numbers, the hustler who can take that action both ways, either right or wrong, and still retain an edge in his favor has a stranglehold on a sure thing. One of them finally figured an angle to do this. He took and laid the odds on point bets but barred the next roll. This means that a decision on that roll in the hustler's favor wins for the hustler, but a decision in his opponent's favor is a standoff and the bet remains to be decided by a later roll.

Usually, when Joe wants to make a point wager at correct odds the hustler is twice as deaf as a post. But with this bar-the-first-roll dodge he not only doesn't have to pass up Joe's offer; he goes out after the business. He flashes a big bank-roll and Joe, who may have been having trouble getting the kind of action he wants just as the bettors on the outside do at Open Craps, goes after it. Joe can get action from the hustler at any time on the points or off numbers either right or wrong, and the hustler, acting as a bank or book, gets enough action to make it well worth while. Smart players often give Harry the Hustler clear and precise but unprintable directions as to what he can do with these bets. But Harry seldom minds that; he expects a beef now and then, and he persists in offering the bets even when there are no takers just on the chance that someone will bite.

Usually, because Joe doesn't even know what percentage is, let alone how to figure it, he never gives this "bar the first roll" phrase much thought. He thinks, "Okay, so the first roll doesn't count. So what? That cuts no ice." If he is a shade smarter than that, he may realize that when the barred number appears on the first roll, the hustler avoids losing. But usually because Joe doesn't think it happens very often, he can't see how that makes any very great difference. He thinks that if there is an advantage, it can't amount to much—anyway not enough to break him. When Joe reads these next paragraphs, he is due for a surprise!

POINT BETS TO WIN WITH THE FIRST ROLL BARRED AT CORRECT ODDS

DON'T BET *that the shooter WILL throw the point 4 before throwing 7 with the first roll barred*. To calculate the hustler's advantage we'll let Joe, the right bettor, wager $1 on each of the 36 possible combinations with two dice for a total of $36. Since the odds on the point 4 are 2 to 1 Harry the Hustler must put up $2 on each wager. Then, supposing for the moment that, after the first roll, all bets are called off, let's see what happens.

If the dice fall exactly as probability predicts Joe gets his $1 back whenever a neutral number appears on that roll or 27 times for a total of $27 and he loses $1 each of the 6 times 7 appears for a loss of $6. When the barred 4 appears Joe only gets his dollar back whereas if it was not barred he would win $2 each time the 4 appeared on that roll. Since the 4 will be thrown 3 times he gets back only $3 instead of $9.

Since Joe invested $36, got back $27 on the neutral numbers and $3 on the 4s for a total of $30 he is short $6 which means that the hustler has an advantage of 16-2/3% *.

---

* Like the field bet at Bank Craps (page 120) two different percentages can be figured for the bar-the-first-roll wagers depending on whether the problem is considered from the hustler's or the player's viewpoint. In each case I have given the highest P. C. whether it be the hustler's advantage or player's disadvantage and listed it for the sake of simplicity as the hustler's advantage.

The same holds true for the point 10.

DON'T BET *that the shooter WILL throw the point 5 before throwing 7 with the first roll barred.* The point 5 can be made 4 ways and the odds are 3 to 2. Using the same method of calculation as above we find that the hustler's advantage is again: 16-2/3%.

The same holds true for the point 9.

DON'T BET *that the shooter WILL throw the point 6 before throwing 7 with the first roll barred.* The point 6 can be thrown 5 ways; the odds are 6 to 5; and the above calculation again gives a hustler's advantage as 16-2/3%.

The same holds true for the point 8.

AT WRONG ODDS

DON'T BET EVEN MONEY *that the shooter WILL throw the point 6 before throwing 7 with the first roll barred.* Ordinarily the hustler doesn't bar the roll when betting even money on this number because he already has 9-1/11% the best of it, but he'll do it if he discovers that anyone is fool enough to take it. Here's why. When the first roll is barred the 9-1/11% edge is calculated on all rolls except the first roll; 100% minus the 16-2/3% edge on the first roll is 83-1/3% which multiplied by 9-1/11% gives a final result of 7-19/33%. Barring the first roll, therefore, gives the hustler a 16-2/3% plus 7-19/33% edge for a grand total of 24-8/33% or about $1.21 on a $5 wager.

The same holds true for the point 8.

POINT BETS TO LOSE WITH THE FIRST ROLL BARRED

These are the bets on which the hustler clips the half-smartened up Joes who have heard that wrong bettors have an advantage.

DON'T BET *that the shooter WON'T throw his point or an off number before throwing 7 with the first roll barred.* The above method of calculation shows that the hustler's advantage is 16-2/3% or about 83¢ on a $5 wager. On this one the Joe who thinks it is smart to bet wrong loses even faster than when he bets right with the first roll barred!

AND DON'T BET EVEN MONEY *that the shooter WON'T throw 6 before throwing 7 with the first roll barred.* The hustler would be a sucker to bet sixes or eights to win at even money, but when he bars that first roll, the shoe is on the other foot. The guys who think they are taking him to the cleaners with a sucker bet are sitting on dynamite! Since they don't know exactly how much edge the sucker bet carries, they can't possibly dope out either how much of an advantage is left when the first roll is barred or who the hell has it.

The answer, of course, is that Harry has it as usual. At even money a wrong bet on 6 or 8 would ordinarily give the wrong bettor 9-1/11% the best of it. Since the first roll packs a 13-8/9% disadvantage the 9-1/11% operates only after the first roll. Therefore, subtracting 13-8/9% from 100% gives us 86-1/9% and that result multiplied by 9-1/11% equals 7-82/99%. Subtract this from 13-8/9% and we have a hustler's advantage of 6-2/33% or about 30¢ on a $5 wager.

This bar-the-first-roll angle not only allows the hustler to bet right or wrong and have an edge both ways, but in some cases it gives him a bigger P. C. than any book or bank would ever have the nerve to take. In the services the hustler offers any bet that gives him an edge and keeps offering that bet until he gets a taker. The hustler knows that the monkey hasn't a ghost of a chance of figuring the percentage for the very simple reason that the hustler can't figure it himself. All he knows is that he has the edge because experience has proved that barring the first roll is a sure-fire method of being a consistent winner.

If you take any of the hustler's proposition bets listed above, you can't kick if anyone ever calls you a chump, and if you take the Bar-Roll bets, you might just as well hand your dough over to the next hustler you meet without bothering to roll the dice for it. He'll get it almost as soon anyway!

Page 178 shows the hidden percentages that are the hustlers' secret weapons—each one a land mine calculated to blow the contents of your pocketbook right out of sight!

PROPOSITION BETS YOU CAN TAKE AND GET AN EVEN BREAK

Many players, even when they know the correct odds on proposition bets, feel there is less wear and tear on their gray matter if they stick to even-money bets. I have, consequently, worked out a list of even-money bets that do give a guy a fair break. If you make these bets, you can be sure that you are not cheating yourself by paying a hidden P. C.

Table No. 13
DANGER!! DON'T TOUCH!! THESE BETS ARE BOOBY TRAPS!

	Advantage Hustler's	P.C. in Cents on a $5 Bet
DON'T BET on one-roll or come-out numbers at bank crap odds	% is same as the banks	
DON'T BET even money shooter won't throw 5, 6, 7 or 8 in 1 roll	11 1/9 %	.56
DON'T BET on one-roll or come-out numbers at less than bank crap odds as high as	41 2/3 %	$2.08
HUSTLER'S HARD WAY BETS		
DON'T BET that shooter will make 6 (or 8) the hard way at wrong odds at high as	45 5/11%	$2.27
DON'T BET that shooter will make 4 (or 10) the hard way at wrong odds as high as	33 1/3 %	$1.67
DON'T BET even money that shooter won't throw any two specified numbers in 1 roll	11 1/9 %	.56
HUSTLER'S TWO ROLL BETS		
DON'T BET even money shooter won't throw 6 or 7 in 2 rolls	3.549%	.18
DON'T BET even money shooter won't throw 7 or 8 in 2 rolls	3.549%	.18
DON'T BET even money shooter will throw 5 or 7 in 2 rolls	4.320%	.22
DON'T BET even money shooter will throw 7 or 9 in 2 rolls	4.320%	.22
DON'T BET even money shooter will throw 6 or 8 in 2 rolls	4.320%	.22
DON'T BET even money shooter will throw 6 or 9 in 2 rolls	12.500%	.63
DON'T BET even money shooter will throw 8 or 9 in 2 rolls	12.500%	.63
DON'T BET even money shooter will throw 5 or 6 in 2 rolls	12.500%	.63
DON'T BET even money shooter will throw 5 or 8 in 2 rolls	12.500%	.63
DON'T BET even money shooter will throw 4 or 7 in 2 rolls	12.500%	.63
DON'T BET even money shooter will throw 7 or 10 in 2 rolls	12.500%	.63
HUSTLER'S THREE ROLL BETS		
DON'T BET even money shooter will throw 2, 3, 11 or 12 in 3 rolls	15.74 %	.79
DON'T BET even money shooter will throw 4 or 10 in 3 rolls	15.74 %	.79
DON'T BET even money shooter will throw 4 or 5 in 3 rolls	4.548%	.23
DON'T BET even money shooter will throw 9 or 10 in 3 rolls	4.548%	.23
DON'T BET even money shooter will throw 5 or 10 in 3 rolls	4.548%	.23
DON'T BET even money shooter will throw 4 or 9 in 3 rolls	4.548%	.23
DON'T BET even money shooter won't throw 5 or 7 in 3 rolls	24.657%	$1.23
DON'T BET even money shooter won't throw 7 or 9 in 3 rolls	24.657%	$1.23
DON'T BET even money shooter won't throw 4 or 7 in 3 rolls	15.625%	.78
DON'T BET even money shooter won't throw 7 or 10 in 3 rolls	15.625%	.78
HUSTLER'S TWO NUMBER BETS BEFORE 7		
DON'T BET even money shooter will throw 10 or 3 before 7	9.09%	.45
DON'T BET even money shooter will throw 4 or 3 before 7	9.09%	.45
DON'T BET even money shooter will throw 5 or 2 before 7	9.09%	.45
DON'T BET even money shooter won't throw 5 or 9 before 7	14.285%	.71
HUSTLER'S BAR-THE-FIRST-ROLL BETS		
DON'T BET that shooter will throw 4 (or 10) before 7, first roll barred	16 2/3 %	.83
DON'T BET that shooter will throw 5 (or 9) before 7, first roll barred	16 2/3 %	.83
DON'T BET that shooter will throw 6 (or 8) before 7, first roll barred	16 2/3 %	.83
DON'T BET even money shooter will throw 6 (or 8) before 7, first roll barred	24 8/33%	$1.21
DON'T BET that shooter won't throw his point or an off number before 7, first roll barred	16 2/3 %	.83
DON'T BET even money that shooter won't throw 6 (or 8) before 7, first roll barred	6 2/33%	.30

Table No. 14

SCARNE'S EVEN MONEY PROPOSITION BETS

BET EVEN MONEY THAT the shooter will or will not throw a

4 or 10	before throwing 7
3 or 9	before throwing 7
3 or 5	before throwing 7
2 or 8	before throwing 7
2 or 6	before throwing 7
5 or 11	before throwing 7
6 or 12	before throwing 7
8 or 12	before throwing 7
9 or 11	before throwing 7
4	before throwing 10
5	before throwing 9
6	before throwing 8
2, 3 or 4	before throwing 7
10, 11 or 12	before throwing 7

ANY ODD NUMBER before throwing an even number
ANY NUMBER BELOW 7 before throwing any number above 7

And to sum up, if you want to avoid cheating yourself, and if you dislike to donate your pay to the *Building Fund For Hustlers' Bank Accounts*, paste these simple rules in your hat.

1. Know the correct odds and don't take any others.

2. Don't bet at all if you can't afford to lose.

And then, after making sure that the hustler and his sidekick, Old Man Percentage, aren't giving you the business, you also want to make sure that the cheat doesn't clip you with his phony dice. (See Chapters 13 and 14 on *Crooked Dice*.)

10

Illegal Craps Is
Big Business

In spite of the fact that gambling today is illegal in most states and the recent enactment of additional state and federal anti-gambling laws, it is definitely big business and gambling at Craps is second only, in the volume of money wagered, to horse racing. Like some other big businesses, it is not freely competitive but monopolistic. If you want to open a gambling house, you would run smack into a large helping of first class trouble within the first ten minutes.

Your first discovery would be that although gambling may be an extra-legal activity, that doesn't mean that you can operate without a license. This license, called an *okay*, is not a visible signed statement that you can hang on the wall behind your cash register, but it carries just as much weight. It has the backing of the political powers-that-be who are, in the end, responsible for and allow whatever illegal organized gambling exists.

But when you contact The Boss and ask him politely if you can open a crap game, that's where the big hitch in your plans develops. His answer is a flat, forceful, "Nothing doing." The combination that has the X on the town not only dislikes competition, but discourages new-comers with remarkable efficiency and the simplest of methods. If you go ahead and try to open a house without an okay, the raiding party will bust in right on the heels of your first customers.

There are such things as *sneak games* but they are one night stands and the operators must be set to blow at a moment's notice. If you should happen to find a location where no combination exists, a spot in some smaller town where the organization is less formal and in which the local fixer does not have the situation well in hand, then you can lay a bet that the spot is not much good for gambling anyway. All the best locations were reserved years ago.

THE OKAY AND THE FIX

Your only chance of getting an okay from the Boss, and for only a small game at that, would be in the event that you had political influ-ence so strong that a refusal would result in political friction—something that the Boss and the combination are experts at avoiding. They even weather the successive changes of political administration with what often seems to be the greatest of ease. Now and then the combination may have to lie low for awhile or move to a new spot. Just before elections they may even close down for a month or so to avoid the introduction of local gambling as a campaign issue. But these dull sea-sons are usually infrequent and seldom last long. When a new set of officials is elected, about all that ever happens is that the combination may have to put a few friends of the new politicians on the payroll and pay a different amount of *ice* to a different fixer.

But let's forget for the moment that you can't open up a casino or a crap game whenever the mood strikes you and see what would happen if the Boss acted as he almost never does and said, "I'll see."

We'll suppose that, after surveying many factors, including the amount of weight he throws, the public attitude, the current political situation in regard to illegal enterprises and your reputation, he finally goes further and says, "Okay." He will at the same time give you a flat figure on the amount of *ice* or *fix* necessary to satisfy him, the politicians that *take* and any other officials, from the top County officials to the local chief of police on down to the cops on the beat, who think they have an *end* coming.

He'll tell you that you have nothing to worry about and to report to him if any official annoys you. He may tell you that the okay came from the *top,* but don't inquire any further as to who is getting what or how much. If you did, your okay would be canceled before you got any further on the general principle that anyone that nosey isn't a *stand-up guy.**

CASINO OPERATION

For a big game of Open Craps with a double-dealer table in a good location and without too many officials asking for an end, it will probably cost you an average of a grand a week.

Once you have an okay, you need a *bankroll man* to supply the necessary capital outlay. This, strangely enough, is the least of your worries because as soon as you have a solid okay, a lot of guys will come around asking to bankroll the game.

At this point, however, you will find that you no longer own the business, but are merely one of the bosses with a piece that amounts to 20% of a small game or 5% or 10% of a big one. In a casino you may be put on the payroll at $300 a week and cut in for 2% or more of the profits, depending upon how much you know about the business.

A location has to be chosen next, a chore that is often accomplished with little or no effort on your part because many politicians are in the real estate business on the side and have pieces of property that they don't mind unloading at a fancy profit. But don't let them stick you with a place next to a church or any neighbors who might put in a beef.

Usually you will rent rather than buy a place because you are never certain when you might have to move. It is also good gambling business practice to rent a second spot as well so that you can make a quick overnight move in case the Boss gives you the office that the cops, having seen too much mention of the game in the papers or heard too many rumors, are going to have to investigate.

And don't neglect to use phony names on your checks, leases, telephone listing and references. If the fix ever goes wrong and you really do get raided without warning, this makes it tough for the prosecution to find out who the bosses are and leaves them free to make the necessary arrangements to spring their employees quickly and without loss of time.

Also any of the bosses that get picked up in the raid will, there

---

* *Stand-up guy:* One who won't squeal in a tight spot but who will stand up for his friends.

being no evidence to the contrary, be held as gamblers who rarely serve a jail sentence and not as operators for whom the penalty is stiffer.

In larger cities, after anti-gambling campaigns on the part of the newspapers, even the combination sometimes has difficulty getting an okay. In those cases the boys usually operate in a small nearby town where the officials handle easier and the ice and rent are cheaper.

Some of these small towns actually compete for the games because, although it is not one of the things the Chamber of Commerce brags about, it does give the local economic situation a boost. Stores, restaurants, hotels, saloons, cab drivers all make money, and out of 20 gambling house employees as many as 15 may be local men.

NO LOCAL PUBLICITY

You might remember, however, that it is usually a good rule in these small burgs not to permit local players to patronize the game. They spread too much talk around town about the size of the game and the big wins and losses. You want the big-time gamblers to hear about this, but not all the neighbors; the less said about a gambling house in its own town the longer it runs.

Besides, the local players are nearly always small bettors and, in any case, you do not want them to come in and lose. You want to bring money into the town not take it away. I know of one Midwestern game which follows this "no local players" policy and has been running steadily for ten years in the same spot.

An average rent for the sort of place you'd need for an open crap game would run to about $300 per week, more or less according to the locality.

The next item on the list is furniture and decorations. If you open a casino, these will set you back nearly any amount you want to pay depending upon how much class you think the joint should have. But if you merely plan a single table of Open Craps you seldom need an elaborate room with fancy decor because the clientele you get, although big-money gamblers, are not fussy and will play Open Craps in a barn if necessary.

Having chosen the house, and remembering that the amount of money you are going to have on hand there during the game might tempt a holdup mob, you should arrange your entrance so that the players will have to pass through at least one other room before they enter the gaming room. As they arrive the outside door is locked behind them and each customer is eyed carefully by the doormen who frisk the customers for concealed weapons and weed out any one who looks like trouble before the second door is unlocked.

THE CRAP TABLE, STICK, BUCK AND BOX

Your most important single piece of furniture is the crap table. If you are doubtful about your fix, you may have to pay $2000 and get a table from a supply house which is portable and breaks down into small pieces for quick moves. Or you can, as many operators do, convert a billiard table for the purpose by laying a bed of cork beneath the baize to eliminate noise and prevent the dice from chipping.

A rail or backboard is built around the table and lined with sponge rubber rail cushion which also prevents wear and tear on the dice and keeps them from dropping dead at the board, thus guarding against the activities of the accomplished dice control artists, some of whom can control the dice when thrown against non-resilient walls or backboards. The box numbers are either painted or chalked on the felt opposite the book's and stickman's positions.

You may also need a *crap stick* at $15 with which the stickman retrieves the dice after each roll although some stickmen do not use it and simply ask the players to throw the dice back. They claim it slows the game and, although the crap stick was introduced for greater protection against the switch artist, the stickmen who do not use it say, "If you can't protect your money without a crap stick, you shouldn't be in the business."

You will also require a *dice buck* at $10 which the stickman places on the point numbers near him to indicate the shooter's point, and a small wooden or plastic container at $20 known as *the box* in which the dice are kept. In play, whenever the players call for a *box-up,* the stickman tips over the bowl, spills the dice across the table and lets the player select another pair.

AND, OF COURSE, THE DICE

And last but not least you need a few dozen sets of dice (five to the set), all perfects true to a tolerance of 1/5000 of an inch and costing $10.00 per set. To make it more difficult for the cheaters who may try to beat the house by switching in work, you should buy your dice made to your order and bearing your own private marks or insignia. You must also make sure that the manufacturer can be trusted not to duplicate your marks for anyone else. As a rule, you will also use the ten to twenty dice you put on the table for one night's play only, and then, after marking them as discards with a monogram canceller ($25) which cuts a circle into the dice, give them to the employees or players or otherwise dispose of them.

Discarding the dice is a precaution both against the wear and tear that will eventually destroy their trueness and upset the P. C. you depend on and against the cheat who, if you did not change the dice for those bearing different marks, would try to duplicate the ones used and switch in dice of his own.

Actually, however, only the operator who is not too smart to the racket depends to any great extent on the marks he may put on the dice. By the time he gets a chance to examine the marks, it is always too late. Dealers and stickmen of the caliber that work at a dice table must not only be capable of catching the crooked move as it is made, but of spotting the guys who might make such moves before they make them.

While the furnishing and decorations are being done, you are busily hiring employees, a job that must be done with care. Your help-wanted advertising is accomplished very simply and efficiently by letting the word go out on the grapevine that you are opening a dice game; the boys will be on your neck looking for jobs in short order. But you must pick them carefully and make sure that each is experienced, a specialist in his job and, above all, trustworthy.

THE LIE DETECTOR AND THE GAMBLERS

In connection with this last and important requirement a recent lie detector test has discovered that among employees in a position to take small sums without immediate danger of being caught, the average percentage of dishonesty is 75%.

In testing the employees of a summer hotel in Arkansas for larceny, the machine put the finger on nine out of twelve bartenders as being guilty of pocketing money that should have gone into the cash register and of having smuggled out occasional flasks of liquor for their own use.

Most of the other employees were also guilty of having stolen from the rooms, cheating guests, tapping tills and raiding hotel supplies. But the eight employees of a dice game concession ran the gamut of the lie detector and turned in a batting average of 100% honesty!

Actually, of course, this test merely shows that they had not done any cheating on the job, and I suspect that the game in the hotel was

Bank Craps using chips. If not, then one of the bosses was working at the tables or an eagle-eyed floorwalker was on duty watching the employees so carefully that stealing would have been dangerous in any case.

Most professional gamblers, like most of their customers, have larceny in their hearts and would follow the bartenders' example if they thought they could get away with it. The lie detector merely reported that they had been honest, but said nothing about what might happen under other conditions. On duty as a rule, the gambling house employee does not steal from the house because it would cost him his job with the combination and he doesn't cheat the customers because it is bad policy and because the steady operation of the P. C. makes it unnecessary.

FLOORWALKERS, DEALERS AND STICKMEN

For an open crap game using a double-dealer table that requires the services of two dealers, two boxmen and one stickman at the same time, you would need the following employees:

Two *floorwalkers* who are usually bosses with a piece of the business and whose duties are those of a manager. They welcome the players, keep an eye on the employees, see that the table is always well supplied with money and relieve the dealers of it when too much has accumulated. In addition to their end of the profits, they also draw down $50 a night.

Five *dealers* who also switch as stickmen and who must be highly experienced and with a great degree of proficiency. The boxman who often has a piece of the game, is usually the smartest of all the employes on the subject of craps. He must know all the correct odds and have a fairly accurate knowledge of the percentages on all wagers. A dealer must be a rapid calculator and be able to outdistance the best bank cashier for speed and accuracy in counting money.

A good dealer can pay off and collect thousands of dollars from as many as thirty players within less than one minute. The faster he works, the more profitable his table will be.

He must also have a phenomenal memory because he must, with many players all making different wagers at different odds at the same time, remember each wager and its odds. He must have good hearing, an even disposition, a sharp eye for monkey business of any description and be immune to the excitement of the play.

In the usual bank crap game these requirements can be relaxed considerably since the dealer's job, due to the use of chips, the presence of the layout and the fact that the smart big-money bettors don't give it much play, lessens the mental strain and is easier.

The dealers must be so wide awake and keenly alert every second that a man can work efficiently at the job only for short periods. A single-dealer table requires two dealers working in alternate shifts of an hour or so each. A double-dealer table needs a crew of four to five dealers. For this nervewracking job the dealer is paid $30 a night depending on how big the game is. Since he works a seven day week, his weekly salary is from $210 plus bonuses and tips.

As a rule dealers also alternate as *stickmen*, but that is not always the case. The stickmen are the croupiers of the dice table, men who must also be fast, experienced workers. They retrieve the dice, assist the dealer by pushing the money toward the players or dealer on the payoff, keep one eye on the dealer to assist him in avoiding errors, one eye on the players to see that they behave, and call the decisions. "Get it down, men!" they chant, "Send it in to the book. Double up and beat the book! Watch it! Here they come. Coming out . . . and he missed it . . . coming out again . . . and he made it the hard way!"

And when the players are slow to bet, "If you don't bet, you can't win. If you don't speculate, you can't accumulate." Their steady stream of patter even contains a word of good advice to the player who cries about his losses, "If you can't afford to lose, don't play."

In the better casinos the stickmen are mostly intelligent and well-mannered and are, as a rule, tall men with a long reach. Because their job is likewise one of constant strain, they also work in shifts, usually of an hour each. They get $30 per night plus tips from winning players. The boxmen are seldom tipped because most players believe them to be operators or bosses rather than employees.

CASHIER, LOOKOUTS AND LUGGERS

One *cashier* who has charge of the bankroll and sees that enough change is always on hand. He keeps the books, makes out pay envelopes, handles advances to employees, does the banking and gets a fresh supply of crisp, new, easy-to-count bills each night. Salary: $40 per night.

Two *lookouts* whose job is to watch dealers, stickmen and players to see that everything runs smoothly. Salary $30 per night.

Four *luggers* who circulate around town, advertise the house by word of mouth and bring players to the game. They are usually paid $25 a head for new players or, in a well-known house, a flat rate of $100 per night plus tips. They furnish their own car and gas.

One *checker or head lugger* who keeps an eye on the luggers and sees that they do their job properly and that they do not lug in any deadheads (no-money players) or troublesome customers. Salary: $30 per night.

Four *doormen* who handle incoming and outgoing traffic at $25 each per night.

One *dice picker* who, when the stickman shouts, "One down" and "Two down" retrieves the die or dice that have bounced over the backboard and on to the floor. One of house's strictest rules is that no one else may pick them up. The dice picker throws the die to the boxman for examination and he, in turn, tosses it to the stickman who places it back in the box. The dice picker also cleans up and runs errands. Salary: $25 per night.

OUTSIDE MEN, DROP ATTENDANTS AND SHYLOCK

Four *outside men,* some stationed at the various approaches to the house to direct the arriving players and one outside the door to examine the credentials of new players and decide whether they can have an okay to go in. If he is in doubt, he checks with the doorman who checks with one of the bosses. Salary: $30 per night.

Four *drop attendants* who stay at the hotel lobbies, sporting centers, clubs, street corners, etc., where the players gather and where the luggers pick them up. Players can always connect with the game even though it may have moved overnight as long as they can locate the drop, a job of detective work that is accomplished very simply by asking the nearest bellhop or cab driver. Salary: $25 per night.

One *Shylock* or loan shark who is not on the payroll but instead pays the house a percentage of his profits. Broke players have a habit of trying to borrow money to continue playing in the hope of getting their losses back. You won't want to be annoyed or have the other customers annoyed by such requests and so you refer them to the Shylock, who, provided their financial standing meets with his approval—and he has it taped better than Dun and Bradstreet does—will make them an overnight loan at 5% interest. And when he says overnight, he means it. If the player doesn't show up the following evening and pay off, his health is due to take a turn for the worse.

Sometimes the Shylock is more lenient with the employees who want loans, giving them until payday to make good rather than just overnight. I knew of one Southern house with about forty employees all of whom were at one time in debt to the Shylock or as the boys say "in the hands of the Philistines."*

THE PAYROLL

You now have thirty-two employees with the following nightly salaries:

	Per Night
2 floor walkers at $50 each	$100
5 dealers at $40 each	200
1 cashier	40
2 lookouts at $30 each	60
4 luggers at $25 each	100
1 checker	30
4 doormen at $25 each	100
1 dice picker	25
4 outside men at $30 each	120
4 drop attendants at $25 each	100
	$875
Total for a seven day week	$6125

Additional expenses include *broke money* ostensibly loaned but actually a gift of from $10 to $50 to any broke player who needs it to

---

* A description published in an English paper in 1737 of the famous Brooks's Club gave the following list of employees common to the gambling house of that day. The list is very similar to that given above although some of the help bear different names.

"A *Commissioner*, always a Proprietor, who looks in of a Night, and the Week's Accompt is audited by him, and two others of the Proprietors.

A *Director*, who superintends the Room.

An *Operator*, who deals the Cards at a cheating Game, called Faro.

Two *Crowpees* who watch the Cards and gather the Money for the Bank.

Two *Puffs*, who have Money given them to decoy others to play.

A *Clerk*, who is a Check upon the Puffs, to see that they sink none of the Money that is given them to play with.

A *Squib*, is a Puff of lower Rank, who serves at half Salary, while he is learning to deal.

A *Flasher*, to swear how often the Bank has been stript.

A *Dunner*, who goes about to recover Money lost at Play.

A *Waiter*, to fill out Wine, snuff Candles, and attend in the Gaming Room.

An *Attorney*, a Newgate Solicitor.

A *Captain*, who is to fight a Gentleman that is peevish about losing his money.

An *Usher*, who lights Gentleman up and down Stairs, and gives the word to the Porter.

A *Porter*, who is, generally, a Soldier of the Foot Guards.

An *Orderly Man*, who walks up and down the outside of the Door, to give Notice to the Porter, and alarm the House, at the approach of the Constables.

A *Runner*, who is to get Intelligence of the Justices meeting.

Linkboys, Coachman, Chairmen, Drawers, or others, who bring the first Intelligence of the Justices meetings, or, of the Constables being out, at Half a Guinea Reward.

Common Bail, Affidavits, Ruffians, Bravoes, Assassins, with many others."

get home and who asks for it. The average here will run about $300 per night.

You also have certain expenses which concern the prevention of beefs—payments to politicians who, although not in power, might want to make a political issue of the game and to shyster newspapermen who sometimes threaten exposure and present demands for hush money.

You may also have a few gamblers on the payroll who never come around because they are paid to keep away—men who don't like it because you and not themselves got the okay to run, locals whom you don't want to employ because they are small-time but who might otherwise beef because you hired some out-of-town boys, etc. This insurance will run to about $200 per night.

Other shakedowns include hard luck stories from neighbors who need fuel oil or rent money and who, unless they get it, may raise civic objections to the kind of business you have brought into their neighborhood. You'll be surprised, too, at the number of people for blocks around who seem to think they class as next door neighbors. Keeping them contented will cost you around $750 per week.

Furthermore, someone is always selling you tickets to some political affair or other, or asking you to kick in to civic causes. And you mustn't fail to buy your share of tickets to the policeman's benefit ball. This eats up another $500 per week. Protection (ice) will cost you about $2,000 per week.

In addition you also need a good supply of crisp, new, easy-to-count bills, at least $50,000 for a double-dealer open crap table with a $300 to $500 limit.

But that's not all. For the first few weeks while you are building up a steady clientele, the action probably won't be consistent enough to pay all your overhead. You should have another $30,000 handy so you won't have to cut into the table money to pay the ice and the nut. Now you know why gambling houses are seldom operated by individuals, but are backed by a combination.

THE SMALL GAMES

There are, of course, thousands of smaller games all over the country that do not have enough business to run every night in the week and which do not have such a big overhead. Some, in spots where the politicians are not so strict about gambling, are sneak games paying no ice. Others pay off the cops on the beat and one or two politicians, perhaps a total of $300 a week for a two-night a week game.

Sometimes the game starts as a big private game and turns into an open game when one of the boys with a bankroll starts to book. He arranges for a place to play by propositioning a club manager or pool-room owner, cutting them in for about 40% of the net profit. That's the deal, although I doubt if any of them ever get their correct share. The bookmaker always makes certain that he gets his first and it's very easy for him to throw a pal playing the outside a few hundred or so on a bet which the latter kicks back later.

As a rule the overhead doesn't run to much, perhaps a dealer and a stickman at $20 per night and a couple of doormen at $15 apiece. The bookmaker himself is usually a crap hustler, or some guy who is just enough smarter than the rest of the boys to know that the P. C. can't be beaten. After all expenses are deducted, a small book of this sort working two nights a week will grind out a couple of thousand a week as the bookmaker's end. These small books, however, often go broke because they usually have a short bankroll and many of them don't really know the racket but just think they do.

But to get back to our big open game with the big weekly over-head. You will want to know if the P. C. and the vigorish can possibly overcome such a terrific nut. And if so, what profit, if any, is left? Okay, here's a look at the other side of the ledger.

With such a nut you'll probably have a $500 limit which is a lot larger than some of you may think at first glance. Suppose, for instance, that you are a big-money player and are shooting. You decide to bet the book $500 to win. Then you throw a 10 on the first roll and take the limit from the book which is $1,000 to $500. You also decide to take it on the box numbers, $1,000 to $500 on the 4, $750 to $500 on the 5, $750 to $500 on the 9, $600 to $500 on the 6 and $600 to $500 on the 8. You pay the book $25 for each of the point and box number bets, a total of $150; and the win bet P. C. against you is $7.07. A *seven* thrown on the next roll of the dice would decide the ownership of $8,700.

THE HOUSE PROFIT

But, in figuring out the house profit on the big open game. I am going to lean way over backward to avoid any exaggeration. Most open games have a limit of $300 or $500, but we'll say that yours is only $300 with a $5 minimum. We'll still wipe out that nut. Watch!

In the private game we discovered that the dice are rolled out on an average of 337 times per hour, but here, because the dealers need time to pay off the many bets made, the rate is slower. By actual clocking in ten different houses for a total of thirty hours, I found that the dice on an open crap table working two dealers, one stickman and two boxmen at the same time roll out on an average of 169 times per hour. Since every 3.37 rolls in the long run effect a decision—either a come-out decision by the throw of a natural or crap, or a pass or miss-out on the point, there are slightly more than 50 decisions per hour.

With two dealers, two boxmen and one stickman, your table will be dealing to from 20 to 25 players betting fives, tens, twenties, fifties, and on up to the $300 limit. Although thousands may be bet against the book on certain bets, we are going to be ultraconservative, and only allow the book a total of $100 worth of action each way on every new come-out bet. We'll give the book $100 worth of action on flat bets, $100 worth to win and $100 to lose.

The 50 decisions per hour multiplied by the $100 wagered on each new come-out to win is a total of $5,000 of which the house percentage earns 1.414% or $70.70 per hour.

On the lose action on all come-outs $5,000 times the house P. C. of 1.402% supplies a profit of $70.10 per hour.

THE EARNING POWER OF THE VIGORISH

Then we need to calculate the earning power of the vigorish. Two-thirds of the 50 decisions or 33-1/3 will be point decisions on which the players will be taking the odds all the way up to the limit. We'll keep our average down to a low $200 worth of right action for the book per point decision and $300 worth of wrong action from players laying the odds.

The 33-1/3 point decisions times $200 of right money gives $6,666 wagered against the book per hour. Of this amount the book collects 4.761-19/21% by picking up the "5%" vigorish, a total of $317.41 per hour.

The wrong bettors wager $300 on each of the 33-1/3 point decisions for a total of $10,000 per hour. Since 4 or 10 will be the point 1/4 of the time, $2,500 will be wagered on these points. The book's P. C. is .813-1/123% or $20.32-1/2.

The numbers 5 or 9 will be the point 1/3 of the time, a lotal of

$3,333-1/3 in wagers per hour. The book's edge is 1.290-10/31 or $43.01.

The numbers 6 or 8 will be the point 5/12 of the time, a total of $4,166-2/3 in wagers per hour. The book's edge is 1.818-2/11% or $75.75 per hour.

We must also add about $100 worth of business for the house on the hard way and one-roll bets for another $10 profit per hour, and the box numbers which get a heavy play in some houses and not so much in others would, on the average, add another $100 of earning power.

Totalling we have:

Flat win bets	$ 70.70
Flat lose bets	70.10
Right point bets	317.41
Wrong point bets (4 and 10)	20.32
Wrong point bets (5 and 9)	43.01
Wrong point bets (6 and 8)	75.75
Proposition bets	10.00
Box number bets	100.00
Total earning power per hour	$707.29

The average crap session in a open game usually starts around ten P.M. and continues to four or five A.M., although sometimes, when a few big bettors are stuck and keep playing the book in an attempt to get even, the session may go right around the clock and through the next evening. Some books put a time limit on this sort of play and announce, "Boys, we quit at twelve noon regardless of whether you are a winner or loser."

On an average, however, the game lasts about six hours. Since there are times when the players will be betting among themselves rather than against the book, I will knock two hours off that and base any calculations on four hours. The hourly earning power times four gives a total for the evening of $2,829.16. At seven nights a week this adds up to $19,804.12.

Your profit and loss sheet at the first week's end should give you a profit of about $7,500.

Then if you continue to get plenty of action, you will probably add a bank crap table to take care of the overflow players who can't push their way into the crowd around the big table. Eventually you may find yourself with the big table and three or four bank crap tables with limits varying from $50 to $300. At this point you are a casino operator.

The lower limit and smaller play cut the average earning power of a fast, double-dealer, bank crap table down to about one third that of a fast, double-dealer, open crap table or $8,000 per week. For catch-as-catch-can play, however, the bank crap table is the more reliable because every bet made earns a P. C. for the house which, in most cases, is higher than that on the open table. When the bank crap table does not have to compete with the open game, its earning capacity is much greater.

The addition of extra tables, of course, increases the size of your payroll, some of the big casinos which carry from six to eight bank crap tables and which can accommodate as many as 600 players at once often use as high as 100 employees. In one resort town a few years ago all the cab drivers in town were on the payroll as luggers and all a player needed to do was step into a cab and say, "To the casino." The driver took him there and the house paid the fare.

HE LOST AND CAME OUT AHEAD!

I know one player who got into one of those cabs twenty miles from the casino and was driven there free of charge. On going into the casino he discovered with some embarrassment that he only had three bucks in his billfold. Ashamed to ask a dealer for a measly $3 worth of chips, he bought three from another player. He stood at one table for awhile, then made a dollar bet, lost it, moved over to another table, hung around a bit without betting, then made and won a few bets and went back to the first table. Here the bank swallowed his few dollars and he was broke.

He then got $5 of broke money from a floorwalker who called a taxi and had him driven back to his hotel twenty miles away. He likes to tell this story because it is one time that he came away with nearly as big a bankroll as when he started and had a forty mile cab ride thrown in!

Some of the resort spots also use an employee we haven't yet mentioned—the *shill*. These are house players who pose as customers, good looking gals sometimes, whose job it is to get the game under way, cheer up the losing players, and continue the play when the action falls off and the house wants to keep the game going because more customers are expected.

The shills, supplied with house money, are not allowed to take any of it out of sight. Formerly, when quitting the table, they would cash in to the dealer and would be met by a *cleaner* who would relieve them of the money. But in most houses today they simply place the money or chips they have left near the Pass and Don't Pass lines so that it is a bit doubtful as to which bet they have made. And after the decision, win or lose the dealer sweeps it in.

Some casinos have additional expenses not listed above because they are set up ostensibly as night clubs with floor shows to attract the customers. The waiters, in a low voice and in a manner that makes the chumps think they are privileged persons tip off the customers that the casino is open. Many of them also think that the gaming room is a sideline when it actually is the tail that wags the dog, the casino operators paying the night club management: rent, the entire overhead of the show and a P. C. of the profits.

In these places even though they have a higher nut to pay—the cost of the show often running as high as five grand a week—Bank Craps is the preferred game because it turns in a profit on every bet and because of lower limit plus higher P. C. the risk is smaller. The cost of the show sometimes, however, is greatly reduced when the actors patronize the tables.

I know one $10,000 a week performer who, after working a three month period, finished owing the management $50,000 in gambling losses. Night club casinos keep him busy for two reasons: he is an exceptional performer with a big drawing power and in the end he pays them for working!

In the resort or transient spots you will also find roulette wheels operated by the casino and Chemin-de-fer, Chuck-a-luck, Blackjack, slot machines, and possibly Hazard or Klondike operated by concessionaires with the house collecting 50% of their take.

If you have never been in a gambling house, one thing about its operation may surprise you. There are never any fights or even any hot arguments. The operators know very well that rowdyism is bad policy and they clamp down on the first sign of it.

ADVICE FROM THE BOSS

On the day you open, if you know your business, you'll gather the help together and give them a little talk which runs something like this:

"Well, boys, you have good jobs with good tips and the work isn't hard. A lot of you live here in this locality and some of you come from other parts of the country. Remember that we can stay in this spot just as long as everyone behaves. We want no complaints or beefs from anyone. I want you to be as polite as possible to all the local people.

"As for the players, remember that if there are arguments, the customers are always right—at least the first time. Except, of course, for smart guys who try to pull fast ones. If a player is losing and looks low, try to cheer him up and never try to win a man's last dollar. If he loses heavy, advise him to quit and remind him that tomorrow's another night. Broke and unhappy players are bad advertising.

"If you notice any funny business such as one customer trying to pick another's pocket or anything like that, don't make a noise about it. Just let me know; I'll take care of him in my office—quietly.

"Remember that anything anyone of you fellows does reflects on this house. Just because we are in the gambling business is no reason why we can't show the players and townspeople that we are gentlemen. I want each boss to see that these rules are lived up to. That's all."

And on the side to the bosses you add, "If one of the employees goes off the beam a little give him a good *cigar** the first time. The next time have him report to me."

HEADACHES

From the player's viewpoint, the moral to this inside look at the economics of the gambling business is obvious: "In the long run you can't win; the house has too big an edge." But if you think the house's profit makes the operator's life a bed of roses, you have another think coming there too. You can get gray hairs in this business like many others—and plenty of them.

In the first place you stand a good chance of having your doctor prescribe a milk diet because you have developed the ulcers that a big percentage of operators get from the headaches they have. They all worry about pinches constantly because even the best okays can go wrong. One outfit I know waited eight months to get an okay for a four month season and invested seventy-five grand. A week before the opening the Governor of the State slapped the lid on all gambling. They lost the $75,000 and eight months of time in which, as they said, "We could have made a *hook up* somewhere else."

Clergymen are bad medicine too and can raise such a fuss at a moment's notice that the *pollys* (politicians) are scared off. Elections

---
* *Cigar:* a bawling out.

are also headaches because you may not only have to close down entirely for a spell, but make sizable campaign contributions to both parties as well.

And you are always only too well aware that your income is entirely dependent on maintaining a steady volume of play. If the tourist season is bad in a resort spot, or if, for other reasons the players don't patronize your joint steadily enough for the P. C. to pay off your terrific nut, you are suddenly not in business any more but are gambling with the players. And you are always apprehensive that an unusually hot or cold spell caught by a fast player will play havoc with your bankroll.

Sometimes, when the dice start passing and won't stop even though you change dice, shift dealers and cross your fingers, you find yourself having to announce, "Sorry, gentlemen, but that will be all for tonight" after which you have to hustle and dig up a new bankroll man before you can reopen.

The tension and uncertainty is so great that, like most operators, you will find yourself wearing a constant glum look—few of them ever smile. And, if you run true to form, the worrying is not only not worth the dough you drag down, but you'll find that you are gambling away most of it at someone else's game or at the races. Or you will try to get smart with it in the night club or real estate business or in Wall Street and in the end prove that other old adage of the gamblers: "In the long run the players all go broke—and the operators too."

11

Gamblers, Hustlers and Cheats

There are five main types of gamblers; the occasional gambler who plays only now and then and usually knows little or nothing about the game on which he wagers his money; the habitual or degenerate gambler who has the fever, is constantly on the lookout for a game and who hopes some day to make a big killing; the dice hustler who knows a little more about dice gambling than the occasional or the habitual gamblers—he favors private dice games where he offers other players sucker dice bets; the dice cheat, a cheat who makes money by cheating at dice, and the professional gambler who gets his living or the greater part of it from gambling.

Most people think that anyone whose livelihood depends upon anything as precarious as gambling must have the best of it and must, therefore, be dishonest. It is true that the professional has an advantage over the other players—he must if he is to make a steady income—but it doesn't necessarily follow that he is a cheat, not unless you consider that charging the other players for the opportunity to play is dishonest.

The professional knows that when any player accepts less than the correct odds or pays a charge for playing, he is bucking a percentage that cannot be beat and must lose in the long run. The professional gets around this by putting himself on the other side of the table. He sees to it that he is the man who operates the game and has the percentage in his favor. He is, actually, not a gambler at all but a business man who supplies a service and makes a charge for it.

Like most charges in legitimate business the rate is fixed according to what the traffic will bear. It is true that P. C. in some games and on some bets is so high that the players have very little chance, but in most casinos there is no rule that the players must play those games or make those bets. The amount of P. C. they pay is directly dependent upon their knowledge of the game and the kind of bets they make. The more they know the less they have to pay.

When they are stuck and in a tight spot there are, of course, many operators who will cop a red hot stove if the owner isn't watching. Many are ex-cheaters, but the majority and especially the successful ones shun crookedness. They know that it is bad business policy, does not pay off in the long run and is unnecessary because the P. C. pays the overhead and expenses, and furnishes a steady profit.

Nor does the term professional gambler really apply to the cheat who makes a business of trimming the chumps with crooked work and moves. Since he is playing a sure-thing and is not risking his money he is not a gambler but a crook. Nor are the employees of the gambling house gamblers. They are workers who earn a salary and make their living from but not by gambling. Like the operators and cheats they are usually habitual gamblers in their off-duty hours but they don't make money then—they lose it bucking a game they know they can't beat.

Because the business man of gambling, the crook who cheats at gambling and the owner and the worker employed in a gambling house are not really gamblers at all, the term professional gambler is a misnomer. But since it is a bit late in the game to replace that term, with some new and more accurate designation, I'll leave it as it is and stick to the customary usage.

Because his business is, except in one state, illegal and has an unsavory connotation the big-time professional usually has a business on the side, night clubs preferably, or a music and vending machine, clothing or liquor business. Because of their interest in anything pertaining to sport some manage prize fighters or own interests in racing, baseball, hockey, professional football, or other sports.

GAMBLING—AND NOTHING ELSE

The habitual gamblers, or degenerates as they are also called, have one track minds. Inoculated with the fever, their thoughts are centered on one thing to the exclusion of nearly all else—the game. They never talk anything but shop, their conversation invariably revolving about how much they lost last night (usually exaggerated) or how much they won (always exaggerated). The only events that get their attention are betting and sporting events and their first question is always the same: "Who do you like and what are the odds?"

The habitual or degenerate gamblers usually acquire stony faces and a set of ulcers from the nightly high tension to which they subject themselves and the habit they have of bottling up all emotion during play. The degenerate seldom moves a muscle of his face to express either dissatisfaction when he loses or pleasure when he wins. The occasional gambler on the other hand makes no effort at all to control his emotions, becoming flushed and excited when he is winning, tense, disgusted and often angry when he loses. The habitual gambler is neither as stony-faced as the professional nor as emotional as the occasional gambler; he usually takes his losses with a sigh, mutters something about this being the last time, and then shows up again the next night as usual.

The habitual or degenerate gamblers have a curiously distorted conception of money and what it means. All live in the hope of that big killing and, when it comes, as it sometimes does, they are never satisfied but want to win still more. Averse to newspaper publicity because it is bad for business they are still extroverts who crave that "big shot" monicker and want to be known by other gamblers as the fastest gambler in town. When they are in the money, well heeled with what they have hoped so long to get, it never sticks to them. They spend it as if they couldn't get rid of it fast enough on big conspicuous cars, at night clubs and on the show girls who, because they are the only ones still around in the early morning hours when the game breaks up, are the girls they usually live with and often marry.

When they are flush they are easily tapped for a loan and when broke they will hock anything they possess to get a new start. As a group they are gregarious, usually joiners who belong to many clubs and lodges, attending all the outings and affairs but seldom the business meetings. Nearly all of them, especially the big money gamblers, are highly superstitious and they carry a wide variety of good luck charms which they stick with even when they lose. If they discarded the charms, they argue, their luck might be even worse!

Many of them are intelligent and well educated; others are nearly illiterate. All of them consider themselves smart. But few, if any, are smart enough to quit when they are ahead of the game or to avoid bucking the other man's game against the P. C. which in their own game earns them a living. And with very few exceptions they all, consequently, die broke.

THE CRAP HUSTLER

This gentleman is a border-line case, half gambler and half cheat. He doesn't usually resort to the out and out crooked work that the cheat employs but gets the advantage he needs to win by the more subtle method of obtaining a favorable P. C. The gambling casino collects a percentage in exchange for giving the player a place and an opportunity to gamble. The hustler just collects it.

When he is working the hustler gets little if any thrill out of gambling; to him it's a job. Because percentage operates over the long run rather than breaking the sucker all at once, the hustler's job is a hard grind. He works the private games, travelling from one to another, looking for one in which the players will go for sucker bets. He will travel a hundred miles in order to find a game whose players will bet even money on sixes and eights and, if necessary, will sit patiently for hours shouting, "I'll lay the gag. Who wants the gag?" until he finally gets takers. He will flash a Michigan bankroll (fat but all singles) to tempt the players into coming after it and betting as the hustler wants them to.

The real gambler may be easily tapped for a loan when he is flush, but don't try to put the bite on a hustler. He is such a niggardly character that he is constantly bumming cigarettes, and when he fails and must resort to smoking his own, he brings out one from an inside pocket. If he brought out the pack someone might try to bum one from him.

His spare time is mostly employed in sitting and thinking—trying to figure out new types of bets which the players won't recognize as sucker bets and which will furnish a satisfactorily high P. C. Only when he is stuck and trying to get out does he forget about P. C. and make bets at the correct odds.

The hustler is a past master at the *cry act*. He always cries that he is out (a loser) and keeps going into his pockets with his winnings so the other players can't clock him. He always exaggerates his losses and

Scarne checking dice and other gambling equipment in a Cuban Money (Open) Craps casino in Havana, Cuba before the Fidel Castro era.

chops his winnings down. To hear him tell it he always loses hundreds of dollars and never wins more than a few bucks. This prevents anyone from trying to put the bite on him and avoids his getting the reputation of being a steady winner which would cause other players to avoid playing with him. If his winnings should be too large to conceal, he counters with a tall story of the even bigger loss he suffered last time. "Always in the red" is the hustler's motto.

He is not a friendly guy. He feels that it is bad policy to make too many friends among the players because he might find himself giving a friend a break, which is no way to win money. The average hustler will work like a beaver hustling a private game and then as soon as he accumulates a fair-sized bankroll will, like any other gambler, go to a casino and try to beat the house. He is hoping to get that big winner by running up his bankroll into the hundred G's and he must go where the money is—to the open or bank crap game. He knows that he is taking the worst of it there just like the chumps who played against him did, but he can't help it. He has the fever.

His main topic of conversation concerns those hustlers—and there have been a few whose names are legendary among gamblers—who started with a sawbuck and ran it up to a quarter of a million in a year's time. The hustler knows that he has little chance that this will happen to him—the same chance the other players had when they bet him even money on sixes and eights—but he is perennially hopeful that the gods of fortune will put their finger on him as an exception to the rule.

The real gambler looks down his nose at the hustler and contemptuously calls him a *nutman* because it is just as hard to get his money as it is that of the nutman who operates a three-shell game and whose swindle is straight highway robbery. When the hustler increases his take by picking up *sleepers* (money bet by other players and forgotten) and by short-changing his opponents, his social status drops a step further and he known as a chiseler.

CHEATS

There are two sorts of cheaters: the amateur, a player who thinks he sees a chance to make some money and doesn't care just how he does it, and the professional—an experienced cheat who is one of the boys, an accepted member of the grift.

If the amateur ever becomes a professional he has to learn the hard way. When he buys his first pair of crooked dice from the local dealer or by mail from a catalog house he is treated like a sucker. They sell him whatever he asks for but they never bother to explain that what he is getting may be years out of date and may, in any reasonably smart company, get him a broken nose. Nor do they supply any instruction sheet explaining the proper way to use the cheating devices. Cheating is an art that is passed along from one generation of cheaters to another strictly by word of mouth. The amateur cheat who orders a mechanical cheating device and doesn't have the savvy he needs to be able to use it properly often finds that it boomerangs and explodes in his face.

When the dice arrive he tries them out on his friends first and, if he clips them successfully, spreads his activities. But sooner or later another and more experienced cheat notices what he is up to. Then the word passes along that "some punk is trying to rob the kids up the street" and his goose is cooked. Experienced cheaters like nothing better than a game in which some amateur is trying to use *work*. They move in and beat him either with his own crooked dice and some angle he isn't smart to or by applying the cross which every cheating method has.

THE CROOKED GAMBLING SUPPLY HOUSES

The gambling supply house catalog is distinctly not the safest place to learn about cheating devices. The dealers' attitude is strictly one of "let the buyer beware." The merchandise listed in the catalogs includes any and everything that has any chance of selling. Many of the items are carried for years after newer developments have made them obsolete and dangerous to use. But that is the customer's worry, not the dealer's; the latter lists the devices just as long as there are chumps who will buy them. Card holdouts, for instance, are still listed at fancy prices and no card sharp who knows enough to come in out of the rain would be caught dead wearing one—because he might be caught dead if he did!

The cheat whose only knowledge of the art and craft of cheating was obtained from a study of the catalog and the writers and gambling exposé lecturers who glean their information from the same source and who are unable to separate the sucker items from the smart stuff are known among the boys as *catalog men*, a highly derogatory term.

The mail-order houses with the fancy catalogs, of which there are about a half dozen in the country, cater largely to the sucker and amateur cheat trade as is shown by the fact that they advertise in magazines of general circulation—the home mechanics and the pulp magazines. Like the spiritualistic and mail order psychic cults who put up a religious front they often operate under the transparent pretense that their products are for magicians only. One catalog states that all goods listed "are sold for these purposes only: Magic tricks and entertainment." It then proceeds to list percentage dice, roulette wheels, keyed punch boards, craps layouts, craps systems and copies of Hoyle. What any practicing magician would want with any of this apparatus is anybody's guess.

The catalog hints that the magicians could use them for exposés. "To really see and be able to demonstrate by having certain items in your possession is a 100% way of doing things. Many hours of fun can be had exposing trades and secrets. We solicit the trade of people in good faith, people that really want these kind of novelties for good uses." If I take them at their word and do a little such exposing, this supply house can certainly have no kick.

When you consider the type of merchandise being sold, some of the other catalog statements also make humorous reading. "Our plant is NEVER closed. You may call at any hour, day or night . . . Sundays or Holidays. A well qualified executive is always cheerfully ready to fill any order. When telegraphing use the following code: PAINT for cards and CUBE for dice." "Our policy, giving the customer a square deal, has resulted in our continued advancement."

Today with the federal enactment of laws banning the interstate shipment of crooked gaming equipment, the professional cheat knows enough not to tangle with the federal government by ordering his crooked dice by mail and, if caught, get a possible federal jail sentence, therefore he gives his business to the local supply house and the small "novelty shops" who have a dicemaker behind the scenes. There are probably 2,000 of these in the country doing an average of $500 worth of business a week. Perhaps one-fifth of this is spent for crooked dice. At an average price of $4 per pair this is 5,000 pair and $20,000 per week, a total of $1,000,000 per year.

The catalog houses hesitate to send big orders through the U. S. mails, usually requiring the purchaser to pick up his own order by messenger. This is apparently the only law they have to worry about; there are laws against gambling but nothing on the books that says that the manufacture or sale of cheating appliances is illegal.

THE DICE MOB

The art of professional cheating has several branches. There are cheats who travel alone, playing single-o against the suckers and, when they can figure an angle to do it, against the house as well. But, since there is safety and strength in numbers and because collusive cheating offers greater possibilities, they more often work in groups known as *dice mobs*.

The various members of the mob each have a particular duty in which they specialize. Except in the steer joint where the *bankroll man* whose capital is needed to back the project is usually the boss, the most important member is the *dice mechanic*. This is the man whose job it is to get the work in and out of the game indetectably and as called for. He must have mastered at least one good switch and be able to use it under fire.

The mob that works the private games may consist of a mechanic and one or more cheats who bet so as to take advantage of the work the mechanic puts into the game. The latter usually keeps his bets small and makes few of them so that, if caught, the big winnings can't be taken away from him since he's not the guy who has them. The member or members of the mob who win the big money are beyond suspicion because they never pick the dice up to shoot.

They don't depend entirely on this misdirection, however. The mobs usually carry an ex-pug or tough guy whose job, in case of a blow and when the mob can't out-talk the victims, is to fight a rear guard action while the cheats beat a retreat. This manoeuvre doesn't always succeed either. The mobs have often been beaten up by a group of angry players, but that never deters them from continuing to pursue the occupation. It's all in the day's work, one of the cheater's occupational hazards.

Dice cheats are doublecross experts in spades and have even been known to cross themselves up. There's the story of the chump who cleaned out three or four dice mobs that were in the game for the express purpose of beating him. And he did it without cheating and by playing sucker bets!

The intended victim was a big politician with a nice fat bankroll and a weakness for Craps. The fact that the boys took him one night for $165,000 hadn't cured him of the habit. But it did make him well known in gambling circles. When the news of that touch got around all the slickers in town laid plans to separate him from more of the same.

They didn't have long to wait. The papers a few days later listed him as among the notables who would attend a forthcoming Tammany clambake. Consequently, when J. P. Banks (which will have to do for a name) boarded the boat, the sharpers were right on deck, all of them well supplied with loaded dice, shapes, and Ts.

The crap game got under way almost as soon as the boat did, and when Banks stepped into it the roughhouse started. He was a right bettor and began taking bets, in his usual manner, all over the place and without paying any attention to correct betting odds. He was taking even money on everything, even on fours and tens—a course that is suicide in any normal game.

But this wasn't a normal game on several counts. In the first place, as soon as those sucker bets went down the hustlers and cheats grabbed for them frantically. Ask any half smart gambler for even money on a bet where he should lay two to one and you can't help but get action.

But there was a hitch. Banks began increasing the size of his bets. He'd take fifty on the point, lose it, take a hundred on the next, lose that, then take four hundred all at even money. It was a hustler's field day. Naturally he had to win once in a while. And when he did, his increased wagers brought back all his losses plus a profit.

In a house game the management protects itself against high, wide, and fancy progressive betting of that sort. The house limit prevents the player from doubling up more than six or seven times in a row. But this game was out in the open and there were no house rules. What's more, every sharper in the crowd, and that meant about half the twenty men in the game, was trying to cover as much as they could of each one of Banks' bets. Each mob tried to prevent the others from getting a look in at this easy money.

Furthermore, because they were all so anxious to clip him themselves, they watched each other like hawks and no one dared rip in with the phony dice that were ready and waiting. And Banks went merrily ahead making sucker bets a mile a minute but increasing or doubling up at the same time and getting back more money on one pass than he lost on the previous missouts. Then a shooter got lucky and made seven numbers and Banks really went to town.

There could be only one finish. He cleaned them out. The smart boys who knew all the tricks had outsmarted themselves. They tried so hard to keep the competition from clipping the chump that nobody clipped him. He broke them instead.

So, *if* you can find a private game in which there are several mobs of sharpers competing for your roll, you can play without worrying about dishonest dice. And, *if* your bankroll is the size of a washtub, you can place the biggest sucker bets in the world and win in spite of it by doubling up. But you might also remember that Mr. Banks managed to do this only once. Since then he has lost all that he won ten times over. He got into a few other games later in which the sharpers present were teamed up.

Your very best bet, unless you can afford to lose, is not to bet at all.

THE STEER JOINT

The other type of dice mob is that which operates the *steer joint* (crooked gambling joint). These boys go out after the suckers and steer them into a specially arranged set-up in which the victim hasn't the ghost of a chance. They really give him *the business*. These "games" may be found wherever there are suckers with money—especially around resorts and racetracks during the season. Sometimes when the mob hears of a big bettor who looks like a promising prospect they travel hundreds of miles and set up a joint just to take that one man. I know of one Eastern mob who went all the way to the West Coast, beat a movie magnate for what they swear was 250 grand, and left immediately by the next train out.

The casino operators are anything but friendly toward the steer joints because they know only too well that a strong beef from a steer-joint victim may create a situation in which the authorities have to put on the heat and close up the whole town.

The mob employs *steerers* whose job is to locate prospective victims and bring them in. Sometimes they are not regular members of the mob but merely players who steer in their best friends. Anyone with larceny in his heart will fill the bill as long as he listens to and gives the nod to the proposition: "Bring your friend around and we'll cut you in for 50% of what he loses." Or it may be 30% or 25% or less, depending on how smart the steerer is. The amount he really gets after it's all over also depends on his knowledge of the racket. If he doesn't bother to add up the victim's losses as the touch is being made his cut will shrink considerably. And if he agrees to come around the next day for the payoff, he may find that the mob has copped a sneak.

The steerer's method of baiting the hook is simple. He merely says, "I heard about a big crap game in town the other day that must be run by a bunch of greenhorns. Believe it or not, they don't charge 5% vigorish—only 3% and they only pick it up on the right bettor." This is calculated to and does make the monkey's eyes glow with interest and the moment he asks, "Where did you say this game was?" he's hooked.

The steerer makes a date with him to look the game over and then tips off the steer-joint operator that he is bringing company. The latter gets busy and has one of the boys rent a hotel room or apartment for the day, covering his tracks with a phony name. If the sucker is just the usual grade another of the boys round up a dozen or more *shills*, local hangers on around the poolrooms who know little or nothing about what the score is except that it isn't on the level. If the intended victim is a habitual gambler who is a bit smart, more experienced shills are obtained. The shills may get anything from $25 to $50 plus bonus depending on the size of the sucker and on how much the shill knows about the racket and how important or tough he may be. The shills who agree to wait for their pay until the end of the week also sometimes find that the mob doesn't live there any more. Bust-out men, however, know enough to demand and get their pay immediately after the game, usually $25 per night whether the joint gets any business or not, plus 10% of each touch.

The shills may be given a hundred bucks among them, told to bet only among themselves and ordered to make sure that they duke back exactly $100 afterward. Or, if the steerer reports that the victim he is bringing in is a big bettor, the operator may give each pair of shills a hundred. "You two bet with each other," he instructs, "and see that I get the $100 back at the finish."

The boys sit around talking about the races or the fight and wait for the steerer and his friend to arrive. The moment the doorbell rings the scene changes quicker than it does when a movie director calls, "Camera. Action!" The book gets behind the money, the mechanic picks up the crap stick and starts boxing up the dice. The rest of the mob and the shills swing into a display of excited, rapid-fire betting that is guaranteed to start the blood racing in the veins of any gambler. When the sucker enters he not only sees plenty of action but the players are betting just the way he likes. If he is a wrong bettor there are plenty of right bettors and vice versa.

He also notices that the situation is as represented: the charge is only 3% and is only picked up on the right bettor. And what's more, there is so much action on the outside that he can get down without even paying the 3%. When the steerer who starts betting immediately, turns and says, "Why don't you get your feet wet?" the chump finds the invitation irresistible. And the moment the monkey puts his first bet down, the stickman gets the office and a set of Tops goes in, or, if the mob is shy a good bust-out man and has the table wired, the squeeze goes on.

They give the chump plenty of excitement for his money although sometimes it is all packed into a few minutes. The steer-joint boys don't fool around and see no reason for any delays. They take the money as fast as they can, sometimes breaking the victim on one shot. And they never fail. Once the victim has lost a few big bets he keeps sending more in to get it back. Although he doesn't know it and unless there is another sucker or two being clipped at the same time, he is the only person in the joint who is gambling—the others are all members of the mob playing a sure thing or shills putting on an act. The amount of money he loses is usually limited only by the amount he has on him and he often comes back again the next night with a new bankroll. Some suckers have been known to come back time after time, always hopeful that their bad run of luck will turn and never suspecting that the whole thing is a swindle.

As an example of the financial possibilities of steer-joint methods Con Baker, the greatest bust-out man ever to rip in a pair of Ts, would never accept less than 20% of a touch, a rate that on one occasion brought him $167,000 in one evening when he fleeced one of America's top oil barons for the tidy sum of $835,000 in a two-hour work day. He always made sure he got it, too. He insisted on counting the bankroll both before and after the game. "I don't trust steer-joint operators," he always said. "They're a bunch of thieves." Added together, Con's touches must easily have gone far past the ten-million mark, and he died at the age of 37 dead broke.

In recent years some dice mobs have specialized in beating book-makers, usually those who have been booking games in small towns and have accumulated a sizable bank account through the operation of Old Man Vigorish. The steerer gives the bookmaker the story that he knows where there is a fast private game that has no one to book it and he rattles off a few impressive names of big executives, wealthy business men, Broadway playboys and movie stars who, he claims, are players. Brought in to have a look, the bookmaker sees a sight nicely calculated to make his eyes pop and his mouth water.

The players are well dressed and their hands are filled with folding money. They are all shouting, "I'll take sixty on the 9," "I'll take a hundred on the 4" without getting many takers. The bookmaker watches and mentally adds up the amount of Vigorish he would collect when these bettors came to the book with this action. The total makes him blink.

"Sure," he says, "I'll book the game." Sometimes, if he's a little bit smart he adds, "I'll bring my own stickman." The boys don't like that idea too much and may try delicately to discourage it, but if he puts his foot down and insists, they don't argue the matter. The bust-out man is simply told that he will have to work from the outside.

The details of the play which takes the bookmaker or anyone else unlucky enough to find himself in a steer-joint are given under the subject of Busters in chapter 13, page 245.

BEATING THE HOUSE

Even the house professional isn't safe from the cannibalistic habit cheats have of preying on their own kind. He may be an old-timer and hep to nearly all the angles, but he is fair game for any cheat who knows a bit more or who can dope out a new method that will take him. A considerable amount of brain power is expended in working out such angles because the professional gambler is the big money gambler and the cheat's winnings may be even more than when he clips Mr. Average Crap Player.

Beating the house is not something the cheats do regularly. These days it's a risky and tricky proposition that nearly always requires something brand-new in the way of angles. But every now and then someone does dope out a new one that works for awhile—until it gets talked about too much. Take a guy that we'll call Horseshoe Harry because that's not his real monicker. He had a nice steady job as dealer at a crap table in Philly and, he sat there night after night wondering how he could safely cop a bundle of it. Every dealer, at some time or other, has tried to figure a way to get some of that dough off the table without being seen, even when he is a part owner.

Harry finally did figure out an angle that had its points. He took a one hundred and a ten dollar bill and carefully pasted them together with rubber cement. The result was something that would have made the Treasury Department sit up and blink—a bill that looked like a C-note on one side and like a sawbuck on the other, in short something that might be termed a C-saw!

Harry also took on an assistant, a player we'll call Frisco, gave him some specific instructions and promised him a split. Then they went to work. Frisco showed up at Harry's crap table, made a few medium-sized bets here and there and then when the heavy betting got under way, made a flat bet to win, putting down a stack of notes, the $100-$10 note on the bottom with the ten dollar side up and 9 tens on top of it. But he neglected to state just how much dough he was betting and Harry neglected to call him on it.

If Frisco lost Harry would scoop in the stack of bills, taking care to keep one eye on the $100-$10 note. Frisco apparently lost $100 but was actually out 9 tens and the two-way note which was worth $110, a total of $200. But he got it back. A moment later, when he asked Harry for change for a hundred and Harry would count out and give him 10 tens, one of which was the gaffed bill.

Then Frisco would make another flat win bet, again putting down the $100-$10 bill topped by 9 tens. When the shooter passed and Frisco won, Harry would reach out, pick up the bills and count them. But, because he turned the stack of bills upside down, he'd get a total of $100 and 9 tens or $190. He would pay off at even money and Frisco, with one loss of $100 and a win of $190, would have $90 profit. Each time he lost he'd be out a Century; each time he won he'd gain $190. The bank would be paying off all the other customers at even money but Frisco would be getting odds of nearly 2 to 1.

The boys did all right for awhile but they forgot to use restraint and finally overdid it. One night one of the bosses, a suspicious egg, noticed that they were neglecting to call the amount bet. Then he gave Frisco's habit of always asking for change for a hundred after every loss a tumble. He walked over just after Frisco had lost a bet, said, "Harry, there's too much dough at this table," and went off with a stack of it which included the gaffed note.

He had no sooner disappeared into the cashier's office than Frisco had his hat and was on his way out. Harry put in a call for a relief and followed suit. He almost beat Frisco to the door. That finished that.

Another dealer solved the problem of copping some of the dough that passed through his hands without being detected by making use of his tobacco chewing habit. Shortly before his shift ended he'd palm a crumbled C-note when he was straightening his pile, then pop some of his tobacco into his mouth, depositing the bill there at the same time. Today the boss who is smart doesn't allow his dealers to chew while on duty.

Trying to beat the house is always a short term proposition. Once the operators rumble the gaff it gets talked about and becomes a dead number fast. That goes for any cheating device. If it gets too much publicity the boys don't dare use it any more. And if you and you and you read the next chapters on crooked dice, cheating is going to be a tougher proposition than it has been.

12

Crooked Dice:
Inside Work

Dice that are everything that they should be are known as *square dice, perfects* or *levels*. The most obvious method of making a "false set" of dice is to weight them so that one or more sides are heavier than the others. J. H. Green, writing in 1880, describes the method then in use as follows:

> The corner spot of the four-side adjoining the five-side is carefully and neatly drilled to the depth of an eighth of an inch. A similar operation is performed with the corner spot of the five adjoining the four-side; so that the two holes, thus made, meet. One of the holes is then covered over with a very strong cement of copal, or other varnish; and quicksilver (sometimes gold is used) is poured into the orifice of the other, which is still open, until it is quite filled; when it is stopped up with cement, and the spots blackened as before.

Opaque dice are a cinch to load. Transparent cubes, as we shall see later, will take only a limited amount of weight which can only be

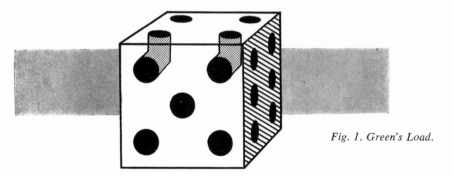

Fig. 1. Green's Load.

placed in certain places. Opaque dice can be loaded as heavily as necessary at any place and on any side. Any part of the die may be drilled, or
the die can be split and the slug inserted. A good dicemaker can plug
the hole or fit and cement the die's parts together so neatly that you
can't spot his surgical operation.

PERCENTAGE OR P. C. DICE

Notice that the load Green described was on the corner of the die
and not in the center of one side. Dice are almost never gaffed so that
the same numbers always come up because even the greenest mark
would rumble that in short order. The load is placed near the edges of
two sides or at the corner where three sides meet so that any of the
opposite unweighted sides will come up, not every time, but more often
than they should. The loaded sides still come up, but the cheat who bets
that they won't wins more bets than he loses. He doesn't have a sure-
thing, but he has a percentage in his favor that pays off in cash.

Sharps have been known to lose in spite of the favorable percentage when Lady Luck was scowling very heavily and when they bet too
heavily in too short a game, but those instances are merely the well
known exceptions that prove the rule. If the dice roll long enough, the
man who knows what numbers are favored, bets those numbers to pass
and lays wrong bets against the others, is going to finish with a fatter
bankroll than when he started. The victim loses because he is playing
against two opponents—the cheat and that invisible but very dependable and powerful gentleman: Old Man Percentage.

Percentage dice, not on the level, are doctored to do two things—
one type is gaffed* to win more often than it should, the other to lose.

* *Gaff.* Any secret cheating device or method, a gimmick. *To Gaff.* To make crooked or
install a gaff. Now you know the origin of the phrase "He couldn't stand the gaff." And "he
blew the gaff" means that he wised up the sucker by explaining the cheating device.

The sharper has the best of it with either. When the dice are fixed to win, he becomes a right bettor; when they are losers, he becomes a wrong bettor.

PASSERS

Passers are cubes so loaded or otherwise gaffed that they favor making passes, thus giving the right bettor the advantage. The 5–3 sides are sometimes loaded on one die and the 5–Ace on the other. This will tend to bring up the 2–4 and 2–6 sides, making the points 4, 6, 8 and 10 the favorites and tending to miss the seven and the craps.

Because the loads in present day transparent cubes must be inserted beneath the paint on the spots, the 4–5–6 sides which bear the most spots can be most heavily loaded and are the most popular variety. Since the Ace–2–3 sides tend to be thrown the most often, the favored points are 4, 5 and 6 while the points 8, 9 and 10 will be thrown less often than usual. When two cheats are working together with these dice, one places big bets on the low numbers to win and smaller amounts or none at all on high points. His partner, a wrong bettor, puts his big money on the high points to lose and bets little or nothing on low points.

MISSOUTS

Missouts are loaded so that they tend to throw more sevens and fewer points. Loaded missouts may be filled so that one die favors the Ace, the other the 2–6; or one die may favor the Deuce and the other the 1–5. Either way the shooter gets more sevens than he has any right to expect.* Some cheaters prefer to have one die favor the ace-deuce-trey, the other the ace-four-five.

The supply house catalogs list a Three Dice Combination consisting of five dice, three filled and two fair all to match at $80.

> "Two of the filled dice are the regular old standby Missouts, Ace and Six Deuce. The third filled die is a strong Deuce Four and when used with the Deuce Six makes the points 4, 6, 8 and 10 the favorites. The filled dice bear a secret mark to avoid the possibility of mixups."

---

* On the come-out the percentage in favor of the shooter's winning with those extra sevens is offset by the fact that the load also brings up more threes (crap) than usual. Cheaters using these dice don't usually bet on the come-out.

   The other kinds of crooked dice (shapes, bevels, capped dice, etc.) to be discussed later, are also made in passing and missout combinations.

Since percentage dice are not sure-fire, you may wonder what happens when Subway Harry is shooting with a pair of Passers that favor the points 4, 6, 8 or 10 and he throws a 5 or 9 for his point. The 4s, 6s, 8s and 10s that he throws next won't do him any good, and his chance of passing is the same as though the dice were fair (odds of 3 to 2). Since this would be taking too much of a chance and since dice cheats, like their dice, usually travel in pairs, Harry's partner merely covers Harry's right bets with wrong ones. Then, no matter whether the dice pass or not, Harry and his partner together neither win nor lose.

When the load or other work used is heavily in the sharp's favor, the percentage is said to be *strong*. And when it is too strong, smart crap players sometimes notice that some numbers appear more than they should and begin to wonder if Lady Luck isn't getting an assist. They eye the cubes and the sharp with a tinge of distrust. In order to prevent rumbles from this class of player and so that the load could be made stronger without being too easily detected, the underworld dicemakers figured that a movable load might be the answer. And they came up with the following very tricky method of gaffing the galloping dominoes.

TAPPING DICE OR TAPPERS

These are always opaque dice, the gaff being impossible in transparent cubes. The interiors contain a drilled out dumbbell shaped channel, a little oil to help the action, and a drop of mercury. When the quicksilver is in the center cavity, the dice are fair. But when the sharp wants the best of it, he taps the dice on the floor "for luck." This jars the mercury, whose surface tension prevents it from running down the connecting channel, and it starts to move. The sharp lets the dice stand in position for a moment while he covers bets and, when the mercury has settled to the corner of the die, he is then throwing a set of loads, either Passers or Missouts.

In order to overcome the disadvantage of having to wait for the slow moving mercury to act, someone concocted another tapping gaff— a weight (made of brass so that a magnet won't detect its presence) which slides back and forth on a slender wire. A ratchet tooth holds it in position at the center until the tapping disengages it. A cup-shaped rubber bumper at the other end makes the fall of the weight noiseless and also serves to hold it in position there.

Tappers are not common because their advantages are outweighed by several faults. They are too complicated to be completely dependable

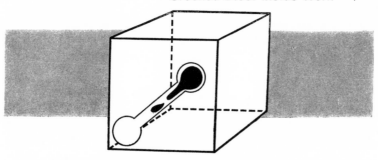

Fig. 2. Phantom view of a tapping die.

and get out of order easily. They have a nasty habit, too, of backfiring on the sharp because the boucing around they get in play sometimes causes the weight to shift unexpectedly and the cheat loses more than the dice are worth before he discovers the fact.

Tappers must be opaque and yet are of no use in the games that ordinarily use opaque dice. The tapping necessary to shift the load is not possible when the dice are in a cage as in Chuck-a-Luck, or when thrown from a cup, as in the counter games. They can be used only in Craps and then only in the games in which the players will stand for opaque cubes. And anyone who will play Craps for real money in this day and age with strangers who use opaque dice should never have been allowed out of his bassinet. In any case, it's a fairly safe bet that he's not in the Armed Forces because a guy who uses his head that seldom would even have trouble passing the psychiatric examination at the induction center. Or am I wrong? Have *you* been using opaque dice in games with strangers?

HOW TO DETECT TAPPERS

Tap the corners to shift the load to the outside and then apply the water or pivot test for loads (see page 220). Sawing the dice in two, the quickest method, will also expose the gaff.

TRANSPARENT CONCAVE SPOT LOADS

Not long after transparent celluloid was invented, some manufacturer who may have suspected that his own Craps losses were due to loaded dice, had the bright idea that transparent cubes would protect him against such skulduggery. It wasn't a bad idea at all. It was, in fact, so good that a lot of players even today still think that he was right.

Even the sure-thing boys had a few bad moments. At first they scowled at the improved product and tried to ignore it. But eventually so many players began to insist on transparent dice that something drastic had to be done, and quick.

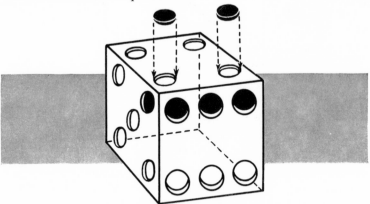

Fig. 3. Transparent dice are loaded with metallic slugs which are placed in the countersunk spots.

It was. One day a dicemaker who had been giving considerable thought to the problem noticed that there were still several places on the die that were not transparent. The paint on the spots was just as opaque as ever. He promptly put a pair of the new-fangled transparent inventions in his vise, drilled a few of the spots just a trifle deeper, painted the bottoms of the holes, inserted thin concave metal slugs, and put another coat of paint back on top. His invention sold—and still sells—like hotcakes in certain quarters, and at fancy prices.

Gold, platinum and tungsten amalgam slugs are used today. The heavier the metal, the thinner the slug and the less likely it is that the player will notice any difference in the depth of the countersunk holes.* If you know what you are looking for, however, you may, by looking through the dice, sometimes find that some holes are slightly deeper than others. But don't count on it. The crooked dicemaker who takes pride in his work avoids this danger by drilling the unloaded spots to the same depth and filling them with paint. One catalog charges extra for this service. "For deep spots to match weight," it states, "remit $10 additional."

---

* The catalog prices give you an idea of the respective worth of the different kinds of loads. Loaded white opaque dice are $25.00 the set. Filled, transparent dice start at $35.00 for amalgam fills, $50.00 for gold fills, and $80.00 for platinum. The manufacturer "recommends the use of platinum or gold unless a very mild percentage is sufficient, in which case amalgam will prove satisfactory."

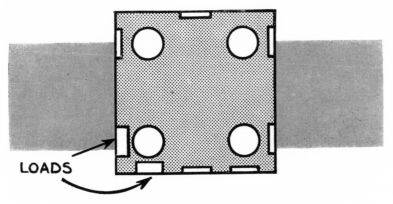

Fig. 4. Loaded spots are sometimes deeper than others but careful dicemakers drill all spots to same depth.

The catalog neglects to mention that, when ordering, you also need to have considerable confidence in the honesty of the dealer in crooked dice. If you don't trust him, you never know when you invest eighty bucks in a set of platinum loads whether the merchandise delivered is as advertised or whether the dealer may not have made a slight error and given you the $35.00 set of amalgam loads instead!

Another tipoff is that, because the dicemaker didn't dare drill too deep, the paint covering the loads may be more nearly flush with the surface than it is in the unloaded spots. The conscientious dicemaker, however, will take care of this angle by building up the paint so that it looks the same in all spots. The only visually discernible difference then is that all the spots are a shade too deep when compared with those in a set of dice that are known to be unloaded.

TRANSPARENT FLUSH SPOT LOADS

Modern transparent casino flush spot dice require considerable more skill to load than dice with recessed spots. To load, the spots are drilled into the face of the die approximately 19/1000 inch. The desired load recessions are first painted, then filled with concave platinum or gold slugs which are painted over. The remaining recessions are filled with paint and the faces of the die are finished off by hand buffing and polishing and, since no recession appears on the die's face, it is called a flush spot load.

DEAD NUMBER OR FIRST FLOP DICE

These are loaded so heavily that the dice fall dead exactly as they should nearly all the time. An opaque die so loaded and carrying some *outside work* (see the next chapter) can be made to bring up one or more numbers (usually one) almost every time. Dead numbers on transparent dice can't be made as strong but can be loaded enough that they will bring up the wanted number about half the time. The strongest transparent load is the Dead Ace which contains twelve slugs altogether. All the spots on the 6 side are filled as well as the two spots on the 4, the two on the 5, the one on the 2 and the one on the 3 that are nearest the 6 side. The Dead Ace is paired up with a die filled to favor the 2–6 so that together they bring up *seven* and the craps, *three*, more often than usual, making it a missout combination.

The smart player can recognize, or at least become suspicious of loads by the way they roll. As they slow down and are just about to come to a stop, a loaded die (when the weight happens to be on the top) may make a sudden and uncalled for last minute quarter turn. It will flop over in an unnatural manner, either forward, to the right or left or backwards. You aren't likely to notice this unless you have seen dice that you knew were loaded in action, but it is a tip-off to the smart crap player and the reason that hustlers don't introduce loads in fast company.

The following tests will show the presence of inside work and every crap player who plays the game with anything but matches should know and be able to use them.

THE WATER TEST

Get a tall glass or bucket of water. Hold the suspected cube just above the surface and drop it gently into the water. Do this several times and note whether some numbers keep coming up oftener than they should. Hold the die with a different number up each time you drop it into the water. See if the die settles evenly or whether it turns over as it goes down. If it turns and the same numbers keep showing, then the strangers you've been playing with are probably not nearly as friendly as they've tried to make out.

PIVOT TEST

If there's no water handy, there's a simpler method which anyone can apply with a certain amount of ease. If you hold the cubes loosely

Fig. 5. The Water Test.

between thumb and forefinger so that there is as little friction as possible, you can make the test without any gadgets. Hold the cube at diagonally opposite corners as shown in Figure 6, with the sides suspected of being loaded on top. Try all four combinations of diagonal corners. If the cube is loaded, and if you have the load on top, it will pull downward, and, if held loosely, the die will pivot between your fingers, the load swinging around to the bottom. When the dice are round-cornered, it requires an extremely light touch to detect loads with the pivot test and the water test shows them up better.

SCRATCH TEST

Your next step is to scratch the paint on the spots opposite the numbers that show too often. If you hit pay dirt by uncovering a small gold or platinum mine, it's your cue to start slugging. In the case of opaque dice, smash them open, or burn them and look for the slugs that remain.

Fig. 6. The Pivot Test for Loads.

FLOATS OR FLOATERS

These are opaque dice of which the catalog says, "they are not weighted or shaped, can be burned and leave no evidence and get by when nothing else will." Sawing them open will expose the gaff, however. Instead of being loaded, they are lightened. One side of the die is sliced off, half the interior is hollowed out, and the side cemented back on. Their name derives from the fact that they are so light that some of them actually float with the hollowed side up when you give them the water test.

Don't make the mistake too many crap players make of thinking that the dice must be fair and square just because *you* put them in the game. They may have been your dice when the game began, but that's no proof that they are still the same pair you purchased.

FILLED TRANSPARENT DICE

F ILLED Transparent Dice with a percentage almost as great as filled White Dice are now made possible by the use of our special platinum and gold spot fill. The spots appear natural and a special reaming assures spots that will always remain tight. Platinum fills, using 24-gauge platinum produce the strongest dice. 24-gauge gold fills are only a degree less effective and where a moderate percentage is sufficient the amalgam filled dice will prove entirely satisfactory.

FILLED TRANSPARENT MISSOUTS

This is a perfect pocket set and for general play will prove most satisfactory. These dice will work on any surface except dirt or a blanket and show a handsome percentage for the Banker at all times. One dice is made to come Ace and the other Six and Deuce, bringing up the numbers 3 and 7. Spots look entirely natural and we suggest ⁵⁄₈-inch dice with slightly round corners for best results. Fair dice to match included with each set, no switching during play.

No. 10G150.	Platinum Filled Missouts....	Per Set	$16.00
No. 10G151.	Gold Filled Missouts...............................	Per Set	10.00
No. 10G152.	Amalgam Filled Missouts........................	Per Set	7.50

FILLED TRANSPARENT PASSERS

While not quite as strong as the Missout Dice, the Filled Transparent Passers will show a very satisfactory percentage, especially when used on a smooth, hard surface giving the dice plenty of action. We recommend the use of the platinum or gold fills in this combination unless a very mild percentage is sufficient, in which case amalgam fills will prove satisfactory. These dice are filled to bring up the numbers 4, 6, 8 and 10 most often and it is not necessary to switch during play. Slightly round corner dice in the ⅝ inch size give best results, fair dice to match with each set.

No. 10G153.	Platinum Filled Passers..............	Per Set	$16.00
No. 10G154.	Gold Filled Passers.................................	Per Set	10.00
No. 10G155.	Amalgam Filled Passers............................	Per Set	7.50

THREE DICE COMBINATION

This is a popular combination set and consists of five dice, three filled and two fair in transparent, all to match. Two of the filled dice are the regular old stand-by missouts, Ace and Six Deuce. The third filled dice is a strong Deuce Four and when used with the Deuce Six makes the points 4, 6, 8 and 10 the favorites. The filled dice bear a secret mark avoiding the possibility of mix ups and complete instructions are supplied with each set.

No. 10G156.	Platinum Filled Three Dice Combination................	Per Set	$24.00
No. 10G157.	Gold Filled Three Dice Combination....................	Per Set	15.00
No. 10G158.	Amalgam Filled Three Dice Combination................	Per Set	10.00

We also furnish three dice sets in various other combinations at the price of the set listed.

Fig. 7. Page from a gambling supply house catalog advertising loaded dice. Prices have, however, jumped 200% above those shown because of the enactment of federal legislation against the interstate shipment of crooked gaming equipment.

A dice mob that knows its business is well equipped with phony dice of assorted shapes and sizes to match any of the common varieties. Or they may take a look in at the game, leave for a few minutes, and return with dice of the proper sort. Dealers in crooked dice advertise that they "can furnish dice in all sizes and colors to meet any emer-

Fig. 8. A Float cut apart to show hollowed interior.

gency." They even list the common garden-variety of Drug Store Dice and say:

> "These are generally off-color and usually have spots sunk deeper than ordinary. To meet this demand we are prepared to match up any common Drug Store Dice. Locate the work you need, and send us your sample and we will produce matching work to order—Tops, Flats, Shapes, Transparent Weight, White Weight, Capped Work."

Even Pee Wee Dice come in for their share of attention.

> "Small dice, especially bone, give the ordinary dicemaker considerable trouble and the work is usually unsatisfactory. However, with our equipment and skilled mechanics, we produce Pee Wee dice that are even stronger than the same work in larger sizes. Our Pee Wee loads are not only filled but hollowed on the opposite sides to insure fast action and make them weight the same as fair dice."

At this point I can hear some of you saying, "Nobody is going to switch crooked dice in on me because mine bear a secret mark so that I'll know when any substitutions are made." Maybe so, but any sharp that isn't hep to such protective devices doesn't stay in the business long. All any proficient member of a good dice mob needs is one quick gander at the marked cube and a few minutes in the nearest men's room. When he comes out, his crooked dice bear a very reasonable facsimile of your secret mark and the sharp wears a grin.

He grins because he knows that from there on if anyone puts in a beef that the dice are not square, and then proves it, the guy who is going to get poked in the jaw is the one whose private mark is on the dice—meaning you!

A special monogram, trademark, or other insignia may protect you for an evening. But the next time you play, the cheats will show up with their phony dice marked to match. Most gambling houses have protective marks on their dice, but they change the designs or the position of the design regularly, using different ones on successive nights.

One secret that has been very carefully guarded by cheats is the method they sometimes use to mark their crooked dice for instant identification. This is important in house games where one and sometimes two sets of five dice each are in use on the table and the cheat has managed to ring in one or more gaffed dice. When a player calls for a box-up, fair dice come into play and the *work* goes into the bowl. The cheat must not only know when his dice come back into play, but must recognize them immediately so that he can take advantage of the P. C. and so that he won't find himself betting against it. He can't pick the dice up and examine them, but he has to be able to identify them at a distance and while they are in action. And yet, at the same time, the other players must not notice any difference in the dice at all. Can you dope out his method of meeting these conditions before you read the next paragraph?

Hold a fair die with the 6-spot on top and the three facing you. Note that a line drawn through the spots on the three slants upward to the right. This is standard dicemaking practice. But when the cheat has his gaffed dice made, he instructs the dicemaker to spot the three so that this line through the spots runs up to the left instead, as on the right hand die, Figure 9. The same dodge can also be worked on the two which should run up to the right when the die is held so that the four is on top. If you see a die mis-spotted in this manner, there is a very good chance that something else is wrong with it as well.

ARE YOUR DICE CROOKED?

Another thing you should remember is that after the cheat has put his crooked percentage dice into the game, he doesn't necessarily switch them out again when he leaves. If he has won any decent amount of folding money, even the $80 he may have spent for a pair of platinum loads can be written off as an operating expense and still leave plenty of

Fig. 9. Cheater's secret identification method.

profit. It is nearly always worth whatever price he has paid for the dice not to have to switch them out again and take that additional chance of being caught.*

This means, of course, that there are at this moment thousands of pairs of P. C. dice of all types traveling around in the pockets of honest players who haven't the slightest suspicion of what they are carrying.

Consequently, the cheat always takes a good look at the dice in play in any game he enters. He may even test them on the pretense that he wants to make sure they are fair. If he finds that they aren't, he knows that someone has saved him some trouble, and he simply makes his bets so as to take advantage of the way the dice are gimmicked. This situation has another advantage as well because, if anyone should rum-

---

* What's more many cheats who use P.C. dice, couldn't switch them out for the simple reason that they can't make a switch. They put the *work* into the game, not with sleight of hand, but by a simple exchange before the game begins.

ble the dice for what they are, the honest chump who owns them is the guy who gets jumped.

Perhaps you will agree that it might be a very good idea if you were to take time out at this point and test your own dice to make sure that they aren't loaded. Apply the tests just given and then, after reading the next chapter, apply the tests given there for *outside work*.

And a word of warning—if you do find that your dice are crooked, get rid of them. *Don't* try to take advantage of the P. C. they supply, even as a joke. It might backfire right in your face. Even the dice cheat sometimes takes a beating with percentage dice.

He may not know, as you probably wouldn't, *exactly* what numbers are favored to come up. On a pair of 3–Ace and 2–5 Passers, for instance, the points 5, 6 and 8 have a favorable percentage, but not the 4, 9 or 10. Sometimes even the cheat doesn't realize this, but thinks, because the dice were sold as Passers, that *all* the points are favored. Consequently when he *overlays* (makes bets larger than usual) on the 4, 9, or 10 because he thinks those points have a P. C. in his favor, he sometimes gets an unpleasant surprise. If the overlaid wager is lost and the winner quits the game, the cheat may have no chance to recoup. More experienced cheats, however, always try to distribute their wagers so that one player won't win so much that he'll quit if the dice happen to roll his way.

Crap hustlers, working on the percentage that sucker bets give them, also lose now and then. They sometimes count too heavily on the fact that the odds are in their favor, and make wagers they can't afford. Then, if the dice go against them, their bankroll is so shortened that they can't place big enough bets to take full advantage of the percentage during the rest of the game.

ELECTRIC DICE

These cubes contain steel slugs and are used over an electric magnet built into a crap table or counter. The slugs used in transparent either concave or flush spot casino dice are made by gluing together 5/1000 inch steel wires to form a grid and punching out circular discs which fit into the countersunk spots. One is inserted in each of the spots on four different sides of the die, leaving the two sides that the operator wants to favor (opposite sides like the 6 and Ace) open.*

---

* Opaque dice are loaded by inserting wire nails which, if the Ace and six sides are to be favored, run through the die from the Ace to the six side.

The magnetic field set up by a concealed electromagnet acts as shown in Figure 10 and brings one or the other of the unloaded sides up. Since the load is so light and since it is on four sides, neither pivot nor water test will detect electric dice. Furthermore their roll is not only natural, but even honest some of the time. However, the moment the operator puts on the squeeze by pushing the button that controls the electro-magnet concealed beneath the playing surface, the electric dice act like trained seals. They are not percentage dice; the action is completely positive. The boys who use these don't intend to give anyone a break.

On the steer-joint crap table the magnetic plate is close to the rail and just beneath the spot where most shooters will throw the dice. If a sucker persists in throwing against the rail at some other spot, the big money only goes down when the shills are shooting the dice above the magnetic area. The pull of the magnet is less noticeable and operates more efficiently on the cubes as they drop down from the backboard than if they were simply rolled across the magnetic spot. Throwing the dice against the rail is, ordinarily, a protective measure, but in the steer-joint the reverse is true. But don't try *not* hitting the rail; you won't like what happens then either!

Electric dice may be either missouts or passers, the latter being most often used. Six-ace missouts have the disadvantages that, because they always bring up one of the numbers 2, 12 or 7, the juice cannot be applied on the 1st roll when 2 and 12 lose and 7 wins. Once the shooter has come out on a point he will always lose when the juice is on because 2 and 12 are no decision and 7 loses, but the smart gambler is likely to become suspicious when too many double-aces and double-sixes appear before the 7 makes him missout.

Electric passers on the other hand throw a variety of points. A pair of electric dice, one die having the 2–5 sides and the other the 3–4 sides open, will throw the numbers 5, 6, 8 or 9. A pair of six-ace trey-four passers will throw 4, 5, 9 or 10.

These dice are as deadly as a cobra and completely positive in action. When steer joint operators are playing a bookmaker, they will take the odds on the point and all the off numbers that can be thrown with the passers in use. When the juice goes off again, the bookmaker is broke!

Either the dealer or a shill on the outside controls the juice by pressing a button concealed beneath the green baize table-covering or by pressing a screwhead on the side or under the edge of the table or a

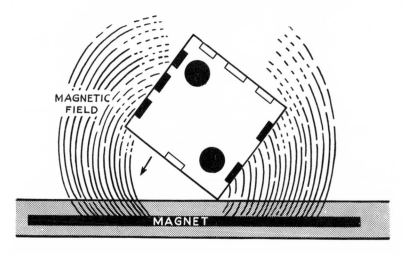

Fig. 10. Electric dice are not loaded as you would expect. Steel loads are indicated in diagram above by black spots. Curved lines of force of magnetic field, pulling on die from sides bring it to rest with the unloaded sides at top and bottom.

foot control. The operation is known either as putting *the squeeze* on or putting *the juice* on.

Reputable gambling houses do not need to *slam bang* by using wired tables. They don't need to; they make handsome profits via the percentage method. Such houses, in fact, don't even consider cheating by this or any other method because it would immediately jeopardize a steady, profitable business that may have taken months or even years to establish. The money that could be made in a few crooked plays would be a drop in the bucket compared to the annual income.

GIANT ELECTROMAGNET

The electric dice users who call in a *juice man* and have him make the house into a *wire joint* are the steer-joint owners who won't pay a bust-out man* a ten percent cut, or the ones who find that the demand for good bust-out men exceeds the supply.

The catalogs list a variety of electromagnets for casino, counter and bar games.

. . . the old reliable counter magnet, time tested and thoroughly satisfactory, complete with five dice made to come any top and bottom

---

* *Bust-out man.* A sleight of hand artist who switches in mis-spotted dice, a method of fleecing the monkey that is just as efficient as electric dice and has the advantage that the table will stand inspection. The smart cheat always prefers sleight of hand methods because they leave no evidence behind as mechanical gadgets do.

GIANT ELECTRO MAGNET

THE Giant Electro Magnet is a recent development in Dice Magnets and is one of the few that will control Transparent Dice with the same positive results that are obtained with white dice. This Magnet is made in two sizes, one 12 inches in diameter with a 10-inch field weighing 15 pounds, and one 18 inches in diameter with a 14-inch field weighing 36 pounds.

The Giant Electro Magnet is operated with three 12-volt 120-ampere automobile type storage batteries and the Magnet Coil, being only ¾ inch thick, can be placed in many places where it would be impossible to use an ordinary magnet. Complete instructions for installing with 45 feet of cable wire, control, and 1 pair transparent electric dice included with each magnet.

We suggest purchasing batteries locally to save carrying charges and they are easily hooked up with our simple instructions. Also the use of a trickle charger is advisable for continual service. If you are unable to purchase these items locally we will supply them at cost.

No. 20G378.   Giant Magnet with carbon foot control and dice......Complete **$125.00**

Fig. 11. Today there are about two firms that manufacture electromagnetic crap tables, and you have to be a known cheater or an underworld figure to purchase such equipment.

numbers desired, batteries placed in any convenient location below or away from the showcase . . . $40.00.

The Super Dynamic Magnet Outfit. Designed and built by one of the country's leading electrical engineers . . . so powerful that a transparent die placed over the plate can be turned over by pressing the control. In play, the action is so natural that it is IMPOSSIBLE TO DETECT whether the current is on or off . . . is controlled with our absolutely SILENT, fire-proof and trouble-proof FOOT CONTROL. These magnets have sold as high as $1500.00 . . . complete with attractive carrying case . . . $150.00.

A popular number is the Electro Money Drawer which is:

. . . designed to meet the needs of the operator of table games. A compact unit attached to any table, magnet being controlled with pressure on the false front of the drawer . . . $45.00.

Prices today on the above and the following magnetic outfits have doubled about twenty-fold. Another example of protective coloring camouflage is the:

Show Case magnet made in the form of a humidor to be hung in the showcase above the cigars and just below the glass counter top. Not a toy or experiment, but a thoroughly practical outfit and one that will give unlimited service.

Opaque electric dice are priced at $1 per pair, transparent loads

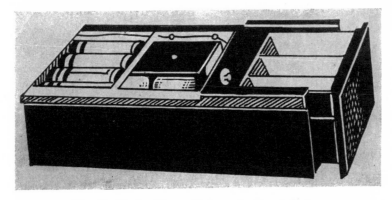

*Fig. 12. Electro Money Drawer showing batteries
and magnetic plate concealed in rear of drawer.*

which are harder to gaff at $10. Electric Chuck-a-Luck cages complete
with dice and magnet cost $100.

THE ROBOT CRAP SHOOTER

One of the cleverest and least known dice gaffs was the one employed not so long ago in a southern resort town by the operator of a
cigar store which was frequented during the racing season by some of
the biggest gamblers in the country. On the counter stood a mechanical
slot machine of the type in which when a penny or nickle is dropped in
five dice, under glass, are whirled around by a turntable.

The operator of this machine had removed all but two dice and
had what amounted to a robot crap shooter. "Nobody," he would re-
mark, "can use the blanket roll or whip shot in this game." He would
shoot with the gamblers for cigars at first and then as they became
interested for real dough. The mechanical gadget became so popular
that at one session some twenty big shot gamblers were gathered at his
counter taking the odds and betting as high as $500 on the point.

Eventually, however, some of them began to notice that the cigar
store owner's luck was what is known as phenomenal. One man clocked
him at winning at least fifty grand during one racing season with his
penny-in-the-slot machine. But mechanical method throwing with the
dice securely under glass where no one could touch them seemed to rule
out all the usual methods of cheating and the gamblers scowled, figured
that maybe it was luck after all, and continued to play.

One day, however, one of them who had lost heavily and altogether too consistently turned to the operator and asked, "How much did you pay for that gadget?"

"A hundred bucks," was the reply. "Why?"

The gambler threw a C-note on the counter. "Okay," he said. "I'm buying it." With which he lifted it off the counter and walked out.

When he took it apart, he discovered batteries and an electro-magnet beneath the turntable that whirled the dice. He found that a screwhead on the bottom edge of the box was a phony and acted as a pushbutton. When the operator dropped a coin in the slot with one hand, his other, resting over the screwhead, applied the squeeze. When the juice was on, one cube always showed either a deuce or five and the other either a trey or four. The operator couldn't miss because he couldn't make a seven but had to make one of the points 5, 6, 8 or 9. And the action was undetectable even by gamblers who could spot the

SHOW CASE MAGNET

T HIS outfit differs from our Counter Magnet in that it is specially designed for use in a glass show case. The magnet coil is made in the form of a humidor to be hung in the show case one inch below the glass and controls a magnetic field of 24 square inches directly in the center of the glass permitting the use of the usual dice mat, either rubber or wood. Not a toy nor experiment, but a thoroughly practical outfit and one that will give unlimited service.

The outfit consists of one humidor coil, 16 dry cells, one floor push or squeeze together with sufficient connecting wire, and five white electric dice made to come any top and bottom numbers desired. Instructions for installing with each outfit and the outfit can be installed complete in a few minutes' time, batteries being placed in any convenient location below or away from show case. Weight complete boxed for shipment 55 pounds.

No. 20G401.   Show Case Magnet complete with 5 dice.................Each $45.00

Fig. 13. Magnet for use in glass show case, built to resemble a humidor.

usual electric dice because the rotary motion covered any unusual ac-tion of the dice which came to a rest before the disk stopped spinning.

The gambler who bought the machine returned it, demanded and got back the money he had lost plus a percentage of the other players' losses and declared himself in as a partner. How much money they won as a team is unknown.

HOW TO TEST FOR ELECTRIC DICE

There isn't any safe method. It can be done very simply by apply-ing a magnet, but there's no point in testing for electric dice in a reputable house, and if you try it in a crooked one, you'll meet the house bouncer but quick and will find yourself sitting in an alley outside, wishing that an ambulance would come along, and still not knowing for sure if the dice were electric or not. If you ever suspect electric dice are being used, your best protection is to take a quick look around for the nearest exit and use it.

Trying to test the table with a piece of steel won't get you anywhere either because the juice is not on continuously. So as to conserve batteries and prevent their going dead while the chump still has folding

---

DICEMAKERS SUPPLIES

No. 213.	Liquid Celluloid Cement	Per Bottle $ .50
No. 214.	Celluloid paint for spots, white, black, red or blue	Per Bottle .50
No. 215.	Straight drills for boring a straight hole in dice	Each .50
No. 216.	Burr drills for hollowing out	Each .50
No. 217.	Quicksilver	Per Ounce 1.00
No. 218.	Polish soap to restore finish	Per Cake .50
No. 219.	Dice Cleaner and Polisher, paste form	Per Jar 1.00
No. 220.	Heel Bark for quick spotting, white, black, red or blue	Per Piece .50
No. 221.	Spotting drills for concave spots, any size	Each 1.00
No. 222.	Spotting drills for birdseye spots, any size	Each 1.00
No. 223.	Spotting drills for double ring birdseye spots, any size	Each 2.50
No. 224.	Special dice jigs for spotting perfect, any size	Each 5.00
No. 225.	Celluloid plugging rope for plugging, white	Per Piece .50
No. 226.	Copper Amalgam for transparent dice	Per Box 1.50
No. 227.	Concave gold slugs for ⅝ size	Each 1.50
No. 228.	Concave platinum slugs for ⅝ size	Each 2.50
No. 229.	Dicemaker's vise, handles all sizes of dice	Each 3.50
No. 230.	Dicemaker's hand drill, handles all sizes dice drills	Each 2.50
No. 231.	Dicemaker's guide for hollowing out (3 examples)	Per Set 2.25
No. 232.	Dicemaker's sand paper, for roughing and finishing, coarse or fine	Per Sheet .25
No. 233.	Dicemaker's glass finishing paper	Per Sheet .25

From the above you may select a complete dicemaker's outfit, getting only those articles actually needed. Equip yourself for any occasion for much less than you would pay elsewhere for a complete Dicemaker's Outfit.

Fig. 14. The supply house furnishes the cheat who is handy with tools all the equipment for making his own crooked dice. Such equipment is now hard to get by cheats.

money in his pants, the juice is put on just before the roll and switched off afterward.

13

Crooked Dice:
Outside Work

A great number of today's dice players are more or less acquainted with some of the facts concerning loaded dice, but their knowledge of the many and varied other methods of gaffing the Memphis dominoes is very sketchy and gives them little protection.

SHAPES

SHAPES are the most common of all P.C. dice, more so even than loads. Any die that is not a perfect cube will not act according to the correct odds and is a shape. After Newton doped out the law of gravitation and dice players began to admit that the fall of the dice is controlled by gravity rather than by the psychic manipulations of some deity, they also realized that lopsided dice would, therefore, tend to settle down most often on their larger surfaces. Ever since then, some dice have been made with unequal sides accidentally on purpose.

SHAPES, BRICKS OR FLATS

These are shaped cubes that have been shaved down on one or more sides so that they are slightly brick-shaped. The amount taken off runs from a light 5/1000 of an inch, to a strong 40/1000, or more, depending on what the cheat thinks he can get away with. If the other players are babes in the wood who can't recognize a strong shape when they see it, that's what goes in. The faster the company the cheat plays in, the weaker the shape. A few thousandths of an inch may not sound like much but there are thousands of users who can testify that it is enough to put a profitable crimp in the odds.

Six-Ace Flats are by far the commonest variety. A few thousandths of an inch are shaved off either the six or ace sides. Since the six and ace sides are still square and all the other sides are rectangles with a slightly smaller area, the dice land and stay more often on the six and ace sides. The dice tend to bring up more sevens and craps than square cubes would and are therefore, *Missouts.**

Fig. 1. Six-Ace Flats.

Another reason for the popularity of Flats is the fact that, being easier to make than loads, they are much less expensive, five bucks a pair being an average price.†

---

* *Passing* shapes can also be made by manicuring one die on the Ace-6 side, the other on the Trey-4 thus favoring the points, 4, 5, 9 and 10. Or the 2-5 on one die can be shaved and the 3-4 on the other to favor 5, 6, 8 and 9.

Shaped missouts are, however, far more common than shaped passers because they are twice as strong. The 6-Ace on one die combines in two ways with the 6-Ace on the other to form 7, but the numbers 2-5 and 3-4 can only combine one way to make any of the favored points, 5, 6, 8 or 9.

† Prices vary considerably because the dice dealer's prices rise in direct proportion to the innocence of the buyer. Five bucks is the price he'd charge a regular customer who knows his way around, but the guy who is buying his first set of crooked dice will be charged whatever the dealer thinks he will pay.

TWO-WAY FLATS are shapes that have been shaved down on two different sides. When a few thousandths of an inch is taken off the six and three sides, for instance, the six-ace and three-four sides are rectangles having a greater area than the two-five sides. The numbers 6, 1, 3 and 4 will appear oftener and when both dice are cut down in the same way, these numbers will combine to form more sevens than would normally appear. They are, therefore, missouts, and cheaters call them *Fast Sevens* or *Four-Way Sevens*. The six-ace and two-five sides, or the three-four and two-five sides, when cut down, act the same.

One of the most interesting things about crooked gamblers is that they aren't choosey about their victims. They will go up against and try to take another gambler just as readily as they will a sucker, provided they can figure an angle that will turn the trick. Plenty of angles have been figured to do just that. For every cheating method aimed at trimming the chumps there is also a doublecross carefully designed to clip the cheat who's using it.

THE CROSS ON SHAPES, for instance, goes like this: Suppose some Joe Blow is using a pair of Six-Ace flats in a payday game. He's betting the dice don't pass and raking in a nice steady profit. Then an old-timer deals himself in, rumbles Joe's gaff, grins without letting it show, and places a few wrong bets. But, before long, he switches over and starts betting that they pass. What's more, he wins. His luck is so hot that it overcomes the percentage Joe's Six-Ace flats are supposed to grind out. Or that's what Joe thinks.

What Joe doesn't know is just exactly what hurts him. The old-timer has copped one of the Six-Ace flats and replaced it with his Trey-4. Joe's cubes were Missouts favoring the seven, but now, without any warning at all, they've suddenly changed to Passers that favor the points 4, 5, 9 and 10. When a crooked die is switched for one of a pair of Missouts, changing it to a passing combination or vice versa, it is said to *split up* the combination and is known as a *splitter*.

When Joe finally discovers what went wrong, as he will some day when he learns more about his racket, he will realize that anyone who tries to cheat with a pair of boomerangs must learn to duck fast.

How to Detect Shapes

The best way is to measure the thickness of the dice with a micrometer caliper which you probably don't have. The next best method is to place the two cubes side by side on a flat surface. Hold one die stationary and turn the other into all possible positions, running your thumb back and forth over the top surfaces of both dice each time. When the shaved surface of one die is on the side and the shaved surface of the second is on top the first die will be taller than the second. Your thumb can detect the difference and when it does, that is your cue to start punching.

BEVELS

Instead of being flat, one or more sides of these dice are convex so that the die tends to roll off the rounded surface and come to a stop on one of its flat sides. The die is beveled by rubbing it on a concave sandpaper block.

BEVELED SHAPES. Shapes which are also beveled are known as *beveled shapes*. Most shapes, in fact, are classed as two-way work because each gaff is usually used in conjunction with some other one. Loads, for instance, are often beveled because it helps make their action more positive.

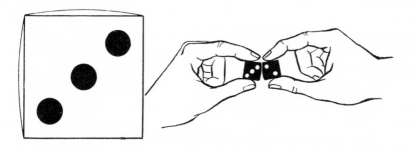

Fig. 2. A beveled die and the wobble test for bevels.

How to Detect Bevels

Use the "Wobble Test." Hold a die in each hand and rub two sides together, trying different sides. When a beveled surface is rubbed against a flat surface or against another bevel, the two dice slip easily against each other and will wobble or rock back and forth.

SUCTION DICE

These have a concave surface which, on a smooth hard surface, tend to stick because a slight vacuum is created. The die is also more likely to remain on the concave side when used on a rough or bumpy surface which would tend to cause a flat sided die to continue rolling. This work is very weak.

BEVELED SUCTION SHAPES. Here the concave surface is combined with a bevel. The die is placed in a vise between two slightly convex plates and squeezed. This is a three-way gaff. The pressure flattens the die giving the two pressed sides a greater area; it makes the pressed sides slightly concave; and it raises a bevel on the other four sides. This die is not square and none of the sides are flat.

On a smooth hard surface the concave sides tend to stick because a slight vacuum is created. Used alone the percentage this would supply would be slight but with the bevel and flat also favoring the same two sides, the P. C. gained is exceptionally strong.

How to Detect Suction Shapes

Apply the wobble test for bevels and look for the two concave sides.

CAPPED DICE

About fifteen thousandths of an inch is shaved off one or more sides of a blank die before the holes are drilled. Then the missing portion is replaced by a sheet of composition that matches the die in every respect except elasticity. The join is invisible and the extra resiliency of the gaffed side or sides tend to make the dice bounce off those sides. This work must be replaced often as it wears out fast and heat often loosens the capping so that the join becomes noticeable.

How to Detect Capped Dice

Press your fingernail or any sharp instrument (a pin or nail) against the surface. The resiliency of the capping can be felt.

And test for loads too. The dealers' advertising copy says:

> Where an extra strong transparent missout set is required we can suggest nothing better than our Capped and Filled Missouts. These are filled with platinum, making them equal to the fastest white dice. For head and head play or pocket use these dice are without equal, stand the very closest inspection and get by in fast company. Made in any color. $50.00 per pair.

Fig. 3. A Capped Die.

The copywriter is being optimistic again. Neither loads nor capping get by in any fast company that deserves the name.

LIQUID CAPPING. For the amateur hustler only. He buys a bottle of liquid or paste which, applied to fair dice, is supposed to give the same effect as capping. It's not worth the $1 he pays. It wears off very quickly and, when warmed up in play by the heat of the player's hands, becomes slightly sticky and picks up dirt.

How to Detect Liquid Capping

Hold the dice in the cupped hands and blow on them. Thus heated and then pressed firmly together the cubes will stick to each other. Rubbing them together sometimes makes the capping peel off.

SLICK DICE

This variety are both square and flat, but some sides are given an extra polishing so that they have a high slippery finish.* The other sides are buffed or roughened. The idea here is that when the dice hit on the smooth sides they will tend to slide to a stop. The advantage player who uses these isn't getting any great amount of P. C. in his favor, but he is playing it safe as far as detection is concerned. Since some sides of ordinary dice get roughened up more than others during normal play, the suspicious player can't be sure that the dice in the game are that way accidentally or on purpose.

---

* Supply houses also sell a powder which, applied to certain sides, gives them a slick "Simoniz" finish.

TRIP DICE

Bevels and shapes are hocussed on their surfaces. Trip dice are gaffed along their edges by various methods known as *Edge Work*. The work is not strong, and, as the manufacturers say, "the operator must continually replace their dice because the life of this type of work is very limited and after a few hours the work is worn down until it is no longer effective."

Just the same, any crap player who wagers money on the game should know that there are such things as Trip Dice because it's the gaff that he doesn't know about that the cheat will use. Whatever disadvantages certain work may have, if we omit mention of it those disadvantages are immediately offset by the fact that it becomes one method the victims aren't hep to and the one, therefore, which may get by.

RAZOR-EDGE WORK

Fair dice are made with several different types of edges. A *razor-edge* die has perfectly square and sharp edges and corners. A *diamond-edge* die has all edges very slightly turned. A third type of edge is known as *slightly turned*, and a fourth, *heavy turned*. A *Light Texas Corner* die has turned edges and a rounded corner. A *Heavy Texas Corner* die has very heavily turned edges and a heavily rounded corner.*

When *all* edges are turned and all corners rounded in the same way the dice are fair. But the cheat sometimes has his dicemaker take a pair of razor edges and turn some of the corners leaving the others sharp so that the dice tend to continue rolling when they hit on a rounded edge and hold when they hit on a sharp edge.

How to Detect Razor-Edge Work

Look or feel with your thumb and make sure that the edges and corners are either all sharp or all turned the same amount. If not they are crooked.

RAISED-EDGE WORK

The dicemaker applies a flatiron to any two opposite sides of the die. The heat raises the edges as shown in Fig. 4 and, having a slightly

---

* Most loads, bevels, flats, suction and capped dice have slightly turned edges and light rounded corners. Razor edges would cut down the strength of the gaff.

greater area on those sides, the die will tend to remain on those sides as a Shape does. The raised edges will also cling when the dice are rolled on a cloth surface.

Fig. 4. Raised Edge Work. All gaffs shown in diagrams are exaggerated.

CUT-EDGE WORK

A cut along the edge of the die at a 60 degree angle causes it, when balanced on edge, to tend to fall in the direction of the cut. Two opposite sides, the Ace-6 for instance, cut on all four edges are slightly pyramidal in shape. Because the remaining four edges of the die would attract attention if left square, they are also cut, but at a 45 degree angle.

How to Detect Cut Edges

See if the angle of the cut on the edge is the same on all edges. If it appears to be a 45 degree angle on some edges and a 60 degree angle

Fig. 5. Cut Edges. Edge indicated by short arrow is cut at
60 degree angle. Long arrow points to 45 degree cut edge

on others the die is crooked. This difference can also be detected by placing the two dice together and running the fingernail over the line left where they join. If the V-shaped crevice that can be felt varies more than others on some sides, it is a V for victory but not yours.

RAISED-SPOT WORK

The catalogs list a number of kinds of work that no cheat who knows his dice ever uses, cubes calculated to appeal to the sucker trade —the amateur or beginning cheat who isn't yet hep to the fact that gambling supply catalogs are even more prone to exaggerate than seed catalogs. Raised spot work falls in this class. The principle is that any slight protuberance on the side of the die will tend to help it roll off that side. In manufacturing, the burr left around the edges of the spots when they are drilled is not polished off. The cheat who knows his way around doesn't use them because of the many far better gaffs and because even the softest mark is likely to feel the raised spot and object.

SPLIT-EDGE AND SAW-TOOTH EDGE WORK

The edges of some sides of the die are serrated with minute cuts on the theory that this will tend to retard the roll when used on a blanket or baize surface. This also classes as sucker work. The supply houses charge $20, but one of the best dicemakers in the business says: "They aren't worth thirty cents."

HEAVY-PAINT WORK

A mild form of loading in which the spots on some sides are filled with a heavy zinc paint.

How to Detect Heavy-Paint Work

So that more paint can be applied, the dice usually have larger spots than they should, the 9/16 inch dice bearing spots of the size normally found on a 5/8 inch die. As with all loads, rounded corners work best. The Pivot or Water test should show that they are loaded. If not, they are too light and won't supply enough percentage to do the cheat any good.

THE PIN GAFF

Another sucker variety, once used but now outmoded. A pin point was embedded in the center spot of the five, its sharp point just flush with the surface of the die. On a baize or blanket surface the point would tend to catch and retard the roll. This work was originally called BRISTLES because pig bristles were used as the gaff.

The methods of making square dice crooked can be combined in a variety of ways. You can have capped fills, capped shapes, capped edge work, razor-edge convexes, beveled shapes, and even that very crooked variety, beveled suction shapes.

And for the dice cheat who is a handy man with tools and wants to "roll his own" the supply house will sell him hand-squared perfect *blanks* (unspotted dice) at 50¢ each as well as the necessary dicemaker's equipment (see page 233).

ROLLERS OR BALL-CORNERED DICE

These are not crooked unless they are doctored in other ways. They are used in some private games because they have the advantage of longer wear than sharp-cornered dice. They are not used by fast company for the reason that they are too easy to control on hard surfaces with the Whip Shot.

If you use sharp-cornered dice as a protection against shapes, remember that they must be replaced regularly because the sharp square edge develops irregularities with use. Any unevenness introduces a percentage favoring one or more sides more than another. Dice that are used too long automatically tend to become P.C. dice in time, and badly manufactured cheap dice are often far enough off to count as shapes when purchased! Moral: Don't use old dice or cheap ones. The odds to which they conform may not be the same as the ones you use when you lay your bets.

Percentage dice are more prevalent than any other kind because little or no sleight of hand is required. The dice cheat can introduce them by various dodges such as exchanging them between games or putting them in just before the game starts and he does not need to switch them out.

The cheat who wants quick action, however, doesn't care for them. Since they operate on percentage, they require time to pay off and the danger is always present that some very lucky chump who managed to bet the right way at the right time over a short period may pull out with his winnings and not give Old Man Percentage an opportunity to even things up in the sharp's favor. The sure-thing boys don't like to play in games of chance that have such a high content of unpredictability. They want to separate the sucker from his folding money with speed, precision, and efficiency.

There's a method of doing that as well, provided the cheat is willing to invest the necessary time in mastering a good clean switch. When he has done that, he forgets P.C. dice and orders a sure-thing variety of crooked work that is as sudden and deadly as a double shot of potassium cyanide.

TOPS AND BOTTOMS

These, also known as *Tops, T's* or *Mis-Spots*, are tops in phony dice. Fifty years and more ago they were called *Dispatchers* for the reason that they sent the mark to the cleaners with dispatch.

These cubes don't bring up some numbers some of the time; they bring up the right numbers at exactly the right time. The action is 100 percent positive and the victim's chance of winning is exactly zero.

Tops are based upon the general principle that players can't see

Fig. 6. Tops and Bottoms as viewed in a mirror.

around corners. If they could see more than three sides of a cube at once, they would notice instantly that Tops not only do not come close to adding to seven on opposite sides, but that some numbers are missing entirely, and others appear twice. Tops usually bear only three different numbers, each one being repeated on the cube's opposite side. (See Fig. 6.) The players on opposite sides of a crap circle see the same numbers when a Top is on the floor between them, but since no one individual can be in two places at once, none of them ever know it.

Amateur cheats, however, don't use those sure-fire cubes because, dangerous as they are to the sucker, they are also loaded with danger for the sharp whose sleight-of-hand isn't top-notch. Although the mis-spotting passes unnoticed during the action of the roll, if the chump ever gets his mitts on a pair of Tops and gives them a once-over lightly, he rumbles the gaff immediately. Consequently, Tops must be switched in and out at a split second's notice, with speed and with smooth, unde-tectable sleight-of-hand. The switch artist who has mastered that never worries about a personal unemployment problem. The mob he signs up with can throw their P.C. dice out the window and depend on Tops to corral all the folding money in sight in practically nothing flat and with 100% efficiency.

If the switch man is good, the chance the sucker has of tagging the cubes for what they are is exceedingly slim. Even the fast-company boys can come a cropper when the T's start rolling! A dice mob can sense a suspicious player with all the celerity of a lie detector. And when he grabs for and examines the dice, the chances are a thousand to one that he'll pick up fair dice. The Tops go in when he's confident that the game is on the level and is absorbed in the betting and the excitement of the game. When you look for them, they're not there; when you don't, they are.

BUSTERS

Tops come in assorted combinations calculated to meet any craps situation. Blitz dice would be a good name for them because their vic-tims are left with the feeling that a steam roller and a couple of General Sherman tanks just rumbled over them. But the gamblers' term, *Busters*, is equally descriptive because that's exactly what happens to the guy who gets in their way—he's busted. If you should ever find yourself in a steer joint and hear someone ask, "Where's Buster Brown?" you'll know that somebody's baby is going to get new shoes—but it won't be yours.

That query is the signal for the *bust-out-man* to *bust in** with Tops that will bust your chance of winning and leave it looking like a punctured soap bubble.

The method of using busters varies with the game being played. In Bank or Private Craps the mechanic uses a pair of Tops so mis-spotted that they make point after point but no seven. Both dice bear three numbers only, each being duplicated on the die's opposite side. Dice mis-spotted in this way will throw only 9 of the usual 36 combinations. There are numerous combinations, a pair bearing the numbers 1, 3 and 5 on each die for instance can only make the combinations 1–1, 1–3, 1–5, 3–1, 3–3, 3–5, 5–1, 5–3 and 5–5 forming the points 2, 4, 6, 8 and 10. The shooter, consequently can't possibly throw a 7 and must pass. Tops that pass are known as *hits*.†

If the dice mechanic is working single-o, he busts in with the hits when he is the shooter. But if you suspect Tops are being used, the shooter is not the only guy you should keep an eye on. When the mechanic has a partner, he busts in both ways—when he is shooting and from the outside when his pal is shooting. The latter throws the dice toward the bust-out man who picks them up, and busts in with the Tops. He repeats the action again later when the shooter wants to have the Tops *ripped* (switched) out.

The shooter uses the Tops for one or more passes, rakes in the dough, then goes back to fair dice and either continues shooting or passes the dice to the next player. The number of passes he makes before ripping the Tops out depends on the action of the players, how well-heeled they are, and the number of passes they'll stand for before scowling suspiciously.

MISSES are Tops that are made to miss the point. When one die bears only the numbers 1-3-5 and the other only 2-4-6, the only combinations possible are odd numbers. Whenever the shooter is trying for

---

* Don't say that someone busted in with a pair of flats or loads, however. Those are always *switched* in. The terms *bust in* and *bust out* apply only to switching Tops.

† Other common passing combinations and the numbers they make are:
  1-2-3 and 1-2-3 which make 2, 3, 4, 5, 6.
  1-3-5 and 1-3-5 which made 2, 4, 6, 8, 10.
  2-3-6 and 2-3-6 which make 4, 5, 6, 8, 9, 12.
  2-4-6 and 2-4-6 which make 4, 6, 8, 10, 12.
  1-4-5 and 1-4-5 which make 2, 5, 6, 8, 9, 10.
  3-4-5 and 1-5-6 which make 4, 5, 6, 8, 9, 10, 11.
  3-5-6 and 3-5-6 which make 6, 8, 9, 10, 11, 12.

Many top cheaters claim that a 2-3-6 pair of Tops are the best as passers because they throw all the points except 10, make fewer hard-way combinations, and consequently arouse less suspicion. Others favor the 2-4-6 combination because the even point numbers 4, 6, 8 and 10 can easily be broken up with a 1-3-5 2-4-6 set of misses which make only odd numbers.

one of the even point numbers (4, 6, 8, 10) with this set of misses, it is impossible for him to throw his point and he must seven out. And when his point is either 5 or 9, a set of 1-4-5 2-3-6 misses makes it impossible for him to throw the point.

Misses are not usually used in private games because the shooter has no legitimate reason to pick the dice up again after he sevens out and thus has no chance to get the Tops out of the game. An exception is when the private or Army game has a cutter who may bust them in and out, because like a house stickman he has the privilege of picking up the dice and throwing them to the next player.

In house games the stickman who rakes in the cubes with the dice stick after the roll and tosses them back was originally introduced into the game as a protection against the switching in of phony dice by the players. But in a steer-joint the stickman himself is usually the bust-out man who does the dirty work. These boys use several different pairs of Tops, both hits and misses, in a manner that gets the money with all the neatness and dispatch of a high class *cannon* (pickpocket) mob or a *heist* (hold-up) mob.

Bust-out men all have their favorite methods of ripping Tops in and out as well as their favorite Top combinations. Some dislike to work with the stick, claiming that it slows them up, others can't work without the stick and others prefer to work from the outside, acting as one of the players. Some use four pair of Tops; others, because it is faster, safer and mistakes are less likely to be made, use only two. In Open or Fading Craps three are most often used—two pair of hits and a pair of misses.

In the steer-joint the mechanics of the operation of clipping the chump go something like this.* The steerer phones in to say he is bringing a sucker—a big oilman. The boys clear the decks for action and the moment the doorbell rings the game suddenly starts rolling full bloom. The book is behind the bankroll, the stickman behind the stick, the shills betting the money with which they have been supplied, and the bosses with the big dough, acting as players, are doing the same. A little room is left between two bosses so that the mark walks into that position.

The dice in the game at the start are all levels. But as soon as the mark starts to bet and the bosses discover whether he is a right or wrong bettor, the office is given and the Tops go in—misses if the chump makes a right bet, hits if he makes a wrong bet. The mark finds that he

---

* Other details of steer-joint operation are to be found in the chapter on *Gamblers, Hustlers and Cheats*, page 207.

can get all the action he wants and then some. The mob always tries to increase the victim's bets as much as possible, figuring that the larger his bets the faster he gets clipped, the fewer moves the bust-out man has to make, and the less chance the mark has of detecting the dirty work. Time is also important; another steerer may be on his way with another monkey.

Suppose the mark is a wrong bettor and has laid $200 to $100 on the 4 which is the shooter's point. The stickman gets the office and pulls the dice in with his stick. As he draws it back, his right hand comes back close to his body and directly over his coat pocket. This pocket has had a specially designed tailoring job, having been built up on the inside so that it is much shallower than usual and divided by partitions so that the pairs of hits and misses are each contained in separate sections. The stickman's fingers dip in and come out with the 1-3-5 2-4-6 misses which do not add up to 4, 6, 8 or 10 any way you look at them.

The chump never glimpses the move because it is covered by the body of the shill who stands close beside the stickman. Sometimes, too, it is the shill's pockets which have been rebuilt, which contain the Tops and into which the stickman's fingers dip. The advantage here is that, in case of a blow, the shill walks off and the stickman can stand for a search. An even smarter method and the one most popular with bust-out men today not only eliminates the necessity for going into the pocket entirely, but makes the whole move quicker and easier. The stickman's hand goes back between his body and that of the shill and, during the second when the end of the stick is out of sight, the shill simply places the proper pair of Tops in the bust-out man's hand.

Once he has the Ts palmed in his right hand, the stickman takes the stick with his left, picks the fair dice up from the table and throws them to the player. Or that is what he seems to do. Actually the Tops are thrown out and the fair dice retained, palmed in the right hand which again takes the stick. (For description, see page 277.)

The dice roll out, the shooter sevens and the chump loses his bet. The stickman pulls the dice in, rips the levels in again, and then moves his hand back for an instant and drops the Tops into the hand that the shill at his side holds ready and waiting.

The bust-out man's job is a nerve wracking one that requires the utmost in timing, speed and smooth precision. His life is no bed of roses at any time. When there are two suckers in the joint, one a right and the other a wrong bettor, he faces a situation he never enjoys. The mark who is a wrong bettor, for instance, has just laid $100 on the 4 and the stickman has ripped in with a pair of deuce-tray-sixes so that the 4 must be made. If the other mark wants to take the odds, the bosses pretend they don't hear him. But that stratagem doesn't always work. The right bettor may go to the book and may even take the limit, say $600 to $300.

The moment this happens those hits on the table are a liability. When the shooter passes, the book will lose five hundred bucks more to the right bettor than the boss picks up from the wrong bettor. But that can't happen here—not in a steer-joint. The bust-out man may have switched the hits in only a moment ago, but suddenly he gets the office to rip in a pair of misses. He has to have them ready and waiting and must bust in on the next roll without fail. Otherwise he's out of a job.

And, if the Tops are still in play, when a player calls for a box-up the stickman must do some more fast smooth work. He has to pick up the Tops, switch them for levels as he throws them into the bowl with the other perfect dice and then spill them all out for a selection. And if he gets the office to put the Tops back again on the come-out roll, when the player throws him the good dice the stickman must again make the switch as he throws them back. Good bust-out men die young; it's hard on the nervous system.

And so it goes. Whenever the majority of the money bet by the chumps is right money, the misses go in and the dice lose; when most of the suckers are betting wrong, the hits go in and the dice win. But whether the dice win or lose, the chump gets clipped both ways and the steer-joint boys simply can't lose. With a good bust-out man behind the stick, the fattest mark can be broken in almost no time at all. After a few losses he tends to make bigger bets trying to get his losses back and he's flat before he knows it. Sometimes the boys break him on one roll.

How do you tell a steer-joint from a game that is on the up and up? Well, if smart gamblers frequent the place and if the game has been operating for several months or longer, it's no steer-joint; those boys don't stick in one spot that long. If the game is a new one, if a stranger brought you there, if there aren't many players around the table and if most of the action is directed your way—then you're in for it. And don't think you aren't. If you think you spot a move and want to object, don't get noisy about it but call the manager and try quietly to get your money back. If you make a fuss that will tip off any other suckers that may be around, you'll get your ears pinned back pronto. The steer-joint boys don't fool.

PERCENTAGE TOPS AND BOTTOMS

Percentage Tops and Bottoms, also known as *One-Way Tops and Bottoms, Double Fives,* or *Double Deuces,* are the newest innovation in mis-spots. Only one of the six numbers on a die is duplicated on the opposite side, usually the deuce or five. A die with two deuces is called a *Double Deuce* by dice cheaters; a die with two fives is a *Double Five.*

A pair of dice may have both cubes mis-spotted, or it may be composed of one mis-spot and one square die. Double Deuces are used together, Double Fives together, and either a Double Deuce or a Double Five may be used with a square die. A pair of Double Deuces will not throw an eleven; two Double Fives will not throw a three. When a square die is used with a Double Deuce or a Double Five all eleven numbers can be made, a fact which makes them difficult to detect in action. A One-Way Top was recently switched into a Reno casino and remained in action for several hours before the dice table personnel got wise.

Here is a comparison of the numbers that can be made and the ways in which they can be made with square dice and with the various One-Way Tops and Bottoms:

Numbers	2	3	4	5	6	7	8	9	10	11	12
Ways to make with											
2 square dice	1	2	3	4	5	6	5	4	3	2	1
1 Double Deuce and 1 square die	1	3	4	5	5	6	5	3	2	1	1
2 Double Deuces	1	4	6	6	5	4	5	2	2	0	1
1 Double Five and 1 square die	1	1	2	3	5	6	5	5	4	3	1
2 Double Fives	1	0	2	2	5	4	5	6	6	4	1

Percentage Tops and Bottoms work both as Passers and Missouts at the same time. Usually, two dice cheats work together; one bets the dice to lose, the other bets the dice to win.

A Double Deuce paired with a square die gives the right bettor in a private game an advantage of 20% on the point Four and 13-7/11% on the Point Five. The wrong bettor lays the odds on the point Nine and enjoys an edge of 16-2/3%; when he lays the odds on the point Ten he has an edge of 25%.

A Double Five paired with a square die gives the right bettor a favorable edge on the point Nine of 13-7/11% and on the point Ten an edge of 20%. The wrong bettor lays the odds on the point Four and has an edge of 25%; laying the odds on the point Five gives him an edge of 16-2/3%.

Two Double Deuces used together as a pair are much stronger. They are seldom used against smart crapshooters unless the cheat is a good dice mechanic capable of switching them in and out of the game. A pair of Double Deuces gives the right bettor in a private game an edge of 80% on the point Four, 50% on the point Five, and 22-2/9% on the point Six or Eight. The wrong bettor has an advantage of 16-2/3% on the point Nine. The point Ten supplies no advantage either way.

Two Double Fives used as a pair give the right bettor an 80% edge on the point Ten, 50% on the point Nine, and 22-2/9% on the points Six or Eight. The point Four has no percentage edge either way.

DOOR POPS

These are a very brazen brand of mis-spotted dice that show 7 or 11 every roll. Since the catalog lists them, there apparently are buyers, but they are strictly for use on very soft marks and then only on dark nights. One die bears only the numbers 6 and 2; the other nothing but 5's! Since anyone but a blind man would tag these cubes as mis-spots, the moment they rolled out, they are of no use except for night play under an overhead light when the chumps can't see anything but the top surfaces of the dice. Strictly for use by cheats who don't know what a real set of Tops is.

THE TAT

In the days before Craps when the common dice games depended upon high scores, Tops were made bearing the spots 4, 5 and 6 to throw nothing but high numbers and with the spots 1, 2 and 3 to throw only low numbers. They were known as *High and Low* dice and sometimes as *Tats*. The 4-5-6 die, still known by the same name although with a slightly simplified spelling, is still used by con-men in a game called *The Tat* or *Up and Down Broadway*.

Like *Three Card Monte* and the *Shell Game*, The Tat is not really a game at all but a swindle disguised as such. The scene of operations is usually a nightclub, cafe or bar in which the Tat mob consisting of two con men, begin by buying a round of drinks for a group of suckers and establish themselves as witty, amusing and somewhat tipsy fellows. One leaves a fair die where someone is likely to see it and, after it has been found, remembers an interesting game played with one die. Or, to make it all seem even more impromptu, the con man may remember the game first and then make a die by pencilling spots on a sugar cube.

Each player puts a dollar in the pot, throws three times, adds the numbers thrown, and the high man collects the money and buys the next round of drinks. It is not long before someone, one of the con men if necessary, suggests larger stakes to make it more interesting. The moment that happens the game does a quick change and becomes a swindle. One of the con men, on his throw, exchanges the fair die for a 4-5-6 Top, called by con men the Tat, and switches it out again after his throw. Since it bears only high numbers he has no difficulty in making high score.

After taking the chumps for as much as they will stand before becoming suspicious of this exceptional run of luck, something that depends upon how smart and how tight they are, the con man who has won departs. The other sticks around a few minutes longer to throw oil on the troubled waters in case anyone tumbles to what has happened and suggests hollering copper.

KNOWLEDGE IS PROTECTION

At this point you are wondering if there is any simple, sure-fire, all-around method of making sure that the dice in the games are levels. I'm sorry, but the answer is: No. Your best protection is to have the information given in this chapter in your head. If you are smartened up to all the gaffs and angles, you will have reduced your chance of being cheated with crooked cubes to a minimum. Phony dice are seldom used in fast company where the players know all the angles. It's too dangerous. The sure-thing boys who don't like to take any chances at all won't take the chance of having their ears pinned back.

Another safeguard, of course, is never to play with any dice but your own. The advice is fair, but the method is impractical because if everyone followed that rule, the game would be solitaire.

Another rule that has whiskers but is still good, nevertheless, is: Don't play with strangers. In fact, don't play with anyone you wouldn't trust with your best girl. And remember that, no matter how friendly he tries to be, or how many mutual friends he says you have, any guy that you met yesterday or the day before is certainly a stranger.

The other old one that "you can't cheat an honest man" has a lot of truth in it, too. Don't team up with some recently acquired "friend" who wises you up to an angle for taking the rest of the boys to the cleaners. The chance is ten to one that he has an even closer friend in the game with whom he is really teamed up for the purpose of taking you.

The only absolutely certain way of never being cheated at Craps is not to play Craps. But if this rule proves a little too tough to follow, you should at least take a good close look at the cubes and make sure that:

1. The dice seven on all sides.

2. All sides are level and not concave, rounded, or with raised spots.

3. All sides are equally polished.

4. The edges and corners are all straight, square and preferably sharp rather than rounded. If rounded, see that all edges and corners are rounded equally.*

5. The spots are all countersunk the same distance and the paint on all spots is the same distance from the cube's surface. Better still use flush-spot dice, but examine them for loads.

6. The dice can pass the pivot or water test for loads.

7. And, whenever possible, use transparent dice.

You should also know where the dice came from and be sure that the guy who bought them didn't exchange them for others on the way from the store to the game. If you can't trust him not to refrain from doing that, you will save money if you look up another game.

If the dice meet the above requirements and if you place your bets according to the correct odds, you have a fair chance of winning. Your only worry, as far as being cheated is concerned, is the mechanic who may switch in dice that don't pass the above tests and the expert whose trained fingers can make even fair dice misbehave with his controlled rolls.

The dice cheat's crooked sleight-of-hand with tips as to how to recognize it when you meet it is the subject of our next chapter.

---

* Fair dice with rounded edges are used in many private games because square edge dice, although they minimize the chance of crooked work, do wear down quickly and have to be replaced oftener. If the dice do have rounded edges, they should *all* be rounded and all in the same manner.

14

Crooks at Work:
Moves

Can fair dice really be controlled or are the rumors to that effect myths? I have been asked this question hundreds of times both during my lectures to servicemen and by gamblers, writers and curious laymen. The answer is: Yes, they certainly can.

The cheat knows very well how difficult it is to put the finger on the man who can make fair dice behave by sleight-of-hand methods. The dice mechanic who uses phony dice may get his ears pinned back if he is rumbled, but the worst that can happen to the dice shark who uses controlled shots is that he gets told to scram. There is no good way of proving for sure whether he really was controlling the cubes or was only trying to look smart by making an unusual or fancy throw.

When he is down to his last few bucks and sees all those $25 and $100 valued chips stacked so high in front of the craps dealer that they touch his chin, there isn't a gambler who hasn't wished that he could make the dice sit up and do tricks. Some of them, consequently, have spent years practicing the art of sharking dice and trying to make that wish come true. They know that the ability to control fair dice may not only enable them to clean up in the private game but beat the house and the smart professional gamblers who carry the big dough as well.

CLIPPING THE SMART BOYS

Prior to the legalization of casino gambling in Nevada, when most tables had not yet been outfitted with sponge rubber side rails, a Greek gambler was clocked as winning at least a million clipping the smart boys with what has since become known as the Greek shot. The measures that casinos have since taken to protect themselves—the throw against the backboard, the sponge rubber rail, the ruling that the players must catch the dice when thrown to them by the stickman and the use of flush-spot dice—all prove that workable and efficient controlled shots do exist. Nevada bank craps tables that do not make use of a string stretched across the center have, in my opinion, been victimized by control shots at one time or another.

Other dice sharks became proficient in making the babies talk on dirt where most games were played and, for that matter, still are. I know one shark who, after softening up an area of dirt a foot square, can stand fifteen feet away, call, "Two sixes!" and throw the dice. They not only land on that square foot, they also show two sixes. This was called the Drop Shot (the shark used to say "when they drop, I col-lect") in the South, the Peekay shot in the Middle West, the Peek Shot in the East and is now usually known as the Whip Shot.

Some Whip Shot sharks specialized in clipping hustlers and the dice mechanics who use phony dice. Pretending to be greenies, they would take all the folding money the hustler would lay when he offered his sucker bet of 5 to 1 on the 4 the hard way. And out would come two deuces! Thousands of so called smart cheaters have wondered why they went to the cleaners when their loaded and shaped dice developed a curious streak of not working as advertised. Their answer is right here: the chump they thought they were going to clip was a dice shark playing dumb and giving them the business with the Whip Shot which can make loaded and P. C. dice do just exactly what they shouldn't do—with trimmings!

Controlled shots are so little known among average players that they have difficulty believing such things are possible even when they see them done. During my lectures whenever I call "Two aces!" and shoot a pair of dice across the table getting two aces, most of the on-lookers apparently think I'm just playing a lucky hunch. They always skeptically demand to see it again. When the same thing happens a second time, they grin and shake their heads, still none too sure that they believe it.

But suppose you have heard on good authority that there are such things as controlled shots. Trying to get some straight dope on odds and percentages is a snap compared to digging up enough information on the methods of the dice shark to enable you to recognize and protect yourself from the controlled shots. You can't walk up to a shark, even supposing you would recognize one when you saw him, and simply ask for the information. His reply, "What the hell are you talking about, buddy?" wouldn't be of much help. He's not going to talk shop with anyone who is chump enough to ask him to give out with information he came by the hard way concerning a shot he has spent years in perfecting and much of whose value consists in its secrecy. He probably had the devil's own time finding out about it himself. He may even have had to pay some old timer a C-note or more for the low-down.

But don't think that *you* can locate a retired dice shark and buy the dope on a few shots for a few hundred bucks. In the first place he may only know one. In the second place he would have to know you about as intimately as his best girl before he'd do business. And even then the chances are that he'd give you the business by holding back the one little but important factor that is the real secret of the trick. The traffic in dice-shark secrets is full of such little snags.

LEARNING THE HARD WAY

Of course, you can send five bucks to the gambling supply houses for the instructions on controlling fair dice which they advertise as having once sold for $40 to $100. But before you do that, read the catalog description given here and then let me give you a preview of what your five dollars will get you.

Can you Control Fair Dice? If not these instructions teach you. How to Control Fair Dice is a complete expose of practically every method in use today by dice manipulators and explains various ways of obtaining results without the use of Loaded or Filled dice. It is not necessary to change dice in a game after you become proficient with any one of the methods described.

The following well known professional secrets are illustrated and described in detail: Pique or Peekay Shot, The Hudson Stack, Hitting the Cushion with one or two dice, The Soft Pad Roll, The Dump Over Shot,

The Marine-Twist or Spin Shot, The Stable Boy's Favorite, Dice Box Holdout for First Flop, Twenty-Six, Indian, etc.

This information has been gathered from all parts of the country and while no one person can expect to be proficient in all methods described, a few hours' practice and mastery of any one will keep any dice man in pocket money wherever there is gambling. In addition to this expose, information is given covering a number of proposition bets any one of which is liable to score wherever tried. How To Control Fair Dice contains practical information compiled by practical men, profusely illustrated and with detailed descriptions enabling the novice to become proficient and expert with practice. These instructions come to you sealed and stapled and CANNOT be returned after seal and staple are broken . . . Each $5.00.

Sounds like a bargain, doesn't it? If you send for it, however, you'll find first that it comes by express and that you have to shell out the express charges. Then, when you open it, you will discover that you have one 8 × 11 sheet of paper printed on one side, one small two by three inch slip of paper and six small glossy photo prints.

The smaller slip of paper lists half a dozen hustler's bets—the information concerning the proposition bets that "are liable to score" which was promised. The other sheet contains about three times as many words as does the advertising come-on above and attempts to describe part of the Blanket Roll, the Peek Shot and one method of Holding it Up in a cup.

What about all those other controlled rolls mentioned in the catalog? Oh, those, as the instructions carefully explain, are merely other names for the same three shots! And if you aren't satisfied with that, you can't very well beef about it because the last line of the copy, which states very plainly that you CANNOT return the instructions after you have seen what you get, should have warned you that you might be due for a let down.

Actually this isn't as much of a swindle as my report might make it appear because if the cheat who is studying to be a dice shark can manage to unscramble enough of the none too clearly worded instructions so that he learns even one of the methods, he should be satisfied that he has received his money's worth. As prices go when you are buying sleight of hand cheating methods, five dollars is dirt cheap.

If the publishers were to ask standard prices for the material I am about to give you—material ninety-five percent of which has never before appeared in any other book—the price of this one chapter alone would set you back several hundred bucks. But perhaps it won't be worth as much to the dice shark after you have read it and studied the instructions that explain how to protect yourself. At least I hope so. A cheating method loses its value in direct proportion to the amount of publicity it gets. When too many prospective victims know the answers, it becomes worthless. Instead of being a safe way to clip the suckers, it is dangerous and the cheat is afraid to use it.

THE LOCK GRIP

The first move the dice shark must learn is the Lock Grip employed for any controlled shot thrown from the hand and using two dice. The dice are held in the bend of the two middle fingers in such a way, see Figure 1, that they *cackle* (rattle convincingly) when shaken but are kept from turning end for end by the pinky, forefinger and thumb.

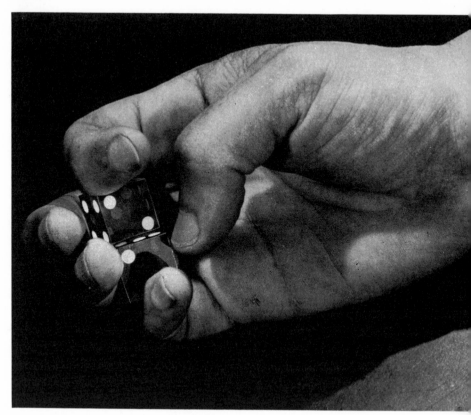

Fig. 1. The Lock Grip.

How to Detect the Lock Grip

The knuckles of the cheat's middle fingers may stick out far enough that they look a bit awkward, but this is tough to see when the hand is in motion. Your best bet is to try to detect him on the pickup. See Blanket Roll below.

THE BLANKET ROLL

This, also called The Soft Roll or Pad Roll shot, is the now famous dodge with which the sharks cleaned up millions in World Wars I and II. Many players have heard of this one, but very few of them are able to recognize it when it hits them. It is still a major money maker and one of the commonest moves in the cheat's repertoire of sleight of hand. One reason for its prevalence is that it is not difficult to do. Even the

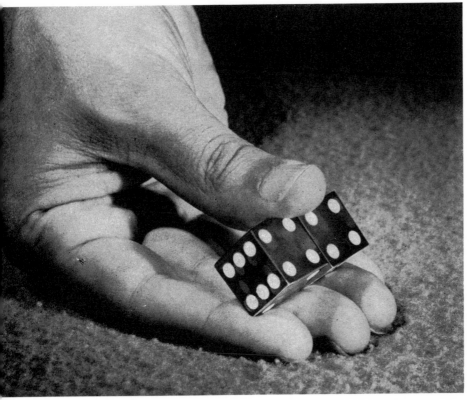

Fig. 2. The Blanket Roll. Manner in which dice are held just before throwing.

cheat who is so clumsy that he trips over his own feet when he dives for a foxhole may have mastered this one.

His first step is to wangle things so that the game is played on a bed, blanket, soft rug, very soft dirt, or any similar surface. Then, when he is shooting, he takes a quick gander at the way the dice lie, and notes the position of the spots that he needs. He reaches out, picks up one die and places it either on top of or next to the second so that certain numbers are on the two sides that face each other.

There are various combinations. Suppose, for instance, that the cheat picks up the dice and holds them in the Lock Grip with either the two sixes, the two aces, or an ace and six facing each other.

He gives them the phony shake and, as his hand comes down to make the throw, the thumb pushes the dice, still together, out toward the ends of his fingers and he rolls them out across the blanket. The dice land together and roll end over end like a pair of cartwheels without turning sideways. Since the sixes and aces are on the hubs of the wheel, they are eliminated and do not appear. The remaining numbers cannot be combined in any manner to make a crap or the natural, 11. On the first roll the cheat can throw a 7 and win, or he can throw a point. But he can't crap out.

And, having thrown a point, his chance of winning is much better than yours. If you throw 4 for a point, you have three ways of winning by throwing 4 again and six ways of losing by throwing 7. But when the cheat has 4 as his point, he picks up the dice and faces any one of the following combinations: 1–4, 6–4, 6–3. With these numbers eliminated by his Blanket Roll throw, the remaining numbers can only make a 4 in two ways, but they can only make 7 in two ways also. Instead of having twice as many ways to lose as he would if he threw the dice fairly, the cheat has a fifty-fifty chance of getting that 4!

If the point is either 5 or 9, the cheat faces the 6–5 (as in the photos) or the 1–2, 1–5, or 2–6 sides and once again has an even chance on what is usually a 3 to 2 bet. He uses the same combinations when 6 or 8 is the point and the odds that were 6 to 5 against him become 3 to 2 *in his favor!*

And if he decides to take 7 to 1 on the 6 (or 8) the hard way, which he would never do ordinarily and which at correct odds is really 10 to 1, the Blanket Roll trims this down to 3 to 1. The other players have 1 chance in 11 of making 6 (or 8) the hard way but the dice shark has 1 chance in 4, a very lucrative prospect indeed. The same holds true for the 4 (or 10) the hard way.

Fig. 3. The Blanket Roll. The dice roll across blanket end over end without turning sideways.

THE EVEN ROLL SHOT

On the first roll, Blanket or Pad Rollers, sometimes place the dice together so that all adjacent sides add to 7 and try to throw the dice in such a way that each cube makes exactly the same number of revolutions.* Because the cubes must stick together slightly as they leave the hand so that they begin to roll at the same rate of speed, some cheats use capping liquid to help make them adhere. This tendency to stick together, and the fact that when they do make the same number of revolutions they stop rolling simultaneously, makes the roll look altogether too controlled and is not very consistently used for that reason.

---

* Or, when trying to make a point, they place the dice together so that as many as possible of the adjacent sides add to that number.

THE CROSS ON THE BLANKET ROLL

In the last war a boatswain's mate first class on one of the big battle wagons won so much folding money with the Blanket Roll that, on being discharged from the service, it filled both his suitcases and, having nothing in which to carry his clothes, he threw them overboard. He not only cleaned out nearly all the other crap players on board, but taught some of his buddies the Blanket Roll and then, after they had each won fat amounts, took them as well. What's more, he clipped the blanket rollers with the Blanket Roll!

When he smartened them up to the shot, he carefully neglected to mention one small technical point of information. He told them that the Blanket Roll is a percentage shot, as it is, but he omitted mentioning that there is one way in which it can be just as positive as a pair of Tops. He didn't say anything about the fact that when the numbers 3 and 4 (or 3 and 3, or 4 and 4) face each other, there are two combinations or points, *the 5 and 9,* that cannot be made with the 1, 2, 5 and 6 that remain on the other four sides of the two dice.

Because his skill at the Blanket Roll was known to the blanket rollers whom he had taught, they always bet the dice to win on his shot. And because even the other players noticed how lucky he always seemed to be when he was shooting, players who wanted to bet the dice to win couldn't get many takers. But the shark soon fixed that. He supplied another player with a bankroll and told him to cover as much of this win money as he could whenever 5 or 9 was the point.

Then, because he carefully faced the 3 and 4 every time 5 or 9 was the point, the blanket rollers who were betting the dice to win lost their shirts to the shark's partner who slipped the dough back to him later. The victims had no reason to suspect anything either; they knew that since the Blanket Roll is a P. C. shot, it can lose. They just didn't know that, on occasion, it can be a sure-fire shot that must lose.

Other cheats have also used this cross but it has always been a well-kept trade secret and the great majority of blanket rollers still do not know it. But if *you* know it, then you know enough not to listen to the guy who says he can show you how to win with the Blanket Roll and who intends later to cross you up.

THE BACKBOARD CONTROL SHOT

This modern percentage controlled shot makes use of blanket, soft rug, or carpet plus a 3-foot high vertical backboard lined with foam rubber. As a rule, throwing the dice against a backboard is a protective measure against dice cheats, but not with this controlled shot. Prior to the time of releasing the dice from the hand, the cheat gives the dice a phony shake, *à la* the spin shot. Then, instead of rolling the dice on the soft surface as in the blanket roll, he lets them fly against the backboard in such a way that both dice hit the backboard at the same time causing the dice to bounce off the backboard onto the soft surface. The momentum causes them to roll back end over end like a pair of cartwheels without turning sideways. If the one-six is one hub of the wheel and the two-five is the other, the only way the cheat can seven out is with a three and four.

THE THREE-CUSHION CONTROLLED DICE SHOT

This highly secretive modern private dice-game controlled throw requires the use of a 3-foot high vertical backboard and two sideboards, each lined with foam rubber. Also needed are a smooth table surface, usually a piece of linoleum, onto which the dice fall and slide to a stop. This controlled shot is very effective because few gamblers believe it is possible to hit a sideboard, backboard, and sideboard and still control the dice. To execute this fantastic dice control shot, the cheat shakes the dice *à la* the spin shot and throws the dice against the right sideboard where they ricochet off the sideboard onto the backboard and onto the second sideboard where they drop onto the smooth playing surface, finally coming to rest with the desired numbers uppermost.

THE WHIP SHOT

This, also called the Peek Shot, the Pique Shot, the Hudson Shot, the Drop Shot, etc., is considerably more difficult than the Blanket Roll, but the dice shark considers the time spent in practicing it a good investment because it is not a P. C. but a positive throw. The expert can throw any number desired with one throw only. Furthermore, it can be used on almost any smooth surface and, once perfected, can clip the smart boys who would rumble a Blanket Roll at once.

The dice are picked up and held in the Lock Grip with the numbers the cheat wants to throw facing skyward. After the shake, the thumb rolls the die out toward the finger tips as in Figure 4. The hand throws them with a motion like the snap of a whip and they go out spinning rapidly like twin gyroscopes without turning over and with the same faces up throughout. See Figure 5.

Fig. 4. The Whip Shot just before throw is made.

Dice thrown in this manner on a hard surface tend to bounce and turn over. To avoid this, the cheat sometimes sprinkles sand or salt on the playing surface to help them slide. When shooting on the ground, he softens the dirt so that the dice will drop dead where they hit without sliding or turning over.

Some cheats use this shot against a board and although they hope to control one die only, it is extremely difficult and requires the greatest of skill. They throw at an angle against the side board so that the dice strike with a glancing blow and continue, still spinning.

House stickmen who know their jobs and who make sure that the players get no chance to set the dice for such a throw make the player place his hand with the little finger edge touching the table, the palm vertical. He must catch the dice as the stickman throws them to him and shake them immediately. If the player fails to catch the dice, they go back to the stickman who throws them to the player again. I mention

Fig. 5. The Whip Shot. Dice are snapped out and spin rapidly keeping the same faces up all the time.

this because, if casino operators take so many precautions to guard against this type of shot, *you* should at least keep your eyes open.

How to Detect the Whip Shot

Watch for a too careful pick-up, the distinctive whip-like motion of the throw, and dice that spin but do not turn over. Salt or sand on the playing surface is suspicious.

THE DICE-TABLE CONTROL SHOT

This new casino dice table control shot is the most difficult dice throw to perfect because it requires perfect aim and timing that can be gained only by long and arduous practice on a regulation casino dice table. This dice throw has taken many a casino operator for a bundle. Prior to the publication of this book, it is doubtful that more than a handful of gamblers and casino operators have had the slightest idea that such a controlled shot ever existed. And I firmly believe that once this book hits the book stands, dice-table manufacturers will make certain that it can't work on their tables.

Most modern dice tables have a sponge rubber embossed zigzag pattern lining the inside of the four 10-inch upright rails that enclose the table's playing surface. However, a bottom inch of this lining, at the juncture of the table surface and the upright rails does not possess the embossed zigzag patterns—it is plain sponge rubber. And this is exactly the spot the dice cheat must hit to control this shot.

The pickup of the dice in order to execute this controlled shot is difficult to detect because only one die has to be maneuvered into position. Immediately after the dice have been offered to the cheater-shooter, he picks them up in such a manner that one die has the desired number uppermost. This die is held palm down between the thumb and the first two fingers of the cheat's right hand flat on the table surface. The cheat lets the dice fly out of his palm-down hand from the table surface giving the one die he wants to control a whiplike snap aiming at the juncture of the table surface and the sponge rubber sideboard. When the spinning die hits this spot of the sideboard (the bottom inch), it bounces off at an angle and drops into the center of the table without turning over, with the desired number remaining uppermost. If the cheat holds the die so that a five is always uppermost, "a hard-way 10" becomes an even bet. The same holds true for the point numbers 6, 8, or 9.

THE GREEK SHOT

The Greek gambler who may have originated this shot and who, in any case, put in plenty of time perfecting it did so because the practice of throwing against a backboard made nearly all the other controlled shots impractical. It is the most difficult shot of all and requires the perfect aim and timing that is gained only by long and arduous practice.

The pick-up on this shot is harder to detect because it is much simpler, only one die having to be gotten into position. In the house where a pick-up is impossible, the cheat needs only a glimpse of one surface as he shakes the die and sometimes gets along without even that by feeling the spots with his thumb,* after which he gives the die a quarter or half turn bringing a wanted number into position.

On the throw, the dice are handled the same as in the Whip Shot but must be thrown so that they do not touch the playing surface until they hit the backboard. The Greek Shot expert aims at the juncture of table and backboard, or floor and baseboard, and both dice must hit that spot together one on top of the other, Figure 6. When they do, the bottom die is boxed in on three sides by the table, the backboard and the die above and does not rebound or turn over. The top die slides off

Fig. 6. The Greek Shot. Dice must be thrown so as to land against backboard as shown below.

and rolls. The existence of this shot is the reason that most dice tables today have sponge rubber rails.

Since the shot controls the lower die only, it is a percentage shot.

---

* This is one of the reasons some houses now use flush spot dice.

But that's plenty good enough. Suppose the cheat is shooting for a high point, a 10 for example. If he can hold up a 6, he has a much better chance of making that ten than if both dice were fairly thrown and he has only one way (6-ace) of missing out with a 7 instead of six ways. Maybe you see now why the estimated million dollars taken by the Greek gambler, who was the champ with this shot and who used it on the big money boys, is not necessarily an exaggeration!

When he works with a confederate, the cheat can take the Greek Shot out of the P. C. class and make it positive. When the point is 10, for instance, the shooter holds up either an ace, 2 or 3 and his sidekick bets the dice to lose. Since the shooter cannot make a 10 when one die shows one of those numbers, he will eventually seven-out and his confederate wins. If 4 is the point, he will hold up a 4, 5 or 6, etc.

How to Protect Yourself Against the Greek Shot

Insist that both dice hit the backboard above the juncture of table and board. This will protect you not only against the Greek Shot but against all controlled shots.

THE REVERSE GREEK SHOT

You should be on your guard against this one because, being easier to accomplish than the Greek Shot, it is more often used. The principle employed is the same except that the shot is not made against a board. It is most often used on the elevated surfaces of bars and counters. The dice are dropped more than thrown from the hand, landing one on top of the other. The weight of the top die keeps the lower one from bouncing or rolling after which it topples off and rolls wild.

How to Protect Yourself from the Reverse Greek Shot

Insist that the dice are thrown against a board.

THE SLIDE SHOT

A fairly easy shot used by hundreds of cheats when throwing the dice from the hand usually on a bar or counter. When the cheat picks up the dice, he grips one with his little finger, (Figure 7), and, in the shake, rattles the other against it, (Figure 8). On the throw, the under

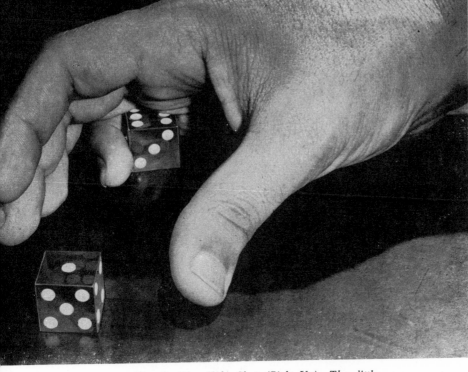

Fig. 7. The Slide Shot (Pick Up). The little finger curls around one die and holds it securely.

side of the little finger touches the bar and the loose die rolls but the one that has been held (the 6 in Figure 9) slides across the bar, spinning but not turning over. The cheat throws the free die out two or three feet, but slides the controlled die only a few inches so that its less natural action is not as easily observed. This can be used like the Greek Shot, either as a P .C. shot to make the point or as a positive shot to miss the point. In bar games where high score is important a high number is held up. It is also used when more than two dice are thrown and no dice cup is used. The shot looks even better with more than two dice since the slide is less noticeable.

How to Protect Yourself from the Slide Shot

The same goes for this one too. Insist that the dice are thrown against the board.

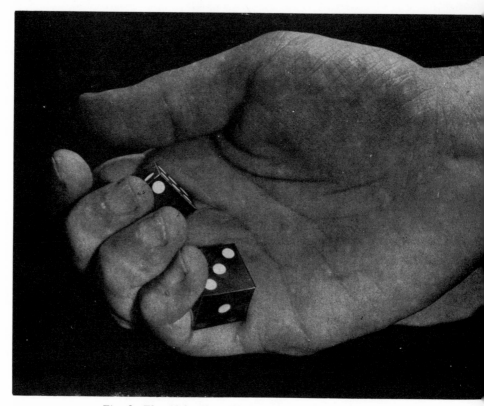

Fig. 8. The Slide Shot (Shake). When shaken the loose die rattles against the one held by the little finger.

THE TWIST SHOT

Used in any two-dice game when a cup is not used. This is the same as the Slide Shot except that the controlled die is held by the forefinger and the number the cheat intends to throw is on its under rather than upper surface. The hand throws the dice with a backhand motion, the side of the forefinger rather than that of the little finger lying along the bar when the dice are released.

How to Protect Yourself Against the Twist Shot

Don't play with guys who have a habit of making one die roll about three feet and the other only six inches or so. And always see that the dice hit a backboard.

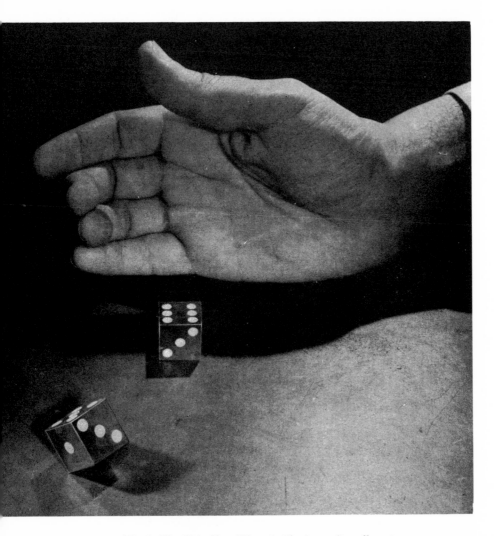

*Fig. 9. The Slide Shot (Throw). The loose die rolls out,
the other slides with the same face up as at the start.*

THE SPIN SHOT

This is another but fancier one on the same principle and is also
used in any two-dice game when a cup is not employed. The dice are
picked up and given a fair shake, neither die being held in position. But
on the last shake, as the hand comes up, both dice are gripped by the
fingers and the cheat takes a quick glimpse at the numbers facing him.
Knowing what they are, he also knows the numbers on the opposite

sides, and if those are the ones he wants, he's all set. If not, he either makes a fair throw or turns one or both dice with his thumb so that a different and more desirable combination will appear. This takes practice but can be done. I can give the dice a perfectly fair shake and throw out any number called with this method.

On the throw the hand comes down, palm facing the bar, and the thumb and fingers simply set the dice down and give them a spin so that they slide out and spin across the bar, without turning end over end. The cheat doesn't use this one all the time; the slide would soon become too noticeable. But he uses it with discretion and on the throws that are important. When he shakes, he holds his hand partly open so that you can actually see both dice rattling around in a thoroughly fair manner. The shake is so convincing that his victims never think to object to the slide.

How to Protect Yourself Against the Spin Shot

Don't play with players who spin or slide the dice more than they should. Always insist that the dice hit a backboard.

THE SWITCHES

The other and important branch of dice manipulation is the ability the dice mechanic must have of switching the fair dice being used for phony ones. There are several for various occasions. I'll start with the simpler ones and work up.

THE MONEY SWITCH

Usually used in street and private crap games, this is the one employed by the less accomplished mechanic who hasn't yet acquired the skill necessary for anything better. There are several methods of handling it. Usually the cheat holds the phony dice palmed in his right hand and a number of bills in his left. In Figure 10 the hand is held so that the camera can see the crooked dice, something the cheat never lets you do. The right hand reaches out, picks up the fair dice (white in the photo to avoid confusion), and, as the player steps back to shoot, his hands come together for a split second. The good dice drop into the cupped left hand beneath the bills and the crooked ones are promptly shaken and tossed out (Fig. 11).

Fig. 10. The Money Switch. Cheat holds palmed crooked dice in right hand and is about to pick up fair dice.

When the cheat wants to take his work out of the game, before passing the dice to the next player he picks them up with his right hand and immediately takes the money from his left. His left hand then peels off a bill, places it on the floor or table and drops the good pair of dice with it. He either retains the bills in his right hand so that they conceal the phony dice until it is his turn to shoot again, or he may put some bills in his pocket and leave the dice there at the same time.

How to Detect the Money Switch

On paper it may sound as though it would be easy to see. In practice it is done so smoothly and quickly that you may have trouble. But keep your eye on the player who changes his money from hand to

Fig. 11. The Money Switch. Fair dice are left beneath bills and crooked dice thrown out.

hand and keeps going into his pockets. And when you spot a suspicious move, pick up the dice at once and examine them.

PALM SWITCH

Now we're getting into fast company. This one requires so much practice that if the cheat who has mastered it would have spent the time learning a trade, he wouldn't have to cheat. He must be able to hold two pair of dice in his hand, rattle them so that they sound like one pair, and throw out either pair as needed!

The dice mechanic uses the Palm Switch to get loads or shapes into the game both when he is shooting and when, as a side bettor, he picks up the dice to throw them back to the shooter. He also uses it to bust in and out with Tops when the shooter is a confederate.

The phony dice are palmed in the right hand and the others are picked up, (Figure 12) by the ends of the fingers. Seen from below, the position is now as in Figure 13. As the hand closes for the shake, the phony dice drop down into the cupped fingers and the fair ones are placed in the palm.

The dice must pass each other like trapeze artists without touching, and, if you think it's an easy matter for the fingers to place two slippery cubes in the exact position and at the exact angle so that the palm of the hand can grip and hold them, try it. Even without the other two dice, you'll have plenty of trouble. Some mechanics practice for years in front of a mirror before they ever attempt the move in a game. Even then it requires plenty of *heart* (nerve).

Figure 15 shows the two crooked dice rolling out and a cheat's-eye view of the palmed pair that are retained.

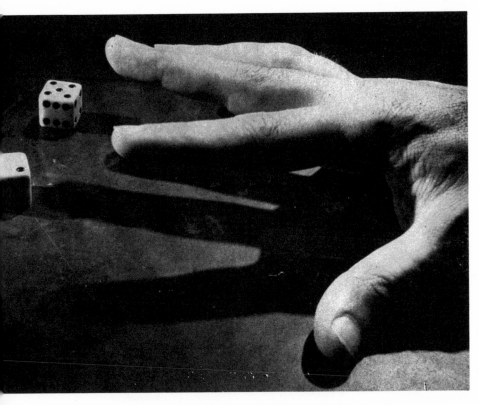

Fig. 12. The Palm Switch. The cheat's right hand reaches out and picks up the dice, holding them at ends of fingers.

How to Protect Yourself Against the Palm Switch

Knowing how it is done may enable you to catch it now and then if you watch like a hawk and suspect the player who picks the dice up too often when he is not the shooter, especially if his hand position looks a bit awkward. And don't hesitate to examine the dice if you have doubts.

TWO-HAND PALM SWITCH

The crooked dice are palmed in the left hand, the fair dice picked up by the right. The crooked dice drop to cupped fingers and right hand places fair dice in palming position in left hand. Then both hands are rubbed together in the characteristic crap shooter's manner when he blows on them to change his luck. When the hands come apart, the fair dice are retained, palmed in the left hand, the phony dice thrown out. A repetition of the move switches the work back out of the game. This switch is usually used in street games.

Fig. 13. The Palm Switch. What you never see is that he has another pair concealed in the palm of his hand.

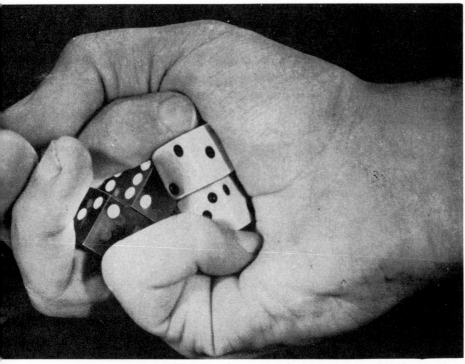

Fig. 14. (above). In one lightning-fast and very difficult move, the positions of the dice are transposed and (Fig. 15 below) the palmed pair is thrown into play.

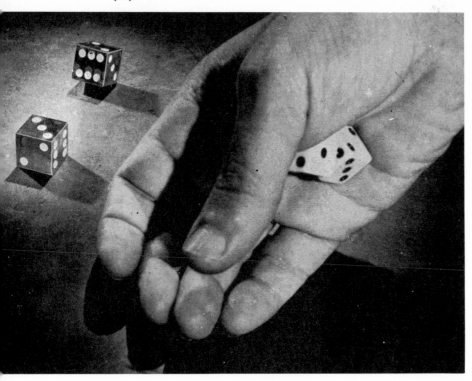

How to Protect Yourself Against the Two-Hand Palm Switch

The cheat must rub his hands together to get the dice in and again to get them out. Look with suspicion on a player who uses this action too frequently. Always examine dice when suspicious.

THE CASINO THUMB PALM SWITCH

This is a fast and very deceptive one-hand switch that is used by the best crooked stickmen and bust-out men in the country. Some, like Con Baker who was the greatest of them all, can do it capably with both hands.

The crooked cubes are palmed in the right hand which always retains a normal relaxed appearance. As the hand reaches out for the fair dice, the second, third and little fingers take the palmed dice and the forefinger and thumb line up the others, (Figure 16). The fair dice are

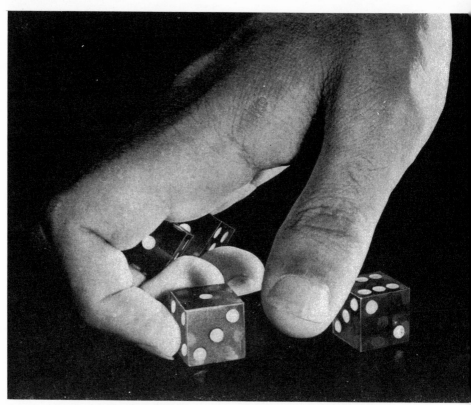

Fig. 16. The Thumb Palm Switch. Second third and little fingers hold crooked dice. The forefinger and thumb pick up others.

pushed back along the thumb and into the crotch of the thumb where they are held as in Figure 17. The phony dice are simply thrown out.

Fig. 17. Thumb Palm Switch. Fair dice are retained in crotch of thumb and crooked dice tossed out.

The expert does the whole move with a smooth practiced ease that would make even a magician's eyes pop.

How to Protect Yourself from the Thumb Palm Switch

This move is the favorite among steer-joint stickmen. After the switch is made, he shifts the stick to the hand holding the dice. If you see that hand pull back near his body and out of sight too often, it may mean that he is going into his pocket with the dice—or sometimes into the pocket of the confederate standing close beside him.

If you ever suspect that you are in a steer joint, don't beef about it out loud—just make an exit through the nearest door—but quick. Those boys aren't fooling.

THE MOUTH SWITCH

There's a story that goes with this one. The guy who first came up with the mouth switch around New York in the 30's beat one money game after another with it and cleaned up handsomely. Known later as The Spitter, he got by with the stunt for nearly a year, hitting a couple of different spots a week and taking out a nice thick wad of cabbage each trip. How much he got away with no one knows, but it must have run into boxcar figures.

He invested first in a consignment of Tops, an ace–2–3 combination that contained only those spots and no others. The Spitter would get into a game and, just before it was his turn to shoot, he'd cough and cover his mouth with his hand. Under cover of that action, he popped a single ace–2–3 Top into his mouth and left it there. Then, when it was his turn to shoot, he reached out with a completely empty hand and caught the dice the stickman threw to him. His little finger curled around one of the cubes as though he were getting set for the Slide Shot. Then his hand went to his mouth and he blew on the dice in the common and characteristic crap player's manner.

You know now where he got the Spitter monicker. He ripped in his misspot by simply spitting it out into his hand. Then he threw it with one of the fair cubes out on the table and held back the third die which he concealed under the bills he held until he had an opportunity to pocket it.

The highest number on the T was a 3 and on the fair die a 6. No matter how often those two cubes were tossed, it was a cinch they'd never show anything higher than a 9, not unless somebody invented something new in the way of arithmetic. If you know for sure that you can't hit a 10 no matter how hard you seem to try, the next step is as obvious as a strip-tease dancer at a Sunday School picnic. All you have to do is bet against the 10.

The Spitter also had all the other angles covered. He made no attempt to rip the die back out again, but simply left it in the game and when the dice were boxed up it went into the bowl and was lost among the others. And he didn't shoot the dice again all evening, the idea being that if a blow came maybe the dealer and stickman would forget that he had ever touched the dice at all.

But every time his die came out of the box, he knew that it was in play because, in addition to having too many spots all alike, a line drawn through the two and three spots did not meet at one corner as they do on correctly spotted dice. Lines through the two spot and three spot ran in the same direction—a variation on the spotting dodge mentioned in the chapter on Inside Work, page 226. Whenever his die was in action, The Spitter began making money in a big way.

Of course, when the house realized that number 10 wasn't appearing anywhere near as often as probability predicts they smelled a rat. And when they gave the dice the double-o, they found the misspot and let loose with a few choice but unprintable words that sizzled like something fresh out of a volcano.

They thought back, of course, and remembered who it was that was so lucky betting against the 10, but they didn't put their fingers on The Spitter because he had been drawing a fat red herring across the trail by putting small bets on the dice to win all evening.

How come? Well, he had a confederate, a guy who didn't know what it was all about but who had no objection to betting the money supplied him by The Spitter as directed and whenever The Spitter gave him the office. His end was maybe a flat fifty bucks and The Spitter met him afterward for the payoff and collected the working capital and winnings. The stooge may have suspected that something was in the wind, but he didn't know just what. For all he could prove, The Spitter was just a lucky egg who was born with a horseshoe in his mouth!

To make it worse or better, depending on how you look at it, The Spitter changed his stooges about as often as he did his razor blades, and more than one casino operator was moping around with a very sad expression on his map wondering how in blue hell those Tops got into the game, who put them in, and why the guys who won were never the same! In some of the joints an aspirin and bromo concession would have been a money maker. But The Spitter's racket was too good to last forever.

One night he walked into a big game on West 48th Street carrying too many slugs of imported bourbon under his belt. He picked up two of the house dice, spit into his hand as usual, and then shot. And *three* dice came rolling out across the table!

You could hear a pin drop from a height of two inches on to a plush rug.

And then, in the middle of this very dead and ominous silence The Spitter, staring at the 3 threes that the dice showed, exclaimed, "Look! Nine the hard way!"

Other versions that the boys tell report him as throwing a three and 2 sixes and saying, "Okay, so my point is fifteen!" and "Gentlemen, the game is Chuck-a-Luck!" You take your choice.

For some reason or other no one has seen The Spitter around since.

This doesn't mean that he was rubbed out. The boys are careful not to take such drastic measures, being well aware that the rap for murder is somewhat stiffer than the one for operating games of chance. His first stop was the alley out back and his second was probably the hospital where he had plenty of time to smile at his quick wit, provided the plaster cast on his face didn't interfere.

Perhaps the reason no one has seen him around since is because they don't recognize the different way his kisser looks after it healed up.

MOVES WITH THE DICE CUP

The following moves are used in bar and counter games in which the dice are thrown from a cup. They are deceptive and employed with great success because the average player thinks that the use of a cup protects him against sleight of hand.

DICE CUP SWITCH: TWO DICE

When the cheat wants to exchange two of the dice employed for loaded dice or for Tops, he makes the palm switch already described and then immediately places the dice cup on top of the palmed dice in the right hand so that it conceals them. The left hand is placed over the mouth of the cup which is then shaken and the dice thrown.

DICE CUP SWITCH: ONE DIE

The crooked die is held in the palm position (see Figure 17). The right hand reaches out and picks up the other dice. One is gripped by the little finger and retained, the others and the thumb-palmed die are tossed into the cup.

In High Dice where the object is to get high score the cheat switches in a 4-5-6 Top on his own throw. In the 26 game, when the dice girls aren't too smart, the cheat who is trying to beat the house switches in as many Dead Number dice as he can. One or two may not be sufficient because most house cups today are trip cups or are lined with deep lateral grooves of ribbed rubber. When thrown from such a cup, the dice do not roll as far and the loads have less chance to act. I know one cheat who, after playing five games, always has five dead aces in.

HOLDING IT UP: FIRST METHOD

The following methods for controlling one die by holding it up in the cup are favorites with cheats in any three or five-dice game such as Buck, Indian, Poker, Drop Dead, etc. Even when five dice are used the cheat who can be sure that one will fall just as he wants it to has an advantage that gets him the money.

He holds the cup as in Figure 18 and moves it toward the dice,

Fig. 18. Holding it Up—1st Method. The first and second fingers pick up dice by snapping them back into the cup.

snapping each one into it in turn with the first two fingers. Or that is what he seems to do. Actually the last die never goes into the cup at all, but is held by the first two fingers against the cup's lip. Figure 19 shows what you never see but what you might see if you could get down under his hand and look up as he shakes the cup.

On the throw the controlled die slides across the bar or counter showing the same number as before. The move gets a lot of use because,

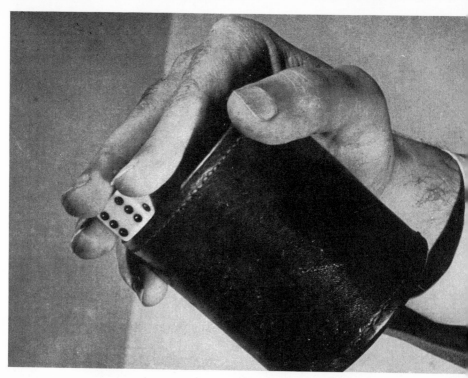

Fig. 19. The last die does not go into the cup but is held during the shake as above and, when the dice are thrown (Fig. 20 below), it slides out without turning over, retaining the same face up as at the start.

since the die never goes into the cup at all, it works just as well with a trip cup as any other kind.

How to Protect Yourself Against This One

Try to make sure that that last die goes into the cup and look with suspicion on the player who uses the pick-up described above.

HOLDING IT UP: SECOND METHOD

In this one the cheat spots the die whose upper face bears the number of spots that will do him the most good and his right little finger curls around it and retains it when he scoops up the dice, the same move as in the Slide Shot, Figure 7. The other dice are all tossed into the cup and the right hand is immediately placed over the mouth of the cup with the little finger and the die it holds going inside. After the cup is shaken, the left hand takes the cup. The right hand is removed and leaves the controlled die resting on the side of the horizontally held cup just within the mouth. Then the dice are thrown and the controlled die slides out without turning over and showing the same face up as at the start. A trip cup with its raised inner lip is your protection here because it upsets this move.

HOLDING IT UP: THIRD METHOD

Very much the same as number two except that the controlled die is held between the index and third finger and lying on the middle finger, the hand flat over the mouth of the cup. Just before the throw is made, the die is left resting on the inner edge of the cup and, on the throw, slides out.

FIRST FLOP DICE* AND THE SLICK CUP

Here's what the catalogs say about this popular cheating device:

Our Special First Flop Dice have met with great success for Indian, Baseball and Poker Dice. Each set consists of five special dice prepared in such a manner that by following instructions you can show a much larger hand than your opponent when desired, both using the same dice.

---

* Also called *Settlers* and *Dead Number* dice.

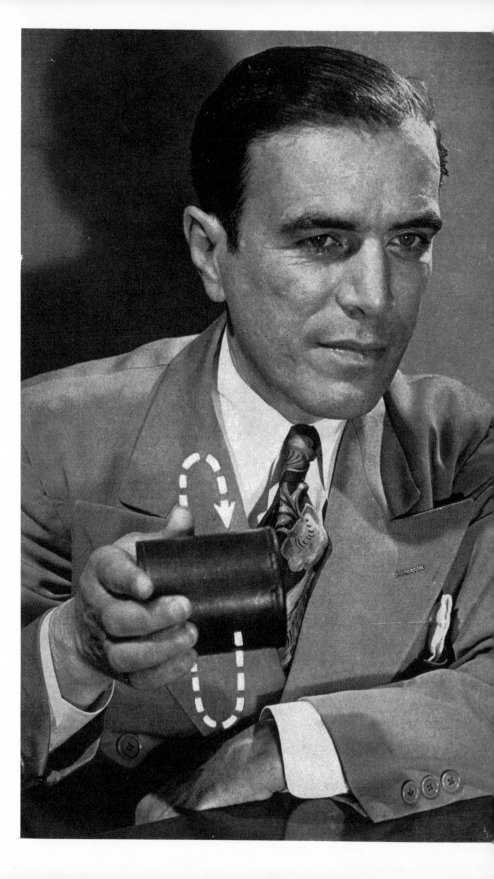

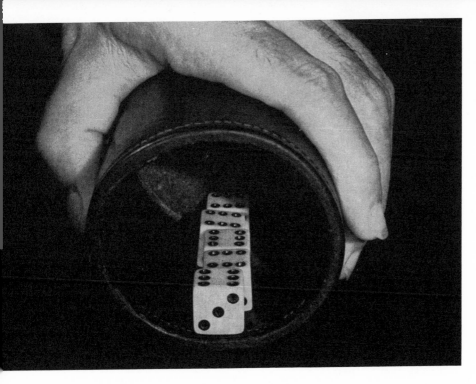

THE SLICK CUP SHAKE. In Fig. 20 (opposite page) the arrow shows the direction and rotary motion of the shake.

Fig. 21 (above) shows how this lines the dice up within the cup.

Fig. 22 (below) Another slight sideward shake causes the loaded dice to tip over and the dice slide out showing desired numbers.

These dice will give much better satisfaction when used in connection with the special dice box listed which has an inside surface made to meet the requirements of these dice. The most practical set is an Ace-Five combination in 9/16 inch white celluloid. Other combinations made to order. Set of 5 . . . $6.25. Special First Flop Box . . . $2.85.

The reason First Flop dice give "much better satisfaction" in connection with the special dice cup is that they are no good to the cheat without it! The cup has a smooth slicked inner surface and when the cheat shakes the cup with an up and down and slightly rotary motion of his arm (Figure 20), the dice, instead of rattling at random inside the cup, spin around the inside surface like horses on a *chump-twister.* *

The centrifugal force lines the dice up within the cup as shown in Figure 21. A last sideward shake just before they are thrown causes several of the dice, all of which are loaded, to tip over so that their loaded sides are down. (The term Dead-Number dice comes from the fact that when their loaded sides are down, they do not rattle in the cup as noisily as the others.)

Although the cheat would not regularly throw five of a kind, as shown in Figure 22, because the chumps might rumble the gaff, he can and does do so when necessary. This is accomplished by giving the shake plenty of the rotary motion. Some cheats use a double combination in which some dice are loaded to bring up one side, some another, so that the same numbers do not appear too consistently.

When he throws, the cheat holds the cup parallel with the counter, shoves it forward a bit and jerks it back quickly so that the dice all slide out without turning. When the victim throws, using the same cup and dice, he doesn't shake or throw properly and the loads do him no good. This could be where the term *shakedown* originated. At least that's what happens to the victim.

The victims aren't always the customers either. The man behind the counter sometimes gets clipped too. There is one difficulty here. Switching in the loaded dice is a cinch but switching the fair cup for a slick cup is tougher because it is hard to find a perfect match. Even if the outside looks the same there is always the chance that the owner will rumble the slicked inner surface.

But a little obstacle like that has never stopped the boys for long, especially if the cup operator gambles for sizeable stakes. One mob of cheaters in the East solved the problem a few years ago so neatly that

---

* *Chump twister:* carnival slang for merry-go-round.

they ended by getting slick boxes into nearly every store, bar and tavern in town.

One of the mob made the rounds giving out with a Bromo Seltzer sales pitch and leaving behind a neatly wrapped sample package with the compliments of the company. When opened, the package was found to contain a handsome leather cup filled with cellophane-wrapped Bromo Seltzer. An advertising sticker which the boys had soaked off a regular Bromo bottle was pasted on the outside of the cup.

Also enclosed was a small printed slip of paper that gave the store-keeper a broad hint in the event he was too dense to get the idea all by himself. It read: "This container can be used as a dice cup for popular bar and counter games—for amusement only."

The moral here, of course, is that you should always look gift horses in the mouth. They might be slick cups!

THE CROSS ON THE CUP

Sometimes even the cheats who buy slick cups with which to cheat their customers get clipped with their own cups. I know of one such operator whose cup backfired to the tune of one grand. The game was called One Flop. Each player had one throw and scored the sum of the spots that appeared on all five dice. High man won and, since aces were low, the storekeeper used Settlers that were all dead sixes.

Trouble showed up when a stranger who seemed to be carrying more drinks than was good for him arrived, played a few games and lost ten bucks. The drunk became annoyed and then a bit belligerent. "I'll bet you two thousand bucks even money that you can't throw fifteen or over," he challenged, producing a bankroll and peeling off C-notes.

The storekeeper whose ownership of a crooked cup was proof that he had larceny in his heart was considering the matter a bit breathlessly when a customer, known to the storekeeper as a big gambler around town walked in and asked for some cigars. As the storekeeper turned to get them, the drunk repeated his offer. The gambler gave him one look, said, "I'll take half that bet," and reached for his bankroll.

The storekeeper's indecision was painful. Then the gambler leaned across the counter and, in a low voice which the drunk pretended not to hear, said, "Your pie-eyed friend thinks, because high score with five sixes is thirty, that the half way point is fifteen and that he's offering an even-up bet. He forgets that low score is five with five aces which makes eighteen or over an even bet. We'd be chumps not to take the bet with an edge like that."

This was the convincer. The storekeeper and the gambler each put up a grand and the storekeeper shook the cup but good. When he could feel that all the numbers were dead in the cup, he slid them out.

And instead of the five sixes that he knew had to show up, he found himself staring pop-eyed at double-fours, an ace, two and three— a total of fourteen! While he was still staring at this impossibility and before he had a chance to recover his balance, the drunk scooped up the four thousand dollars and made a wavering, but hasty bee-line for the door.

And the storekeeper still can't dope out what happened because, when he shook the dice again, he threw sixes just as he should. He never tumbled to the fact that all five of his dice were switched out and then back in again. And he wouldn't believe it if you told him because he had his eyes glued on the drunk watching for a phony move every second.

He saw none for the very good reason that the stranger made none. But the gambler whom the storekeeper knew did. He made a switch that is a simple and barefaced move but which, covered by the proper misdirection, does the job with efficiency and dispatch. The gambler had five Settlers that were differently loaded in his left hand when he stepped into the store. He picked up the dice on the counter with his right hand just as the storekeeper turned to get the cigars he asked for. Then, as the drunk repeated his proposition, and the store-keeper turned back, he tossed those from his left hand into the cup.

When he said, "I'll take half that bet," his right hand went to his pocket, left the storekeeper's dice there and came out with a roll of bills. Then, after the explosion but before the smoke had blown away, he reversed the same moves unnoticed by the storekeeper who was dazedly watching the drunk depart, trying to collect his well-scattered wits, and cursing inwardly because he couldn't object that his dice shouldn't act as they did without admitting that he had begun by cheating the drunk in the first place.

If you have ever been cheated with any of these moves, it may be some satisfaction to know that the guy who cheated you has probably been clipped by one or more of them too. The cheat never draws the line anywhere. Another cheat is not only fair game but often an even better sucker than the honest chump.

That's a good reason for not cheating in itself, although I can think of even better ones.

**How to Protect Yourself from the Dice Shark
When a Cup Is Being Used**

Use a *trip cup* which contains obstructions on its inner surface that make the dice tumble as they are thrown and prevents the shark from sliding them out. Some cups have a trip rim; others are lined with ribbed rubber. An ordinary cup can be made into a trip cup very simply by gluing small pieces of leather or wood in various places on the inner surface.

If a trip cup is not available, you can insist that the dice be well shaken and that the cup be turned completely upside down on the throw so that the dice bounce on the playing surface and do not slide out. Don't hesitate to examine the dice.

15

So You Have a System?

Today there are more betting systems advertised for sale on how to beat the dice tables in Las Vegas than at any other time in history. A couple of decades ago the only magazines that would publish a gambling system advertisement was a pulp magazine. But, today, due to the want of advertisements, periodicals such as *Time, Newsweek, New York Times, New York Daily News, Chicago Tribune* and other respected publications have dropped their high standards and accept gambling system ads that the seller guarantees when put to use will beat the Las Vegas casinos. These get-rich-quick betting systems sell from $25 to $100. No wonder these advertisements have graduated from cheap pulp magazines to our leading and respected national periodicals.

The crap-game operator and dice hustler earn money by making Old Man Percentage work for them. The dice cheat earns money by beating the dice chumps with crooked dice. And the Johnny-Come-Lately crap player, knowing nothing about the mathematics of the game, sees some high roller win a bundle at the Las Vegas craps table and wishes he were in his shoes. Then when home he reads an ad in his local paper of some dice system that the author states is infallible, or he reads an advertisement in some national magazine and invests thirty-five bucks or more in an instruction sheet that promises to tell him "How to Beat the Las Vegas Dice Tables" simply by following a certain betting method.

ROTHSTEIN SYSTEM

The Rothstein System uses the general principle on which most dice systems are based. It is our old friend the Martingale, double-up, or progressive system in disguise, and it is more commonly employed at the dice table than at any other gambling game. It is advertised this way:

THE ROTHSTEIN SYSTEM

Did you ever try to beat the RACES? It cannot be done. And you cannot beat crap games any more than you can beat the races. Crap games are MADE TO WIN for the house. Unless you use a SYSTEM.

The Rothstein Crap system is a simple mathematical progressive way of placing bets on the layout. And if the system is adhered to, STICK TO THE SYSTEM, it will win. Figures do not lie and this system is nothing but a simple play of figures.

Anyone that can count 1-2-3-4-5-6 etc., can use the ROTHSTEIN SYSTEM. We sold it to a man in Ohio and he wrote back inside of a week and told us he made $225.00 with the system.

It is guaranteed to win if you FOLLOW THE SYSTEM. The only thing that can keep you from winning is the house man. He does not like a system player and can, if he wishes, bar anyone. All that is required is that the house fades your bets. Not a crooked move of any kind.

This system once sold for $3.00. Today it sells for $20! It should also be obvious to anyone who "can count 1-2-3-4-5-6" that if a man had a guaranteed winning system, peddling it to all comers at twenty bucks is the last thing he would do. Actually, this ad does not misrepresent the facts as much as some of them do. After stating that the system is guaranteed to win, it actually tells, in the next-to-last sentence, exactly why the system won't work!

Here's the dope. Your first step is to place 1 chip on the Pass line. If you lose, you bet 3 chips, and if you lose that you bet 7 chips. Each time you lose, you double your last bet plus 1. If you win after your first bet, you are ahead 1 chip; after the second bet, 2 chips; after the third bet, 3 chips, etc. And each time you win, you go back and start the progression over again with the 1-chip bet.

"Sometimes," the instructions read, "the dice go clear around the table before they make a pass. This is unusual but it will happen. Nevertheless they *must* pass some time and, while it may take the heart out of players to keep piling chips up, the chips will all come back when a pass is made and there will be surplus chips with them. THIS IS A SYSTEM THAT NO HOUSE MAN LIKES TO SEE USED AGAINST HIS GAME."

That last sentence is strictly off the beam, since stickmen have a habit of crying, "Double up, men! They're bound to change. Double up and beat the bank!" The house likes to see the system used because in trying to win small amounts steadily the player must make many bets; and the more bets he makes, the more the house earns in percentage.

Before I put my finger on the big hitch in the whole scheme, let me first describe another variation of the progressive system known as:

THE WATCHER, OR PATIENCE SYSTEM

The instructions on this one lead off my warning that you must have plenty of patience, and, incidentally, $500 to $1,000 capital. With those two requirements the system is guaranteed to win $10 a day, rain or shine, day in and day out. Don't be greedy, the writer warns, just be satisfied with the ten bucks per day and everything is Jake. "This system has been tried and is recommended by some of the smartest dice players in the country."

This time, instead of betting the dice to win, you are to bet the dice to lose. Much stress is laid on the fact that you must watch the dice and not make any bets until after four successive passes have been made. Then bet $10 that they lose on the fifth. This clever little dodge saves you the loss of four $10 bets! Since a penny saved is a penny earned, you're already making money!

You have a far better chance betting the dice to lose on the fifth pass than on the first because the odds against five successive passes being made are 31 to 1. It's practically a sure thing. You'll lose such a proposition only once in 32 times. Then you take your $10 and leave. Don't be greedy and be tempted to try the system twice in the same night.

And, if you should lose that 31-to-1 shot? You merely bet $20 that the dice will lose on the next pass. The odds against six passes being made are 63 to 1. If, by any strange streak of fate, you lose that one, too, bet $40 that they don't pass. The odds are 127 to 1 against seven successive passes. You can hardly ask for better odds in your favor than that.

I know one player who bought and played this system for four weeks. He came away every night wearing a broad smile and with a $10 profit. Of course, sometimes he had to wait hours before four passes were made in a row so that he could begin betting, but he expected that; instructions told him he needed plenty of patience.

But one night he had a little difficulty. When he walked into the casino, he had won $10 a night for four weeks and was $280 ahead of the game. When the fourth pass was made, he bet $10 on the next. The shooter sevened. He bet $20 and the shooter threw an Eleven. He bet $40 and the shooter sevened again. He bet $80, and a point was bucked right back. He bet $160 and began sweating. But he had faith in the system; it was guaranteed to win. A missout *had* to come sometime, and when it did he'd be $10 ahead once more.

Then the shooter crapped out with Two-Sixes and my friend relaxed, all smiles, but only for a moment. The house made no move to pay off.

"Hey," the player asked, "I had $160 down to lose. Don't I get—"

The stickman gave him a sour look. "Something wrong?" he asked, pointing to the space on the layout which read "Bar" "Two-Sixes". "In case you don't know, that means there's no payoff, but you don't lose either."

My friend scowled. He was learning fast now. The system sheet hadn't said anything about a stand-off, but he began to see that it gave the house two whacks at his dough. There was nothing he could do, however, but let the $160 ride on the next come-out and hope for any crap except Two-Sixes.

The dice came out—a natural with a Six-Five. The house raked in the $160, and my friend, now shy a total of $310, reached shakily for his roll, counted off $320 and threw it on the table.

Then he bumped head-on into another very hard fact that the system had failed to stress.

"Sorry, sir," the box man said, "but you can bet only three hundred. That's the limit at this table."

Now what? If he bet the $300 and won, he would still be a $10 loser. If he lost he'd be shy $610 altogether. The guaranteed system hadn't said anything about a situation in which he'd lose no matter what happened. He'd forgotten that one little line in the ad which read: "All that is required is that the house fades your bets."

While he was trying to make up his mind the dice came out and the shooter sevened. His hesitation saved him $300. But he was still shy $310, thirty bucks more than the $280 it had taken him four weeks of patient waiting to win.

This is also the flaw in the Rothstein System. In fact, every progressive system eventually runs smack up against the house maximum betting limit and explodes in the player's face. Take a close look at the usual house betting limits and you'll see that the spread between the minimum and maximum betting limits prevents the system player from doubling up more than six or seven times. A 25¢ to $25 top, for instance, allows him to bet 25¢ and then double by betting 50¢, $1, $2, $4, $8, and $16. If he loses each bet he's sunk, because the seventh doubling up would take him above the limit. The same thing holds true of the 50¢ to $50 and the $1 to $75 or $100, the $2 to $200 or $300, and the $5 to $500 limits.

One book on dice systems even introduces the subject by warning the player to find out the rules governing the limit of the stakes before beginning to play. "The best system," it adds, "is worthless unless the house allows adequate margin for raising the stakes." The writer then wades into a complex explanation of the Patience system as applied to all sorts of games and neglects to mention that *all* houses do have a limit that *does not* allow an adequate margin for raising the stakes. This booklet today bears a $20 price on its cover and is sold for $15 "while they last." It has been in print for years.

There are also a few things wrong with the advice to watch for four passes before betting and then put your money on the fifth pass because the odds against its being made are 31 to 1. Those are the odds that five successive passes won't be made, all right, but you are *not* betting that five passes won't be made. You are betting that the *next* pass won't be made. There's a slight difference. The odds on that are, as always, slightly less than 50–50. (When the Two-Sixes are barred you have a 49-23/77% chance.)

The author of the above-mentioned booklet has a couple of other system secrets that deserve passing mention. "Practice craps in your home for thousands of shots before you dare enter a gambling house. By doing so you will acquire the necessary intuition for guessing the results of the next shot." Any reader who follows this plan and successfully develops intuition of that kind should set up as a fortune-teller.

And the last word on all the systems in the book is the one in which you are advised to play *against* the player using a progressive system! You always bet the same amount he does and "whenever his guess is wrong you have won as many progressive stakes as he has lost. He has to do the guessing, which is the real trick in every game." This writer not only believes in the maturity of chances (which is what his "watching" tactics imply) but also in the gamblers' superstition that the odds are against the guesser! But even at that, he's a little bit smart; he writes a book on systems instead of playing them.

THE HOT AND COLD SYSTEM

This one is a lulu. The gambler who advertises it for sale promises the player that "with this system you will be betting they win *every time* the dice are *hot* (making passes), and betting they lose *every time* the dice are *cold* (not passing)."

You think this sounds impossible? You'd pass it up because there just couldn't be any way to make certain that you would be betting they win during every hot spell and betting they lose during every cold spell? Strangely enough, the method given tells you exactly how to do that, and for only $5.

Before you read further, see if you can dope out a way to do it. I warn you, however, that once you've got the answer it won't make a killing.

Here's the method. Whenever a player makes a pass, you begin betting the dice to win. If he continues through a hot spell of passes, you're on it. And the moment he throws a missout you begin, with the next roll, betting the dice to lose. Now you're sure to be on any cold spell. And as soon as another pass appears you switch back again. The moment that someone makes a long series of either passes or missouts you are in the big money. Sounds good, doesn't it?

Here's the catch. The instructions forgot to say what would happen when a pass is followed by a missout, then a pass, then a missout and so on, passes and missouts coming alternately. What would happen? Playing the hot-and-cold system, you would lose every single bet during the time the dice acted that way.

And, because this system requires that you bet on every decision, the price you'll pay the house in percentage before you discover for yourself what's wrong will be a darned sight more than the five bucks the system cost you. The house and the guy who sells the system make the money—but you lose.

THE PLACE BETTING SYSTEM

This is one of the favorite crap systems used by some of the so-called smart bigtime gamblers. When chance is working in its favor, this system appears so certain to win the money that many a player using it has been told by casino bosses in no uncertain terms to scram and take his business elsewhere.

Here's the method of betting. The high roller usually bets the maximum limit, although lesser amounts can be wagered. For example, he puts $300 to win on each of the six place bets: 4, 5, 6, 8, 9 and 10, wagering a total of $1,800. The moment one of these numbers is made, he collects his winning bet and calls off the $1,500 bet on the remaining five place numbers. Place bets can be called down any time in most casinos throughout the country.

Whenever a FOUR or TEN is made the player wins $540 (at 9 to 5 odds). When a FIVE or NINE is made he wins $420 (at 7 to 5 odds). If a SIX or EIGHT is made he wins $350 (at 7 to 6 odds). The high roller and also the worried dice game operator figure that he has six numbers, the 4, 5, 6, 8, 9 and 10, going for him, against the bank's lone number, 7. And because he believes he is only paying the bank a percentage on one place bet, he thinks he must eventually beat the bank.

Since those six place numbers can be made in 24 ways and the SEVEN can only be made in six ways, the odds are 4 to 1 in favor of the system player's winning either $540, $420 or $350. But if the losing SEVEN appears before one of the six place numbers is thrown, which is 1 in 5, the system player loses $1,800. Even so, it looks like a good bet to the system player because if he makes a couple of FOURS or TENS he's beating the game.

To find the fallacy here we must discover whether the player pays the bank a percentage on the bets he calls down, and if so, how much? To do this we must analyze a series of 36 bets.

Let's suppose that the system player in a single dice session makes 36 such $1,800 place bets, and let us assume that the dice fall exactly as probability predicts and each of the 36 combinations on the dice are made. Craps and ELEVEN: will be made 6 times out of the 36 rolls, but since they do not affect a decision, we can ignore them and consider only 30 bets of $1,800 for a total of $54,000 wagered.

The numbers FOUR and TEN will each be made three times, or six times altogether, and the player retrieves his $1,800 plus $540 in winnings six times out of 30 for a total of $14,040. The numbers FIVE and NINE will each be made four times, or eight times altogether. The player will retrieve his $1,800 eight times plus $420 in winnings each of the eight times, for a total take-in of $17,760. The numbers SIX and EIGHT will be thrown five times each, a total of ten times, and the player retrieves his $1,800 plus $350 in winnings ten times, for a total of $21,500. These winning totals add to a grand win total of $53,300. Subtracting this win total from the $54,000 wagered, we get a loss of $700, or 1.296%.

This brings up one of the most unusual percentage problems in Craps. Why should this system player pay a smaller overall percentage than the percentage on any single place bet? This is because the system player in this instance is actually laying $1,800 to $540, $1,800 to $420, or $1,800 to $350, instead of taking the odds. Hence, when the percentage is computed on the sum risked, it decreases in ratio. However, this percentage reduction is only a paper reduction.

THE RIGHT AND WRONG WAY SYSTEM

This two-way betting system has been a conversation piece for many old-time private-crap-game hustlers for years. It recently popped up again in a $10 booklet published by a Nevada gambling-supply house, and the writer assures the reader that he can beat any banking crap game simply by betting the dice to lose and win at the same time.

The writer advises the system player to bet heavily right from the start because in a short time the management will realize he has a sure-fire system and will bar him from further playing. The idea is for the system player to win as much as he can before being barred.

Here's the method the system writer describes.

The system player walks up to a bank-crap table and places a $60 bet on the Don't Pass or Lose line before the come-out. The shooter on the come-out throws a point number, either 4, 5, 6, 8, 9 or 10 and the system player takes $60 worth of place odds on the point. (See pages 115–118 for place bet odds.)

You begin to see what the theory is now? If the shooter fails to make the point, the system player, who has taken $108 to $60 on the point FOUR (or TEN) will lose his place bet, but will win the $60 bet on the Don't Pass line, thus breaking even. But if the shooter makes the point FOUR, the system player loses the $60 bet on the Don't Pass line, but wins $108 on the FOUR, for a $48 profit. If the point number is FIVE or NINE, the system player breaks even or wins $24 on either point; on the points SIX or EIGHT, he breaks even or wins $10!

According to the author of this booklet, since the player must either break even or win, he can't lose, barring naturals and craps on the come-out.

This statement leaves us breathless. Since this system is based on betting the Don't Pass line, it is utterly impossible to bar naturals and craps on the come-out.

But let's forget this little gem and go on to our analysis of what actually happens to the player who bets the system over a long crap session.

Let's take 360 dice decisions and bet $60 wrong and right. We bet $60 on the Don't Pass line 360 times for a total of $21,600. Out of the 360 decisions, SEVEN or ELEVEN will appear 80 times on the come-out, losing the system player $4,800. Craps will appear 40 times, but since 10 of these craps will be standoffs, due to the bar on the Two-Sixes or the Two-Aces, the system player will win only 30 times for a total of $1,800. The points FOUR or TEN will appear 60 times, compelling the system player to wager $60 each of the 60 times for a total of $3,600 more. The system player breaks even 40 times when the point is missed and earns $48 each of the 20 times it is made for a profit of $960. The points FIVE or NINE appear 80 times, compelling the system player to bet $60 each of the 80 times for a total of $4,800. He breaks even 48 times when the point is missed, and he wins $24 each of the 32 times it is made for a profit of $768. The points SIX and EIGHT will appear 100 times, and the player is forced to bet $60 each time for an additional total of $6,000. The system player breaks even the 54-6/11 times when the point is missed, and he wins $10 on each of the 45-5/11 times it is made for a profit of $454.55.

If we add the system player's winnings of $1,800 on the craps, $960 on the FOURS and TENS, $768 on FIVES and NINES and the $454.55 on the SIXES and EIGHTS, we get a winning total of $3,982.55. Subtracting this total from the $4,800 our system player lost on the naturals, we find that his net loss is $817.45, and, since the system player risked a total of $36,000 playing the system, his rate of loss is 2.27%.

THE FIVE-WAY CRAPS BETTING SYSTEM

This old five-way craps betting system was brought back to life by an extensive advertising campaign in a number of national newspapers and magazines including the *New York Times, Time* magazine, and *Newsweek*. The advertisement promised that for the sum of $35 the buyer with this system was sure to beat the dice tables in Las Vegas, Reno, Bahamas, Puerto Rico, London, Monte Carlo. The advertisement continues as follows.

"ACTION ON EVERY ROLL!"
BET LIKE THE PROFESSIONAL INSIDERS DO

The most talked about dice instruction in America. Put this new knowledge to immediate use for astounding result. By placing only 5 bets and having all numbers in your favor . . . including the 7. After making his point and your 5 bets are placed any number that comes out in each roll 2, 3, 4, 5, 6, 7, 8, 9, 10, 11, 12. YOU WIN! Only if the shooter's point comes back in two rolls, you don't win. You play two rolls after making his point and make $10 to (approx.) $200 (according to the amount bet).

NOW YOU SAY, PROVE IT! O.K.

Get a pair of dice. Play for as many shoots as you like, and you be the judge. Make your point on the 1st roll, then see if you can repeat the same back in 2 rolls. If you don't, YOU'RE A WINNER EVEN IF YOU HIT A 7. Keep track of the score you make, then see your results after 40 to 50 shoots or more.

BET ON IT! MAKING MONEY IS EASY . . . WHEN YOU KNOW
HOW. BET THE SOURCE THE EXPERTS USE . . .
"ACTION ON EVERY ROLL"

Allow 2 to 3 weeks for Delivery.
Send Money Order plus 80¢ for
Overnight Delivery!

Three weeks after your $35 check has cleared, you receive by special delivery a sheet of instruction as follows.

"The following is how the system works. Place a $35 bet on DON'T PASS or lose line before the shooter comes out for a point. The odds are 15 to 1 on the 11, or 4 to 1 on the 7, on the first roll. If you're worried about a 7 or 11 coming out on the first roll, then you could lay the odds on the number he comes out with on the box number of the point made. After he hits his point, you bet the boxes and Field as follows: Place $10 on #6, $10 on #8, $5 on the Field, $5 on Box 4 or 5 whichever number doesn't appear in the Field, depending on where you are playing—in Las Vegas, Bahamas, San Juan or in any legalized casino only. Now, you've GOT TO WIN on every roll—unless he hits his point. We suggest you take your bets down after his 2nd roll."

The first error. The system sheet reveals that the writer knows nothing about craps odds when he says that the odds on an 11 or 7 on the comeout are 15 to 1 and 4 to 1 respectively. The true odds are 17 to 1 on the 11 and 5 to 1 on the 7. Let's skip this little gem and continue with the analysis of this system.

The system player walks up to a dice table in a Nevada or Puerto Rican casino and places a $35 bet on the Don't Pass or Lose line before the comeout. The shooter on the comeout throws a 7 or an 11 and the system player loses his $35. The odds say that this will occur on the average of 8 times out of 36 comeout throws. The system sheet states that if you're worried about a 7 or 11 coming out on the first roll, then you could lay the odds on the number the shooter comes out with. This statement leaves us breathless. How anyone can lay the odds on the point when a 7 or 11 has been thrown on the comeout is beyond me. But to get on with our analysis of the system, let's skip the 7 and 11 and 2, 3 or 12 (craps) on the comeout and say that the shooter throws a 4 on the comeout and see what happens. As things now stand, the player has $35 riding against the point 4. Now the system instructs the player to switch and bet right, but instead of making one win bet as described in the popular Right and Wrong Way System the player is told to make four such win bets. He is told to take $10 worth of odds on the number 6, $10 on the 8, $5 on 4 (no field number) and $5 on the Field. The system player has a total of $65 in wagers on the craps layout. If the shooter throws a seven he collects $35 on the wrong action and loses $30 on the right action. If the player makes his point number 4 and sevens out on the following roll, the system player loses $60 and collects $14 on the place bet 4 for a loss of $46. In short, the system is a very bad adaption of the Right and Wrong Way System described previously because the player is paying a hidden percentage on five bets instead of two.

THE FIELD BETTING SYSTEM

On one of my recent surveys I ran into a curious situation in an illegal gambling joint near an eastern army camp that was patronized by many servicemen. The layout had a 2-3-4-9-10-11-12 Field and I noticed one soldier to whom the rest of the layout seemed to be a blank. All his bets went on the Field. And his manner of betting made it obvious that he was playing a system. I began watching him with considerable interest because it was the first time I had ever seen a player at Bank Craps try to match his system against a space that had such a high P. C. against him as the 11-1/9% that the Field layout carries.

He had a lot of fun for awhile, increasing his bets when he lost and dropping back to his original $1 bet whenever he won. But it wasn't long before I saw him lose six times straight. Then he put $39 on the field, lost again, hesitated a second, went into his pocket, brought out his billfold and took out everything that it contained—an even $80. His hand trembled as he put it down on the Field. If he lost this one his bankroll was going to consist of whatever loose change he had.

The dice came out. A six! He watched the banker scoop in his eighty bucks and then turned and left the casino without even stopping to ask for broke money. I followed him, introduced myself and told him about the survey I was making. And I asked him what in blazes he was doing playing a double-up system against the Field with a 11-1/9 P. C. against him. Then I had to explain what a P. C. was. He didn't know what I was talking about!

"Okay," he said, "maybe that's the catch. But you're wrong calling it the Double-Up system. I read about this system in a recent issue of a men's magazine and the writer said the double-up system was no good, that it is strictly a house come-on. He showed that with his system you risk nearly 50% less and make three times as much profit."

"That's interesting," I said. "And where's *your* profit?"

"Okay, so it didn't work, but it sure looked good on paper."

"They all do," I told him and added, "After losing that last Field bet, if you'd had more money how much would you have bet on the next roll, according to your system?"

The soldier shook his head. "I don't know. The article didn't say. The Field wasn't supposed to lose more than seven times in a row. After the seventh miss it said that the eighth roll would bring up a Field number every time! It was sound as the Bank of England." Then he pulled a clipping from his pocket and handed it to me. It bore a chart like this:

THE FIELD BETTING CHART
ALLOWS FOR 6 CONSECUTIVE MISSES

Roll	Bet	Cumulative Amount Bet	Gross Return on a Win Including Amount of Last Bet	Net Profit
1	1	1	2	1
2	2	3	4	1
3	4	7	8	1
4	9	16	18	2
5	19	35	38	3
6	39	74	78	4
7	80	154	160	6

"I see," I said. "If a Field number doesn't appear for seven rolls you've invested $154. If you win anywhere along the line you are ahead from $1 to $6; but if you lose you are out $154. Quite a system. On the second bet you double up, on the next four you double up and add one; on the last you double up and add two. Since you add after you double up it's *not* a double-up system. That's quite a difference!"

My next step was to hunt up a copy of the magazine article and give it the double-o. The article titled: *All This and Seven, Too* consisted of a solid four and one half pages of text and tables spread over nine pages.

The writer led off with some fancy claims. "This, my friends, is a system to win at dice, in any honest, standard $100 limit (and up) gambling house in the land . . . Don't say it can't be done. It can. The mathematical odds prove it. The system to be divulged to you proves it; the results prove it." No mention is made of the fact that going out and making a million with the system instead of broadcasting the secret to all comers would also help prove it!

Then he makes a crack that implies that there are no gambling houses that do not cheat by saying that there "are supposed to be" places that use honest dice. And he adds that the system won't work unless the dice are honest. In other words, the system is bound to win only you won't find a place where you can use it!

The writer appears to think that crooked dice are the means houses all employ to earn their money. Somebody should take him aside and tell him about percentage and how it operates.

He gets even funnier as he goes along. "Everybody knows, of course," he says, "that in normal betting the odds are against the dice."

And he explains that this is the reason the "professional crapshooters are wrong bettors and bet the dice to lose" and that "the house wants you to ride the dice." After which he advises the reader to bet right just as the house prefers. "You *can* take the dare and bet with the dice. Take chances now and then? Yes. Make big bets? Yes. But stick to The System when you do it, and you'll come out all right. You'll make that killing." And a little further along he gets down to cases. ". . . If the idea of $17 to $35 (profits) per hour for every C-note in your roll appeals to you, read on."

But when you do read on you find yourself blinking at this one. "The System . . . is not based on mathematical frequencies alone. It is a subtle blending of those odds together with practical probabilities and the innate human gambling instinct, with certain checkmates on your emotions." When anyone puts the odds, practical probabilities (whatever those are), the gambling instinct and emotional checkmates all into one cocktail shaker and mixes them up, the drink you get has a kick like an angry mule.

In addition to the $160 minimum bankroll that the writer said had been necessary he also adds that the player must have:

1. A banker's cool head.
2. A gambler's nerve.
3. Patience (where have we heard that before?)
4. A clear mind.

You must also keep a careful and accurate count of the successive number of bets made and the cumulative amount of your bets, and you must be content with a banker's, not a crapshooter's profit. I'll add another requirement he apparently doesn't know about! You also need a complete lack of knowledge of percentage. Because if you know how P. C. operates you won't touch the system with a forty-foot pole even with gloves on.

Let's take a look at the soldier who was playing the system on the Field and at the way the house P. C. that the article didn't mention affects him. In the first place the article says that the Field pays even money on 3, 5, 9, 10, 11 and 3 to 2 on 2 and 12 if the bet is over $1, even money if it is less. He doesn't care or doesn't seem to know that if the layout and payoff odds vary from this description that the house P. C. will also be different. And he seems to think that all layouts carry a Field of the kind he describes when, as a matter of fact, about one out of a hundred answer his description.

The usual Field numbers, as on the layout I found the soldier playing, are 2, 3, 4, 9, 10, 11, 12. The P. C. for the house is 11-1/9%. The writer says the dice will roll out 360 times per hour, something that could happen only if the system player was the only person at the table making bets. The actual figure is about 169 times per hour. But I won't argue the point; I'll call it 360. The soldier who tried the system was, according to the chart, betting amounts of from $1 to $80 each roll. The average for 360 rolls, in the soldier's case, was about $4 per roll. At 360 rolls per hour he would be betting $1440 per hour which, multiplied by the house P. C. of 11-1/9%, means that the house has earned $160 on the action.

This happens to be exactly the amount of bankroll that the writer says is needed to play the system. In short, if you got an even break in the luck playing this system and with the dice rolling 360 times per hour, the house would have earned your $160 bankroll in one hour. And this little detail is a matter the author overlooks entirely!

In the following few months I heard from gamblers all over the country that the Field bet which usually got very little play was getting heavy action. Some of the boys couldn't dope it at all. "All of a sudden a lot of 'smart guys' start playing the Field for no good reason. And to top it off they are using a system. Can you beat it!" Some of the boys knew the answer. They had seen the magazine article. Their reaction was: "I wish that sheet would run an article along those lines every month. It's a shot in the arm for new business. Plenty of boys who never played before are trying the system."

All of which reminded me where the writer found his system. He says that his informant was "the former owner of a small gambling emporium." No wonder the system recommends bets on the Field!

But to finish off the Field Betting System. The writer says that the next best bet on the table is point play. After some very confused mathematics he comes up with the promise that "the System will turn in a minimum of $70 per hour profit" and it only "requires that just one point in eight be made . . ." A glance at the Point Play betting chart which he gives shows that if the shooter should miss out nine times in a row the system player has lost an investment of $227.

Of course this isn't supposed to happen. Why not? Well, and hold your hats on this one, he says that there's a difference between theoretical mathematical frequencies and the frequency with which the points actually do come up. He attaches a chart showing the results of 1,000 consecutive throws of the dice which he made at home and deduces, because his results do not agree exactly with what probability says can be expected, that we can throw the old outworn mathematical law of averages out the window. Boy, page Mr. Einstein! This writer not only is cooking on the front burner; he has boiled over and ruined the stove!

But the worst is still to come. His 1,000 home-made rolls also showed that Snake-Eyes and Box Cars (craps 2 and 12) came up oftener than the theory of probability states can be expected and that 7 (also crap 3) came up less often. Therefore, says he, this "brings us to a strange conclusion but one stoutly supported by the evidence; that Snake-Eyes and Box Cars on every roll are a good bet."

Since either of these points can only be expected to come up 1 out of 36 times in the long run, he appends a chart 16 inches long showing you how to bet progressively in case the Snake-Eyes doesn't show up as soon as it should. If you tried to paste this chart to your cuff so you could have it handy and make sure that you were betting in the proper manner the blamed thing would reach clear up to your shoulder!

The way you do it is place $1 bets on the deuce the first 28 times the dice come out. If you win anywhere along the line, you start back at the beginning again with one buck. But if no deuce shows up you increase your bets to $2 each for the next 16 rolls, then up them to $3 for 9 rolls, then to $4 for 7 rolls. When you reach 141 rolls you find yourself betting 88 bucks with a total investment laid out of $2,630. If the deuce shows the next time you win $98. If it doesn't you are out the two and a half grand plus.

Of course, this isn't supposed to happen either. Who ever heard of rolling the dice 141 times and not having a deuce show up at least once? It sounds awfully good if you don't look at it too hard which is just what we are going to do. So as to avoid too many fractions I'll give the system player another three rolls and make it an even 144. Two aces can be expected to appear 1/36 of the time or on an average of 4 out of 144 rolls. But that's no guarantee that 4 double-aces *must* appear on *every* 144 rolls. Eight double-aces may come and then again there may be none.

Suppose, for instance that the two aces were thrown eight times within the first 28 rolls. According to the magazine's chart the system player betting $1 on Snake-Eyes is ahead $220. Then Snake-Eyes fail to show for 141 rolls. That wipes out the $220 profit and $2,410 more besides. And, at the rate of 360 rolls per hour (given by the author of the article) this hits you within thirty minutes!

Don't ever make the mistake of using a system that supposes the law of averages to be a law. It's not. It's an approximate statement of what will probably happen in an infinite number of throws of the dice—and that leaves a hell of a lot of room for the unexpected to barge in and clip you with a haymaker.

The article also states that "The System does not advice an odds bet on a line point unless that point has not appeared within the span of its chance probability. There is no guarantee that 10 or 4, whose mathematical odds are 11 to 1, will come up on the 12th roll, or before 7, but at least, after 11 rolls you have a better chance." Duck boys, there's our old friend Maturity of Chances, the gamblers' pet fallacy, horning in again!

He also mentions in passing that the correct odds on the Snake-Eye bet are 35 to 1 and that the house only pays off 30 to 1. But he never even hints at what you know this means if you have read my previous chapters and absorbed a few of the facts I've given about percentage and its operation. He doesn't mention the word percentage once in the whole article. He gives no sign of knowing that the house's edge on this come-out bet is a sweet 13-8/9% nor that the reader who bets on two aces with his system is paying the house 13-8/9 cents on every dollar bet. With an even break in the luck and at 360 rolls per hour, he will pay the house at least $160 per hour.

The house P. C. that is in there grinding away on every bet is unbeatable by any system. If it weren't, all the gambling houses in the country would have had For Rent signs tacked to their front doors long before now.

THE SYSTEM THAT WORKED!

You can't beat *the* game but now and then a gambler does beat a game—and with a system. Recently a big book at Open Craps in the South was taken by one player for an amount estimated by the house clockers and other players at close to $150,000.

The man who did it was a smart gambler with a very cute angle. What's more he started with the kind of a bankroll that the boys call a *spit*—a small ten-dollar bill. Strictly a wrong bettor, he placed all his bets down on the outside so as to avoid paying any vigorish to the book. His action was slower this way but he stuck to it, laying the odds on Off Numbers and on Points, and making flat lose bets on which he had the 1.414 P. C. in his favor.

He had been following this same policy for months without much success, had, in fact, been hanging around the game for some time without a dime. But then those storms that all gamblers hope for set in. His lone sawbuck began to grow until it became a couple of grand. From there on his bets were mostly at $300 to $200 and $150 to $100 and the right bettors began to go to him for action because they didn't have to pay him the 5% vigorish that the book charged. He was getting an even-up gamble on the points and earning the 1.414 percentage on his flat bets to lose. And his lucky streak continued.

The book definitely doesn't like such a situation when it happens too often and particularly not on such a large scale. The gambler knew this and tried to keep the book happy by throwing it a little business now and then, preferably on tens and fours and once in a while on sixes and eights. But when his bank roll reached $10,000 the house became skittish.

The bosses couldn't stand seeing him take all that action away from the book and, rather than tell him to take his business elsewhere, they decided to play him from the outside in an attempt to knock him out, break him and get rid of him. One of them took a twenty grand bankroll of the book's money and went to work. When the gambler wanted to bet $500 they lose the boss said "$1,000" and the player, with a 1.414 P. C. in his favor took it. But when the boss took the odds on the points he ran into trouble. When the player wanted to lay $1,000 and the boss asked for $2,000 he got "No" for an answer and had to be content with the smaller bet.

Playing it smart and with his lucky streak still going strong he cleaned the boss of the book's twenty grand and then quit for the night. But the next night he was back again. Ordinarily, the book might have told him that they didn't care for his business, but they were short $20,000 and they wanted it back. The other bosses, using the book's money, went after him on the outside again. But his luck still held and they lost too. This went on for a month, until one night when the player packed up he was ahead a total of nearly one hundred and fifty grand. He didn't show up the next night and hasn't shown since. Unless he is going up against another game somewhere else, it could be that he is the one gambler in a thousand who is smart enough to quit for good when he is ahead of the game. But I wouldn't bet on it.

The bosses, of course, realized after losing their first $50,000 that they shouldn't be doing what they did. But watching the book lose all that action was aggravating. And losing fifty grand is always a barrier to clear thinking and sensible action. They realized that the gambler's smart play made him, in effect, the book—a book that got the action because it charged no vigorish. They knew that when they took the odds they had an even-up gamble and that when they bet $1,000 on a flat bet to win that they were paying him $14 in percentage. But they were trying so hard to recoup that they acted like any player who is stuck— they hoped against hope that they could hit a lucky streak that would overcome the P. C.

When a player can walk into a game, take away the book's action, force the bosses to play him on the outside and make them place right bets—the story has humor. But the snapper is this: the house didn't go broke during the month that this smart apple took them for more than a hundred grand as you might expect. The money the book earned from the other players during that same period not only wiped out the loss but added up to a profit! Breaking a book or a bank is not as easy as the long-haired boys who write gambling sequences into their fiction and movie scripts would have you believe.

P. S. If you think you can do what this player did, be sure to remember one thing. His system worked in the only way any system ever paid off—because he had Old Man Percentage playing ball on his side.

And remember that the P. C. is usually known as the "house percentage" because it favors the house—not *you*.

THE CRAP HUSTLERS' PRIVATE GAME SYSTEM

The smart private-crap-game hustlers whom I have seen in action have their own sure-fire winning system. They manage to get Old Man Percentage to work for them instead of against them. It goes something like this:

Since the hustlers know that the odds in Private Craps favor the wrong bettor, they usually bet wrong. They rarely shoot the dice, but, instead, fade the center or make one or more wrong flat bets because these bets give a favorable edge of 1.414%. When 4, 5, 9 or 10 is the point, they lay the correct odds, but since these wagers give them no percentage they hold them down to a minimum. When the point Six or Eight appears, and they are laying even money, they increase the size of their bets so as to be sure to earn that 9-1/11% edge.

Even with this betting advantage, they still refuse all further action if a player makes two passes. The reason they give for this is that they avoid any chance of going broke while bucking a shooter who might run into a long winning streak. This action, they say, serves as their maximum betting limit and prevents other players from winning too much of their cash in too short a time and then quitting the game. The system works and they earn money with it—against players who don't know the correct odds.

SCARNE'S BANK CRAP SYSTEM

This is the bank-crap betting system I used at the crap tables I visited in this country during my casino survey.

I used this system not to win money but to cut down my crap losses during my survey. I selected the bank-crap bets with the smallest house percentage and systematised them. The bets used were the Pass Line bet, Come bet and Free Odds bet on the point which carried a house edge of .848%.

Neither the crap dealers nor the casino bosses like to see this system used at their tables. Not because they are afraid it will break the bank—the dealers don't like it because it makes considerably more work for them than usual; the casino bosses don't like it because each bet made involved in the system gives the house the smallest favorable percentage at Bank Craps.

This system is not guaranteed to beat the bank because, like all other systems, the player is bucking adverse odds. But it will cut the bank's earning power to a rock-bottom minimum and increase your chances of winning as against those of the average crap player.

Here's the method:

Bet a chip on the Pass line before the come-out. If the shooter throws a natural or crap, again bet a chip on the Pass line. If the shooter throws a point number, 4, 5, 6, 8, 9 or 10, you take the odds on the point. You received the correct odds on this bet since the bank levies no charge. (See page 152).

On the next throw of the dice, you bet 1 chip on the come, and if a 4, 5, 6, 8, 9 or 10 is thrown, you take 1 chip's worth of odds on this number. You again receive the correct odds because of your come bet.

With a rate of loss of .848%, you can expect to pay $84.80 on $10,000 worth of action, and $848 on $100,000 worth of action. So, you see, all systems are worthless, even the best of them.

The only way to take full advantage of the free odds is to make your Pass or Come Bet a minimum (or multiple) of ten ($10).

If you want to shave the bank's percentage down a bit more—to .832%—simply bet the Don't Pass and Don't Come space and lay the free odds.

16

Scarne's Rules for Other Dice Games

There are many parlor games using dice and game manufacturers are constantly issuing board games based on current events, politics, real estate, or on other games such as football, baseball, hockey, boxing, etc., in which dice determine the moves of the counters. Since these games are so numerous and many of them exceedingly short-lived, the rules given here are limited to the most popular betting games currently played in casinos, stores, clubs and bars—games in which the loser is penalized either by losing a bet or having to pay the check or for the drinks.

Nearly all of these games have been completely neglected by previous rule book compilers and have not appeared in print before. For the first time each game has been analyzed to find out whether the game is an even-up proposition, and if not, who has the advantage. In the banking games the percentages in favor of the banker are given.

Both the names and rules of some of these games vary in different parts of the country. The commonest method of play is the one given here, except when it is either strategically or mathematically unsound, in which case the error has been corrected.

Some players do not distinguish between similar games such as Indian and Poker dice and they play one nearly the same as the other. In these cases I have set down the methods of play that are most dissimilar.

The great majority of dice games to be found in other game books are hundred-year-and-more-old games that are seldom played today probably because the rules given are nearly always incomplete.

CORRECT ODDS IN DICE GAMES USING 2, 3, 4 OR 5 DICE

Dozens of different private and banking dice games are played today and their names and rules vary in different parts of the country. For example, some players do not distinguish between similar games such as Hazard and Chuck-a-Luck.

The great majority of these games make use of from two to five dice, and nearly all the hustler's sucker or proposition bets are made on throws of two, three, four, or five dice. They usually involve either the combined total or the appearance of one or one of several possible combinations of hands such as one pair, two pair, three of a kind, etc.

The following tables show the various combinations, the number of ways they can be made, and the odds against making them in one trial. These tables will enable the player to analyze most of the dice problems he will meet. Reference to the correct odds shown here will show whether a proposition bet is or is not a sucker bet. These odds will also enable the player to figure the house's favorable percentage in a banking game. The tables also give you the answers to odds problems that arise in other dice games. The method for figuring the house percentage is given on pages 54 and 55 in chapter 2.

TABLE OF COMBINATIONS AND WAYS

Two Dice

Specific Hands and Combinations	Number of Ways	Odds Against, in One Trial
One Pair	6	5 to 1
A Specific Pair 1		35 to 1
No Pair	30	1 to 5
A Specific No Pair 2		17 to 1
Total Combinations of All Non-Specified Hands	36	

Three Dice

Specific Hands and Combinations	Number of Ways	Odds Against, in One Trial
Three of a Kind	6	35.0 to 1
A Specific Three of a Kind	1	215.0 to 1
One Pair	90*	1.4 to 1
A Specific Pair	15	13.4 to 1
No Pair	120	4.0 to 5
Total Combinations of All Non-Specified Hands	216	

* Although there are actually only six one pair, from aces to sixes, the figure 90 above gives you the total number of ways of holding a pair plus one of the other 5 numbers on the third die. The same holds true for most of the hands shown in the following tables.

Four Dice

Specific Hands and Combinations	Number of Ways	Odds Against, in One Trial
Four of a Kind	6	215 to 1
A Specific Four of a Kind	1	1295 to 1
Three of a Kind	120	9.8 to 1
A Specific Three of a Kind	20	63.8 to 1
Two Pairs	90	13.4 to 1
A Specific Two Pairs	6	215 to 1
One Pair	720	4 to 5
A Specific One Pair	120	9.8 to 1
No Pairs	360	7.6 to 1
Total Combinations of All Non-Specified Hands	1296	

Five Dice

Specific Hands and Combinations	Number of Ways	Odds Against, in One Trial
Five of a Kind	6	1295 to 1
A Specific Five of a Kind	1	7775 to 1
Four of a Kind	150	50.8 to 1
A Specific Four of a Kind	25	310.0 to 1
Full House	300	24.9 to 1
A Specific Full House	10	776.6 to 1
Straight	240	31.4 to 1
A Specific Straight	120	63.8 to 1
Three of a Kind	1200	5.5 to 1
A Specific Three of a Kind	200	37.8 to 1
Two Pairs	1800	3.3 to 1
A Specific Two Pairs	120	63.8 to 1

Five Dice (cont.)

Specific Hands and Combinations	Number of Ways	Odds Against, in One Trial
One Pair	3600	1.2 to 1
A Specific One Pair	600	11.9 to 1
No Pair	480	15.2 to 1
	————	
Total Combinations of All Non-Specified Hands	7776	

Note: When Straights do not count, the number of No Pairs increases to 720.

Five Dice, Aces Wild

Specific Hands and Combinations	Number of Ways	Odds Against, in One Trial
Five of a Kind	156	48.8 to 1
A Specific Five of a Kind (No Aces) .. 31		249.8 to 1
Five Aces	1	7775 to 1
Four of a Kind	1300	4.9 to 1
A Specific Four of a Kind (No Aces) .. 260		28.9 to 1
Full House	500	14.5 to 1
A Specific Full House (No Aces) 100		76.7 to 1
Straights	1320	4.8 to 1
A Specific Straight 660		10.8 to 1
Three of a Kind	2400	2.2 to 1
A Specific Three of a Kind (No Aces) 480		15.2 to 1
Two Pairs	900	7.6 to 1
A Specific Two Pairs (No Aces) 180		42.2 to 1
One Pair	1200	5.5 to 1
A Specific Pair (No Aces) 240		31.4 to 1
	————	
Total Combinations of All Non-Specified Hands	7776	

Note: The words in parentheses (No Aces) mean that you cannot make such a hand. Example: No matter what numbers show on the dice, it is impossible to make a four-Ace hand (with Aces wild). If you threw four Aces and a Deuce, you would have five Deuces; if you threw two Aces and a pair of Deuces you would have four Deuces, etc.

TABLES OF NUMBERS AND WAYS

Two Dice

Numbers	Ways	Odds Against, in One Trial
2 (or 12)	1	35.0 to 1
3 (or 11)	2	17.0 to 1
4 (or 10)	3	11.0 to 1
5 (or 9)	4	8.0 to 1
6 (or 8)	5	6.2 to 1
7	6	5.0 to 1

Three Dice

Numbers	Ways	Odds Against, in One Trial
3 (or 18)	1	215.0 to 1
4 (or 17)	3	71.0 to 1
5 (or 16)	6	35.0 to 1
6 (or 15)	10	20.6 to 1
7 (or 14)	15	13.4 to 1
8 (or 13)	21	9.3 to 1
9 (or 12)	25	7.6 to 1
10 (or 11)	27	6.6 to 1

Four Dice

Numbers	Ways	Odds Against, in One Trial
4 (or 24)	1	1295.0 to 1
5 (or 23)	4	323.0 to 1
6 (or 22)	10	128.6 to 1
7 (or 21)	20	63.8 to 1
8 (or 20)	35	36.0 to 1
9 (or 19)	56	22.1 to 1
10 (or 18)	88	13.7 to 1
11 (or 17)	96	12.5 to 1
12 (or 16)	125	9.3 to 1
13 (or 15)	140	8.3 to 1
14	146	7.8 to 1

Five Dice

Numbers	Ways	Odds Against, in One Trial
5 (or 30)	1	7775.0 to 1
6 (or 29)	5	1554.2 to 1
7 (or 28)	15	517.4 to 1
8 (or 27)	35	221.1 to 1
9 (or 26)	70	110.0 to 1
10 (or 25)	126	60.7 to 1
11 (or 24)	205	36.9 to 1
12 (or 23)	305	24.4 to 1
13 (or 22)	420	17.5 to 1
14 (or 21)	540	13.4 to 1
15 (or 20)	651	10.9 to 1
16 (or 19)	735	9.5 to 1
17 (or 18)	780	8.9 to 1

BACKGAMMON

Backgammon, one of the world's most ancient games, has been played for thousands of years in all parts of the world. It was played in

Egypt, Greece, and Rome, and probably derives from the even earlier oriental game of Pachisi (Parcheesi), in which the movements of counters on a board are governed by the throw of dice. It was played throughout the Middle Ages in Europe as Tables until Chess became the more popular game in the 15th century. In the early 17th century improvements in the game gave it a tremendous revival and it swept Europe under various names: Backgammon in England, Gammon in Scotland, Tric-trac in France, Puff in Germany, Tarola Reale in Italy. Another craze for the game occurred just before World War I, and it is still widely played in the Middle East as Tric-trac. Incidentally, the word Backgammon has been ascribed to the Welsh words *back* and *gammon* (little battle), and also to the Saxon *bac* and *gamen* (back game).

Backgammon as played today is simply a bigtime fashionable illegally operated gambling game, infested by hundreds and hundreds of dice hustlers and cheats. Untold millions of dollars change hands nightly at the game, most of which eventually winds up in the pockets of backgammon hustlers. The introduction of the doubling block has made Backgammon the bigtime gambling game that it is. For example, in some close big money games, the doubling block moves almost as fast as the dice. What may begin as a $100 game can easily double and redouble to $25,600, and since the stakes are tripled when an opponent is backgammoned, a single game can cost the loser $76,800. The biggest Backgammon winning that has come to my attention was the $250,000 three-day score made by three American Backgammon hustlers on the French Riviera.

Anyone can learn the rudiments of the game in a half hour or so, but to become an expert or hustler at the game requires considerable knowledge of dice.

Requirements

1. Two players; three or more sometimes participate in the stakes (see Chouette, page 328).

2. *The Board.* A rectangular board is divided into two halves by a vertical *bar.* One half is called the *inner* (or home) *table;* the other the *outer table.* (Traditionally the inner table is the one nearest the light.) The players, designated *Black* and *White,* face each other. Twelve alternately colored triangles, called *points,* project from each

side of the board toward the center. The players sit on opposite sides of the board.

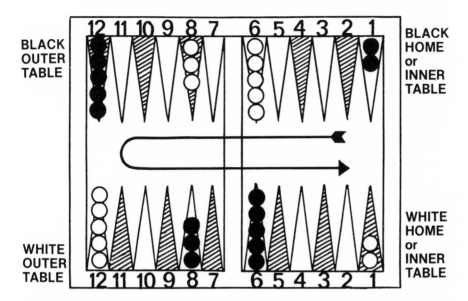

A Backgammon board layout and the location of the black and white men at the start of game. Arrows show the direction of black's moves. Whites move in the opposite direction.

3. *Pieces.* Each player has 15 checkerlike pieces (often called *men* or *stones*) of contrasting colors, usually black and white. Their starting positions are shown in the illustration. The movement of White's pieces is from Black's inner table clockwise to White's home table. Black's pieces travel in the opposite direction.

4. *Dice.* Each player has a dice cup and two dice.

5. *Doubling Cube.* A large die whose faces are numbered: 2, 4, 8, 16, 32, 64.

Notation

Each point is numbered as in the diagram although the numbers do not appear on the board. The initials B and W indicate which side of the board the point is on. A move lists the point moved from and the point moved to. *Example:* White, B12–W6, B1–B3 means: White moves one stone from Black's 12 point to White's 6 point, and one stone from Black's 1 point to Black's 3 point. If more than one stone makes the same move, the number of stones being moved is added in parentheses as: B1–B3 (2).

Start of the Game

Each player throws one die from his cup and the player throwing the highest number has the choice of seat and color of men. If both players throw the same number they throw again. The player throwing the highest number is the winner and plays first by using the numbers on both his own and his opponent's dice. Thereafter, the turn of play alternates and each player throws both his own dice.

The Play

The object of the game is for each player to move his 15 men toward the inner table on his own side of the board, and then *bear* them off the board. White moves clockwise, Black moves counterclockwise. The first player to bear all his men off wins the game.

The numbers on the two dice, taken separately, show the number of points over which the men may be moved. When one man has been moved the number of points indicated by one die, the other number may be used either to move the same man further or to move another man. When a player throws a doublet (both numbers the same) it counts double. A 6–6, for instance, counts as four sixes, a total of 24 points, not 12. Since a doublet consists of four numbers, the player may move as many as four men, or stones.

The player must attempt to use both (or all four) numbers if he can. If he can use only one number, he must try to use the higher (or as many as can be used of a doublet.) If none of the numbers thrown are usable, the play passes to his opponent.

The Moves

A point is open to a player when it is not occupied by two or more of his opponent's men. A player who has two or more men on one point has *made* that point and his opponent's men may not land on it. A man may pass over a closed point in using the total of both numbers on the dice provided each number could be played separately.

A single man on a point is a *blot.* When a man of the opposite color lands on that point the blot is *hit,* and the man originally there is taken off and placed on the bar. A man *on the bar* may *enter* again when a number is thrown that will place the man on an unoccupied point of his opponent's home table. All men on the bar must be reentered before any other moves may be made. When a player has two or more men on a point it is said to be *blocked,* and an opponent's man may not come to rest on the point although it can move past the blocked point. If a player blocks six adjacent points and has one or more of his opponent's men behind it, he has made a *prime.* If he blocks all six points of his home table when his opponent still has one or more men on the bar, he is said to have *shut-out.*

Bearing Off Men

Once a player has advanced all 15 of his stones or men to his own inner table, he may start *bearing off,* which consists in removing men from the board. The first player to bear off all his 15 men wins. A man may be borne off any point whose number shows on either die. *Example:* If White rolls 4–3, he may remove a stone from W4 and another from W3. Instead of bearing off he may also use the numbers to move inside his inner table.

When a number rolled is higher than the highest point on which a player has any men, he bears off from the next highest number. If, after having started to bear off, a man is hit, it goes to the bar and must enter, and come around again to the inner table, before the player can continue bearing off.

Scoring

The first player to bear off all his men wins the game. If the loser has borne off at least one man, and has no man left in the winner's inner table, he loses a *single* game. If he has not borne off a single man, he loses double (*Gammon*). If, in addition, he has a man left in his opponent's inner table or on the bar, he loses triple (*backgammon*).

Doubling

Backgammon is played for an agreed base stake which may be increased by *doubling* during play, and by *gammon* and *backgammon* (as above). An automatic double occurs when equal numbers are thrown on the first roll, and both players roll again. (Automatic doubles may be waived by agreement, and, if not, are usually limited by agreement to one or two per game.)

Either player has the right to offer the first voluntary double before casting, and this right alternates thereafter. The opponent must agree to play at the double stake, or forfeit the game and the stake. If he accepts the double, the game continues at the increased stake. The player who offered the double may not immediately double again. The privilege of making the next double falls to his opponent and if he doubles, the first player either resigns and pays the double stakes or accepts and the game continues with stakes that are four times the original amount. There is no limit to the number of doubles that may be made but the option of offering doubles alternates between players. These doubles are cumulative and in addition to increases from gammon or backgammon.

Additional Rules

The following additional rules will cover most irregularities that may occur:

1. After the game has started, if it is seen that some of the men have been set up in the wrong position, the game must be started again.

2. The dice must be thrown from the box onto the player's right-hand table. If the dice are thrown out of the right-hand table, or if they are tilted and do not rest flat on the surface, or if either die is touched by either player during the throw or before the player has called the numbers showing, the throw is faulty and must be thrown again.

3. A player must not throw his dice until his opponent's play has been completed.

4. After a player has moved a man and taken his hand from the piece, he cannot change his play.

5. If a player moves incorrectly, his opponent can demand that the error be corrected provided he does so before he has made his own throw.

Backgammon Opening-Move Strategy

There are really three distinct styles of playing Backgammon:

1. *The Running Game.* It is usually adopted by a player when he gets several high throws at the outset of the game and everything is subordinated to full speed ahead and no concern about his opponent's moves.

2. *The Block Game.* The object of this strategy is to block as many points in a row as possible to impede opponent's progress. This is purely a defensive game.

3. *The Back Game.* With this type of strategy, a player, instead of trying to rush his men forward, concentrates upon doing everything possible to delay his own forward progress, which he does by endeavoring to have his own men set home and reentered in his opponent's inner table, making points, so that later they may hit the opponent's blots.

Actually, there are two kinds of Backgammon players, those who depend entirely on the element of chance to win and those who put their trust in the fascinating factor of skill. While skill plays a very important part in winning Backgammon, still the element of luck is always present. Therefore of paramount importance to a winning player is an accurate knowledge of the odds in the various dice throws that arise during play. For instance, suppose you wanted to calculate your opponent's chances of a 2 or a 3 compared to the probability of his throwing a 6 or a 7. This can be figured out as follows: The total number of different combinations that can be made with two dice is 36 (see Combination or Ways Table, page 314). A single 2 can be made on the dice in 12 different ways. It can be made a double, and it can be made with any of the other five numbers on the dice. *Examples:* 1–1, 2–6, 6–2, 2–5, 5–2, 2–4, 4–2, 2–3, 3–2, 2–2, 2–1, and 1–2. Hence the chances of throwing a 2 in one throw of the dice is 23 to 12, or less than 2 to 1 against. It is obvious of course that a double can be thrown only one way, but there are two ways to throw any other number, such as 4–2, or 2–4.

The player with a special knowledge of two-dice mathematics need only apply it with intelligence to have a decisive advantage over his opponent whose plays are contrary to the mathematical chances. It takes a knowledgeable player to tell whether or not he is facing a worthy opponent on the first few throws of the dice. A player who fails to play his opening moves correctly cannot be expected to play a good game. To aid such a player, the following examples depict all the first throws with two dice and the best way to play each to gain the best advantage. The various parts of the board and the different points mentioned that follow may be readily located by looking at the diagram on page 319. It also shows the setup for the start of the game.

The best doubles plays to make at start of game are as follows:

1. A 6 and 6 throw: Move two men from your opponent's 1 point to his bar point. Move two men from your opponent's 12 point to your

bar point (a very strong throw). Another strong play is to move three men to your bar and one man to your opponent's bar point.

2. A 5 and 5 throw: Two men from your opponent's 12 point to your 3 point.

3. A 4 and 4 throw: Move two back men from your opponent's 1 point to his 5 point and two men from your opponent's 12 point to your own 9 point.

4. A 3 and 3 throw: There are two excellent ways of playing this throw which are as follows: Move two men from your 6 to your 3 point, and two men from your 8 to your 5 point. Move two men from your opponent's 12 point to your 7 or bar point.

5. A 2 and 2 throw: Move two men from your opponent's 1 point to his 5 point.

6. A 1 and 1 throw: The best opening throw of two dice: Move two men from your 8 to your bar point, and two men from your 6 to your 5 point.

The best regular throws and plays at start of game are as follows:

1. A 6 and 5 throw: Move one man from your opponent's 1 to his 12 point.

2. A 6 and 4 throw: Move one man from your opponent's 1 to his bar point, and one man from opponent's 12 to your 9 point. This is a weak throw.

3. A 6 and 3 throw: Move one man from your opponent's 1 point to his bar point and one from opponent's 12 to your 10 point.

4. A 6 and 2 throw: Move two men from your opponent's 1 point to his bar and 3 point.

5. A 6 and 1 throw: Move one man from your opponent's 12 point to your bar point and one man from your 8 to your bar point. A strong throw.

6. A 5 and 4 throw: Move one man from your opponent's 1 point to his 5 and one man from his 12 to your 8 point.

7. A 5 and 3 throw: Move two men from your opponent's 12 point, one to your 10, and one to your 8 point.

8. A 5 and 2 throw: Move two men from your opponent's 12 point, one to your 11, and one to your 8 point.

9. A 5 and 1 throw: Move one man from your opponent's 1 point, one to his bar point. A weak throw.

10. A 4 and 3 throw: Move two men from your opponent's 1 point, one to his 4 point and one to his 5 point.

11. A 4 and 2 throw: Move one man from your 8 and one from your 6 to your 4 point.

12. A 4 and 1 throw: Move two men from opponent's 1 point, one to opponent's 2 point and one to opponent's 5 point.

13. A 3 and 2 throw: Move one man from opponent's 1 to opponent's 4 point and one from opponent's 12 to opponent's 11 point.

14. A 3 to 1 throw: Move two men, one from your 8 and one from your 6, to your 5 point.

15. A 2 and 1 throw: Move one man from opponent's 1 point to opponent's 2 point and one man from opponent's 12 to your 11 point. The weakest throw of the dice.

Backgammon Strategy

Now that we have discussed opening-move strategy, we continue with the following abbreviated tips, hints, and strategy that are essential to good Backgammon playing.

1. The most important strategy of Backgammon is to start the two men on the opponent's table as soon as possible to prevent their being blocked. These two men are the weakest members of your forces and you should bring them to safety without any delay. Once you form this habit you will have improved your game many times.

A good double early in the game will prevent these men from being blocked; even a small double will help in this direction. Also, if your two furthermost men are on your opponent's 5 point, it will slow the progress of your opponent's men as they arrive at his home table. If you advance these two men to your opponent's bar point, it is also a valuable advantage, but at the start of the game it is wise to hold them on the 5 point just in case you decide to switch to a back game.

2. Avoid taking unnecessary chances. This follows next in importance to advancing your outposts. The beginner usually attempts an overbold game, taking all kinds of chances to make point. This is a very bad habit, for the reckless type of play generally ends in a lost game.

3. The primary objective of a strong opening is to obtain the advantageous points that will slow up the advance of your opponent's two men in your home table. The most important point to secure first is your 5 point, then your bar point, which furnishes you a powerful blockade on your opponent's two outposts. While some players prefer the bar point before the 5 point, all agree that the bar point and the 5 point are

the two strongest points to secure. Next in order comes your opponent's 5 point, which permits the escape of your two outposts.

4. Another important factor to keep in mind is not to crowd your men on your points. Getting a long string of 6 or more men on any point limits your position and places a number of your men out of play. Also, avoid playing your men on to the low points in your home table, as these men also are out of action, and the position puts you at a disadvantage.

5. Never take up a blot in your home table, unless certain that you can block that point. Remember that the men reaching your home table have theoretically traveled all around the board, and their value is much greater than your opponent's two men in your home table. If your opponent's men are hit in your home table, they are only set back a few points, whereas if your men are hit in your home table, they must retravel 19 points to again reach the point where they were hit.

6. Do not expose a man to being hit unless the risk means a greater risk for your opponent if he takes advantage of it.

7. Another vital tactic that is important to learn is that of shutting out your opponent by closing your home table. This basically consists of blocking all the points in your home table so that if you hit an opponent's blot on some other part of the board, he will be unable to restart that man and must rest idle while you continue to play.

8. When forced to leave a blot, always attempt to keep as far away as possible from your opponent's men. A blot seven points away from your adversary can only be hit with a combination throw, and the chances of doing this are about 5 to 1 at that distance. If you are forced to leave a blot within 6 points of your opponent, leave it as near as possible, one point away being safest. Also, when leaving a blot, try to choose a point which is more likely to be covered next throw.

9. When the numbers thrown on the dice are not available to make points, be sure to use them to make preparations for securing points. If your opponent is a safe distance away, spread these builders so that the following throw will permit you to make another point.

10. The expert Backgammon player always knows at all times exactly how far ahead or behind he is of his adversary. The best way to determine your comparative strength or weakness is as follows: First, pair any men you and your opponent have on opposite points, then calculate how many points your unpaired men are from the home table. Then by making the same calculation with your adversary's unpaired men and comparing the total you can estimate which player is ahead.

Once your position is known, you will know just when you must change your tactics or resort to a back game.

11. If your adversary is ahead of you when bearing off, never play up from your 4 or 3 points while still having a large number of men on your 6 point. *Example:* Suppose that your 6 point is loaded with six men and you obtain a small throw of a three and a two; it would be wiser to move up two men from your 6 point, rather than play the men up from the lower points. The two men played forward from the 6 point would leave only four men on that point, and a lucky throw of double sixes would clear these men from the board and give you a possible chance of overtaking your opponent. If you had played up the low throw from the 4 or 5 points, the double sixes would still leave two men on your 6 point, and the chances of hitting two more sixes in the next few throws would be highly improbable.

12. After sending one or two of your opponent's men to the bar and having three or more points blocked in your home table, do not fail to spread your oncoming men so that you can make a new point in your home table or be ready to rehit his men as they reenter.

13. Guard against decoy blots left by your opponent, especially if he is an experienced player. Make doubly sure that the blots are forced or attempted at a great risk, and before hitting same, make certain that his home table is not closed so that if your men are rehit they will be locked out on the bar.

14. If your adversary has locked your two outposts in his home table on his one point and has already brought all his men into his home table and is bearing off his men, the only chance of victory you have is to hold these men in position in the hopes of forcing him to leave a blot as he bears his men. If he should open another point in the midst of his men, endeavor to split up your two men, leaving two blots which form a greater menace to him, as you still have the opportunity of hitting him with the favorable throw and you are putting him in a position where an unfavorable throw on his part may force him to hit one of these blots which then may reenter and send his man or men back to start over. If you can establish your two outposts on the 5 point in your opponent's home table, you are quite safe from any effective block of these two men, and your outside men can then be advanced with more effective action.

15. As the game nears the end and the contest is tight, the men must be advanced to the home table in the fastest manner possible. One way of doing this is to make plays that will carry a man from one table

to another. *Example:* If you have a man on your opponent's 10 point and a three is thrown, move this man across the table to your 12 point; a play that takes the man into your outer table. If you had a man on your 12 point and six is thrown, the play would be to move this man into your home table. Playing your men so that they can go from one table to another permits you to gain the maximum amount of speed in bringing them home.

16. In throwing off, when your home table is closed and your opponent has men on the bar, the safest procedure is to move your men up in your home table rather than to take men off for the throws. This opens up the high points in your home table, so that your adversary can enter on these points, which removes the danger of his hitting you on reentry.

17. In throwing off, when your opponent still has a man or men in your home table, try and keep an even number of men upon the points nearest the bar to avoid an unnecessary blot.

18. In throwing off, after your opponent has passed your men, try to bear off with the fastest possible speed. Remove as many men as possible with each throw, and when certain throws compel you to move up, try to cover the vacant points. A home board with all points covered is more quickly cleared in bearing.

Chouette

This variant of Backgammon is played by three or more players although it is still a two-handed game. The players cast dice for precedence, and the one throwing the highest number becomes the *man in the box;* second highest is *captain* for all the others, and they rank below the captain in accordance with the numbers they throw. Players who tie throw again to determine their rank.

The play is between the man in the box and the captain. Other players may advise the captain, but in case of disagreement he himself has the final decision as to how a move shall be made. If he wishes to double and any of his partners do not want to take the risk, they resign and forfeit their stakes to him. He continues the game on his own responsibility assuming all risk. The man in the box then decides whether to accept the double or resign.

If the man in the box doubles, each opponent must accept individually or pay the current stakes and resign. If the opponent of the man in the box resigns, the next highest player in standing who accepts the double takes his place at the board as the new captain.

If the player in the box wins the game, he stays in the box, and the next member of the team in order replaces the losing captain. If the man in the box loses (including loss by refusal of a double), he becomes the lowest-ranking member of the team. His place in the box is taken by the winning captain, and the next player in order moves up to captain. When a game ends, the player in the box collects from or pays to each remaining active member of the team the full value of the stake at that time.

Partnership Backgammon

Backgammon can be played, like many other two-player games, in partnership—two players versus two, or three against three. In the two-against-two partnership game, one member of each team plays against a member of the other, their Backgammon boards arranged so that rolls of the dice can be seen by all four players. On each side, one player plays Black, while the other partner plays White. The members of only one team roll the dice; one casts for Black and his throws are used by the Black players on both sides, the other rolls for White and his casts are used by both White players. When any player has borne off all his pieces, his team wins the contest.

Dutch Backgammon

This game is played in the same way as Backgammon except that all the men or stones start on the bar, and each player must enter all his 15 men before advancing any of them. He may not hit a blot until he has moved at least one man around to his own inner table.

Turkish Backgammon

In this variation, which is also called Moultezim, the play is the same as in regular Backgammon except for the following:

1. All 15 of White's men start on Black's 12 point and Black's 15 men start on White's 12 point. Black must move all of his men the full 24 points around the board: first to the right from White's 12 point in the White outer board, into White's inner board, then into his own inner board, and off to the left (instead of the right as in regular Backgammon). White also moves in a counterclockwise direction: from the outer board and into the White inner board and off to the right, the same as in the regular game.

2. Both players must get to their own outer boards with their first men before moving a second one from the starting point.

3. One man on any spot is a point.

4. Men are not hit or sent home; there are no blots. Therefore since you cannot stop on top of any man, the most important point of strategy in Moultezim is to create a prime in order to block your opponent. However, the rules of the game do not permit a player to create a prime commencing at the starting point of his opponent; that is, on this section of the board a player must leave one point open.

Greek Backgammon

Greek Backgammon, commonly called Plakato, is played like regular Backgammon except for the following:

1. All 15 of White's men are on the Black one point, and all of Black's men are on the White one point. All the men must move the full 24 points, in the same direction as they do in regular Backgammon.

2. A player can stop on an opponent's man but he cannot remove the piece from the board. That is, the player can leave his man on his opponent's point and the opponent cannot move his man until the player moves his man off.

Gioul

This Middle East variation is played like regular Backgammon except for the following:

1. The men are arranged on the board and move in the same direction as in Greek Backgammon.

2. As in the case of Turkish Backgammon, the men are not sent home.

3. One man stopping anywhere is considered a point, while six men in a row constitute a prime.

4. When a player rolls a double, he plays it as in regular Backgammon, but in Gioul, he continues playing the succeeding doubles all the way to double sixes. *Examples:* If double ones are cast, the player first plays the double ones, followed by double twos, double threes, double fours, double fives, and double sixes. If double fours are rolled, the player plays the double fours, followed by double fives and double sixes. All moves are made before the opponent makes his next roll.

5. If a player cannot complete all of his doubles, he forfeits the rest to his opponent. *Example:* Suppose double fours are rolled and the

player is able to play the double fours but he cannot play the double fives, or can only play one five, his opponent will then complete playing the fives and also play the double sixes. If, in turn, the opponent is unable to finish the doubles, the play of that toss is then considered finished and the opponent makes a new roll.

Acey Deucey

An elaboration of Dutch Backgammon which is a favorite of the United States Navy, Marine Corps, and merchant marine. It is a game for two players and uses a pair of dice which are usually thrown from the hand, although a cup is used in tournament play. Thirty counters, or men, are used, 15 of each color, and an Acey Deucey mat or a Backgammon board is used.

Each player *peewees* a die, that is, each rolls a die, and the player throwing the highest number has the first move. If both throw the same number, the throw is made again. If Black moves first and enters his men on the spaces 1 to 6, White must enter his men on the spaces directly opposite—24 to 19. Black moves to his right and around the table toward White's starting spaces (counterclockwise), and White moves in the opposite (clockwise) direction toward Black's starting spaces. Black may, if he likes, enter his men on spaces 12 to 7 and move in the opposite (clockwise) direction, in which case White must enter on spaces 8 to 13. The players always move in opposite directions.

Each player's object is to enter and move his 15 men through one complete circuit of the board and take them off before his opponent succeeds in doing the same. Men are entered on the board and moved according to the numbers appearing on the dice, either number being played first and each number being played separately. If a player throws "fifty deuce" (5–2) he may enter one man on the 5 space and move it ahead two spaces or he may put two men in play, one on the 5 space and one on the 2 space. The same rule applies to the movement of the men, both numbers thrown being used to move one man or each number being used to move different men. As in checkers, once the player has moved and lifted his fingers from the man, the move may not be retracted.

Any number of men of the same color may occupy the same space. Two or more men of the same color on one space make that space dead for opposing men, who may not land on it. If a man lands on a space occupied by a single opposing man the latter is *booted,* or *kicked,* and must be removed from the board and reentered on the starting spaces. It may be reentered at any time.

A pair of men on the space do not constitute a block past which the opposing pieces may not move but merely prevent opposing men from landing on that space. If Black has a man on space 1, White has a pair each on spaces 5 and 3, and Black throws 4–2, Black may not move his man the total of six spaces because each number thrown must be used separately. He cannot use either the 4 or the 2 because these moves would bring him to spaces 5 and 3, which are occupied by opposing pairs. If he threw 4–3, however, he could move his man three spaces and then four spaces.

Doubles. When a pair of like numbers (two threes, two fours, etc.) are thrown, the player moves his men double the amount thrown. If two fours are thrown he makes four moves of four spaces each.

An Acey Deucey Throw

When ace-deuce is thrown the player moves one man three spaces, or one man one space and another, two spaces. Then he selects any double number he desires and moves accordingly. If he selects double fives he makes four moves of five spaces each. After these moves are completed he takes an additional throw of the dice. If the player cannot use any part of his acey-deucey throw or cannot select a double that he can use entirely, he uses whatever part he can and loses the balance including the right to make an additional throw.

Taking Off

When all 15 men have moved around the board and are within the last six spaces, they are taken from the board according to the throw of the dice. They may also be moved forward within the last six spaces toward the last space on the board. This is often done in order to pair men and prevent booting when an opponent still has a man to enter. If a man is booted when men are being taken off, he must be reentered in the starting spaces and moved around the board again until he reaches the last six spaces before the taking-off process may be resumed.

When there are no men on the space whose number is thrown and when all the men remaining are so close to the last space on the board that they cannot move the number of spaces indicated by the throw, a man on the next highest space to the number thrown is taken off. For example, if there is a man on the opponent's first space and three on his third space and a throw of 5–6 is made, since none of the men can be moved that many spaces, two of the men on the next highest (third) space are taken off. If one player covers six adjacent spaces with pairs it is known as a *Hindenburg Line* and completely blocks his opponent from moving past that section of the board until the arrangement is broken up.

Stakes

Players usually play for a specified amount per game or for so much a man. In the latter case the player who first takes off all his men wins the game and collects from his opponent as many units as the opponent has men left that have not been taken off. If the stakes are a nickel a man and the losing player has five men left, he loses 25 cents.

Ten Things Every Winning Acey-Deucey Player Must Know

1. Learn the rules so thoroughly that you can recall them instantly and correctly.

2. The best form of practice is to play alone. Many hours of enjoyment and heightened skill will be your reward.

3. Take your time and study each play thoroughly before making it.

4. Pay attention to your own game and try not to discuss your or your opponent's plays during the game.

5. Never touch a man (piece) until you are certain you are going to play it.

6. Don't take too great risks during the game, because a good sound game is generally a cautious one.

7. Try and play with better players, as this is one of the best means of improving your game.

8. Do not rattle the dice or tap on the table when it is your opponent's turn to play—instead use that time to analyze the men on the board.

9. When moving a man, don't play hunches—play the odds.

10. Lose with good grace and sportsmanship, and remember that the main purpose of the game is entertainment.

European Acey Deucey

While the pieces are set on the board as for regular Backgammon, this variant differs as follows:

1. On a roll of acey-deucey (1–2), the stakes are doubled and the player may use the roll of 1–2, name any doublet he wishes, move his doublet and also the complementary doublet, and roll again. (The com-

plement of a number is its difference from 7. Thus, having named 3–3, the player next uses 4–4.) Of course, if the player is unable to use any portion of the roll, he loses the rest of the acey-deucey privilege. *Example:* A player rolls 1–2, moves, names 5–5, moves, but can then move only three 2's. He loses the fourth 2 and does not roll again.

2. To bear off, the player must roll the exact number of the point on which he has men. *Example:* The player rolls 6–2 having men on all points but 6 point and 2 point. He has no move. But with any pieces outside his own table, he may move the men inside his home table. With all in the home table, however, only bearing off is permitted.

Russian Backgammon

In this variation, no men are placed upon the board at the start, but each player enters his men by throws of the dice—both players enter in the same home table and both move in the same direction around the board to the opposite table. Bearing off is the same as in Backgammon. After having entered two or more men, a player is at liberty either to continue entering his men with any subsequent throws, or to move the men already entered. When a blot is hit, the owner must reenter it before he makes any other move. But at any other time a player must move men already entered to use his full roll, even if unable to enter any additional of the original 15 off the board. Except on a player's first roll of the game, doublets are used twice over; he can not only play the upper faces of the dice twice over, but the bottom (opposite) faces also, and can throw again before his opponent. After each thrown doublet the player continues to throw until he fails to throw a doublet, in which case he plays the numbers thrown and the throw passes to his opponent.

Tabard Backgammon

This variant is played like regular Backgammon except that all of Black's pieces are set up in White's inner and outer tables, while all of White's men are set up opposite these in Black's inner and outer tables. There are the same number of pieces that there are on the same points as in the regular game and the play from there on is identical.

Snake

In this variation, which is played primarily as a basic practice game, Black pieces are set up as usual (five on B6, three on B8, five on

W12, and two on W1), but White has only six men on the board, two each on B1, B2, and B3, the other nine being on the bar. All other rules are as in regular Backgammon.

CHUCK-A-LUCK

A very old dice game originally called Sweat-Cloth in England and known in this country, where it appeared about 1800, as Sweat. Later it came to be known as Chucker-Luck and finally as Chuck-Luck, Chuck-a-Luck, and simply Chuck. More recently it has been known as The Bird Cage.

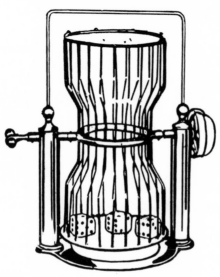

Since the numbers on the back line of the Hazard layout (the three-dice Hazard originally called Grand Hazard) are the same, are called "the Chuck numbers" and are paid off at the same odds, the two games are very closely related.

Rules

Three dice are tumbled in a wire cage called the Chuck cage and the layout bears the numbers 1, 2, 3, 4, 5, 6. The players place their bets on the numbered spaces of the layout, and if the player's number appears on one die, the bank pays off even money; if this number appears on two dice, the bank pays 2 to 1; and if on all three dice, the bank pays 3 to 1. In casinos the limit is usually $5, $10 or $25.

336 / Scarne on Dice

In the casinos today it is the occasional gambler and the women who give the cage its action. It is also found at outings and bazaars where, when he gets action, it is an outing hustler's dream. "Three winners," the dealer shouts, "and three losers every time!" This come-on sounds good and is apparently believed by the non-thinkers who play the game, but it is considerably shy of the truth.

Suppose we test the dealer's claim by putting one dollar on each of the six numbers and spin the cage. If the three dice show three different numbers, the house takes in $3 and pays out $3. So far it's even-up. But notice what happens whenever two dice show the same number. Suppose that two 3s and a 4 are thrown. The bank pays $2 on the 3 and $1 on the 4 but collects $1 each on the 1, 2, 5 and 6. There are two winners and four losers and the house pays out $3 and collects $4 for a dollar profit. And if three of a kind are thrown, there is one winner and five losers; the house pays out $3 and takes in $5 for a $2 profit.

To find out what this advantage in favor of the house amounts to in percentage, we consult our *Three Roll Table* and find that 216 combinations can be made with three dice which in the long run will consist of 120 no pairs, 90 pairs and 6 threes of a kind. Suppose that we continue to cover each numbered space on the layout with $1 bets and spin the cage 216 times. We will wager $6 each of 216 times for a total of $1,296. In 120 spins we can expect to get no pairs. Each time we lose $3 and win $3 and in the end come out even, having bet $720 and taken down $720.

But on the 90 spins on which pairs appear, we wager a total of $540. We take down $270 on the double numbers at 2 to 1 and $180 on the third number at even money, a total of $450. Our loss is $90.

On the 6 times that three of a kind appear, we wagered a total of $36 but at 3 to 1 take down only $24 for a loss of $12.

Our total loss of $102 divided by the total amount we wagered or $1296 gives us the percentage in favor of the house as 7-47/54%.

Some impatient Bird Cage operators apparently feel even this P. C. is not strong enough because they gaff the cage as well, using electric dice and an electro-magnet in the table beneath the cage.

Electric dice are loaded in such a way that they bring up either one of two opposite sides. The three chuck dice are all loaded alike and when the juice is on either a pair or three of a kind must appear. If the open sides are the six and ace, the dice will show 3 sixes, 3 aces, a pair of sixes and an ace, or a pair of aces and a six.

The tipoff on the electric cage is the fact that the distance between the floor of the cage and the table in which the magnet is concealed is not as great as on a fair cage.

The Cross on the Cage

You can also lose even when you operate the game yourself. Suppose you are the chairman of a lodge entertainment committee and you want to provide a few games of chance for the members of your annual outing. But you are smart; you have a suspicion that last year when you made a deal with a professional for a percentage of the profits that he made more out of it than the lodge did. You want to avoid that this time so you decide to rent the cage and have it operated by a lodge member.

You go to a dealer who handles gambling equipment and put the proposition up to him. "I want to rent a chuck-a-luck cage. But you won't need to supply an operator. We'll run it ourselves."

Curiously enough the dealer doesn't object the way you were afraid he might. "Okay," he says. "But if my man doesn't go along with it, I've got to know where you're going to use the cage. I can't rent it unless I know that the spot is okay. Otherwise the cops might pull a raid, grab the cage, and you wouldn't be able to return it."

That sounds reasonable enough so you give him the information he wants, pay the rent in advance (which is usually equal to the retail cost of the cage and dice if you bought them outright) plus a deposit to insure the safe return of the cage. The dealer requires the deposit because it has happened that the entertainment committee has smashed the cage in a fit of anger on discovering that, instead of making a profit for the lodge, they have lost heavily.

Why does it lose? Well, when the dealer wraps up the cage you don't get quite the same article that you do if his operator were going to accompany it. The dice it contains are loaded. Then a couple of the dealer's friends show up at your outing or bazaar and put down the limit in folding money on the numbers they know the dice favor. Instead of clearing the expected profit, the lodge loses its shirt and the entertainment committee gets a new chairman!

If you hire a Chuck-a-Luck operator, you get the short end of the deal; and if you don't, you get clipped even worse. There is not only more than one way to skin a cat, but there are dozens of ways to clip a chump.

Crown and Anchor

This fast banking game, very popular among the British and Australians is now being played by many American servicemen. Three dice are used each of which carry the six symbols: Crown, Anchor, Heart, Spade, Diamond and Club. A layout carries the same symbols.

The players place their bets on the symbols on the layout and the banker throws the three dice from a cup. The payoff, even money on singles, 2 to 1 on pairs, 3 to 1 on three of a kind, shows that the game is actually Chuck-a-Luck in disguise and the advantage for the bank is the same 7-47/54% as in Chuck.

My advice is the same as for Chuck-a-Luck: Don't play it. The game is too fast and the P. C. too high to beat.

KLONDIKE

This is both a counter and casino banking game.

Counter Klondike

Five dice are used and are dropped through a chute that contains a series of inclined planes which trip the dice. The banker throws first and then each player throws in turn trying to beat the banker's original throw. The bank takes all ties.

The scoring is similar to Indian Dice, the combinations or hands made, in descending order of value, are: five of a kind, four of a kind, full house, three of a kind, two pairs, one pair. No pair and straights (numbers in sequence) have no value. The dice that do not help make one of these combinations do not count, a pair of deuces with a six having the same value as a pair of deuces with any other number. The ace is high, the deuce low.

Casino Klondike

This is similar to the counter game except that two dice cups and two sets of five dice each are used together with a layout which offers the player three different types of bets: *Win, Lose,* and *To Beat Two Aces.* A bet on a *Win* space wins for the player if he beats the banker's throw; a bet on a *Lose* space wins if he scores less than the banker's throw; a bet on the space marked *To Beat Two Aces* wins if he throws two pair or more.

The Banker throws first on the Klondike space and lets his dice remain there. The player on his left throws next, using the second set of five dice, and the others follow in rotation from left to right. The bank pays even money on all bets and collects or pays off on each wager after each player's turn. The bank takes all ties.

BANK'S FAVORABLE PERCENTAGE. On the Win and Lose bets, the bank's advantage obviously lies in the ties and it works out at 5.195 + %. On the Beat Two Aces bet, the P. C. is twice as strong: 11.111%. The method of computing both percentages is given below in detail.

The P. C. makes cheating unnecessary and in most casinos the game is not gaffed. But fly-by-night operators sometimes use First Flop Dice so that the dealer can throw high at will. Electric dice can also make Klondike a sure-fire proposition.

Method of Calculating the P.C.

The probability that any specific combination (or hand) will be thrown by the bank is the number of ways that combination can be made divided by the total number of combinations possible with five dice. The probability that any two combinations will be thrown in succession (first by the banker and then by the player) is the product of their separate probabilities.

The *Combination Table* (p. 315) shows that the numbers on five dice can be combined in 7776 ways of which 720 ways are *no pairs.** The probability that the banker will throw no pair is, therefore, 720/7776, and the probability that the player will throw no pair is the same. The probability that both banker and player will each throw a *no pair* in succession is 720/7776 × 720/7776 or 518,400/60,466,176. In other words there should be 518,400 ties of *no pair* out of 60,466,-176 throws.

---

* Straights excluded.

A specific *pair* (such as a pair of deuces) can be made in 600 out of 7776 ways for a probability of 600/7776 and the probability that it will be tied is that fraction multiplied by itself or 360,000/60,466,176. If there are 360,000 pairs of deuces, there will be like numbers of pairs of threes, fours, fives and sixes, a total of 2,160,000 ties of *pairs*.

A specific two-pair combination (such as a pair of deuces and a pair of threes) can be made in 120 out of 7776 ways. And 120/7776 × 120/7776 gives us a probability of 14,400 ties of this two-pair combination out of 60,466,176 throws. Since there are 15 different two pair combinations, there is a total of 15 × 14,400 or 216,000 ties of *two pairs*.

A specific three of a kind combination can be made in 200 out of 7776 ways. And 200/7776 × 200/7776 gives us a probability of 40,000 ties of this three of a kind combination out of 60,466,176 throws. Since there are 6 different three of a kind combinations, there is a total of 6 × 40,000 or 240,000 ties of *three of a kind*.

A specific full house can be made in 10 out of 7776 ways. And 10/7776 times 10/7776 supplies a probability of 100 ties out of 60,-466,176 throws. Since there are 30 different full house combinations, there is a total of 30 × 100 or 3,000 ties of *full houses*.

A specific four of a kind can be made in 25 out of 7776 ways. And 25/7776 × 25/7776 gives us a probability of 625 ties out of 60,466,-176 throws. Since there are 6 different four of a kind combinations, there is a total of 6 × 625 or 3,750 ties of *fours of a kind*.

A specific five of a kind can be made in only 1 out of 7776 ways. And 1/7776 × 1/7776 gives us a probability of 1 tie out of 60,466,176 throws. Since there are 6 different five of a kind combinations, there is a total of 6 × 1 or 6 ties of *five of a kind*.

Summary: In each 60,466,176 throws, the probability is that there will be—

518,400	ties	of	No pair
2,160,000	"	"	Pairs
216,000	"	"	Two pair
240,000	"	"	Three of a kind
3,000	"	"	Full house
3,750	"	"	Four of a kind
6	"	"	Five of a kind

3,141,156 ties of all sorts

Since all these 3,141,156 ties win for the banker, he has an advantage of 3,141,156 ties divided by 60,466,176 throws or *5.194 + %*.

To get the P.C. on the *Beat Two Aces* bet, we add the 720 ways that no pairs can be made to the total of 3600 ways that pairs of twos, threes, fours, fives and sixes can be made for a total of 4320 ways that will *not* beat two aces and will win for the bank. These losing throws subtracted from the total of 7776 ways leaves 3,456 combinations that will beat two aces and lose for the bank. Subtracting losing from winning throws, we find that the bank has 864 more ways of winning than losing, an advantage on the *Beat Two Aces* bet of 864/7776 or *11.111%*.

HAZARD

There used to be two games of Hazard, the 700-year-old Hazard played with two dice from which Craps evolved and a three-dice Hazard played with a layout and called Grand Hazard. Writers of game books have long confused them; even today they think that Grand Hazard is Chuck-a-Luck.

Today, in this country, Craps has superseded the two-dice Hazard. But the three-dice Grand Hazard is one of the most popular banking games in the country and is known simply as Hazard.

Occasional gamblers like it because its action is fast, because of the great variety of bets the layout carries and because, being completely unable to calculate its none-too-easy-to-figure percentages, they seldom have the slightest idea what they are up against. Some players even believe that the house percentage is the same on all bets.

The players see payoff odds running as high as 180 for 1 and, even if they knew that the correct odds are 215 to 1, they'd still make the bet

because $180 for $1 is a lot of money. Even the banker eyes ten or twenty dollars on such a bet nervously because, if the player wins, it means a payoff of $3,600 which will take even the higher percentages found in this game a considerable time to get back.

The smart gamblers who know a little something about P.C. also play it but they stick to bets that have low percentages and avoid the sucker propositions some of which have a P.C. as high as 30-5/9%. The banker likes both kinds of action, smart and dumb; it balances the layout.

The usual limits at Hazard are $5, $10 and $25 with exceptions made occasionally for big bettors.

The foregoing layout and three dice are employed. The players place their money on the various spaces of the layout and the banker, behind the layout, drops the three dice through a Hazard chute which sometimes contains a series of inclined planes called steps down which the dice roll. Or they are thrown from a Hazard cup.

The game is one of the fastest for the players and one of the most profitable for the bank because all bets are decided *every time* the three dice are thrown.

Chuck Number Bets

A bar running across the top of the layout is divided into spaces each of which bears one of the numbers 1, 2, 3, 4, 5, 6. These bets are paid off at the same odds as at Chuck-a-Luck. If one ace appears when the three dice are thrown, the bank pays off players who have bet on the 1 space at even money; if two aces appear, it pays off at 2 to 1; if three aces appear, it pays off at 3 to 1. The same holds true for each number. The house P. C. is the same as at Chuck-a-Luck: *7-47/54%*.*

High and Low Bets

When a player puts his money on the space marked high, he wins if the sum of the spots showing on all three dice after the throw totals 11 or more, provided the high score is not made with three of a kind (3 fours, 3 fives or 3 sixes) in which case the bank wins. Bets on the Low space are won by the player when the total is 10 or less and provided the Low score is not made with three of a kind.

The fact that the banker collects on three of a kind (sometimes

---

* See Chuck-a-Luck, page 335–337, for method of calculating this P. C.

called triplets) on this bet is what gives him a favorable P.C. There are 216 possible combinations with three dice (6×6×6) of which 108 are high and 108 are low. Since there are 6 ways to make triplets out of 216 and 3 will be high and 3 low, the bank's advantage is 3 throws out of 108, a probability of 3/108 or 1/36. Expressed in percentage, the banker has a favorable percentage on the High (and also on the Low) space of *2-7/9%*.

Odds and Even Bets

Here again the banker wins when triplets appear. If your money is on the Odd space, you win when the sum of the spots is odd except when odd threes of a kind (3 aces, 3 threes, or 3 fives) appear. Since there are 108 odd and 108 even numbers, the bank's advantage is the same as on the High and Low bets, *2-7/9%*.

Raffles

A bet on this space placed opposite a certain three of a kind (as three aces) is a bet that that particular triplet will appear on the next throw. Since there is only 1 way of making a specific triplet out of 216 combinations, the correct odds are 215 to 1. The bank pays 180 for 1 which is actually only 179 to 1 and thus has a favorable advantage of 36 ways or throws out of 216. In percentage this is 36/216 or 1/6 of 100, an edge for the bank of *16-2/3%*.

Any Raffle

A bet there is a wager that any one of the triplets will appear. The correct odds are 35 to 1 and the bank pays 30 for 1 which means 29 to 1. The bank has an advantage of 6 ways out of 36 and 6/36 of 100 equals an edge for the bank of *16-2/3%*.

Across the bottom of the layout there are spaces bearing the numbers 4 through 17. A bet placed on one of these numbered spaces is won by the player when that number appears as the sum of the three dice thrown. The following breakdown gives the percentage and method of computing it for each number.

FOUR can be made in 3 ways (1-1-2, 1-2-1, and 2-1-1) out of 216 ways. Since there are 3 chances in 216 or 1 in 72, the correct odds are 71 to 1. When the bank pays 60 for 1 which means 59 to 1, it has an advantage of 12 ways in 72. 12/72 or 1/6 of 100 is an edge for the bank of *16-2/3%*.

Some banks pay 60 to 1, have an advantage of 11 ways in 72 for an edge of *15-5/18%*.

SEVENTEEN. Same P.C. as number FOUR.

FIVE can be made in 6 out of 216 ways and the correct odds are therefore 35 to 1. When the bank pays off at 30 for 1 (29 to 1), it has an advantage of 6 ways in 36 for a P.C. of *16-2/3%*.

When the bank pays 30 to 1, its P.C. is *13-8/9%*.

SIXTEEN. Same P.C. as number FIVE.

SIX can be made in 10 ways out of 216 and the correct odds are therefore 20-3/5 to 1. When the bank pays 18 for 1 (17 to 1), it has an advantage of 3-3/5 ways in 21-3/5 ways and 36/216 or 1/6 times 100 equals an edge for the bank of *16-2/3%*.

When the bank pays 18 to 1, its P.C. is *12-1/27%*.

FIFTEEN. Same P.C. as number SIX.

SEVEN can be made in 15 ways out of 216 and the correct odds are therefore 13-2/5 to 1. When the bank pays off at 12 for 1 (11 to 1), it has an advantage of 2-2/5 ways in 14-2/500 1/6 which is a P.C. of *16-2/3%*.

When the bank pays 12 to 1, its P.C. is *9-13/18%*.

FOURTEEN. Same P.C. as number SEVEN.

EIGHT can be made in 21 ways out of 216 and the correct odds are therefore 9-2/7 to 1. If the bank pays 8 for 1 (7 to 1), it has an advantage of 2-2/7 ways in 10-2/7 ways or 2/9 which is a P.C. of *22-2/9%*.

When the bank pays 8 to 1, its P.C. is *12-1/2%*.

THIRTEEN. Same P.C. as number EIGHT.

NINE can be made in 25 ways out of 216 and the correct odds are therefore 7-16/25 to 1. When the bank pays 6 for 1 (5 to 1), it has an advantage of 2-16/25 ways in 8-16/25 ways or 11/36 which is a P.C. of *30-5/9%*.

When the bank pays 6 to 1, its P.C. is *18-53/54%*.

TWELVE. Same P.C. as number NINE.

TEN can be made in 27 ways out of 216 and the correct odds are therefore 7 to 1. When the bank pays 6 for 1 (5 to 1), it has an advantage of 2 ways out of 8 or 1/4, which is a P.C. of 25%.

When the bank pays 6 to 1, its P.C. is *12-1/2%*.

ELEVEN. Same P.C. as number NINE.

The same advice goes for this game as for Bank Craps. If you must play it, give yourself at least half a chance to win. Play it smart and remember that the higher the P.C. against you, the smaller is your chance of coming out ahead of the game. The banker is bound to get your money in the long run, but if you stick to low P.C. bets, he'll have to work longer for it.

P.C. IN FAVOR OF THE BANK ON ALL BETS AT HAZARD

Bets	Correct Odds	When Bank Pays	The P.C. Is	When Bank Pays	The P.C. Is
CHUCK NOS.					
Singles		Even money			
Doubles		2 to 1	7 47/54%		
Triplets		3 to 1			
HIGH .... ⎱		Even money	2 7/9%		
LOW .... ⎰					
ODD .... ⎱		Even money	2 7/9%		
EVEN .... ⎰					
RAFFLE	215 to 1	180 for 1	16 2/3%		
ANY RAFFLE	35 to 1	30 for 1	16 2/3%		
4 ⎱ 17 ⎰	71 to 1	60 for 1	16 2/3%	60 to 1	15 5/18%
5 ⎱ 16 ⎰	35 to 1	30 for 1	16 2/3%	30 to 1	13 8/9%
6 ⎱ 15 ⎰	20 3/5 to 1	18 for 1	16 2/3%	18 to 1	12 1/27%
7 ⎱ 14 ⎰	13 2/5 to 1	12 for 1	16 2/3%	12 to 1	9 13/19%
8 ⎱ 13 ⎰	9 2/7 to 1	8 for 1	22 2/9%	8 to 1	12 1/2%
9 ⎱ 12 ⎰	7 16/25 to 1	6 for 1	30 5/9%	6 to 1	18 53/54%
10 ⎱ 11 ⎰	7 to 1	6 for 1	25%	6 to 1	12 1/2%

THE LAS VEGAS BIG SIX

The Big Six, or Jumbo Dice Wheel, is a giant wheel of chance five feet in diameter which, with its pedestal, stands eight feet high. It is the most popular of the casino side games and often earns the house $1,000 or more per day.

There are 54 spaces around the rim of the wheel's surface, each of which shows one side of three dice bearing different combinations of the numbers 1 through 6. There is a layout which also bears the numbers 1 through 6. The players *cover* (put their money on) one or more num-

A Big Six dice wheel found in many Nevada casinos

bers on the layout and the dealer spins the wheel in a clockwise direction. Projecting *posts* (nails) on the outer edge of the wheel's rim separate the spaces and pass by a leather indicator at the top. When the wheel comes to a stop, the section in which the indicator rests is the winning combination.

This is how one of the "Gaming Guide Souvenir Booklets," which most luxury casinos distribute free to hotels and casino guests, describes the payoff odds.

IT's THE BIG SIX FOR BIG THRILLS. You'll enjoy a thrill a minute at this spell-binding Wheel of Fortune. If you put $1 on 1 and the wheel stops at 1-2-3, you get back $1 plus the $1 you invested since the 1 showed only once. If the wheel stops at 1-1-2 you get back $2 plus the $1 you invested since the $1 shows twice. This holds true for all the numbers, i.e., if you play $1 on 5 and the wheel stops on 4-5-6, you get back $1 and your dollar. If it stops at 5-5-5, you receive $3 and your $1.

If you are still not convinced that this is the game for you, the Big Six dealer will explain further advantages of the game. He tells you that "there are three winners and three losers on each and every spin of the wheel." He illustrates this by putting a silver dollar on each of the six numbers on the layout, then he points to a space on the wheel marked 1-2-3 or a space marked 4-5-6 and tells you that if the wheel stops on either of these spaces the player who wagered $1 on each of the six numbers on the layout can't lose any money. The player would win three $1 bets and lose three $1 bets, thus breaking even. He demonstrates this by collecting the three silver dollars on the losing numbers and uses them to pay off the three winning numbers. "Nothing," he adds, "could be fairer than that."

What the casino booklet and the dealer fail to point out is the fact that there are only six sections on the wheel that are dead even and contain three different numbers. The other 48 sections contain 24 doubles (pairs), and 24 triplets (three of a kind). This arrangement gives the Big Six operator a favorable advantage of 22-2/9%, which is much too large for any player to overcome.

Here, without the help of algebra, trigonometry or differential calculus, using only simple grade-school arithmetic, is the proof that this is the correct percentage.

The wheel bears 54 sections of which 6 have no pairs, 24 have pairs, and 24 have three-of-a-kinds. Let's put a $1 bet on each of the six numbers on the layout, spin the wheel 54 times, and assume that the "law of averages" is strictly enforced and that each of the 54 spaces appears once as a winner. We wager $6 on each of the 54 spins for a total of $324.

In 6 spins of the wheel we get "no pairs," winning $3 and losing $3 each time. We come out even, having bet $36 and taken down $36.

On the 24 spins in which pairs appear, we have wagered a total of $144. We take down $72 on the double numbers at 2 to 1, and $48 on the single numbers at even money, a total of $120. Our loss is $24.

On the 24 spins in which three-of-a-kinds appear, we have wagered a total of $144 and at 3 to 1 take down only $96 for a loss of $48.

Our total loss of $72 divided by the total $324 wagered gives us the percentage in the operator's favor of 22-2/9%, or, in decimals, 22.22+%.

Since your average rate of loss is 22-2/9¢ on each dollar wagered, do you still think the Big Six is as attractive a proposition as the booklet and the dealer tried to make out?

Some Big Six wheels have fewer than 54 sections—48 or 30 or some other number—and the dice arrangements on their winning sections vary as well. The more triplets there are on the wheel, the greater the operator's percentage.

HIGH DICE

Also Called Beat the Banker and Two Dice Klondike

A very popular and very fast counter game usually operated by dice girls. It is also a deceptive game because it looks as though it should be easy to beat but is not.

A pair of dice are thrown from a cup. Banker and player each throw once, the banker first. The player must throw a higher number than the banker to win. The banker takes all ties.

The game is an even-up proposition except for those ties which constitute the house percentage. To calculate this we simply need to find out how many ties the law of averages says can be expected to be thrown in the long run. The banker stands to throw the number two (with two aces) once out of 36 throws. The player's chance of throwing two aces is the same, and the chance that they will both throw two aces in succession is 1/36 times 1/36 or 1/1296. A tie with two aces will be thrown once out of every 1296 times in the long run.

Since *three* can be thrown in 2 ways (1-2 and 2-1), the banker will throw it 2/36 of the time and the player will do the same. 2/36 times 2/36 is 4/1296 which means that a tie of three will be thrown 4 times in 1296 throws. If we make this same calculation with each number from 2 through 12, we get the results listed below:

No.	Chance of a Tie		
2	1/36 x 1/36 =	1/1296
3	2/36 x 2/36 =	4/1296
4	3/36 x 3/36 =	9/1296
5	4/36 x 4/36 =	16/1296
6	5/36 x 5/36 =	25/1296
7	6/36 x 6/36 =	36/1296
8	5/36 x 5/36 =	25/1296
9	4/36 x 4/36 =	16/1296
10	3/36 x 3/36 =	9/1296
11	2/36 x 2/36 =	4/1296
12	1/36 x 1/36 =	1/1296

Adding, we find that we can expect to throw a total of 146 ties out of 1296 times. This is a favorable percentage for the bank of *11.265%* which amounts to 56¢ on a $5 wager. In the long run the bank earns the amount of your bet every nine throws.

If the banker pays the player when the latter throws two aces, there are 144 ties and the P.C. is reduced to *11.111%*.

UNDER AND OVER 7

This is an old timer that is still going strong. It gets a steady play because it is simple, easy to learn and so deceptive in appearance that the average player looks at it, scratches his head and can't understand why the operator of the game doesn't go broke in short order. The game is popular with the operators because they know that their chance of losing is nil, that it is one of the biggest sucker games ever to come down the pike, and that the P. C. for the house, although the player can't see it, is as strong as they come.

The game is usually operated by hustlers. Two dice, a dice cup, and the layout shown below are used, the design sometimes being simply drawn on the pavement with chalk or scratched on the ground.

The player puts his money on any one of the three spaces and

Under 7 **2 3 4 5 6**	**7**	Over 7 **8 9 10 11 12**
EVEN MONEY	5 FOR I	EVEN MONEY

throws the dice. If he bets on UNDER 7 and throws any of the numbers under seven, the bank pays him off at even money. The same is true of the OVER 7 space. If he puts his money on the 7 space, he is paid off at 5 for 1.

It all looks as if the operator were bending over backward to give the customers a fair chance to win. He's bending over all right, like the leaning tower of Pisa, but in the other direction. Here's the breakdown.

Since there are 6 ways out of 36 to make *seven,* the player who puts his money on that space can expect to win 1/6 of the time. If the operator paid off at 5 to 1, it would be an even-up proposition. But that 5 *for* 1 on the layout actually means only 4 to 1. The operator only pays off $4 when he should be paying $5. This is a P. C. in his favor of 16-2/3% or 81-2/3¢ on every $5 bet.

Some of the *Under and Over 7* operators go even further when the chumps will stand for it and pay off only 3 to 1 for a nice hefty 33-1/3% advantage.

Of the 36 combinations with a pair of dice 15 will add to the numbers on the UNDER 7 space. The player has 15 chances out of 36 to win which means that the correct odds are 7 to 5 against him. The operator only pays off even money and again has a favorable advantage of 16-2/3%. The same holds true for the OVER 7 space.

No matter where you place your money you are bucking a stiff P. C. of at least 16-2/3 (and sometimes even 33-1/3) which will grind down your bankroll almost as fast as if you had your pocket picked. *Under and Over 7* is the biggest sucker game of them all. When you see it, do a right about face and a hasty retreat on the double-quick.

FOUR FIVE SIX OR THE THREE-DICE GAME

This game is so popular through the northwestern United States, in western Canada and in Alaska that it has taken the place of craps among servicemen. Most players believe it is an even-up game with no advantage for the banker.

As many players may play as can crowd around the playing surface. Three dice are used, being thrown from a cup. Each player puts the amount he desires to wager down in front of him and the banker who covers all bets, plays against each player in turn. After the first round, the next player on the banker's left becomes the banker and so on.* The banker shoots first.

When either banker or player throws (a) the combination 4-5-6, (b) any pair and a 6, or (c) three of a kind, it is a winning decision. If (a) 1-2-3, or (b) any pair and an ace is thrown, it is a losing decision. When any pair is thrown and the third die is a 2, 3, 4 or 5, the number on the third die becomes the shooter's point. If his opponent fails to score a winning or losing decision and also throws a point, the player whose point is highest wins.

A tie is a standoff and is no decision. When a player does not get a pair and does not throw either 4-5-6 or 1-2-3, the roll is neutral and he must continue shooting until he wins, loses, throws a point, or ties.

Since the banker wins and loses according to exactly the same deciding throws as does the player, there would seem to be no advantage in his favor. Or it looks that way until we break it down. A glance at the *Combination Table* on p. 315 shows that there are 216 different combinations possible with three dice of which 120 are no pairs, 90 are pairs and 6 are three of a kind.

Of the 90 pairs 1/6 can be expected to have a 6 as a number on the third die, a total of 15. There are 6 ways to throw three of a kind and 6 ways to throw 4-5-6, a total altogether of 27 winning ways.

The losing throws: any pair with an ace and 1-2-3 can be made in 15 ways and 6 ways respectively for a total of 21 losing ways.

Point numbers (any pair with a 2-3-4-5) can be made in 60 ways (the 90 ways pairs can be made minus the 30 ways pairs with aces and sixes can be made).

All these winning and losing and point number ways added together show that just half of the possible 216 ways are of importance or 108 ways. The other 108 rolls are neutral and do not effect any decision.

The banker's advantage lies in the fact that he always throws first. Out of 108 rolls he can expect to win 27 times, lose 21 times and throw a point 60 times. Considering the winning and losing decisions only for the moment, he has an advantage of 6 winning ways in his favor, a P. C. of 6/108 times 100 or *5-5/9%*.

If he throws a point, his opponent takes the cup and throws, and

---

the 5-5/9% is now in his favor. But while the bank always has this P. C. on his throw, the player has it only when the banker throws a point or 60/108 of the time. (On the other 48 throws, the player never gets a chance to shoot.) 60/108 of 5-5/9 leaves a favorable overall percentage of 3-7/81% for the player.

Subtracting the player's percentage from the banker's percentage leaves a 2-3/8% advantage in the banker's favor. This is about 12¢ on a $5 bet.

Because they think it is an even-up game, many players pass up their opportunity to be the banker when it is their turn. The 2-38/81 P. C. is consequently always working against those players and grinding them down. The game is an even-up proposition only if each player takes his turn at banking so that the P. C. works for as well as against him.

CRAPLESS CRAPS

A rare innovation on bank crap layouts is one in which both craps (2, 3 or 12) and the natural 11 are considered as point numbers. Usually when played this way the layout does not carry a Don't Pass line and place betting is not permitted. At first glance the prospect looks very inviting as does the dealer's explanation which goes about like this: "When you put your money on the Pass Line, this layout prevents your losing on the come-out with a crap. This layout gives the front line player a better run for his money than any other in the country. On the others you had four ways to lose with a crap on the come-out. Here that's impossible. You either throw a 7 on the come-out and win or you make a point. On the other layouts you'd lose when you threw a deuce; here, if you can make it again before a 7 you win."

The player listens to this sales promotion, remembers all the time he has thrown craps and lost, and decides that the house must be run by newcomers to the business who aren't quite hep to what they are doing. He consequently plays the Pass line, thinking that it must have an even smaller P. C. against him or perhaps even a P. C. in his favor.

Perhaps when I tell you that the hustlers have been introducing this same idea into private games, you will begin to realize that there must be a screw loose somewhere. There is. The players seem to forget that although craps do not lose for them, neither does 11 win on the come-out, and that the crap numbers as points are tough to make before a 7.

If you add up all the winning and losing rolls as we did in calculating the house advantage on the flat win bet in Craps (page 95), you will find that the edge for the bank on the pass line and for the hustler who is fading the shooter or placing a flat lose bet is almost 4 times the 1.414% of Craps. It is *5.380%*.

These layouts usually do not allow place betting but the hustlers in the private games will lay you the odds on any of the points 2, 3, 11 or 12. They lay 5 to 1 on the 2 whose correct odds are 6 to 1 and which gives the hustler an edge of *14-2/7%*. The same goes for 12. He lays you 2-1/2 to 1 on the 3 whose correct odds are 3 to 1 and has an edge of 12-1/2%. The same is true of 11.

TWENTY-SIX

This was a favorite banking counter game in the Midwest back in the 1950's. Due to anti-gambling crusades its popularity fell off in that area for a time, but recently I have witnessed its resurgence in various sections of the country, the dealers usually being dice girls.

Ten dice and a cup are used. The player selects any number from 1 through 6 as his point. He throws the ten dice thirteen times and totals the number of times he has thrown his point number. The object is to throw 26 or more point numbers.

Dice MUST Roll Across Board—Clear of Dice Cup
Please Pay In Advance   Call Point-Before-First Roll of Dice
13 Shakes, 10 Dice for 25¢
The below awards are ordinarily used but are subject to change by the proprietor
We Pay In Trade Only

11 or less—pays $1.00	*26 or more—pays $1.00*
13 even——pays .50	*33 or more—pays $2.00*

Most 26 game operators use a score sheet giving rules and payoffs like those above. Note that the payoffs appear to be: 4 to 1 if the player scores 26 points or more, 8 to 1 for a score of 33 or more, 4 to 1 for a score of 11 or less, and 2 to 1 for a score of exactly 13.

The operators have known from experience for many years that the game earns a handsome profit, but they have never known either the correct odds or the exact house percentage. For years one gambling supply house has carried a note in its catalog stating that the percentage in favor of the house is "about 17%," an obvious guess with no math to back it up. In the following text you will find for the first time in print anywhere the exact house percentage to three decimal places.

The reason that no one has ever before come up with these answers is that if we attack the problem using the standard binomial formula we immediately run into computations using fantastically large figures.

At the very start when we try to compute the odds against throwing exactly 26 points with 13 throws of 10 dice (or 130 throws of one die) we bog down in complications such as the following. The number of combinations of n things taken r at a time or $_nC_r$ is

$$\frac{n\,(n-1)\,(n-2)\ldots(n-r+1)}{r!} \quad \text{or} \quad \frac{n!}{r!\,(n-r)!}$$

And then, since the probability that an event will happen at least r times in n trials is the sum of the probabilities that it will happen in n, n—1, n—2, . . . , r times we get a formula (or are you still with us) that looks like this:

$$P^n + {_nC_{n\text{-}1}}\,P^{n\text{-}1}\,Q + {_nC_{n\text{-}2}}\,P^{n\text{-}2}\,Q^2 + \ldots + {_nC_r}\,P^r\,Q^{n\text{-}r}$$

In our particular problem, $P = 1/6$, $Q = 5/6$, $n = 130$, and $r = 26$. If we substitute these values, we have this:

$$\left(\frac{1}{6}\right)^{130} + \frac{130!}{129!}\left(\frac{1}{6}\right)^{129}\left(\frac{5}{6}\right) + \frac{130!}{128!\cdot 2!}\left(\frac{1}{6}\right)^{128}\left(\frac{5}{6}\right)^2$$

$$+ \ldots \frac{130!}{26!\cdot 104!}\left(\frac{1}{6}\right)^{26}\left(\frac{5}{6}\right)^{104}$$

Given above are the first three and the last terms only. There are 105 such terms altogether. But before we even bother to write them all out, let's take a look at the first one: $\left(\frac{1}{6}\right)^{130}$. If you tackle that with a table of logarithms, you'll come up with an answer (if we haven't stumbled arithmetically anywhere along the line) of 6919.5×10^{-105}. And that decimal, if you make the multiplication indicated is an infinitesimal bit of nothing that looks like this: .0000000000000000000000 000000000000000000000000000000000000000000000000000000000000 00000000000000000000069195.

There are 104 other such terms to be calculated and then added together. Since each term is progressively larger we could work out the last few terms and not bother with the infinitesimally small fractions that precede it, but that is still a major headache.

Several years ago the Harvard Computation Laboratory put a battery of calculating machines to work and come up with a whole book full of answers. Since the binomial formula is used in many problems and so often requires staggering amounts of arithmetic, they constructed a set of Cumulative Binomial Probability Distribution Tables which give probability fractions for a wide range of values of n, r, and P. And because Dr. Frederick Mosteller, Chairman of the Department of Statistics, had seen a copy of *Scarne on Dice* and was aware of the 26 game problem, he saw to it that the calculating machines were asked to provide figures for the terms n = 130 and P = 1/6.

When 10 dice are rolled 13 times (the same as one die being rolled 130 times) the probability of throwing 33 or more points is, according to the table, .00747. This means that the player will obtain a score of 33 or more 747 times in 100,000 games. We multiply this probability fraction by 8 because the payoff is 8 to 1 and get an expected gain of .05976.

We obtain probability fractions for the other scores from the tables, multiply by the payoff, and get expected gains in each instance as below:

$$
\begin{aligned}
\text{P of 26 to 32} &= .17458 \times 4 = .69832 \\
\text{P of 33 or more} &= .00747 \times 8 = .05976 \\
\text{P of 11 or less} &= .00529 \times 4 = .02116 \\
\text{P of 13 exactly} &= .01691 \times 2 = .03382 \\
\end{aligned}
$$

Total expected gain ...... .81306

This means that for each $100 bet the player can in the long run expect to win $81.306 and lose the difference, or $18.694. Since the operator retains $18.694 out of each $100 bet the favorable advantage for the house is 18.694% or about 18.7%.

Another reason why some people have miscalculated this problem is that the payoffs listed on the sheet are misleading. The sheet clearly states that on a bet of 25¢ the player is paid $1 when he gets 26 or more. This looks like odds of 4 to 1. But the dealer puts the player's quarter in the cash register before the game begins and it is not returned to the player when he wins. The player receives $1 *for* the 25¢ he wagered which is odds of 4 *for* 1, or odds of 3 to 1.

And even with a P.C. of 18.7% in their favor the dealers some-times cheat. A common method is to cut down the player's chance for a high score by holding out one die now and then so that the player only throws nine dice. The house doesn't use loads because if the players noticed a certain number coming up more often than usual, they would select that for their point. But players attempting to beat the house do switch in loads (Dead Number dice).

Another cheating method, called Pushing the Pencil is worked by having the dice girl short a player on the count by putting down fewer points on the score sheet.

When the house pays off in trade, as the score sheet insists in big type, the operators' profit is even higher because a buck's worth of merchandise didn't cost the operator that much. If his markup is 50%, each dollar of merchandise he pays out actually costs him only fifty cents.

Also, don't believe that WE PAY IN TRADE ONLY line. If the dealer knows you, and you have money and want to play for cash, the "trade only" rule goes out the window. A player who wins a couple of times and receives eight drinks stops playing because by then he is in no condition to continue. But if he receives $8 in cash, he'll stick around trying to win more, an outcome that is unlikely since he's bucking an edge of 18.7%.

BARBOOTH OR BARBUDI

A favorite among Greek and Jewish players played mostly in Can-ada and large cities such as Detroit, Chicago, New York and other cities bordering on southern Canada. It is a dead even game, shooter and fader each having an exactly even chance.

Any number can play, usually as many as can sit around a regula-tion poker table. Two dice, thrown from a cup, are used. Each player rolls one die and the high man becomes the first shooter. Unlike Craps the shooter does not specify the amount of his wager but the player on his right, called the *fader*, bets any amount up to the limit that the shooter will not win and places it in the center of the playing surface. The shooter may cover the bet, may allow other players to take all or part of the bet, or may refuse the wager and pass the dice. The fader also has the privilege of refusing to fade and passing his opportunity to fade. The other players make side bets on whether or not the shooter or fader will win.

After his bet has been covered the shooter throws out the dice for one roll. If the number thrown does not effect a decision the dice pass to the fader who takes one roll. If his roll is also no decision, the shooter throws again; and shooter and fader continue to throw alternately until a decision is effected.

When a shooter throws a losing decision or loses because the fader throws a winning decision, the dice pass to the fader who becomes the next shooter. A shooter retains the dice and continues to shoot as long as he continues to win. The game provides no mathematical advantage for either the shooter or fader and is known as a dead even game. A house employee known as a *cutter* takes a charge of 2.5 percent of the amount of each winning bet. A bookmaker or banker is usually available to accept side bets for a charge of 5 percent, which is divided equally among the bookmaker and house cutter.

As many can play as can fit around a poker-sized table. Two small peewee (.375-inch) dice and two dice cups are used. The shooter and fader, beginning with the shooter, alternate throwing the dice until a decision has been achieved. If a shooter or fader throws 3–3, 5–5, 6–6, or 6–5, he wins. If he throws 1–2, 1–1, 2–2, or 4–4, he loses. All other throws are meaningless. If the shooter loses with a throw of 1–1, 2–2, or 4–4, or if the fader wins with a throw of 3–3, 5–5, or 6–6, then the dice pass to the fader who becomes the next shooter. If the shooter loses with a throw of 1–2 or the fader wins with a throw of 6–5, the shooter retains the dice.

Although the small opaque dice used are easy to switch and load the method of play in which shooter and fader throw alternately makes any use of percentage dice impractical. Tops cannot be used because ripping them in and out on every roll is too tall an assignment for the best of dice mechanics. The things to beware of are the Slick Cup used with First Flop dice and controlled shots with the cup (see Chapter 14).

INDIAN DICE

Any number can play and five dice are used. The players throw one or more dice to determine the order of play, high man playing first, next highest second, and so on.

Sixes are high, deuces low and aces are wild, that is can be counted as any number desired. The first player may take as many as three throws but may stand pat after the first or second if he so desires. Following players may not take more throws than the first player.

After the first throw, the player may put aside any of the five dice and place the others in the cup for his second throw, or he may rethrow all five. He repeats this process of selection after the second throw, and may throw any or all of the five dice the third time, including any of those which he set aside on his first throws.

The object is to secure high poker hands which rank in the following order: five of a kind, four of a kind, full house, three of a kind, two pair, one pair. No pair and straights do not count. Whatever the dice show after the last throw is the final value of the hand.

As an example, the first player throws two fives and the other dice show two, three and four. Unless he wants to throw all five again in the hope that he will throw something better than a pair, he places the two fives to one side and throws the remaining three dice in an attempt to better his hand similar to the draw in Poker. If he throws ace, three, four this time, and if the ace is wild, he places it with the two fives and has three of a kind. He then throws the last two dice in an attempt to get another five, or a pair which will give him a full house.

Each round is called a *leg*. If it is a two-handed game, the player winning two out of three legs wins the game. When there are more players, they are all entered in two legs. The lowest man in the first leg plays a two-handed game with the lowest man in the second leg and the loser pays the check.

If two players tie for low man in any leg, they play it off in the same way. When played as a betting game for stakes, the high man in the first leg plays a two-handed game with the high man of the second leg. When played for drinks, low men play off, loser paying the check. If two or more men in any leg tie, they also play it off.

The game is an even-up proposition, each player having an equal chance.

BUCK DICE

Any number can play and three dice are used. Each player throws the dice to determine the order of play, the player making highest score goes first, next highest second, and so on.

The low man then throws one die and the number thrown becomes the *point number*. The high man begins by throwing all three dice, scores one point for each point number thrown. He continues to throw as long as he throws point numbers which are added as he goes along.

When he fails to throw a point number on any throw, the dice pass to the next player.

The object is to score exactly 15 points, called *Buck* or game, and each player, as he reaches this score, drops out of the game until only one player remains who is the loser and who foots the bill. If a player whose number is close to 15, on his next throw, reaches a total above 15, the throw does not count and he must throw again. Any three of a kind (not point numbers) is a *Little Buck* and counts 5 points. When the point number appears on all three dice, it is *Big Buck* or *The General* which counts 15 points and eliminates the player no matter what score he has previously made.

When played on a bar, three crosses, called bucks from their resemblance to the end view of a sawbuck, are drawn on the bar with chalk. The center of the cross is erased when the player throws his first point number and one arm of the cross is erased for each additional point number thrown. When all three crosses are rubbed out, he has scored fifteen.

In one popular variation, the additional rule is added that when the shooter has 13 point numbers to his credit and 2 to go, only two dice are thrown, and when he has scored 14 and has only 1 to go, only one die is thrown.

The player shooting first has a slight advantage.

HOOLIGAN

A popular bar game played for drinks, low man paying, or played as a betting game. Any number may play and five dice are used with a cup. Score is kept on a sheet ruled into boxes that bear the numbers 1 through 6 and the letter H for Hooligan which is a straight (a throw of 1–2–3–4–5 or 2–3–4–5–6). Each player throws dice to determine order of play, high man going first, next highest second, and so on.

Each player takes three throws per turn, called a *frame*. After the first throw, he may select any number as his point.

He then puts all dice bearing this point number to one side and throws the remaining dice a second time. If one or more point numbers appear on this throw, those dice are also put aside and a third throw is made with any dice that remain. If, after the first or second throws the player has thrown five point numbers, on his next throw he uses all five dice again.

After the third throw, the point number is multiplied by the number of points thrown to get the score for that frame. If the player has thrown 5 threes, his score is 15, if 7 sixes, his score is 42, etc.

If in coming out for any number (that is on the first roll) a Hooligan is thrown the player is credited with 20 points for Hooligan. If, however, a player has tried for all of the points with the exception of Hooligan he must then try for Hooligan on the last frame and is allowed three throws.

The player is not required to select a point number after the first throw, but may, if he likes, pick up all five dice and throw again for a point and he may do the same after the second throw.

On each succeeding turn the player must shoot for a different point number than any played previously so that at the end of seven turns, which constitutes a game, he will have shot for each of the point numbers: 1, 2, 3, 4, 5, 6 and for Hooligan.

The scores for each frame are added and the player having the highest total score wins, or when played for drinks, the low man or sometimes the two lowest men pay.

As an example, if the first player throws 3 deuces and a pair of threes, he may select either the deuce or three as his point, or if he likes, he may pick up all five dice and throw again, selecting his point from among the numbers thrown on his second throw, in which case none of the numbers can be scored which appeared on the first throw.

When 3 deuces and a pair of threes are thrown, the logical choice is to select the deuce as the point, place the three dice that show deuce to one side, and throw the remaining two dice for the second throw. If he should now throw 2 deuces for a total of 5, the player then throws all five dice for the third throw. If he should throw 3 deuces on this last throw he has made a total score of 8 deuces or 16 points.

If on the second throw 1 deuce is thrown, that die is placed to one side and the remaining die is thrown for the third and last throw. If a deuce is thrown this time, the player scores 10, and if not, the player has made 4 deuces altogether for a score of 8 for that frame.

On his next turn the deuce is dead and he must shoot for some other point.

Hooligan is also played as a banking game in which the player does not shoot against an opponent but tries to reach as high a total as possible. The player usually pays a quarter to play and the operator pays off various amounts (usually in trade rather than cash) for high scores. Sometimes a score between 84 and 89 inclusive will get the player $1, a score between 90 and 93 is paid off at $2, and so on, but the payoff varies with different operators and in different places.

It is impossible to figure an exact house percentage on this game because different operators pay off differently, and because the players have a choice as to the order in which they select their points and the way they play them. The number of throws is also a variable factor. A perfect score is 335.

POKER DICE

Similar in some ways to Indian Dice. It is usually played with five poker dice whose sides bear the playing card denominations: Ace, King, Queen, Jack, Ten and Nine although the usual spotted dice are sometimes used, Ace being high followed by 6, 5, 4, 3 and 2 in that order. The Ace is also sometimes played wild.

Any number can play and each player throws one die to determine the order of play, highest man going first, next highest second, and so on.

The object is to throw the highest poker hand in either one or two throws as desired. After the first throw, the player may stand pat or may draw (as in draw poker) by throwing one, two or three of the dice again. The object is to secure high poker hands which rank as follows: five of a kind, four of a kind, full house, straight (any five cards or numbers in numerical sequence), three of a kind, two pair, one pair.

The extra die or dice not included in one of the above hands do not have any value. If a player throws 4 jacks, for instance, the fifth die does not help to decide the winner in case of ties. Tying players throw off. In the two-handed game the best three hands out of five win.

CHICAGO OR ROTATION

This probably derives from the similar pool game called Chicago. Any number can play and two dice are used, and any player may go first. On the first round each player throws once and tries to make a 2. If successful, he scores two points, if not he scores nothing. On the second round each player shoots for a 3 which if made scores three points. All of the eleven number combinations possible with two dice (2, 3, 4, 5, 6, 7, 8, 9, 10, 11 and 12) are played for in this manner beginning with the lowest. The player having the highest total score after all numbers have been shot for is declared the winner.

BASEBALL

Baseball fans go for this one. A two-person game with two dice and several counters to represent men. A diagram representing a baseball diamond and a nine-inning box score chart are drawn.

Each player throws once and high man has choice of throwing first or second. The player up at bat (throwing the dice) throws until he has three outs counted against him after which the number of runs he has made in that inning is entered on the box score and his opponent throws. The player with the highest number of runs at the end of nine innings is the winner.

SCORING: The numbers 3, 4, 5, 6, 7 or 8 are strike-outs or put-outs except that when either 4 or 8 are thrown the hard way (with 2–2 or 4–4), they are walks and put a man on first base. When 6 is thrown the hard way (3–3), it is a double play and two outs are scored against the shooter.

Number 9 is a one base hit called a single.

Number 10 is a two base hit or double.

Number 11 is a three base hit or triple.

Number 2 and number 12 are home runs.

If a runner is on first when a walk is scored, he advances to second base. A single advances all runners one base; a double, two bases; a triple, three bases; a home run brings all players in. A run is scored for each player crossing home plate.

PIG

Any number of players may play and one die is used. Each player throws to decide the order of play, low man going first, next highest second, and so on.

The first player throws the die as many times as he desires, adding the numbers on the upper face of the die each time. If he throws an *ace*, it cancels out whatever score he has made on that turn and he must pass the die to the next player. He may stop throwing and pass the die to the next player at any time, and if he does so before throwing an ace, he is credited with the sum of the numbers he has thrown on that turn.

As usually played, the player who first scores 100 points is the winner. Since this gives the player who throws first an advantage because, all else being equal, he has the best chance of reaching 100 first, the rule is sometimes made that each player must be allowed an equal number of turns.

When a player reaches 100, those players who have not yet had a turn in that round are allowed to throw, and if any of them also go over 100, the highest man is declared the winner. The game is still not an even-up proposition because now the last player has the advantage since he knows what previous scores have been made and, unless he throws an ace, can continue shooting until he makes a higher score and wins.

If all players are to have an equal chance, the game should be played in sets with as many games per set as there are players and with the first throw of each game rotating in turn around the circle of players. In the first method of scoring, this will allow each player to go first once in each set, and in the second method will allow each player to go last once in each set.

Warning: Don't think that because Pig is such a simple game that it can't be beaten and that it is safe to play with strangers. I suspect that the game was invented by the con men and is simply a variation of their favorite swindle The Tat dressed up in new clothes. In The Tat the victims are clipped by switching in a mis-spotted die that bears nothing but high numbers. In Pig the con man, on his turn merely needs to switch in a die which has 2 sixes and no ace.

THIRTY-SIX

Any number can play and one die is used. Each player puts a stake in the center forming a pool and each one throws the die to determine order of play, low man going first, next highest next, and so on. The players throw the die in turn and continue to throw, adding each number thrown to the previous one and calling out the totals. The object is to reach 36 or approach it as closely as possible without passing it. Players passing 36 are busted. The player who comes closest to 36 wins. Ties divide the pool. Most players throw again at 32 or less; stop at 33 or more.

PUT AND TAKE DICE

Any number can play and two Put and Take dice are used. One die bears numbers such as 1, 2, 3, 4, 6, (or some similar combination) and the word: *All*. Each side of the other die bears either a P or T.

Each player puts a stake in the pot and each player throws the two dice in turn. If a P and a 4 appear, the player puts four more units into the pot; if T and All appears, he takes all the money in the pot; if P and All appears, he must put in an amount equal to that in the pot, etc.

Dice cheats cleaned up with this one when it was popular a few years ago by using misspotted dice and sometimes loaded or shaped dice.

PUT AND TAKE TOP

This is the same game but a top is used instead of the dice. The top is eight-sided and the sides are usually marked P-1, T-1, P-3, T-3, P-4, T-4, P-ALL, T-ALL.

Both the Put and Take and High and Low Tops can be crooked, and switched in and out of the game as required. Most tops are gaffed with edge work, the edges being rounded on some sides and sharp on

others. The top will tend to roll off the sides with the rounded edges and stop on the sides whose edges are sharp.

Some tops have alternate edges bevelled so that when the victim spins the top clockwise with his right hand (the normal manner), it always lands Put. The cheat spins the top counter-clockwise and always takes. The crooked supply house lists fair Put and Take tops at 75¢ each, controlled tops at $10.

Gaffed High and Low Spinning Tops numbered from 1 to 8 have a central spindle which projects farther on one end of the top than the other. It is so beveled that high numbers always come up when the cheat is spinning. When he passes the top to the next player, he pushes the spindle down through the top so that the end that projected farthest becomes the short end and what was the upper side of the top becomes the bottom. This end for end reversal is the same as reversing the direction of the spin and the victim finds that he can only throw low numbers.

Both the Put and Take and High and Low Tops can be tested by changing the direction of the spin to see if that has any effect on the result. Not playing with strangers, and that includes anyone you haven't known since you were knee high to a pup, is also a help.

When the Put and Take tops, the High and Low tops and another type bearing names of race horses are fair but are banked with a layout, the P. C. in favor of the banker goes as high on some tops as 40%.

ACES

Also called *Aces To The Center, Deuces To The Left, Fives To The Right*. This is one of the most fascinating of all dice games. It is very popular in the Far East particularly the Philippines. In the swank social clubs in Manila the players each possess their own cups bearing their names.

Any number can play and each player must have a dice cup and five dice. Each player throws five dice and the player throwing the highest poker hand (Ace is high and 6, 5, 4, 3 and 2 represent King, Queen, Jack, Ten and Nine respectively) takes any seat and is the first shooter; the player throwing the second highest hand sits on his left and shoots second; and so on. Tying players shoot again.

The first shooter begins by throwing five dice. Each thrown die that shows an Ace is placed in the center of the playing surface; all Deuces are passed to the player on his left; all dice showing Fives to the player on his right. The player continues to throw until he either fails to throw an Ace, 2 or 5 or until he has no more dice left. It then becomes the turn of the next player on his left who has dice to throw.

Players who have no dice left remain in the game because other dice may pass to them from the other players at any time.

When all but one die have been placed in the center the player throwing the last Ace with the last die is declared the loser. When played for drinks the loser pays the check. When played for a wager the player throwing the last Ace is declared the winner and takes the pot.

This game, like Barbudi, is almost impossible to cheat. Percentage dice such as shapes and loads would give the cheater no advantage because the dice pass from one player to another. On his own throw with the last die, a cheater might switch in a mis-spotted die that lacked an Ace so that he could not throw an Ace and lose. But, since the players on the left and right usually grab the die when a 2 or 5 is thrown, it would be almost impossible to switch it out again.

HELP YOUR NEIGHBOR

Again becoming popular, this is one of the oldest dice games in existence.

Three dice and a cup are used. Each player throws three dice and the player who makes high score shoots first, the player with the next highest score sits at his left and shoots second, and so on. Tying players shoot again.

No more than six players can play. Each player has his own number, the first shooter being number 1, the second number 2, and so on. If there are only three players the first shooter takes the numbers 1 and 2; the second shooter has 3 and 4; the third shooter has 5 and 6. If there are only two players, the first takes the numbers 1, 2 and 3; the second, 4, 5 and 6. If there are five players the 6 is a dead number and if there are four players the 5 and 6 are dead.

Counters or chips (usually 10 to each player) are used. Each player at his turn throws the three dice and each player whose number (or numbers) appears must place one counter in the center for each such number. For example, if there are six players and the first shooter throws a 3 and two 5s, the number 3 player places one counter in the center and the number 5 player puts out two counters.

The player who gets rid of all his counters first is declared the winner and takes the pot. The player on the first shooter's left begins the following game.

LIAR OR DOUBTING DICE

A popular game on transpacific liners and in the Far East, it is now gaining rapidly in popularity in the United States.

Any number can play. Five dice are used with a dice cup. Each player throws five dice and the player throwing the highest poker hand (Ace is high and 6, 5, 4, 3 and 2 represent King, Queen, Jack, Ten and

Nine respectively) takes any seat and is the first shooter; the player throwing the second highest hand sits at his left and shoots second; and so on. Tying players shoot again.

At the beginning of play each player places before him three units of bet. The first shooter shakes the dice, turns the cup upside down, and lifts it, shielding the dice from view with his hand. He then announces the value of his hand but need not state the truth. The player on his left must either accept the statement or call him a liar.

If the first shooter's statement is doubted and if he has at least as good a hand as he called, the doubter puts one unit of bet into the pot. It then becomes the doubter's turn to throw and he plays against the player on his left, and so on around the table.

If the first shooter's statement is accepted as true by the player at his left, it becomes the latter's turn to throw. He may use all the dice originally thrown or leave as many of them as he cares to and throw the others. As the first shooter did, he covers the dice he throws and must then announce that the five dice have a value that beats the hand which the first shooter announced and which was accepted. The first shooter then either accepts or doubts this statement, and this process continues until one of the two players has doubted a hand which the other player has actually thrown or bettered. The doubter then puts one of his units of bet into the pot.

When a player has placed all three of his units of bet into the pot, he drops out of the game and the other players continue until only one player is left who still retains one or more of his original three units of bet. This player is declared the winner and takes the pot.

The player on the left of the first shooter begins the next game.

MARTINETTI

Also called *Ohio* or *Centennial.*

Any number can play. Three dice, a cup, individual markers for each player (usually coins of different denominations) and a layout numbered from 1 to 12, as shown below, are used.

1	2	3	4	5	6	7	8	9	10	11	12

Each player throws the three dice and the player making high score shoots first. The player making second highest score sits on his left and shoots second, and so on. Tying players shoot again.

The first shooter then throws the three dice. If an Ace is thrown, he places his marker on space number 1 on the layout. If he fails to throw an Ace, the dice pass to the player on his left.

If he throws an Ace, he may also use a Deuce on the same throw, and if he throws both an Ace and Deuce, he may use a three-spot and advance his marker to the second and third layout spaces accordingly. He may also use any two or three numbers thrown and add them together to form the number needed. For example, the numbers in a throw of 1–3–6 can be combined in various ways to produce the additional numbers: 4, 7, 9 and 10.

Each player continues throwing as long as he continues to throw numbers he can use.

If a player throws a total which he needs but which he overlooks, any opponent who can use that number may, as soon as the shooter has passed the cup, call the number and make use of it by advancing his marker. If two players call the number at the same time, the one who is first on the shooter's left may use the number.

The player whose marker first travels from 1 to 12 and back to 1 again is declared the winner.

PAR

One of the newest and most interesting of dice games, played mostly in the Middle West.

Any number of players can play, six or seven making the best game. Five dice and a cup are used.

Each player throws five dice and the player throwing the highest poker hand (Ace is high and 6, 5, 4, 3 and 2 represent King, Queen, Jack, Ten and Nine respectively) takes any seat and is the first shooter; the player throwing the second highest hand sits on his left and shoots second; and so on. Tying players shoot again.

The first shooter throws all five dice on his first throw. He may then use as many of the dice as he likes, but not more than four, and throw again. He may then continue throwing but must always, after the second throw, leave one additional die on the table each time. Or he may discontinue throwing on any throw.

The object of the game is to make the dice total 24 or more. If, after rolling the last die, the number is less than 24 the player must pay the unit of bet times the difference between his score and 24 to each of the other players. For example, if his total is 20 he would pay each player four times the unit of bet.

If he gets an even 24, the player neither gains nor loses and the dice pass to the next player on his left.

If he exceeds 24, the amount in excess of 24 becomes his point. For example, if his total is 27, three is his point. The player then throws all five dice once and for each three-spot that he throws he collects three times the unit of bet from each of the other players.

SHIP, CAPTAIN, MATE AND CREW

Also called *Mariner, Battleship,* and *Destroyers.*

Any number may play and five dice thrown from a cup are used. Each player throws a single die to determine the order of play, highest man going first, second highest second, and so on. Tying players throw again. The deal rotates to the left.

Each player, in turn, is allowed three throws and first tries to get a 6, 5 and 4 in that order, the 6 representing the *Ship*, the 5 the *Captain*, the 4 the *Mate*. If a 6 and 5 appear on the first throw the player puts those dice aside and rolls the remaining three dice trying to get a 4. If a 6 and 4 appear on the first roll, the 4 cannot be used until a 5 has been made and the player sets aside the 6 only and throws four dice on his next throw.

When the player has succeeded in getting a 6, 5 and 4 in that order, the points on the remaining two dice constitute his score, called the *Crew*. If he has not used all of his three throws he may, if he likes, use any remaining throws of the two dice in an attempt to make them show a higher total.

The player who has made Ship, Captain and Mate and whose two remaining dice show the highest score is the winner and takes the pot into which each player has contributed equal stakes. If the two high players tie, it is considered a tie for everyone and another round is thrown. The player to the left of the first shooter in the first round becomes the first shooter in the second round.

GENERAL

Puerto Rico's most popular dice game, played in bars, clubs, and homes throughout the island, is *Generala* or, in English, General. In bars it is usually played for drinks, low man paying, but I have also seen thousands of dollars change hands at a single General game session. Because it contains an element of strategy which few other dice games do not have, it is in my opinion a very fascinating game. Since so many American tourists now visit Puerto Rico, I suspect it may soon become equally popular in this country. For that reason I include the rules for General here.

Any number may play, singly or in partnership. Five dice are used with a dice cup. Score is kept on a sheet ruled into boxes. The players' names are entered across the top, and down the left hand vertical column are the numbers 1, 2, 3, 4, 5 and 6 followed by the poker hands: Straight, Full House, Four of a Kind, and Small General (five of a kind), as shown on pages 371 and 372. The Big General listing is not necessary.

Value of Poker Hands and Point Numbers

Five of a kind, known as the "Big General" when made on the first throw, automatically wins the game, regardless of the score. Five of a kind made on the second or third throw is known as the "Small General" and is valued at 60 points.

Four of a kind made on the first throw is valued at 45 points, on the second or third throw 40 points.

A full house made on the first throw is valued at 35 points, on the second or third throw 30 points.

A straight (1, 2, 3, 4, 5 or 2, 3, 4, 5, 6) made on the first throw is valued at 25 points, on the second or third throw 20 points. Aces (1) may be used as "wild" in making a straight, but they can only be used to equal a 2 or 6. They cannot be used to equal a 3, 4 or 5 to make a straight. This is the only time during the play of the game that aces may be wild.

The point numbers (1, 2, 3, 4, 5 and 6) are valued at their total spot value. Example: three sixes, 18 points; or two fives, 10 points; or four aces, 4 points, and so on.

The Play of the Game

Each player throws the five dice to determine the order of play, holder of lowest valued hand going first, next lowest second, and so on. In determining partners, two lowest and two highest hands are partners. The dice and cup pass to the left, clockwise.

Each player may take either one, two or three throws per turn, called a "frame." A complete game consists of ten frames, unless some player throws a general.

First Throw of the Dice

The player shakes the five dice inside the cup and throws them onto the bar or table. If he throws a pat poker hand, such as four of a kind, full house or straight, he enters his score on the sheet. If, however, he throws any other hand, a pair, two pair and so on, he has the following option.

He may put aside one, two, three or four dice and throw the left overs, or he may throw all five dice again. Example: If the player has thrown a total of two or three sixes, he may decide to hold the sixes and try to better the hand by throwing the remaining dice. This is similar to holding certain cards and drawing to improve the hand in Draw Poker.

Second Throw of the Dice

The same rules apply as in the first throw, except that a general becomes a small general and the value of the poker hands diminish.

Third Throw of the Dice

After the third throw, if a small general, four of a kind, full house or straight has not been made, the player may select any number for his scoring point number. Example: His hand is made up of three aces, a five and six. Since the best score he can make with the ace (1) is 5 points, it is to his advantage to name the aces as his point and enter 3 points along side number 1 on the sheet. Or, if his hand shows a pair of two's, a pair of four's and a five, his best bet is to name the two's as his point number and score $2 + 2 = 4$. He would then enter 4 points on the sheet in the 2 line.

However, after a score has once been entered on the sheet, the player cannot shoot for that hand or point number again. On each succeeding turn of play, the player has one less hand or point number to shoot for so that, at the end of the game, the player will have shot and entered a score for each of the ten frames.

Following is the final score of an actual game played by four Puerto Ricans.

	Tito	Juan	Raul	Mario
1	0	0	4	3
2	4	6	6	4
3	9	9	6	6

	Tito	Juan	Paul	Mario
4	8	8	12	12
5	20	10	15	20
6	12	0	18	18
Straight	25	25	20	25
Full House	35	30	30	30
4 of a Kind	40	40	45	40
Small General .	00	00	00	60
Total	153	128	156	218

Note: Mario with a total of 218 points was the winner of the game. And because the game was played at $1 a point, Raul owes Mario $62 (the difference between his final count of 156 and Mario's 218). Juan owes Mario $90 and Tito owes Mario $65.

YACHT

Yacht is often called an English version of General. Its plan is similar. Five dice are thrown from a cup, each player in rotation may throw the dice three times in each round, and there are 12 rounds in all. After each round, a player may leave standing such dice as satisfy him and throw the rest. Various dice combinations are assigned scoring values: yacht (five of a kind) scores 50; big straight (2, 3, 4, 5, 6) scores 30; little straight (1, 2, 3, 4, 5) scores 30. Also, full house (three of one kind and two of another), four of a kind, and choice (any five dice) each scores the total number spots showing on the five dice thrown in that turn. Sixes scores as many times six as there are sixes among the five dice. Likewise the fives, fours, threes, twos, and aces. At the end of each turn, the player must designate his five dice to count in one of the 12 categories shown on the scorepad.

Hand	Maximum	A	B	C	D
Yacht	50				
Big straight	30				
Little straight	30				
Four of a kind	29				
Full house	28				
Choice	30				
Sixes	30				
Fives	25				
Fours	20				
Threes	15				
Deuces	10				
Aces	5				

In each turn a player must select a category not previously selected; therefore at the end of the game (12 rounds) he will have selected each category once. He may select a category even though it will score zero for that round. At the end of the 12 rounds the score is added and highest score wins.

CRAG

This game is similar to Yacht, except that only three dice are used and in each turn a player may throw the dice only twice (or may stand on his first throw). Also there are 13 categories (rather than 12) in this game: *Crag* is a pair plus a third die that makes the total of the spots on all three dice, 13; this counts 50. *Thirteen* consists of any three dice whose spots total 13, and counts 26. Three-of-a-kind counts 25. *High straight* (4, 5, 6), *low straight* (1, 2, 3), *even straight* (2, 4, 6) and *odd straight* (1, 3, 5) count 20 each. Sixes, fives, fours, threes, twos, and aces are counted in the same manner as in Yacht. Also a special score sheet is ruled off, as in Yacht.

DOUBLE CAMEROON

This is another version of Yacht, but in this game ten dice are used. There is also another important difference: After the player's third throw in each turn, he must divide his ten dice into two groups of five and select a category for each. There are ten categories, thus each player has five turns in all. The categories are as follows: five of a kind, counts 50; *large cameroon* (2, 3, 4, 5, 6), counts 30; *little cameroon* (1, 2, 3, 4, 5), counts 21; full house, sixes, fives, fours, threes, twos, and aces each count the total number of spots on the five dice selected that match that category. A special score sheet is used, as in Yacht.

GOING TO BOSTON

This game, played with three dice, is also known as Yankee Grab and Newmarket. It can be played with any number of players, each of whom contributes equally to the pot and each of whom has three throws with the dice. Each player plays as follows:

On the first throw, the highest die must be set aside, and the two others retained for another roll. On the second roll, the higher die is kept and the lower is used for last roll. When two dice are equal, one must be used for the last roll. After the third throw, the player's total is the sum of the three dice.

MULTIPLICATION

This game is played in the same manner as Going to Boston, except that the last die thrown is the multiple of the sum of the two former ones. That is, if a 3 and 4 of the first two throws have been put aside, and the last thrown die is a 6, the player's total score is 6 times the sum of 3 and 4, or 42.

HEARTS DUE

In its original form, this game is played with six special dice, each with the letters H E A R T S on its respective faces. However, six regular dice may be used, 1 being H; 2, E; 3, A; 4, R; 5, T; and 6, S. The players take turns in making one roll with all six dice and score as follows:

H (1)	5
H–E (–2)	10
H–E–A (1–2–3)	15
H–E–A–R (1–2–3–4)	20
H–E–A–R–T (1–2–3–4–5)	25
H–E–A–R–T–S (1–2–3–4–5–6)	35

When doubles, triples, etc., are thrown, only one of the letters or numbers counts. The exception to this is when three H's (1's) are rolled; then the entire score of the play is canceled and the player goes back to zero score.

17

Scarney Dice®

Several years ago I created Scarney Dice—with which over 40 exciting different dice games can be played. While these Scarney Dice games can be played with two or more standard dice by considering the 2 and 5 spots on each die to indicate the word "dead," they are considerably more enjoyable when played with the specially created Scarney Dice. Each die of these dice is marked with 1, 3, 4, and 6 spots, plus the word *dead* repeated on two opposite sides.

While there are over 40 different games, due to limited space only the rules of play for Straight Scarney Dice, Scarney 3000, Scarney Put and Take Dice, Scarney Duplicate Jackpots, Scarney 21 Up and Down, Scarney Bingo Dice, Scarney Black Jack, Scarney Chemin De Fer, Scarney Pie-Eyed Dice and their variants are listed in this chapter. The complete Scarney Dice game set (which contains a set of 5 Scarney Dice, chips, dice cup and an 80-page book that contains the complete rules for the more than 40 Scarney Dice games) can be purchased at most gift and game stores.

A set of five Scarney Dice. Each die is marked with 1, 3, 4 and 6 spots, plus the word "DEAD" repeated on two opposite sides.

STRAIGHT SCARNEY DICE

Requirements

1. Two or more players.
2. A dice cup.
3. A set of five Scarney Dice. Each die is marked with 1, 3, 4, and 6 spots, plus the word *dead* repeated on two opposite sides.
4. A set of multicolored chips.

Seating Positions and Turn of Play

The players seat themselves at any places around the table. Where they sit for the moment is irrelevant. To determine seating position and turn of play, each player shakes the five dice in the cup and throws them onto the playing surface. The player throwing the highest five-dice number total selects any seat he wants, the player throwing the next highest number total sits to his left, and so on. Dice showing the word *dead* count nothing (zero). Once the seating has been arranged, the holder of the highest number total starts the game and is referred to as the *shooter*. From then on, each shooter's turn of play moves to the left, clockwise, from player to player.

A complete game consists of seven frames. At the completion of each game, the right to start the next game passes to the player at the immediate left of the player who won the previous game.

Scarney Dice Bonuses

When a throw is made without a *dead* die showing, the shooter scores the total point value of all the numbers plus the point value of any one of the following Scarney Dice bonuses that may have been made:

1. *Big Scarney*, which is any five of a kind including five *dead* dice

made on any one throw of any frame, wins the game and pot regardless of the scores.

2. *Any four of a kind* (numbers only), made on any one throw, receives a bonus of 40 points.

3. *Any Full House,* which is three of a kind and a pair (numbers only), made on any one throw, receives a bonus of 30 points.

4. *Little Scarney,* which is four *dead* dice, made on any one throw, receives a Little Scarney bonus of 25 points. The four *dead* dice are put aside and are out of play.

5. *Any three of a kind* (numbers only), made on any one throw, receives a bonus of 20 points.

6. Any two pairs (numbers only), made on any one throw, receives a bonus of 10 points.

Bonus hands, which include one or two *dead* dice, do not count.

The Ante

Each player before the game gets started antes (puts) an agreed-upon equal number of chips into the center of the playing surface known as the *pot*. All players must ante in turn, starting with the first shooter and rotating clockwise.

The Play

The shooter places the five Scarney Dice into the cup and after a proper shake promptly throws them on the playing surface. If five *dead* dice or any five of a kind are made on any one throw, the shooter calls "Big Scarney," wins the game, and takes the pot regardless of the score. However, if one, two or three *dead* dice (known as *craps*) are thrown, they are put aside and the remaining aces, threes, fours, and sixes (known as *live dice* or *numbers*), are put back into the cup and thrown again. In short, with the exception of Big Scarney and Little Scarney, every dice throw that shows one or more dead dice is a scoreless hand and the dead dice are put aside and are out of play. The remaining numbers are put back into the dice cup and thrown again. When a throw is made without a dead die, it is referred to as a *live throw* or a *point score,* and the total points of all the thrown numbers plus any bonus that may have been made are credited to the shooter. Once a shooter has thrown a point score he may do one of these two things:

1. He may call "pass," or "stay," and enter the points on his score

card as his frame score, and pass the dice and cup to the opponent on his left, or

2. He may call "hit," which means he wants to throw again to try to better his frame score. Should he make a point score on his next throw, the total of the thrown numbers plus the bonus points, if any, are added to his score for a new frame total. *Example:* The shooter on his first throw scores 17 points. He calls "hit," and throws a second time scoring 16 points plus a three of a kind bonus of 20 points for a total of 36 points. Adding these 36 points to the 17 points gives him a new frame total of 53 points. However, if the shooter throws one or more *dead* dice on his second throw, it cancels out the 17 points made on the first throw and the shooter has nothing (zero points). When the shooter has one or more live dice in play, he may *hit* and continue to throw until he *passes* and enters his scored points as his frame score. Or, he may continue to throw until he *craps out* (when all five dice are *dead*) and enters a zero as his frame score. And so it goes, to the left, clockwise, from player to player, until each player has completed seven frames and the game ends.

When a player has a single live die in play he may, if he likes, take the remaining die, put it in a cup, and call "Opposite." He then shakes and turns the cup mouth down onto the table and lifts the cup. When a player calls "Opposite," he accepts the die's *bottom* number as his point score rather than that of the top. *Example:* Opposite, when throwing a three, is four; a four is three; an ace is six; and a six is ace. A *dead* die is *dead*, be it opposite or not.

The Double-Down or Double-the-Score Option

Before the first throw of each frame and after a dead throw (scoreless hand), the shooter may double down if he cares to. The double-down option gives the shooter an opportunity to double the points, if any, of his next throw. Whenever a shooter elects to double down, he must ante one chip into the pot and call "Double down," before throwing the dice. If the shooter succeeds in throwing a point score, the total points thrown are doubled. When doubling down, only the point score total is doubled; Scarney Dice bonuses remain the same. *Example:* The shooter throws a point score of 15 points plus a three of a kind, 20 points bonus hand. He simply doubles the 15 points for a total of 30 points and adds the 20 points, getting a grand total of 50 points for the throw.

The above rule holds true except when the double down involves only one die; then only the numbers ace and six are doubled. The three and four are still scored at 3 and 4 points. When a player wants to double down on a single die's opposite side, he calls "Double the opposite."

Note: A player is only permitted to double down before the scoreless hand. A player is not permitted to double down when possessing a point score. To repeat, a player can only double down before the first throw of each frame or after throwing a dead or scoreless hand.

How to Score a Scarney Dice Game

After the first shooter's frame score has been entered on the score sheet, the player seated to the first shooter's left becomes the next shooter. And so it goes to the left, clockwise, from player to player until each player has shot seven frames and the game ends. Exception: When a player shoots Big Scarney, this immediately ends the game regardless of the score. When a player craps out, zero (0) is entered on the score card as his frame score.

Score is kept on a score pad which allows for a single and cumulative game score. A game consists of seven frames for each player. A player with the highest score wins the game and takes the pot—except when Big Scarney (any five of a kind including five *dead* dice) is made on any one throw of any frame; this automatically wins the game and takes the pot regardless of the scores. Should two or more players have identical high game scores, one or more extra frames are played by each of the high scorers until the tie is broken. The following is a sample score sheet of a Straight Scarney Dice game played by four players:

Frames	A	B	C	D
1st	10–10	33–33	9–9	0–0
2nd	12–22	6–39	52–61	26–26
3rd	9–31	6–45	18–79	45–71
4th	0–31	8–53	36–115	0–71
5th	0–31	0–53	27–142	32–103
6th	16–47	12–65	26–168	0–103
7th	0–47	32–97	0–168	0–103
Game scores	47	97	168	103

In the above game, player C, scoring 168 points, is the winner and takes the pot. The score for each player's frame is written down to the left of the dash, the cumulative score to the right. In the right-hand column the score for each frame is added to the previous total and brought down to a new total. Thus, each player always knows what the score is and how far ahead or behind he is.

PARTNERSHIP STRAIGHT SCARNEY DICE

Partnership Scarney Dice is a game for four players, two against two, as partners. The rules for Scarney Straight Dice apply with the following exceptions and additional rules:

1. Each player throws five dice for partners; the holders of the two highest number totals (*dead* dice count nothing) are teamed up against the holders of the two lowest. If three- or four-way ties occur on the throws for partners, one or more extra throws must take place until the ties are broken. Partners seat themselves opposite each other, and the holder of the highest total number is the first shooter. From then on the turn of play moves to the left, clockwise, from player to player.

2. At the completion of a game (seven frames for each player), partners' game scores are added together and the side with the highest total score takes the pot. Winning partners divide the pot equally.

Note: Team play can be extended to six persons, three against three.

SCARNEY 3000®
The World's Best Family Dice Game

Scarney 3000 is the world's most exciting bar, club, and home dice game. It is the favorite dice game of the members of the John Scarne Game Club of my hometown of Fairview, New Jersey. Another John Scarne game creation. A game consists of an undetermined number of rounds of play, and the player who first obtains a score of 3000 points or more wins the game and receives the difference in points between his total and that of each of the losing players. The complete Scarney 3000 game set can be purchased at most gift and game stores.

Requirements

Any number can play, each playing for himself. Five Scarney Dice, a dice cup, and pencil and paper to keep score are used to play the game.

Seating Positions and Turn of Play

They are the same as those prescribed under Straight Scarney Dice, page 376.

Point Values of the Dice

Any dice throw which contains one or two *dead* dice is a point-scoring throw and each *dead* die is valued at 50 points. A dice throw containing three, four, or five *dead* dice is a bonus hand (see Point Values of Bonus Hands). The only time the point numbers (1's, 3's, 4's, and 6's) have any value is in bonus hands. Otherwise they are known as "bust dice" and count nothing, zero points.

Point Values of Bonus Hands

Any dice throw containing three or more dice of the same number, aces, threes, fours, sixes, is considered a bonus hand when accompanied by one or two *dead* dice on the same throw, or if one or more *dead* dice appear on the next toss. Throwing a *dead* die with a bonus hand or on the next roll is known as "confirming the bonus."

Any dice throw containing three or more *dead* dice is also a bonus hand but needs no confirmation because *dead* dice are point-scoring dice.

Bonus hands are valued as shown in the table that follows.

Rules for Bonus Hands

1. If a dice throw contains a bonus hand plus one or two *dead* dice, the hand is confirmed and all points scored on the hand including 50 points for each *dead* die count.

Bonus Hands	Point Values	Bonus Hands	Point Values	Bonus Hands	Point Values
3 DEAD	200	4 DEAD	400	5 DEAD	3000
3 Aces (1's)	100	4 Aces (1's)	200	5 Aces (1's)	3000
3 Threes (3's)	300	4 Threes (3's)	600	5 Threes (3's)	3000
3 Fours (4's)	400	4 Fours (4's)	800	5 Fours (4's)	3000
3 Sixes (6's)	600	4 Sixes (6's)	1200	5 Sixes (6's)	3000

2. If a dice throw reveals a potential bonus but does not include a

dead die, the bonus hand is not confirmed and the player must put aside the bonus dice and throw the remaining dice or the five put-aside dice whichever the case may be. If this subsequent throw contains one or more *dead* dice, the bonus hand is confirmed and all points made on the hand count.

3. If the confirming throw does not contain a *dead* die but does contain another potential bonus, the player throws again in an attempt to confirm all points made on the hand.

4. If the confirming throw does not show a *dead* die, the potential bonus hand is busted and all previously made points for the hand plus the potential bonus points are canceled out. The player scores zero points for the hand and passes the dice and cup to the player on his left.

5. A bonus throw made up of *dead* dice does not require confirmation since they are point-scoring dice.

The Play

At each turn of play, unless a player throws a bust hand, he must throw the dice until he scores a minimum of 200 points. Then he can do one of two things: (1) he can "stand" (pass) and enter his score on the score sheet and pass the dice and cup to the player on his left, or (2) he can continue to throw the dice in an attempt to better his score. If, however, he throws a bust hand, his turn immediately ends, he scores nothing, and the turn of play passes to the player on his left.

The Play in Detail

1. The shooter shakes the five dice inside the cup and throws them onto the table. If he fails to throw a *dead* die or a bonus hand, he calls, "Bust," and passes the dice and cup to the player on his left, his turn of play being ended.

2. If the shooter throws a hand whose point total is less than 200, such as *dead*–3–4–6–6, he counts aloud 50 points for the *dead* die and puts it aside with the *dead* side facing upwards.

3. He returns the non-scoring (3–4–6–6) dice back into the cup and throws these four dice again. The second throw shows *dead*— 3–6–6, the shooter counts aloud 50 for the *dead* die, puts it aside with the previously scored *dead* die, and calls aloud his point total which is now 100.

4. He next places the three non-scoring dice (3–6–6) back into the cup and throws them again. This throw reveals two *dead* dice and a 6. The shooter adds the 100 points for the two *dead* dice to his 100 previously scored points and calls aloud 200. He then puts the two *dead* dice aside with the two previously put-aside dice.

5. Since the shooter has scored the required 200 points for a score to be valid, he may do one of two things: (1) he may call "Stand," and pass the cup and dice to the player on his left and enter the 200 points to his credit on the score sheet, or (2) he may call "Hit," and throw the remaining non-scoring die in an attempt to better his 200 point score. If, however, the shooter throws the non-scoring die and it fails to show *dead*, the hand is busted and the player scores nothing for the hand. But, if the throw produces a point-scoring *dead* die, its 50 point value is added to the previously scored 200 points, and he calls "250" aloud. The player then may as before stand or hit, and throw out the five put-aside dice and continue the same procedure of play as described above until he decides to stand or until he busts.

6. If during his turn of play, a player should throw a potential bonus hand, the rules as described under Rules for Bonus Hands apply.

7. The procedure of placing point-scoring dice aside and rethrowing the non-scoring dice continues until one of two things happen: either the player throws a bust hand and loses the dice as well as all points scored for the hand, or the player says, "I stand," and enters his scored points which must be 200 or more for each round of play. The dice and cup are then passed to the player on his left.

8. A player never enters his hand score until he decides to stand and his turn of play is finished.

End of Game

The game ends when a player scores 3000 or more points. By so doing, he wins the game and gets credit for the point difference between his score and that of each opponent.

Following is a sample score sheet of a Scarney 3000 game played by four persons. The score for each player's turn of play is written down to the left of the dash and the cumulative score to the right. This makes it known to each player at all times what the total score is and how far below or above the 3000-point game mark each player is. Bust hands are not entered on the score sheet. Player D, the winner of the game,

A	B	C	D
200—200	200—200	450—450	600—600
450—650	200—400	200—650	800—1400
200—850	550—950	200—850	1900—3300
950—1800	200—1150	300—1150	
1050—2850		650—1800	
2850	1150	1800	3300

with 3300 points is well over the 3000-point mark for game. Because the game was played for points, A owes D 450 points, the difference between his final game score of 2850 and D's 3300. B owes D 2150 points and C owes D 1500 points.

Note: For players who prefer a longer game, a 5000-point game is recommended.

PARTNERSHIP SCARNEY 3000

This is four-handed Scarney 3000. Two players are teamed against the other two. The rules for Scarney 3000 apply with the following exceptions and additional rules.

1. Each player throws five dice for partners, holders of the two highest number totals (*dead* dice count nothing) are teamed against the holders of the two lowest. If three- or four-way ties occur on the throw for partners, one or more extra throws must take place until the ties are broken. Partners seat themselves opposite each other, and the holder of the highest number total starts the game by becoming the first shooter. From then on, each player's turn of play moves to the left, clockwise from player to player.

2. The score sheet heading is marked "They" and "We." Each player enters his hand score under his partnership heading and when a partnership's score totals 3000 or more points, the game ends and each of the winning partners collects the total point difference between their total and that of the losing partnership.

Note: Team play can be extended to six persons, three against three.

SCARNEY PUT-AND-TAKE DICE

Scarney Put-and-Take Dice is without a doubt one of the best poker-style betting dice games in history. It combines the ante and pot-building flavor of Poker, the double-down psychology of Black Jack, and the thrill and chance uncertainty of dice throwing.

Requirements

Scarney Put-and-Take Dice can be played by as many players as can sit around the playing surface. Three Scarney dice, a dice cup, and a set of gaming chips are used to play the game. The main objective of the game is to throw *Scarney* (any three of a kind including three *dead* dice), which wins the game and takes the pot.

Selecting Seating Positions and Turn of Play

Each player shakes the three dice inside the cup and throws them onto the playing surface. The player throwing the highest total (*dead* dice count zero) takes any seat and is the first shooter. The player throwing the second highest sits on his left and shoots second, and so on. Tying players continue to throw until the ties are broken. Upon completion of a round, the right to start the next round goes to the player on the left of the previous winner.

The Ante

Each player, before the round (game) gets started, antes (puts) an agreed-upon equal number of chips in the center of the playing surface, known as the pot. Each player must ante in turn starting with the first shooter and rotating clockwise.

The Play

Each player's turn of play is governed by the following rules:

1. The shooter places the three dice in the cup and, after a proper shake, promptly throws them onto the playing surface.

2. When the thrown dice show two *dead* dice and a number, known as a *put*, the shooter must pass the dice to the player on his left and contribute to the pot an equal number of chips as there are spots on the third numbered die. *Examples:* The shooter throws two *dead* dice and a four; he must put four chips into the pot. The shooter throws two *dead* dice and a six; he must put six chips into the pot; and so on.

3. When the thrown dice show a double (two identical numbers) and a single (different number or a *dead*), known as a *take*, the shooter takes from the pot an equal number of chips as spots shown on the single die and throws again. *Examples:* The shooter throws two threes and a *dead* die; since a *dead* die counts zero, no chips are taken from

the pot. This is known as a *push* or *standoff* and the shooter throws
again. The shooter throws two fours and a six; he removes six chips
from the pot; and so on.

4. When the shooter throws three singles (three different numbers) or two singles and a *dead* die, such as 1–3–6, 3–4–6, 3–4
dead, and so on, the throw does not count and the shooter throws again.
This is known as a *split, in-between, neutral,* or *no decision throw*.

5. When a shooter throws a three of a kind, including three *dead*
dice (1–1–1, 3–3–3, 4–4–4, 6–6–6, or *dead-dead-dead*), he calls
"Scarney," is declared the winner of the round, and takes the pot.

6. Before any throw of the dice the shooter may, if he cares to,
call "Double down." The double-down option gives the shooter an opportunity on a possible hit to take double the number of chips from the
pot as the take indicates. *Example:* The shooter's throw is 4–4–6. He
simply doubles the 6 and takes 12 chips from the pot. If when doubling
down, however, the shooter throws a put, he must put double the number of chips that the put indicates. *Example:* The shooter's put shows
dead-dead–4. He simply doubles the 4 and puts eight chips into the
pot.

7. To emphasize: A player continues to throw the dice until he
throws a put and passes the dice to the player on his left; and so it goes,
from player to player, until a player throws Scarney and wins the pot.

8. Should the number of chips in the pot be reduced to five or less,
each player puts into the pot an amount equal to the original ante.
Should a player throw a take on a double down and the number of chips
in the pot is less than the take calls for, there is no redress; he simply
takes the remaining chips in the pot and a new round gets underway.

SCARNEY DUPLICATE JACKPOTS

Scarney Duplicate Jackpots is one of the most thrilling and fastest-
action dice games ever invented. The object of the game is to win the
jackpot by throwing the same three-dice number total as did the previous shooter. Dead dice count zero (0); number dice their spot value.
Example, 1 spot, one point; 3 spots, three points, etc.

Requirements

Any nuumber can play. It makes an excellent four-, five-, six-, or
seven-person game. Three Scarney dice, a dice cup, and a set of gaming
chips are used. *Dead* dice count zero.

Seating Positions and Turn of Play

To determine seating positions and turn of play, each player shakes the three dice in the cup and throws them onto the playing surface. The player throwing the highest three-dice number total (*dead dice count zero*) takes any seat and is the first shooter. The player throwing second highest sits on his left and shoots second; and so on. Tying players shoot again. Upon completion of a game, the right to start the next game goes to the winner of the game.

The Jackpot Ante

Each player, before the game gets started, antes (puts) an agreed-upon equal number of chips into the center of the playing surface known as the *jackpot*. All players must ante in turn, starting with the first shooter and rotating clockwise.

The Play

The first shooter places the three Scarney dice into the dice cup and, after a proper shake, throws them onto the playing surface. There is no action for the first shooter on his first throw. He merely calls the total of the three thrown dice and passes the dice cup and the three dice with the same numbers face up toward the player to his left whose turn it is to play. From then on, the rules governing each shooter's turn of play (one throw with three dice) are as follows:

1. If the shooter throws (matches) the exact same number total as the previous shooter (the player to the shooter's right) he calls "Scarney," wins the game, and takes the jackpot. *Example:* The previous shooter made a total of 13 points (3, 4, and 6). Upon completion of his throw he passed the cup and three dice—with the 13 points face up—to the next shooter. If the next shooter throws any three-dice combination totaling exactly 13 points, he calls "Scarney" and takes the jackpot.

2. If the shooter throws a lower number total than the previous shooter, he must put one chip into the jackpot for each point number below the previous shooter's total. *Examples:* The previous shooter's total was 15; the next shooter throws 10 and puts five chips into the jackpot. The previous shooter's total was 16; the next shooter throws 4 and puts 12 chips into the jackpot. The cup and dice, with the same numbers upward, are passed to the next player.

3. If the shooter throws a higher number total than the previous shooter, he simply passes the cup and dice with the total upward to the player on his left.

4. If the shooter throws three *dead* dice, called craps, zero points is his score; each player except the shooter must put five chips into the jackpot. The shooter then passes the dice and cup to the next player. And so it goes, to the left, clockwise, from player to player, until a shooter wins the game and jackpot by throwing the exact same number total as did the previous shooter on his right.

SCARNEY 21 UP AND DOWN

Anyone can learn to play the game in a few minutes, yet it is an unending source of entertainment for children and adults alike. Scoring is the direct opposite of that in Straight Scarney Dice. With the exception of Big Scarney, only *dead* dice count. That is, the object of the game is to win the pot by bringing the players' combined total of thrown *dead* dice to exactly 21—and then follow with a throw of numbers (no *dead* dice) called, confirming the throw.

Requirements

1. Any number may play, singly or in partnership. Needed are five Scarney dice, a dice cup, and a set of gaming chips. Score is kept by oral count.

2. For seating positions and turn of play, see Straight Scarney Dice Rules of Play, page 376.

The Ante

Each player, before the game gets started, antes (puts) an agreed-upon equal number of chips into the center of the table, known as the pot. All players must ante in turn, starting with the first shooter and rotating clockwise.

The Play

The first shooter begins by throwing five dice. If one, two, three, or four *dead* dice (called crap or craps) are thrown, they are counted aloud and put aside. The remaining numbers (dice) are thrown again.

The shooter continues throwing, each time adding aloud each crap (*dead* die) thrown to the previous total. The shooter continues to throw the remaining numbers until he fails to throw a *dead* die. Whereupon, the dice and cup pass to the player on his left.

If all five dice show *dead,* either on the second throw or after any number of throws, they are added to the score and all five dice are thrown again by the same shooter; any subsequent *dead* dice thrown are added to the running total. And so it goes, until the shooter fails to throw a *dead* die and his final total score is the second shooter's starting number. If the first shooter threw nine *dead* dice, the first *dead* die thrown by the second player is numbered 10, and so on. This continues until one player throws a *dead* die which brings the total to exactly 21; but the game does not end unless his next throw is comprised of numbers (no *dead* dice).

If a *dead* die appears on the next throw, the total is 22. If two *dead* dice appear, the total is 23 and the shooter continues throwing and adding *dead* dice to the total until no *dead* die is thrown. Whenever a player's starting number is 22 or more, all subsequent thrown *dead* dice are subtracted from the total until the shooter fails to throw a *dead* die. *Example:* If a player's starting number is 25 and he throws a total of 11 *dead* dice and then fails to throw a *dead* die, the total number is now 14. To emphasize: Whenever a player's starting total is 20 or less, all subsequent thrown *dead* dice are always added to his starting total. But when a player's starting total is 22 or more, all subsequent thrown *dead* dice are subtracted from his starting total. If a player's total reaches zero, his next thrown *dead* die is counted as 1, and the second *dead* die is 2, etc.

Chip Penalties

Whenever a player's *dead* dice total passes the magic 21 mark, he must put one chip into the pot for each *dead* die he throws below or above 21. *Examples:* The player's starting number is 19 and he throws 6 *dead* dice for a new total of 25. Since he is 4 over 21, he must put four chips into the pot. The player's starting number is 23 and he throws 7 *dead* dice for a new total of 16. Since he is 5 under 21, he must put five chips into the pot. And so it goes, until the end of the game. *Note:* Some players prefer to pay only a one-chip penalty for passing the magic 21 mark instead of one chip for each thrown *dead* die below or above 21.

For this ruling to be valid, it must be mutually agreed upon by all players before the start of the game.

The End of the Game

The game ends when a player hits 21 exactly and then throws numbers (fails to make a *dead* die on his next throw). When this occurs, the player calls "Game," is declared the winner, and collects the pot—except when Big Scarney (any five of a kind including five *dead* dice) is made on any one (single) throw. Big Scarney automatically wins the game and takes the pot, regardless of the *dead* dice total. Upon the winning of the pot, the right to start the next round and throw first goes to the player to the left of the previous winner.

SCARNEY BINGO DICE

Scarney Bingo Dice combines the psychology of Bingo, the probabilities of Poker, and the constant fascination of dice throwing.

Requirements

Any number can play. Needed are three Scarney dice, a dice cup, a set of gaming chips, and a standard 52-card deck of playing cards. Each player throws the three dice; the player throwing the highest score (*dead* dice count zero) takes any seat and is the first dealer and shooter. The player throwing second highest sits on his left and shoots second, and so on. Upon the completion of the game, the right to start the next game goes to the player on the left of the previous winner.

Preparation to Start the Game

The player who is to shoot first shuffles the deck of cards and puts them face down on the table to his right. The player to his immediate right cuts the cards. Next, the player who is to shoot first deals 16 cards one-at-a-time face up onto the center of the table forming four rows of four cards each (vertically and horizontally). The rest of the deck is set aside and do not come into play.

Value of the Cards

Kings count 13 points; queens, 12; jacks, 11. All other cards have their face values: tens, 10; nines, 9; eights, 8; sevens, 7; sixes, 6; fives, 5;

fours, 4; threes, 3; twos, 2; and aces, 1. The suits (clubs, diamonds, hearts, and spades) have no value relative to each other and do not count.

The Ante

Each player, before the game gets started, antes (puts) an agreed-upon equal number of chips aside known as the pot. All players must ante in turn, starting with the first shooter, and rotating clockwise.

The Play

Each player at his turn makes one throw of the three dice. When a thrown number or a combination of numbers (*dead* dice count zero) matches the value of one of the face-up cards, the player must turn it face down. A player can only turn one card face down at each turn of play. However, if two or more cards can be turned face down, the player may choose which card he will turn face down. *Example:* The shooter's three-dice throw shows a 3, 4, and 6. With such numbers, the player may turn face down any one of the following cards: 3, 4, 6, 7, 9, 10 or king (13), providing such cards are resting face up on the table. When a player throws a number total whose point value fails to match the point value of a face-up card, it is a no decision throw and he passes the dice and cup to the player on his left.

When a player throws Scarney (any three same-numbers or three *dead* dice), he can elect to turn face down any face-up card he wants; or he can refuse to turn a card face down and pass the dice and cup to the next player.

When a player turns face down the fourth or last face-up card of any vertical or horizontal row, he calls "Bingo," and receives one chip from each player. When a player goes bingo two ways by turning a card face down, he calls "Double Bingo," and receives a Double Bingo bonus of two chips from each player. When a player goes Double Bingo by turning a corner card face down, he calls "Double, Double Bingo," and collects a bonus of four chips from each player. The players continue to throw in turn until one player turns face down the sixteenth or last face-up card resting on the table. When this happens the player calls "Bango," wins the game, and rakes in the pot.

SCARNEY SPEEDY BINGO DICE

Scarney Speedy Bingo Dice is a very interesting variation of Scarney Bingo Dice and is recommended to players who desire a much quicker-ending game. The same rules of play as for Scarney Bingo Dice apply with the following exceptions and additional rules:

1. Any number can play. Four Scarney dice, a dice cup, a set of gaming chips, and a standard 52-card deck of playing cards are used.

2. Any four of a kind (four same-numbers or four *dead* dice) made on any one throw, known as *Bingo,* automatically wins the game and takes the pot regardless of the positions of face-down or face-up cards.

3. Three of a kind and three *dead* dice count only their point value.

SCARNEY BLACK JACK

Scarney Black Jack possesses the hit, stay, and double down features of the casino card game of Black Jack; in addition, it offers the player a greater chance of participation with the throwing of the dice.

Requirements

Any number can play, usually as many as can sit around the playing surface. Two Scarney dice, a dice cup, and a set of gaming chips are used. The object of the game is to get a higher count (total value of thrown dice) than the banker-shooter, up to but not over 21. Should the player throw the dice and force his total over 21, he loses his bet and sacrifices any chance to beat or tie the banker-shooter.

Count Value of the Dice

Each *dead* die counts 10; each one (ace) counts 1 or 11 according to the discretion of the shooter; and each three, four, or six count their spot value.

Selecting the First Banker

To determine the first banker and seating positions, each player shakes the two dice in the cup and throws them onto the playing surface. The player throwing the highest total becomes the first banker and selects any seat he wants. The player with the next highest sits to his left and so on. Dice showing the word *dead* count 10. Once the seating has been arranged, each player, starting with the player to the banker's left, places the number of chips he wants to bet in front of him. The banker, who accepts all bets within the limit, shoots against each player in turn. The player shoots first and the banker second. And so it goes, to the left, clockwise, from player to player, around the table.

Rules Governing Shooter's Turn of Play

The shooter places the two Scarney dice in the cup and, after a proper shake, throws them onto the playing surface.

1. When the shooter, on his initial throw, makes a *natural black jack* (a *dead* die and a one or ace), he calls "Black jack," and it becomes the banker-shooter's turn to play. If the banker-shooter also makes a natural black jack, it is a standoff or push. No one wins, no one loses. If the banker-shooter fails to throw a natural black jack on his first throw, the banker-shooter loses and pays the shooter at 2 to 1 odds.

2. When the shooter's first throw shows a count of 20 or less, the player may elect to hit (throw) or stand (not to throw). If he is satisfied with his count he says "Stand," or "Good," and passes the dice and cup to the banker-shooter.

3. If he is not satisfied with his count and elects to throw to try and better his count, he can do one of two things—he can either throw one die, called a *one shot*, or throw both dice, called a *two shot*. Examples: (*a*) The player's first throw shows a 4 and a 3 for a count of 7. The player decides to take a two shot; he says "Hit the 7" and again throws out the two dice, which show a 6 and 4 for a new count of 17. (*b*) The player hits the 7 with a one shot which shows a 10 count. He has a new count of 17. (*c*) The player is satisfied with his count. As mentioned before, he says "I'll stay," or "Good," and passes the dice and cup to the banker-shooter. (*d*) The player throws a number that forces his total over 21, which is called a *bust*. The banker-shooter collects the player's bet and pushes the cup and dice to the next player.

4. *The Double Down.* After his first throw, and at no other time, a player may elect to double his bet and make only one additional throw, which can be either a one shot or a two shot. This is known as a double down. The player must then double his original bet by putting up an amount equal to his original bet.

Rules Governing the Banker-Shooter's Turn of Play

1. The banker-shooter follows the same throwing rules described above for the shooter.

2. If the shooter made a natural black jack and the banker-shooter fails to do so, the banker-shooter pays the player 2 to 1 odds for his bet. If the shooter and the banker-shooter each throw a natural black jack, it is called a standoff or push, in which case no one wins. It's a tie or standoff.

3. When the banker has a count of 16 or less, he must throw again.

4. When the banker has 17, 18, 19, or 20, he must stay—he cannot throw again.

5. When a banker has a count of 17 with an ace and a six—called "a soft 17"—it is an optional play. He can elect to stay or throw at his own discretion.

Final Settlement

1. When the banker's count goes over 21, he must pay the player still in the game.

2. When the banker's count is higher than the player's, he collects the player's bet.

3. When the banker's count is lower than the player's, the banker pays the player's bet at even money.

4. When the banker and the player have the same count, it's a standoff or push, and neither wins.

Rules Governing the Bank

1. After the first banker has been selected by the procedure set forth under "Selecting the First Banker," he shall bank five complete rounds (five turns of play for each player).

2. Upon completion of these five rounds, the bank shall pass to the player on the first banker's left, and each five rounds thereafter shall move to the left clockwise.

3. A banker deciding he no longer wants the bank may pass the bank to the player on his left before the completion of the five rounds— provided there are no uncompleted bets remaining on the board.

SCARNEY CHEMIN DE FER

Chemin de Fer is one of the most popular card games found in fashionable European casinos. Now, its dice counterpart, Scarney Chemin de Fer—a private banking game but possessing all the thrills and excitement found in its casino forerunner—can be played right in your own home or club. Unlike Baccarat, Chemin de Fer, or Black Jack, Scarney Chemin de Fer is an even-up game. There is no advantage for the bank or player.

Requirements

Five Scarney dice, a dice cup, and a set of gambling chips are used to play the game.

The Game

Scarney Chemin de Fer can be played by two, three, four or more players each playing against the banker. The object of the game is to beat the banker by making either one or two throws and hold a combination of dice totaling as close as possible to 9, or to a two-digit number ending in 9. *Dead* dice count zero (0) points. When the total of the dice is a two-digit number, only the last digit has any value. *Examples:* A count of 17 has a point value of 7, a count of 19 has a point value of 9, a count of 23 has a point value of 3, a count of 30 has a point value of 0, and so forth.

Selecting the First Banker

To determine the first banker and seating positions, each player shakes the five dice in the cup and throws them onto the playing surface. The player throwing the highest five-dice total becomes the first banker and selects any seat he wants. The player throwing the next highest sits to his left, and so on. Dice showing the word *dead* count nothing (zero). Once the seating has been arranged, the banker starts the game and each player's turn of play moves to the left, clockwise, from player to player.

The Banker's Turn of Play

Before the play begins, the banker establishes arbitrarily his own betting limits. *Example:* He may declare that while he's the banker, the bets are from one to five chips. Once the betting limit has been established and before the banker throws the dice, each player must place his chip bet directly in front of himself, toward the center of the table. Once the players' bets have been placed, the banker puts the five Scarney dice into the cup and after a proper shake throws them onto the playing surface, and adds their sum total and abides by the following rules:

1. If the banker on his first throw makes a 7, 8, or 9 for his point number, his turn of play ends. If the point is 9, it is called La Grande. If it is 8, it is called La Petite. If it is a 7, it is called a Natural. The banker's point is noted by each player—since this is the number he will try to beat.

2. If the banker on his first throw makes a 0, 1, 2, 3, 4, 5, or 6, as his point, called a Hit Number, he must draw (throw a second time). However, he is only permitted to throw the *dead* dice, if any, made on the first throw. He cannot pick up and throw a numbered die—nor can he throw only some of the *dead* dice. He must throw all the *dead* dice made on the first throw on his second throw. *Examples*: The banker's first throw shows a 6, 4 and three *dead* dice for a count of 10 and a 0 (zero) point number. Because zero is a Hit Number, the banker must throw a second time and the throw must be made with the three *dead* dice. The banker has no option, he cannot throw one or two of the *dead* dice—he must throw all the *dead* dice made on the first throw, which in this instance are three.

3. If the banker makes five numbers (no *dead* dice) on his first throw, he cannot throw the second time because he has no *dead* dice to throw even though his count may be a Hit Number such as 0, 1, 2, 3, 4, 5, or 6.

Once the banker has made his point with either one or two throws, the point number is noted by each player. The banker, then, passes the dice and cup to the player on his left, who shall be referred to as the first player.

Player's Turn of Play

The first player places the five Scarney dice into the dice cup, and after a proper shake throws them onto the playing surface and follows the same rules as the banker-shooter to attain his point number.

1. If his point is lower than the banker's, the banker collects the bet from the first player.

2. If the first player's point is higher than the banker's, the banker pays the bet.

3. If the first player and the banker have the same point, it's a stand-off and neither wins.

Once the first player's turn of play ends, the second player's turn of play begins, and so it goes, clockwise, from player to player until each player has had his turn of play and a new round gets underway.

Rules Governing the Bank

The following rules govern the bank:

1. After the first banker has been selected by the procedure set forth under Selecting the First Banker, he shall bank five complete rounds (5 turns of play for each player).

2. Upon completion of these five rounds, the bank shall pass to the player on the first banker's left and, each five rounds thereafter, shall move to the left clockwise.

3. A banker deciding he no longer wants the bank may pass the bank to the player on his left before the completion of the five rounds—provided there are no uncompleted plays remaining on the board.

SCARNEY PIE-EYED DICE

This drinking fun game is only recommended for adults who have a sense of humor and are not allergic to drinking as well as to club memberships where dice throwing for drinks is permitted by law.

Any number can play (the more, the merrier) and five Scarney dice are used with a dice cup. Each player throws the five dice once to determine the order of play. The player who throws the highest total (*dead* dice count zero) goes first, next highest second, and so on. Tying players throw again.

Although the playing rules are extremely simple, you may get pie-eyed following them. Each player gets three throws. Each player in turn, for his first throw, shakes the five dice inside the cup and throws them onto the bar or table. If he throws one, two, three, or four *dead* dice, he puts them aside and throws the leftover numbered dice (1, 3, 4, 6) a second time. The same holds true for the third throw. The first player to throw five *dead* dice orders a drink—a double rye with celery tonic, vodka with chili sauce, or anything the bartender claims he can mix.

The next player to throw five *dead* dice must drink it, no excuses accepted, on penalty of being tossed out of the game. The third player to throw five *dead* dice foots the bill for the drink. The number of rounds depends upon the amount of punishment the players can take. *Note:* If you want to speed up your drinking, change the ordering, drinking, and playing rules to four *dead* dice instead of five. *Note*: Many players prefer to play Scarney Pie-Eyed Dice with two Scarney dice. A player makes one throw of the two dice at each turn of play. The first player to throw two *dead* dice orders the drink, the next player to throw two *dead* dice must drink it. The third player to throw two *dead* dice pays for the drink.

ADDITIONAL RULES FOR SCARNEY DICE GAMES

If you observe the Scarney Dice rules of play, you will have interesting and enjoyable games. You will also avoid arguments that might arise during play. Follow the rules of the game you are playing and insist that other contestants do the same.

1. If a die comes to rest cocked at an angle on a chip or any irregularity on the playing surface, and if there is a difference of opinion as to which side faces up, the player to the shooter's right shall stand at the shooter's position and shall decide the outcome by stating which top surface of the die appears to be upward from that position.

2. If playing on an elevated surface, and one or more dice fall off the playing surface, the throw is *no-dice*. It does not count and the dice must be thrown again.

3. If a throw is made and one or more dice still remain in the cup, the throw counts and the player must throw the remaining die or dice to complete the throw.

4. When a score is agreed upon and written down, it may not later be set aside. Proven mistakes in addition on the score sheet must be corrected. If the error is noted during a play of a frame, the frame must be completed before the error is able to be corrected.

5. A player during his turn of play, and at no other time, may ask the scorekeeper to call out the scores.

6. If a player shoots out of turn, and it is discovered before the next shooter's first throw, his turn of play does not count. The next turn of play reverts back to the player whose turn it would have been if no irregularity had occurred.

7. If a player fails to give the dice a proper shake; or if, after the

shake, he looks into the cup before throwing; or if he acts in a way that causes an opponent to believe he is trying to control the dice roll; then the other players may reprimand the shooter and may call for a proper shake. If an irregularity occurs a second time, other players may call the throw dead and the offending player is barred from further play.

18

Skarney®—The Best in Card Games

Skarney, the first really new card game concept of this century, can be played in more than 30 different ways. However, due to limited space the rules of play for only Skarney Partnership and Skarney Singles appear in this chapter. Skarney Partnership is one of the most bizarre, exciting, and charmingly exasperating partnership card games in history. It has bluff as in Poker, scores big like Canasta, and is played like no other game. It has the flavor of Pinochle, the partnership understanding of Contract Bridge, and the suspense of Gin Rummy. And withal, it has an inner world and logic of its own, taxing the capacity of the most inveterate card player. I am especially proud of Skarney because the games are my own invention, which I've taken the creator's liberty of naming Skarney. The complete Skarney set can be purchased at most gift and game stores.

SKARNEY PARTNERSHIP

Requirements

1. Four players, two against two as partners.
2. Two standard 52-card decks, with four added jokers shuffled together and used as one, a total of 108 cards.

The Game

A game consists of seven deals or hands and terminates at the end of the seventh deal, in which a final score is attained by each partnership. The partnership with the higher score wins the game. The winners of the game score the difference between their total game and that of the losers. Should both partnerships have identical scores, the game is a tie. The four jokers and the eight deuces are wild and can be used to represent any card of any denomination or any card of any denomination and suit their holders dictate.

Melds

The whole game of Skarney pivots around the combinations of three or more cards of the same rank and three or more cards of the same suit in consecutive order, which players singly or in partnership seek to form in order to score points and special bonuses for their side. The four jokers and the eight deuces (twos) are wild and can be used to represent any card the holder dictates. For instance, three or more cards of the same denomination (such as three queens or two queens and a wild card) or three or more cards of the same suit in consecutive order (such as three of hearts, four of hearts, and five of hearts, or the three of hearts, wild card, and five of hearts) when legally placed face up in front of a player are called a *meld*. That is, cards are melded as soon as they are placed face up on the table with the evident intent to meld. If the exact location of a melded card is in doubt, any player may ask that the meld be clarified.

There are two basic kinds of Skarney melds: a *group* and a *sequence*. Each basic meld is subdivided as follows:

1. *A natural group meld* is a combination of three or more cards of the same rank.

2. *A mixed group meld* is a combination of only one wild card

(deuce or joker) with two or more cards of the same rank. But only one wild card can be used in a mixed group meld.

3. *An independent deuce group meld* is a combination of three or more deuces. An independent deuce group meld of three or more deuces is commonly referred to as a *deuce spread,* or a *silver spread.*

4. *An independent joker group meld* is a group of three or four jokers. An independent joker group meld is commonly referred to as a *joker spread,* or *gold spread.*

5. *A natural sequence meld* is a combination of three or more cards of the same suit in consecutive order. An ace can be used only to form a high sequence meld such as ace, king, queen of the same suit. It cannot be used to form a low sequence meld such as ace, deuce, three of the same suit.

6. *A mixed sequence meld* is a combination of only one wild card (deuce or joker) with two or more natural cards of the same suit in consecutive order. When a mixed sequence meld is placed on the table, the exact position of the wild card indicates the natural card it is meant to represent. It should be noted that a joker or a deuce can be used as a king of any suit in a sequence meld such as ace, wild card, queen. It cannot be used to form a low sequence such as ace, deuce, three of the same suit.

It is possible to meld 13 cards of the same suit in a natural or mixed sequence (two, three, four, five, six, seven, eight, nine, ten, jack, queen, king, and ace) with or without one wild card. To emphasize, at no time can more than one wild card be part of a Skarney meld—except when deuces or jokers are melded separately to form an independent deuce group meld or an independent joker group meld.

Laying Off Cards. As in Rummy the addition of one or two cards to a meld already placed on the table is known as a *layoff* and the act of adding one or two matching cards to a meld already placed on the table is known as *laying off.*

After the partnership has fulfilled its initial meld contract, a player at each turn of play, in addition to placing legal melds on the table, may extend his or his partner's previous meld or melds by laying off (adding) one or two matching cards or a matching card and a wild card to a specific melded group or sequence. Players are not permitted to lay off on melds of the opposing partnership. Detailed rules governing natural and wild card layoffs are as follows:

1. *A natural group meld* comprised of the king of spades, king of

diamonds, and king of clubs is lying on the table. The melder of this group or his partner holds three or more kings. At his turn, he is permitted to lay off only one or two of these kings on the king group meld. However, the three kings he holds can be melded as a separate group meld and must be placed in front of the melder. They cannot be placed in front of his partner.

2. *A mixed group meld* comprised of the king of spades, king of diamonds, and a wild card (deuce or joker) is lying on the table. The melder of this group or his partner holds two kings. At his turn, he is permitted to lay off one or both of the kings on the mixed group meld.

3. *A natural sequence meld* comprised of the five of hearts, six of hearts, and the seven of hearts is lying on the table. The melder of this sequence or his partner holds the four of hearts, eight of hearts, and the nine of hearts. At his turn of play, he is permitted to lay off only one or two of these cards. He can extend the sequence meld on one or both ends by laying off a single card, such as the four of hearts or the eight of hearts or both—or he can lay off the eight of hearts and the nine of hearts—but never is he permitted to lay off more than two cards on any one meld at any one turn of play.

4. *A mixed sequence meld* comprised of the five of hearts, wild card (deuce or joker), and the seven of hearts is lying on the table. The melder of this sequence or his partner holds the four of hearts, eight of hearts, and the nine of hearts. At his turn of play, he is permitted to lay off only one or two of these cards. He can extend the sequence meld on one or both ends by laying off a single card such as the four of hearts or the eight of hearts or both—or he can lay off the eight of hearts and the nine of hearts—but never is he permitted to lay off more than two cards on any one meld at any one turn of play.

Wild Card Layoff

A player at his turn is permitted to lay off a wild card (deuce or joker) on either a natural group or natural sequence meld belonging to his partner providing the wild card is accompanied by a natural matching card that will extend the meld, and the meld does not already contain a wild card such as a mixed group or mixed sequence meld. In addition, a player is permitted to lay off one or two deuces on an independent deuce group meld, and one joker on an independent joker group meld.

Swapping a Wild Card

One of the many fascinating features of Skarney is the often present possibility of the holder of a natural card exchanging it for a wild card (deuce or joker) that is part of a mixed meld belonging to his opponents. A player under no conditions is permitted to exchange or swap a wild card for a natural card from either his own or his partner's meld. Rules governing the swapping of a wild card for a natural card are as follows:

1. If a partnership has a mixed group of three or more cards resting on the table which includes a wild card, an opponent at his turn may swap the wild card for a same rank card of a missing suit.

2. If a partnership has a mixed sequence meld of three or more cards resting on the table which includes a wild card, an opponent at his turn may swap the wild card for a natural card that the wild card is meant to represent

3. A player is permitted to swap a wild card in an opponent's meld or melds at any time during the play of the hand but only at his proper turn of play. Failure of the partnership to fulfill its initial contract meld does not alter this ruling.

4. To reiterate, a player under no condition is permitted to swap or exchange a wild card for a natural card from either his or his partner's melds.

5. A player at his turn of play and before melding or laying off can swap from as many mixed melds as possible and from one or both of his opponents at the same turn of play.

Note: Whenever a wild card is swapped from a mixed group or a mixed sequence meld, that meld becomes a natural meld. Whenever a wild card and a matching natural card are laid off on a natural group or sequence meld, that meld becomes a mixed meld. It is not unusual to see the same meld change from a mixed meld to a natural meld or vice versa several times during a hand.

Contract Melds

The first meld by each partnership in each of the seven deals must meet the exact initial meld requirement as described by contract. Only one player of each partnership is required to fulfill the initial meld contract.

To simplify matters we shall call an initial basic group meld (natural group meld, mixed group meld, deuce spread, and joker spread) made up of only three cards a "group." We shall call an initial basic sequence meld (natural sequence meld and a mixed sequence meld) made up of only three cards a "sequence." To reiterate, no part of a contract meld can have more than three cards when first placed on the table. Nor can the contract melds be made up of a combination of *groups* and *sequences*. They must be either all groups or all sequences.

CONTRACT REQUIREMENTS FOR FIRST MELD

1st Deal: 3 Three card groups or 3 Three card sequences
2nd Deal: 3 Three card groups or 3 Three card sequences
3rd Deal: 3 Three card groups or 3 Three card sequences
4th Deal: 4 Three card groups or 4 Three card sequences
5th Deal: 4 Three card groups or 4 Three card sequences
6th Deal: 4 Three card groups or 4 Three card sequences
7th Deal: 4 Three card groups or 4 Three card sequences

Skarney or Hand Bonuses

When a player melds or lays off his last card or cards in his hand, he calls "Skarney," ending the hand. This is also known as Rummy, or Going Out. The partnership going Skarney receives the following designated Skarney bonus for each of the seven hands or deals that follow:

BONUSES FOR GOING SKARNEY

First hand ..... 100 points
Second hand ... 100 points
Third hand ..... 100 points
Fourth hand .... 200 points
Fifth hand ..... 300 points
Sixth hand ..... 400 points
Seventh hand .. 500 points

When a player draws the last card of the stock and does not go Skarney, the hand ends without that player offering a potential discard, and the partnership scoring the higher number of points wins the hand and receives a *hand bonus* equal in point value to the Skarney bonus designated for the specific hand. In case each partnership scores the same number of points, the hand does not count and the same dealer deals again.

Skarney Shutout Bonuses

Should a player go Skarney (on the fourth, fifth, sixth, or seventh hand) when putting down his partnership's contract meld (four three-card melds) and the opposing partnership has not put down their contract meld, his partnership receives a Skarney *shutout bonus* (also referred to as Skarney blitz, or a skunked bonus) of 200 points in addition to the Skarney bonus for the specific hand. When a player is trying for a shutout bonus, it is said that "He's blitzing."

Point Count of Each Skarney Card

At the end of each hand, cards melded on table are credited as follows: tens, jacks, queens, and kings are referred to as high cards and each counts 10 points. Threes, fours, fives, sixes, sevens, eights, and nines are referred to as low cards and each counts 5 points. Aces known as stop cards count 15 points each. Deuces and jokers known as wild cards count as follows:

An independent joker group meld of three or four jokers also known as a joker spread or gold spread counts 100 points for each joker. When a single joker known as a lone joker is part of a mixed group or a mixed sequence meld, it counts 50 points. Each unmelded joker caught in a player's hand is referred to as a penalty card or disaster card and counts 100 points against the holder. An independent deuce group meld of three or more deuces also known as a deuce spread or silver spread counts 50 points for each deuce. When a single deuce known as a lone deuce is part of a mixed group or mixed sequence meld, it counts 25 points. Each unmelded deuce caught in a player's hand is referred to as a penalty card or calamity card, and counts 50 points against the holder. All other unmelded cards (threes to aces) caught in a player's hand, even though they may form melds, are also referred to as penalty cards and are deducted at amounts equivalent to their melding values. So that the reader can see the card counts at a glance, they have been placed in tabular form.

Joker (part of a mixed group meld or a mixed sequence meld)		50 points
Jokers (3 or 4 forming an independent joker group meld)	each	100 points
Deuce (part of a mixed group meld or a mixed sequence meld)		25 points
Deuces (3 or more forming an independent deuce group meld)	each	50 points
Ace		15 points
10, jack, queen, and king	each	10 points
3, 4, 5, 6, 7, and 9	each	5 points

POINT SCORING FOR PENALTY CARDS

Cards Left in Player's Hand at the End of a Hand

Joker	minus 100 points
Deuce	minus 50 points
Ace	minus 15 points
10, jack, queen, and king	each minus 10 points
3, 4, 5, 6, 7, 8, and 9	each minus 5 points

How to Select Partnerships

Partnerships are determined by prearrangement or by cutting. Rules to determine partnerships by cutting follow.

1. The four players seat themselves at any four places around the table, where they sit is for the moment irrelevant.

2. Any player may shuffle the pack and offer the pack to any other player for a cut.

3. For the purpose of cutting for partners and seating positions, the cards rank Ace (high) K-Q-J-10-9-8-7-6-5-4-3-2 (low).

4. Each player cuts a group of cards from the pack immediately exposing to the others the bottom card of his group. Players cutting the two low cards become partners. So do the players cutting the two high cards. Although it may be agreed to keep the same partnership throughout several games, any player may nevertheless at the end of a game demand a new draw for partners and seating positions.

5. If two, three or four players cut cards of equal rank, the suits then rank spades (highest), hearts, diamonds, clubs (lowest).

6. If two players cut identical cards, they must cut again, but the cut of the other two players stands.

7. If in cutting, a player draws a joker or exposes more than one card or cuts one of ten cards resting either at the top or bottom of the pack, he must cut again.

8. The player who has cut the highest card may choose any seat. His partner sits opposite him. The opposing partnership takes the remaining seats.

The Shuffle and Cut

1. The player who cut the lowest card in the cut for partner position starts the game by dealing the first hand. From then on the deal moves to the dealer's left clockwise.

2. Dealer shuffles the cards. Any player may call for and shuffle the pack any time before the cut, although the dealer has the privilege of shuffling the pack last. Special care should be taken to shuffle the cards

thoroughly after each hand because the groupings of the previous melds cause the cards to become segregated in ranks and consecutive suits.

3. Dealer puts the pack of cards face down on the table to his right. His opponent to his right has first privilege of cutting the cards. If that player refuses to cut, any other player may cut. If all the other players refuse to cut, the dealer must cut the cards. He cannot refuse! At least twenty-five cards must be in one portion of the cut deck. Explanation of a cut: To divide the pack into two or more packets of at least 25 cards each and then reassemble them in a different order.

The Deal

Dealer, starting with the player on his left, deals each player including himself 11 face down cards, 1 at a time in clockwise fashion. The remainder of the undealt cards are placed face down in the center of the table forming the stock.

If the 108 card pack is too bulky to hold to deal, the dealer may lift off a portion from the top of the card pack as close to 44 cards as he can estimate and deal from this portion. If he holds any cards after the deal, they are replaced on top of the pack, or if the dealer took less than 44 cards to begin with, he takes additional cards from the top of the pack to complete the deal and any leftover cards are replaced on top of the pack.

The Actual Play of the Hand

Each player, at his turn, starting with the player on the dealer's left and continuing clockwise around the table, does as follows:

1. He draws the top card of the stock.

2. He may, if he chooses, exchange a natural card for a wild card from each of his opponent's melds.

3. After his partnership has fulfilled its initial meld requirement, he may, if he chooses, place on the table before him any possible melds and lay off, either two or one cards, on each of his and his partner's previous melds.

4. He removes a potential discard from the cards he is holding, turns it face up, and offers it to the player on his left by extending it toward him and asking "Do you want this card?" The player may do either of two things, accept or refuse the potential discard. If he refuses it, he replies "I don't want it," and the potential discard is then offered to the next player, and so it goes from player to player in a clockwise fashion. Should one of the players accept the potential discard, he must say "I'll take it." This action ends the turn of play for the player who

offered the card. Or, if each player in turn refuses the potential discard, the player who offered it must keep the card and return it to his hand, and his turn of play is ended. If however, a player's potential discard is either a wild card or an ace, it may be offered only to the player's opponent on his immediate left—and if the opponent accepts it, he loses his turn to pick the top card of the stock. If he refuses it, the player who offered it must keep it. He is not permitted to offer it to the other players. An ace or wild card offered as a potential discard is referred to as a *stop card*.

A player cannot offer his last accepted potential discard (nor an identical card) immediately but must wait until his next turn of play. *Example:* If his last accepted potential discard was the six of hearts, he cannot offer it until he has offered one other card first. Moreover, if he has another six of hearts in his hand, the same restriction applies.

If a player has one card left in his hand after either melding or laying off or doing both, he is not permitted to offer it as a potential discard. He simply says "Last card," and retains it in his hand. And so it goes, from player to player until the end of the hand.

Giving and Receiving Information

A player during his turn and at no other time may:

1. Ask any other player how many cards he holds. The question must be answered correctly. However, a player must announce when he has only one card in his hand.

2. Ask the storekeeper what hand is being played or to announce the cumulative score. He may also ask the point value of the Skarney bonus for the hand being played.

3. Call attention to the correct contract meld requirement if his partner is in the act of making an initial meld.

4. Before melding or indicating by word or action that he holds a Skarney hand ask, "Partner, may I go Skarney?" It is strongly recommended that only this phrase be used. Partner must reply "Yes," or "No" (nothing more), and the answer is binding. However, a player may go Skarney without asking permission of his partner. For further information, see Irregularities in Asking Permission to go Skarney, page 417.

End of Hand

When a player melds or lays off the last card or cards in his hand, he calls "Skarney," ending the hand. This is also known as rummy, or going out. The partnership going Skarney receives the designated Skarney bonuses for each of the seven hands as shown on page 411. Should the cards in the stock be exhausted before any player has gone Skarney, the hand ends and the partnership scoring the higher number of points wins the hand and receives a hand bonus equal in point value to the Skarney bonus designated for the specific hand. In case each partnership scores the same number of points, the hand does not count and the same dealer deals again.

When the number of cards in the stock is low (ten or less cards), any player is permitted to count the number of cards remaining so as to know the number of rounds left.

How to Score a Hand

The following steps are used to determine the score. The partnership is credited with the total value of all cards melded. These points are added, and from this sum is subtracted the total penalty point values of the cards remaining in the partner's hands. The net balance is the partnership's score at the end of the hand and this may occasionally be a minus score. Note that all cards left in the hand count against the player regardless of whether or not they could have been melded. Should a player commit a rule violation during the hand and a penalty has been assessed, then penalty points for such offense are charged to the offender and deducted from the partnership's total hand score.

The partnership that went Skarney or won the hand with a higher number of scored points is credited with either a Skarney bonus or a hand bonus for the designated hand as stipulated under Skarney or Hand Bonuses (page 405) and this figure is entered on the score sheet. The scores for each hand are then added to (or subtracted from, as the case may be) each previous cumulative score, if any. In this manner, players can not only check the score and Skarney bonus for each hand but also have a cumulative total at the end of each hand.

To speed up the arithmetic in scoring, first group together your partnership's penalty cards. Second, remove enough cards, if possible, from yours and your partner's melds whose point values equal those of the penalty cards. These and the penalty cards are put aside as they no longer enter into the scoring. Third, add up the point values of yours and your partner's melded cards still left on the table, and from this amount deduct any penalties assessed for irregularities. The balance is the partnership's hand score. The counting process will be further speeded up if the melds are stacked in separate piles of 100 points whenever possible.

End of Game

The game ends upon completion of the seventh hand and the partnership with the higher total score wins the game and gets credit for the point difference between both scores. See the sample scoring game that follows:

Score Sheet	They	We
First hand scores	130	65
Skarney bonus	100	
Total scores 1 hand	230	65
Second hand scores	195	50
Skarney bonus	100	
Total scores 2 hands	525	115
Third hand scores	295	345
Skarney bonus		100
Total scores 3 hands	820	560
Fourth hand scores	180	230
Skarney bonus		200
Total scores 4 hands	1,000	990
Fifth hand scores	160	375
Skarney bonus		300
Total scores 5 hands	1,600	1,665
Sixth hand scores	265	15
Skarney bonus	400	
Total scores 6 hands	1,825	1,680
Seventh hand scores	195	—280
Skarney bonus	500	

Total games scores . . They 2,520   We 1,400
—1,400 We's score
They wins by . . . . 1,120 Points

First Hand: They go Skarney, scoring 130 points + 100 points Skarney bonus. We score 65 points. The score at the end of the first hand is 230 to 65 in favor of They.

Second Hand: They go Skarney, scoring 195 points + 100 points Skarney bonus. We score 50 points. These scores are added to the score of the first hand, showing They leading We at the end of the second hand by 525 to 115.

Third Hand: We go Skarney, scoring 345 points + 100 points Skarney bonus. They score 295 points. These scores added to the previous cumulative scores show They with 820 points and We with 560.

Fourth Hand: We go Skarney, scoring 230 points + 200 points Skarney bonus. They score 180 points. The scores at the end of the fourth hand are 1,000 to 990 in favor of They.

Fifth Hand: We go Skarney, scoring 375 + 300 points Skarney bonus. They score 160 points. At the end of the fifth hand We is leading They 1,665 to 1,160.

Sixth Hand: They go Skarney, scoring 265 points + 400 points Skarney bonus. We score 15 points. The score at the end of the sixth hand is They 1,825, We 1,680.

Seventh Hand: They go Skarney, scoring 195 points + 500 points Skarney bonus. We score minus 280 points. They's game total is 2,520 points. We's game total is 1,400 points. So, They's winnings for the game are the difference in scores or 1,120 points. At one-tenth of a cent a point, partnership They collects $1.12 from partnership We.

ALTERNATE SKARNEY

This is a most fascinating variation of Skarney and my favorite. It is highly recommended to the experienced Skarney player who wants his Skarney game to have greater scope leading to more possibilities for skilled card maneuvers and more opportunities for error. This is all due to the fact that Alternate Skarney possesses two sensational progressive game features, such as (*1*) Each of the seven initial (contract) meld requirements becomes a bit more difficult to attain with each succeeding deal. (*2*) The point value of each of the seven succeeding Skarney or Hand Bonuses increases by 100 points in direct relation to the attainment of the contract meld—thereby making for a more balanced scoring game. The rules governing Skarney apply in full for Alternate Skarney, except as follows:

CONTRACT REQUIREMENTS FOR FIRST MELD PLUS POINT SCORE FOR EACH SKARNEY AND HAND BONUSES

Deals		Bonuses for Winning the Hand
1st Deal	Any 3 three card melds comprised of 3 groups, 3 sequences or a combination of both	100 points
2nd Deal	3 three card groups	200 points
3rd Deal	3 three card sequences	300 points
4th Deal	Any 4 three card melds comprised of 4 groups, 4 sequences or a combination of both	400 points
5th Deal	2 three card groups and 2 three card sequences	500 points
6th Deal	4 three card groups	600 points
7th Deal	4 three card sequences	700 points

SAMPLE SCORING OF AN ALTERNATE SKARNEY PARTNERSHIP GAME

Score Sheet	They	We
First Hand Scores	130	65
Skarney Bonus	100	
Total Scores 1 Hand	230	65
Second Hand Scores	195	50
Skarney Bonus	200	
Total Scores 2 Hands	625	115
Third Hand Scores	295	345
Skarney Bonus		300
Total Scores 3 Hands	920	760
Fourth Hand Scores	180	230
Skarney Bonus		400
Total Scores 4 Hands	1,100	1,390
Fifth Hand Scores	160	375
Skarney Bonus		500
Total Scores 5 Hands	1,260	2,265
Sixth Hand Scores	265	15
Skarney Bonus	600	
Total Scores 6 Hands	2,125	2,280
Seventh Hand Scores	195	—280
Skarney Bonus	700	

Total game scores .. They 3,020   We 2,000
                                    —2,000 We's score
Total game scores .. They wins by .... 1,020 Points

First Hand: They go Skarney scoring 130 points + a 100 point Skarney Bonus. We score 65 points. The score at the end of the first hand is 230 to 65 in favor of They.

Second Hand: They go Skarney scoring 195 points + 200 points bonus for Skarney. We score 50 points. These scores are added to the score of the first hand showing They leading We at the end of the second hand by 625 to 115.

Third Hand: We go Skarney scoring 345 points + 300 points Skarney Bonus. They score 295 points. These scores added to the previous cumulative scores show They with 920 points and We with 760.

Fourth Hand: We go Skarney scoring 230 points + a 400 point Skarney Bonus. They score 180 points. The scores at the end of the fourth hand are 1,390 to 1,100 in favor of We.

Fifth Hand: We go Skarney scoring 375 points + a 500 point Skarney Bonus. They score 160 points. At the end of the fifth hand We is leading They 2,265 to 1,260.

Sixth Hand: They go Skarney scoring 265 points + a 600 point

Skarney Bonus. We score 15 points. The score at the end of the sixth hand is We 2,280, They 2,125.

Seventh Hand: They go Skarney scoring 195 points + a Skarney Bonus of 700 points. We score minus 280 points. They's game total is 3,020 points. We's game total is 2,000. So, They's winnings for the game are the difference in scores or 1,020 points. At one-tenth of a cent a point, partnership, They collect $1.02 from partnership We.

Additional Rules

The rules that govern irregularities are designed to define the offense and provide adequate remedy in all cases where a player accidentally, carelessly, or inadvertently violates a rule of the game and gains an unintentional but nevertheless unfair advantage. An offending player should be ready to pay a prescribed penalty graciously. The general rules governing irregularities follow:

1. When an irregularity has been committed, a player may draw attention to it and give or obtain information as to the penalty applicable to it. The fact that a player draws attention to an irregularity committed by his partnership does not affect the rights of the opposing partnership.

2. After attention has been drawn to an irregularity, play shall stop and not be resumed until all questions in regard to rectification and to the assessment of a penalty have been determined. Either player of the offended partnership has the right to impose a penalty without consulting his partner.

3. A penalty may not be imposed until the nature of the offense has been clearly stated; however, a penalty once paid, or any decision agreed and acted upon by the players stands, even though it may later be adjudged wrong.

4. The right to penalize an offense or irregularity is forfeited if a player of the offended partnership (*a*) waives the penalty, (*b*) consults with his partner as to the imposition of a penalty before a penalty has been imposed, (*c*) calls attention to an opponent's irregularity after he or his partner has drawn a card from the stock.

5. Rectification or validation proceeds as provided in the following irregularities applicable to the specific offense. When these irregularities are appreciated and the penalties invoked, arguments are avoided and the pleasure and enjoyment which the game offers are materially enhanced.

Dealing Out of Turn. Should a deal out of turn be discovered before the first play, the deal stands and the first play is made by the player whose turn it would have been if no irregularity had occurred. In this case, the deal passes as though the cards had been dealt by the correct player. But should a deal out of turn be discovered after the beginning of the first play, the deal stands and play continues from that point. In this case, the deal passes as though the irregular deal had been correct.

Misdeals. There must be a new deal if:

1. It is discovered during the deal that the cut was omitted.

2. During the deal the dealer exposes any card other than his own.

3. Before each player has made his first play, it is discovered that any player was dealt an incorrect number of cards. If such discovery is made after each player has made his first play, the play continues without correction.

4. Before each player has made his first play, a card is found faced up in the stock, or a foreign card is found in the pack or in a player's hand, or it is discovered that a card is missing from the pack.

Irregularities in the Draw from the Stock. The following rules cover irregularities in the draw:

1. If a player draws the top card of the stock and sees or exposes another card or cards of the stock in the process, he must show the card or cards so seen or exposed to all the players and replace them. In addition, he must show his drawn card to all the players before placing it with the cards in his hand. The player whose turn it is to play next may either take the top card of the stock or shuffle the stock and cut before drawing from the stock.

2. If a player draws two or more cards from the stock and puts them in his hand, he must forgo his draw for as many turns as the number of extra cards he has drawn. He must offer a potential discard at each turn and may not meld, lay off, or swap wild cards until after his next legal draw.

3. If a player draws from the stock before the preceding player has offered a potential discard, the draw stands, and the player loses his turn to accept the potential discard and the offender is not permitted to meld or lay off until his next turn of play.

4. If a player draws from the stock when it is not his turn, he must show the card erroneously drawn to all players and replace it on the

stock. The player whose turn it was to play may either take it as his draw or shuffle the stock and cut before drawing.

Irregular Deck During Play. An irregular deck during play is one in which:

1. A card is found face up in the stock. It must be turned and shuffled with the rest of the stock and cut.

2. A foreign card is found in the pack. It must be removed. If it is in a player's hand, it is removed and replaced immediately by the top card of the stock.

3. One or more missing cards are found and no player admits to their ownership. They should be shown to all players, then put into the pack, which is shuffled and cut.

Stop-Card Irregularity. If a player's potential discard is a stop card (joker, deuce, or ace) it may be offered only to the player on his immediate left, and if that player accepts the stop card, he loses his turn to pick the top card of the stock. If he refuses the stop card, the player who offered it must keep it. He is not permitted to offer the stop card to the other players. If, however, the player accepts the stop card and draws from the stock inadvertently, he must show the card erroneously drawn to all the players and replace it on the stock. The next player may, if he chooses, take the card as his draw or shuffle the stock and cut before drawing. There is no penalty for this infraction.

Last-Card Irregularity. When a player holds only one card in his hand, he cannot offer it as a potential discard. When holding only one card, a player must announce "Last card," in a voice that all can hear. Second, he must hold the card so that its value is hidden from the other players' views. If, however, a player inadvertently exposes the value of his last card, there is no penalty, but the player may be reprimanded. If the player repeats the infraction, his partnership is penalized 50 points for each new offense.

Potential Discard Irregularities. The following covers potential discard irregularities:

1. If a player offers a potential discard without drawing, he must draw the top card of the stock if attention is called to the irregularity before the next player has drawn. If the next player draws before attention is called, the offending player must take the next top card of the stock and play reverts to the other player.

2. If a player at his turn has refused the potential discard either by word or action, the decision stands. He cannot accept the refused potential discard under any conditions.

3. If a player at his turn has accepted a potential discard either by word or action, the decision stands. He cannot refuse the potential discard under any conditions.

Illegal Contract Melds. If it is discovered during a player's turn to play that he has:

1. Placed on the table as a contract meld an insufficient or illegal meld, (*a*) he may correct the irregularity by putting down sufficient melds from his hand, in which case he may rearrange the cards put down in error providing he makes use of all melded cards; or (*b*) he may return to his hand one or more cards put down in error and rearrange all his melds from melded cards and cards in his hand, in which case his partnership is penalized 100 points.

2. Placed on the table an illegal or insufficient contract meld and cannot remedy the situation, he is permitted to return the cards to his hand and the penalty to his partnership is 10 points.

Irregularities in Melding and Laying Off. After a partnership's contract meld has been fulfilled and a player has laid down a meld or melds, he cannot pick them up and replace them in his hand. Nor is he permitted to rearrange them in any other kind of meld. Cards once melded and laid down on the table remain as legal melds. The same ruling holds true for a one- or two-card layoff on either partner's melds. If a player lays down an illegal meld or layoff and attention is brought to it, he is permitted to correct the irregularity or replace the cards in his hand and the penalty for the infraction is 50 points. If, after an illegal meld or layoff, the next player draws a card from the stock before attention is called to the error, the illegal meld or layoff stands as a legal play.

Irregularities in asking Permission to Go Skarney. The following cover irregularities in asking to go Skarney:

1. At his proper turn of play and before melding or laying off cards, or indicating he has the necessary melds to go Skarney, a player may ask, "Partner, may I go Skarney?" It is strongly recommended that only this phrase be used. Partner must reply either "Yes," or "No" (nothing more), and the answer is binding. If the player fails to abide by the answer, his side is penalized 100 points.

2. If a player calls "Skarney" without asking his partner's permission and finds he cannot go Skarney, his partnership is penalized 100 points and the cards (if any) that the player may have exposed in attempting to go Skarney are returned to his hand.

3. If the player after asking the question, but before receiving a

reply, melds or lays off, indicates a meld or layoff, withdraws the question, or gives any other information; or if the partner, in giving a negative answer, transmits information, either opponent may demand that the player go Skarney (if he possibly can) or not go Skarney.

4. If after asking his partner's permission to go Skarney and receiving an affirmative answer to the question, a player states he cannot go out, his partnership is penalized 100 points and the cards (if any) that the player may have exposed in attempting to go Skarney are returned to his hand.

5. If a player who receives a negative answer to the question "Partner, may I go out?" proceeds to attempt to meld all of his cards, he must rearrange these melds so that at least two cards will remain unmelded. The two cards or more remaining unmelded are returned to his hand and offender must offer a potential discard and the partnership is penalized 100 points.

Score Corrections. Here are the important points of rules of scoring:

1. When a score is agreed upon and written down, it may not later be set aside. Proven mistakes in addition or subtraction on the score sheet may be corrected at any time prior to the start of a new game. If the error is proven after the first draw of any hand, the hand must be completed before the error can be corrected.

2. Once a partnership has counted its cards and announced its total score and the score is entered on the score sheet and a new hand has started, the partners cannot call for rectification of some previous mistake they have made. Players are not required to inform their opposition that they have committed an error or failed to lay off a card or failed to meld to their best advantage, nor are they required to notify the opposition that they are calling an incorrect count to their disadvantage.

3. A player who inadvertently mixes his melds with the rest of the cards before counting them forfeits their count.

4. A player who inadvertently mixes an opponent's melds with the rest of the cards before they are counted may not dispute that opponent's claim to their point value.

SKARNEY SINGLES

Double-Deck Skarney Singles is just like Skarney Four-Handed Partnership except that everyone plays for himself. You can use all your knowledge in Skarney Four-Handed Partnership to good advantage except that the partnership factor is missing. Yet it is different enough to create novel and exciting situations that could never arise in partnership play. The official rules for Skarney Four-Handed Partnership apply with the following exceptions and additional rules:

1. Two, three, or four players, each playing for himself.

2. Each player is required to fulfill his initial contract meld.

3. A player at each turn of play may swap (if possible) a wild card (deuce or joker) from one or more melds of each and every opponent.

4. A player is only permitted to lay off cards on his own melds. To emphasize, a player is not permitted to lay off cards on opponent's melds.

5. When a singles player goes Skarney by putting down his contract meld, he receives the Skarney shutout bonus only if each and every opponent has failed to put down a contract meld.

SKARNEY STRATEGY

The following are the 20 basic points of Skarney strategy:

1. Learn the rules of the game so that you can recall them at a moment's notice.

2. Pick up your 11 dealt cards one at a time.

3. Take time out to arrange your hand in ranks and suits.

4. Don't give the strength of your hand away by saying you have a weak hand, or no wild cards, or a strong hand and many wild cards.

5. When putting down a contract meld, do not expend vulnerable wild cards in mixed melds too freely when no great urgency presses.

6. Think twice before offering a stop card (ace, deuce, or joker) to your left-hand opponent—especially when he holds only a few cards.

7. When holding a weak hand, accept all matching potential discards. When holding a strong hand, think twice before accepting a nonmatching potential discard.

8. Before melding and laying off, study your opponent's mixed melds for possible wild-card swaps.

9. Study your natural and mixed melds and your partner's for possible layoffs and lock-ups.

10. When melding and laying off, try to keep one wild card in your hand to help a possible Skarney hand.

11. The safest potential discard to offer your opponents is a card of the same rank they have previously refused.

12. Remember the potential discards taken by your partner and try to feed him the like—or hold same for possible layoffs on partner's melds.

13. Try not to leave yourself with just one wild card as your last card.

14. Wild cards without natural pairs near the end of a hand are expendable—too many may be a handicap.

15. Try to put down your mixed meld so that the wild card will be as safe as possible.

16. It's mathematically best to meld groups rather than sequences, better for laying off cards.

17. Think twice before saying "No" to the question, "May I go Skarney?"

18. You should play for Skarney whenever it appears that the prolongation of the hand will benefit your opponents more than yourselves.

19. Don't discuss or criticize your partner's play during the play of the hand.

20. Study the score at the end of each hand.

Probabilities in a Skarney Hand

In Skarney, as in all card games of skill, there is a mathematical basis for many correct plays. But mathematics plays only a minor part of Skarney strategy. You do not have to be a mathematician to play well, nor do you have to memorize mathematical rules laid down by anyone. There are, of course, some probability factors in Skarney, which are apparent even to the beginner. It should be obvious that you have a better chance of making a 3-card natural group meld than a 3-card natural sequence meld when you hold a pair of kings than if you hold a king and queen of spades. In fact the odds are 3 to 2 in favor of the natural group. The reason, there are six kings to draw from and there are only four cards (two aces of spades and two jacks of spades) to draw from to make a 3-card natural sequence.

The number of ways that 11 cards can be dealt to a player out of a total of 108 cards is a figure with 15 digits—approximately 344,985,-000,000,000. But this does not represent the number of different Skarney hands because a ten of hearts, for instance, in a group meld is not different from a ten of diamonds or a wild card. The number of significantly different hands that can be dealt in Skarney is very much smaller—approximately 3,500,000.

On the average, you will be dealt one or more wild cards per hand (11 cards) and you are better than a 3 to 1 favorite to be dealt at least one wild card. Your whole hand, on the average, in approximate figures will be:

Wild cards	1 (plus)
Aces	1 (minus)
High cards	3 (plus)
Low cards	6 (minus)
Total	11 cards

Your hand will have two natural pairs (or longer sets) and will for example be: deuce, ace, 3–3, queen–queen, jack, 9, 8, 6 and 5. The most disconnected hand in Skarney is one containing no matched cards and no wild cards, but you will be dealt a hand of this type about once in 3,000 deals.

Techniques in Playing for Skarney

The principle of mobility is a general principle common to most card games of skill. In Skarney to keep your hand fluid and to be prepared for most contingencies is of utmost importance. In playing for Skarney, the desired flexibility can be maintained by forming as many two-way melds incorporating the same cards in both groups and sequences as you possibly can. For instance, among your cards you hold three three-card sequences, the seven, eight, nine of diamonds; seven, eight, nine of spades; and the seven, eight, nine of clubs. These same three three-card sequence melds can be switched to three three-card groups, such as 3 sevens, 3 eights, and 3 nines. It becomes quite a problem to some players when holding twenty or more cards to segregate the melds in their proper manner. I have seen many players holding a Skarney hand but unaware of it and never going Skarney simply because the hand was not arranged properly. This is especially true when a few wild cards are among the large number of cards a player is holding. The best advice that can be given is to take your time when sorting out melds in your hand, because who knows, a simple rearrangement of melds may spell Skarney for you.

Tactics When You Need a Contract Meld

A contract meld of three three-card groups or three three-card sequences is fairly easy to obtain. Possession of one or two wild cards, for instance, practically assures it. But don't rush to put down mixed melds (melds possessing a wild card) unless they are fairly safe from being stolen (swapped for a natural card) by your opponents. Otherwise it is best to wait even several rounds in order to put down natural melds or closed mixed melds. That is, providing your opponents have not as yet put down their contract meld.

If your opponents have fulfilled their contract meld and your side has not, by all means get down on the board (if possible). It is best to gamble a stolen wild card (deuce or joker) than to be caught with a 50- or 100-point penalty card in your hand. As play progresses, the urgency for putting down a contract meld increases to the point where its desirability can no longer be weighed too delicately.

A contract meld of either four three-card groups or four three-card sequences is difficult to get unless you happen to be dealt two or three wild cards. With no wild cards, it is really tough. The general principles as to when you should put down your four three-card contract melds are simple. You should almost always go down as soon as you can. Only very seldom may you indulge in the luxury of waiting for a more desirable contract meld. Always remember Skarney Four-Handed Partnership is a partnership game and partners must cooperate in putting down a contract meld. Some players holding a contract meld wait for their partners to meld, hoping to go Skarney after their partners fulfill the contract meld. Skarney Partnership, like Contract Bridge, is a partnership game and to win at Skarney, as at bridge, partnership cooperation is required. So when you have an opportunity to fulfill a four three-card contract meld in the early part of a hand, do so and try for a big scoring hand. The 200, 300, 400, 500, 600, or 700 points for Skarney bonus is big—but so are the penalty cards your opponents may be caught with.

Getting your contract meld down has obvious advantages. It is your race toward going Skarney. It gives your partner a chance to meld groups and sequences, plus laying off on your melds, and vice versa. It also relieves your partner of the pressure of trying to attain the contract meld. Last but not least, it puts the pressure on your opponents, and at times causes them to put down mixed melds with vulnerable wild cards. But as you may already have discovered, it may be to your disadvantage to put down either a natural or mixed contract meld during the early stages of the hand. It makes it easier for your opponents to choose safe potential discards and reduces the flexibility of your own hand. Therefore, you will have to weigh the advantages against the disadvantages such as being left with four or five disconnected cards in your hand, after fulfilling your contract meld.

The necessity for making such decisions arises frequently in Skarney, and the player who consistently uses good judgment will win many more games than his opponents.

To succeed in blitzing, some luck and considerable psychological bluffing on your part and your partner's are required. You both must keep poker faces and play it cool so as not to alert your opponents to the fact that you are attempting a blitz. And, always remember: When you have a good reason to fear that your opponents may go Skarney quickly—it is wise for you, if possible, to unload—put down all your melds and layoffs be they natural or mixed melds.

The Subtle Art of Potential Discarding

Skarney is a game of deduction and counter deduction. (1) You must try to figure out what cards each opponent is holding in his hand so that (*a*) you won't give them any useful cards and (*b*) you won't be holding cards for an impossible or unlikely meld. (2) You must try to figure out what cards your partner is holding in his hand so that (*a*) you'll be holding cards you can lay off on his possible melds and (*b*) you'll be offering potential discards that are useful to your partner. Therefore, good potential discarding is both offensive and defensive. Offensively, you want to build up or maintain a hand that will give you a contract meld and a fair chance to go Skarney. Defensively, you want to make the attainment of these objectives as difficult as possible for your opponents.

At the very beginning of the hand the question of what is and what is not a safe potential discard is not too important. On the first few rounds any potential discard is usually accepted by one of your opponents or partner. You should not worry at this point because more often than not some one will take almost every card coming his way, if he needs it or not. Such a player is referred to as a "garbage picker." What you should do at the beginning of the hand is to concentrate on building your own hand and keeping your opponents in the dark regarding the strength of your hand. However, during the middle of the hand, prior to your opponents' fulfillment of their contract meld, you cannot do better than to match your opponents' previous potential discard with a similar rank card. If one of your opponents offers a five, you should retaliate and offer a five if you have one and can spare it. The presumption is that he does not have a pair left in a rank that he has offered so early. Sometimes you will be wrong, but more often you will be right.

If you hold a lone ace (stop card) it is usually wise to offer it to your left-hand opponent. Again the presumption is that he will not accept it for fear of losing a pick from the top of the stock. Think twice, however, before offering an ace or a wild card in the later phase of the hand.

The foregoing advice on potential discards is intended to apply in any situation where the two partnerships are on equal or near-equal terms. The partnership trailing by several hundred points is bound to accept nearly every potential discard that might come its way hoping to net hundreds of points more than you could make by going Skarney quickly.

Once your opponents have put down their contract meld, each of your potential discard plays must be thoroughly analyzed, more so if one of your opponents holds his last card. You must be ultrasafe in offering a potential discard. Study your opponents' and your own melds (if any) very carefully and then think twice before making the play. Owing to the luck (chance) aspect of Skarney, the most skillful potential discarding cannot guarantee success every time.

Acceptance and Refusal of Potential Discards

Prior to either side having fulfilled its contract meld, there is no need to consider taking a potential discard when it matches a card in your hand or gives you a meld: just take it with a feeling of gratitude to the giver. But, when the offered card does not give you a match or a meld, the problem of taking it poses a dilemma. It frequently happens that an opponent tries to pass his partner a card of the same rank as previously taken. When such a condition prevails, it may be good tactics to take it even though it doesn't help your hand. You can always offer it back later on if you must.

An important question that often arises at the beginning of a hand is whether to try for a big score and take almost every card that comes your way or to accept fewer valuable cards and try for Skarney. However, not every hand is suitable for a big score. Often a player is dealt

11 cards which are better adapted for a fast contract meld and a quick Skarney—providing the player gets an assist from his partner. Such a decision depends on the score. If your partnership is far ahead, you should play for Skarney, only accepting a potential discard that gives you a meld or extends a meld. If your partnership is far behind—and all other things being even—try for the big score. The necessity for making such decisions arises frequently in Skarney and the player who consistently uses good judgment will be the winner. Should you be offered an ace (stop card) in the early stages of the game and you are bent on trying for a big score—accept it when first offered. It very often is part of the opponent's meld or matched aces and he is offering it as bluff card so as not to break up any of his other matched sets or melds. If you have what you consider a possible Skarney hand, don't take it, because a disconnected ace is a difficult card to get rid of when your opponents have put down their contract meld.

When both partnerships are down with melds, you should be extra cautious in accepting an opponent's potential discard. Take a careful look before accepting or offering a potential discard. Observe all melds on the table. At this stage, it is fairly easy to tell what card is good or bad for your side or your opponents'.

Most beginners at this stage of the game are tempted to accept an opponent's potential discard merely to extend one of their own melds. By all means, do not accept an opponent's potential discard that he cannot get rid of by laying it off on one of his own melds.

Should you have no quick chance of going Skarney, and your partner holds very few cards in his hand, accept all potential discards from your partner, thereby giving him the opportunity to go Skarney. And last but not least, think twice before offering or accepting an ace or wild card when both partnerships are down to their last few cards.

Defense Against Opponents Who Have Many Cards

Going Skarney? Should the opponent be the ones who are holding big hands of 20 or more cards by taking every potential discard that comes their way, your best defense is, of course, to go Skarney and catch them with a boodle of penalty cards. Partners should cooperate in this situation. For instance, it may easily be that both partners would be in good position to go Skarney if their side puts down its contract meld. In this situation, one of the two partners may have to injure his own Skarney hand by using a couple of wild cards to fulfill his partnership's contract meld. The question arises, which partner should it be? Obviously the one who can best spare the wild cards—but how can one tell? One good indication that the partner has an excellent chance to go Skarney and is merely waiting for his partner to put down the initial meld is that he is not trying to further build up his hand and is refusing most potential discards, and usually offering the drawn card as his potential discard. Consequently, this player's partner should be the one to make the sacrifice and put down the contract meld.

Protecting Your Jokers and Deuces

One of the most important factors in skillful Skarney playing is the use of a wild card. Do you hold it in your hand and wait until you can deploy it in a safe (locked) mixed meld but by so doing take a chance of getting caught with it in your hand? Or do you meld it in an open mixed meld and hope your opponents don't steal it? I can't help you on this one because there are billions of possible hands in Skarney and each requires a different strategy, so you'll have to use your best judgment on how to deploy the wild card. But, whenever you are faced with a decision on whether to use a joker or a deuce in a locked (safe) mixed meld, consider the fact that the joker counts 50 points and the deuce 25. The penalty against you if you are caught with a joker in your hand is 100 points, a deuce 50 points. Hence, there are times when you should use a joker in an open mixed meld, other times a deuce. It all depends on whether your opponents are trying for a contract meld or going for Skarney. Also to be taken into consideration are the opponents' chances of stealing (swapping) the wild card. At times, too many wild cards pose a question. For instance, you hold three jokers. If melded as a joker spread they count 300 points. You wonder if the 300 points are better than a try at the Skarney bonus by using the jokers in mixed melds where they are worth only 150 points, plus the chance of being caught with them in your hand for a disaster penalty of 300 points. Such decisions can only be appraised at the time of happening. There is no cut and dried rule that fits wild cards.

Asking Permission to Go Skarney

When you are ready to go Skarney, you may, according to the rules, ask permission of your partner. But, remember you are not obliged to ask that question. Ask it only if there is a reason for you to do so.

You should not ask permission whenever your hand clearly indicates what to do. *Example:* If you are able to go Skarney on the seventh hand and win the game at the same time, you should not ask the question. Your partner does not know your hand and it is conceivable that he may give a negative reply. Neither should you ask permission if you are sure that you shouldn't go Skarney because you don't want to risk the possibility of an affirmative reply.

You should ask permission of your partner any time you are really interested in his opinion. For instance, you suspect that the handful of cards your partner is holding contains a number of wild cards whose penalty point values could possibly reduce your hand score to a minus score, but of course you cannot be sure about it. By putting the question to him, you are giving him the opportunity to say "No," if he actually has the hand you suspect. In that case, he will put down all possible melds at his next turn and you may or may not go Skarney on the next round. But, if his is not the type of hand you expected, he will say "Yes."

Expert Skarney players will also sometimes ask permission with the definite expectation of getting a negative reply. For instance, if a partner has just stolen a joker or two from his opponent's melds and has a great many cards in his hand and has not melded any cards as yet, it is obvious that he does not want the hand to end at this stage. By asking him, you simply advise him of the strength of your own hand. He will surely answer "No," and will have acquired the knowledge that as soon as he puts down his melds you will try to go Skarney. If he judges, however, that prolongation of the hand would be more profitable, or by chance he cannot meld as he would wish, he will still not meld, and at your next turn, you should ask again, etc.

For more detailed information and strategy of winning play for all 30 Skarney variants, read *Skarney,* a 145-page book which I wrote several years ago.

19

Skarney Gin®

The World's Best
Two-Handed Card Game

"What card players the world over need is a great two-handed card game." I have said this for many years, and now it seems Skarney Gin fills the bill. It is truly the most fascinating and exciting two-handed card game in history. Regular Gin Rummy, unlike Skarney Gin, is basically a gambling game. Leave the stakes out of Gin Rummy and it falls flat on its face as a nongambling game. Skarney Gin, however, is a great family pastime. For the millions of married couples Skarney Gin is the ideal two-handed game.

Skarney Gin is the game that I honestly believe will soon displace regular Gin Rummy as America's favorite two-handed card game. It outclasses regular Gin Rummy not only in fun and excitement but in strategic planning. The reasons for the above statements are: (1) Skarney Gin makes use of three melds, groups, sequences, and poker straights—whereas regular Gin Rummy employs only groups and sequences. This factor alone gives Skarney Gin greater scope and flexibility, causing the player to commit more errors than he would in regular Gin Rummy. (2) The ten-card initially dealt hand in regular Gin Rummy always remains the same during play. In Skarney Gin the ten dealt cards held by a player fluctuate. They may increase to twenty or more cards, decrease to one, increase to ten or more, remain the same, or dwindle to zero when a player goes Skarney or gin. This unusual and fascinating scientific aspect of Skarney Gin makes the game much more interesting and requires greater player concentration than regular Gin Rummy. (3) Although Skarney Gin is a scientific game, poor players win occasionally, so that everyone becomes convinced that he plays well. In no other card game do you find so many self-proclaimed local champs.

TEN THINGS EVERY WINNING SKARNEY GIN PLAYER MUST KNOW

1. Learn the rules so thoroughly you can recall them instantly and correctly.

2. Minimize mechanical errors by picking up your dealt cards singly.

3. Don't break up a possible meld at the start of the hand to withhold a doubtful card from your opponent.

4. Study your contract meld before putting it down. However, it usually pays to put down poker straights rather than groups or sequences.

5. Risk adding to opponent's meld rather than offer a live potential discard.

6. Late in the hand, think twice before offering an ace (stop card) as your potential discard.

7. It usually doesn't pay to accept a potential discard only for its layoff value.

8. When purposely holding back your contract meld, make sure to study the score.

9. When putting down poker straights, it is best to meld them in sets of threes rather than sets of fours, fives, or sixes—the reason is, there are more opportunities for layoffs.

10. Don't play hunches—play the odds.

STANDARD RULES FOR SKARNEY GIN

Requirements

1. Two players—although the game may involve three or four players, only two of these may be in play against each other simultaneously.

2. A standard 52-card deck. It is recommended that two packs of cards with backs of different colors be used in the play. While the dealer is shuffling for the deal, the nondealer is giving the other pack a preliminary shuffle, after which it is set to one side. It is shuffled again by the loser of this hand before he deals the next hand.

Point Scoring for Penalty Cards

Melded cards resting on the table at the end of a hand count zero. Only the cards left in a player's hand at the end of a hand are scored. Even though they form melds they are counted as penalty cards against the holder. The ace is the highest-ranking penalty card, having a value of 15 points. The king, queen, and jack are valued at 10 points each. All other cards have their numerical face value, such as deuce 2 points, three 3 points, four 4 points, etc. The suits have no value.

So that the reader can see the penalty card counts at a glance, they have been placed in tabular form.

POINT SCORING FOR PENALTY CARDS
LEFT IN HAND AT END OF GAME

Cards	Points
Aces	Minus 15 each
Kings	Minus 10 each
Queens	Minus 10 each
Jacks	Minus 10 each
Tens	Minus 10 each
Nines	Minus 9 each
Eights	Minus 8 each
Sevens	Minus 7 each
Sixes	Minus 6 each
Fives	Minus 5 each
Fours	Minus 4 each
Threes	Minus 3 each
Twos	Minus 2 each

Melds

The following three types of melds are permitted in Skarney Gin.

1. *Group Melds*. Three or four cards of the same rank such as three or four eights, three or four kings, etc.

2. *Sequence Melds*. Three or more cards of the same suit in consecutive order. *Examples:* three, four, five of hearts; or eight, nine, ten, and jack of spades. Aces, however, may be used in both low and high card sequences. *Examples:* ace, deuce, three of spades; queen, king, ace of clubs. Aces, however, cannot be used in a round-the-corner sequence such as king, ace, deuce of diamonds.

3. *Poker-Straight Melds*. Three or more cards of various suits in consecutive order. *Examples:* poker straights such as the three of clubs, four of diamonds, five of spades; or ten of diamonds, jack of hearts, queen of clubs, and king of diamonds, etc. Aces, as in sequence melds, may be used in both a low or high card run or straight. *Examples:* ace of hearts, deuce of diamonds, three of clubs; or queen of spades, king of hearts, ace of clubs, etc. Aces cannot be used in a round-the-corner straight such as king, ace, deuce.

Contract Melds

The first meld made by each player in each and every deal (hand) until the completion of the game must meet the exact initial contract meld requirement of three three-card melds, a total of nine cards. The three three-card melds may be comprised of any of the following: (*a*) three three-card group melds; (*b*) three three-card sequence melds; (*c*) three three-card poker-straight melds; (*d*) any three three-card meld combinations made up of groups, sequences, and poker straights. *Examples*: (1) one three-card group, one three-card sequence, and one three-card poker straight; (2) one three-card group and two three-card sequences; (3) one three-card group and two three-card poker straights, etc. To emphasize, no part of a contract meld can have more than three cards when first placed on the table, nor can the contract meld be comprised of more or less than three three-card melds.

Selecting Dealer and Starting Position

By mutual consent either player may shuffle the deck of cards. Each player cuts a group of cards from the deck. Player cutting the low-faced card deals first. In case of a tie, players cut again. The loser of a hand deals the next hand.

If players want to cut for seat position, the player cutting low takes his choice of seat.

The Shuffle and Cut

Dealer shuffles the deck. Opponent may call for a shuffle at any time he likes prior to the cut, though the dealer retains the privilege of shuffling last. Dealer must offer the deck to opponent for cut. If opponent refuses to cut, the dealer must cut his own cards before starting the deal. When cutting, at least ten cards must be in each cut portion of the deck.

The Deal

Dealer deals the opponent ten cards and himself ten cards, the opponent being dealt the first card off the top of the deck and so on alternately, until the dealer gets the last, twentieth card. The remainder of the deck, called the stock, is placed face down on the table between both players. It is advisable to spread the stock out fan-shaped on the table to minimize the chances of inadvertently drawing and seeing any cards other than the one to which the player is entitled.

The Actual Play of the Hand

Each of the two players in turn, starting with the non-dealer, does as follows:

First, he takes (draws) the top card of the stock (the remainder of the undealt cards which are face down on the table).

Second, once a player has fulfilled his contract meld, he may, if he chooses, place on the table before him any possible melds and any possible one- or two-card layoffs on each of his previous melds. A player at each turn of play is not permitted to lay off more than two cards on each previous meld. Nor is a player permitted to lay off cards on his opponent's melds.

Third, he removes a potential discard (remember, I said "potential discard") from the cards he is holding, turns it face up in his hand and offers it to his opponent by extending it toward him, asking, "Do you want this card?" The opponent may either accept or refuse the potential discard. If he accepts it, he replies, "I'll take it." This action ends the turn of play for the player who offered the card. If the opponent refuses the potential discard, the player who offered it must keep the card and return it to his hand, and his turn of play is ended. A player cannot offer the same potential discard he just accepted from his opponent at his subsequent turn of play. *Example:* A player accepts his opponent's potential discard, which is the six of spades. He cannot offer the six of spades to his opponent until he has offered another card first.

Fourth, if a player's potential discard is an ace, and the opponent accepts it, the opponent loses his turn to pick the top card of the stock.

Fifth and last, should a player hold one card in his hand, he is not permitted to offer it as a potential discard. He merely says "Last card" and keeps it.

A player during his turn and at no other time may ask his opponent how many cards he holds. The question must be answered correctly. And, so it goes from player to player until the hand ends by a player getting rid of all the cards in his hand by going Skarney—or two cards remain in the stock. When a player draws the fiftieth card from the stock and puts down his melds and layoffs, if any, the hand ends then and there without the player offering a potential discard.

To reemphasize, a player at each turn of play after having put down his contract meld may meld and lay off one or two cards on each previous meld as he wishes. A player is not permitted to lay off cards on his opponent's melds.

Note: In Skarney Gin, to minimize the chances of not picking from the stock at a player's turn of play, the following rule should be enforced. Once a player has refused a potential discard, he must immediately pick a card from the top of the stock. The strict observance of this rule will avoid many arguments between players as to whether a player at his turn of play has or has not taken a card from the stock.

How to Score a Hand

1. When a player, after having laid down his contract meld gets rid of every card in his hand, he calls "Skarney," ending the hand. This is also known as *gin,* or *going out.* The player who goes Skarney receives a 20-point Skarney bonus plus a total point count of all the cards that his opponent holds in his hand at the end of the hand even though

they form melds. *Example:* A player goes Skarney. His opponent holds seven cards comprised of four tens, two fives, and one ace. The player who Skarneyed scores 65 points. The penalty value of his opponent's seven unmelded cards, plus 20 points for going Skarney, makes a total of 85 points. His opponent does not score.

2. When a player goes Skarney or gin, and his opponent has failed to put down his contract meld, the 20-point Skarney bonus for the hand is doubled to 40 points and is known as *double Skarney,* or *double gin*.

3. When a player has drawn the fiftieth card (the last card, leaving two in the stock), the hand ends without that player offering a potential discard—and the player holding the lower penalty point total in unmelded cards in his hand wins the hand and gets credit for the point difference between both totals. *Example:* The hand ends and player A is caught with 15 points in unmelded cards in his hand. Player B has 36 points in unmelded cards in his hand. Player A is the winner of the hand and scores 21 points, the difference between both totals. Should both players tie, a no-hand is declared and the same dealer deals again.

End of Game

A game terminates at the end of any hand in which a total of 200 or more points is scored by either player.

How to Score a Game

1. Winner of the game scores the difference between both totals.

2. Winner of the game gets a *game bonus* of 200 points for winning.

3. An extra 25 points known as a *box bonus* is added to each player's score for each hand won.

4. Should a player score 200 points or more before his opponent scores any points at all, winner gets a 200-point game bonus plus a 200-point shutout bonus—plus all other credits. Following is a sample scoring of a Skarney Gin game, using my new game scoring method. The hand score for each player is written down at the left, then a dash followed by the cumulative game score to the right. This makes it known to each player at all times how far ahead or behind he is.

SAMPLE SCORING OF A SKARNEY GIN GAME

	You	Opponent
	44-44	
		64-64
	36-80	
	40-120	
	27-147	
		70-134
	120-267	
Game scores	267	134
Box bonuses	125	50
Game bonuses	200	
Total scores	592	184
Minus loser's score	−184	
Your net winnings	408 points	

First Hand: You go Skarney. Your opponent is caught with 24 points in unmelded cards (penalty cards). You score 24 points plus a 20-point Skarney bonus—a total of 44 points.

Second Hand: Your opponent goes Skarney. You are caught with 44 penalty points. Opponent scores 44 points plus a 20-point Skarney bonus. A total of 64 points. At the end of the second hand your opponent leads by 64 to 44.

Third Hand: Two cards are left in the stock. No one goes Skarney. You hold 9 penalty points, your opponent 45. You score the difference, 36 points. At the end of the third hand, you lead 80 to 64.

Fourth Hand: You go Skarney. Your opponent is caught with 20 points in unmelded cards (penalty points). You score 20 plus a 20-point Skarney bonus for a total fourth-hand score of 40 points. The cumulative game score at the end of the fourth hand is 120 to 64 in your favor.

Fifth Hand: You go Skarney. Your opponent holds 7 penalty points. You score 7 plus a 20-point Skarney bonus for a fifth-hand total of 27 points. The score at the end of the fifth hand is 147 to 64 in your favor.

Sixth Hand: Your opponent goes Skarney. You are caught with 50 penalty points. Your opponent scores 50 plus a 20-point Skarney bonus, or 70 points in all. At the end of the sixth hand the score reads 147 to 134 with you in the lead.

Seventh Hand: You go double Skarney. Your opponent holds 80 points in unmelded cards (penalty points). You score 80 plus a 40-

point double-Skarney bonus for a total seventh-hand score of 120 points. The 120 points puts you well over the 200 mark with a total of 267 and gives you game. You have five boxes, a total of 125 points at 25 points each, your opponent has two boxes worth 50 points; these are added to the scores. You add a game bonus of 200 points for winning the game. Your grand total is 592. Your opponent's is 184. So your point winnings for the game are the difference in scores, or 408 points net. At one-tenth of a cent a point, you collect 41 cents from your opponent.

ADDITIONAL RULES FOR SKARNEY GIN

If a player accidentally, inadvertently, or purposely violates a rule of the game he must pay a prescribed penalty. The right to penalize an offense or irregularity is forfeited if the offended player (*a*) waives the penalty, or (*b*) calls attention to an opponent's irregularity after he has drawn a card from the stock.

Misdeals

A misdeal is declared, and the dealer of the hand immediately starts a new deal, whenever any of the following improprieties are discovered (there are no penalties for the dealer or the responsible player):

1. If a card is turned over any time during the deal.

2. If either player or both players have been dealt an incorrect number of cards.

3. If a player deals out of turn and the error is discovered before a play has been completed.

4. If a player looks at an opponent's card or cards during the deal.

5. If a card is found face up during the deal.

6. If, however, a card is found face up in the stock, it must be properly turned, the stock shuffled and cut, and play continues.

Irregularities in the Draw

Here are problems that may arise when drawing:

1. If a player inadvertently picks off the stock two cards instead of one or inadvertently sees the face of the card below the one he has just taken, or his opponent has reason to believe that he has seen it, then his opponent at his turn of play, may, if he likes, look at the face of the top

card of the stock and take it or shuffle the stock and cut before drawing from the stock.

2. If a player draws from the stock before his opponent has offered a potential discard, he loses his turn to accept the potential discard. Furthermore, he cannot meld or lay off until his next turn of play and the penalty to the offender is 25 points.

Imperfect Deck During the Play

The following are the rules when a faulty deck is discovered:

1. There must be a new deal by the same dealer:
   - (*a*) If it is discovered that the deck has one or more duplicate cards.
   - (*b*) If a foreign card (not from either deck) is found in the deck during the deal or in the stock at any time before a player goes Skarney.
   - (*c*) If it is discovered while the hand is still in play that the deck has fewer or more than the standard 52 cards.

2. If, however, a card of the other deck, when two decks are being used, is found in the stock, it shall be eliminated and play continues.

3. If it is discovered after a player goes Skarney or the hand is over that the deck has fewer or more cards, it has no bearing on that or previous hands.

Irregularities in the Potential Discard

Here are rules covering discards;

1. If a player offers a potential discard without drawing, he must draw the top card of the stock if attention is called to the irregularity before his opponent has drawn. If the opponent draws before attention is called, the offending player must take the next top card of the stock and the play refers back to the opponent, and the offender on his next turn to play may not meld or lay off until his subsequent turn to play.

2. If during the play a player should refuse a potential discard either by word or action, he cannot then decide to take it. His refusal to accept it is his final decision on that card.

3. If a player at his turn has accepted his opponent's potential discard either by word or action, the decision stands. He cannot refuse the potential discard under any condition.

4. A potential discard once offered cannot be returned to the player's hand and another potential discard substituted; the play stands.

Illegal Contract Melds

If it is discovered during a player's turn to play that he has placed on the table as a contract meld an insufficient or illegal meld, the following can be done:

1. He may correct the irregularity by putting down sufficient melds from his hand, in which case he may rearrange the cards put down in error providing he makes use of all melded cards. The offender is penalized 25 points.

2. He may return to his hand one or more cards put down in error and rearrange all his melds from melded cards and cards in his hand, in which case he is penalized 25 points.

3. If a player errs by placing on the table an illegal or insufficient contract meld and he cannot remedy the situation, he is permitted to return the cards to his hand and he is penalized 25 points.

4. If a player errs by placing on the table more than nine cards (3 three-card melds) as his contract meld, he may correct the irregularity by returning the extra cards to his hand. There is no penalty for the infraction providing no cards from the hand are used to help achieve the contract meld.

Irregularities in Melding and Laying Off

The following details rule melding and laying-off irregularities:

1. After a player's contract meld has been fulfilled, and he puts down an additional meld or melds, he cannot pick them up and replace them in his hand. Nor is he permitted to rearrange them in any other kind of meld. Cards once melded and laid down on the table remain as legal melds. The same ruling holds true for a one- to two-card layoff.

2. If a player lays down an illegal meld or layoff and attention is brought to it, he is permitted to correct the irregularity and replace the card or cards in his hand. The penalty for this infraction of the rules is 25 points.

3. If after an illegal meld or layoff, the opponent draws a card from the stock before attention is called to the error, the illegal meld or layoff stands as a legal play.

4. If a player melds or lays off cards before drawing a card from the stock, and attention is called to the error, the player must draw a card from the stock and return the illegal melds and layoffs to his hand, and he cannot meld or lay off until his next turn of play.

Stop-Card Irregularity

If a player's potential discard is an ace, commonly known as a *stop card,* and if the opponent accepts the ace, he loses his turn to pick the top card of the stock. If the opponent refuses the ace, the player who offered it must keep it. If, however, the opponent accepts the stop card and draws from the stock inadvertently, he must show the card erroneously drawn to his opponent and replace it on the stock. The opponent may, if he chooses, take the card as his draw or shuffle the stock and cut before drawing. There is no penalty for this infraction.

A Last-Card Irregularity

When a player holds only one card in his hand, he cannot offer it as a potential discard. When holding only one card, a player must announce "Last card," in a voice that his opponent can hear. If, however, a player inadvertently does offer his last card, there is no penalty, but the player may be reprimanded. If the player repeats the infraction, he is penalized 25 points for each new offense.

Score Correction

If a scoring error is made, the following rules prevail:

1. When a score is agreed upon and written down, it may not later be set aside. Proven mistakes in addition or subtraction on the score sheet may be corrected at any time prior to the start of a new game. If the error is proven after the first draw of any hand, the hand must be completed before the error can be corrected.

2. Once the winner of the hand has verified his point count for the hand and entered it on the score sheet and a new hand has started, players cannot call for rectification of some previous mistake they all have made. A player is not required to inform his opponent that he has committed an error or failed to lay off a card or failed to meld to his best advantage, nor is he required to notify the opposition that he is calling an incorrect count to his disadvantage.

3. A player who at the completion of a hand inadvertently mixes his or his opponent's penalty cards with the rest of the cards before they are counted may not dispute that opponent's claim to their point value.

SKARNEY GIN DOUBLES

This exciting and scientific variation of Skarney Gin is recommended to the Skarney Gin players who want their game to have greater scope plus a reward for skillful preplay card analysis and psychological bluff. The addition of these two scientific maneuvers leads to a more strategic and greater point scoring game. This feat is accomplished by simply adding a pass, double, and redouble bidding system to Skarney Gin. This bidding system corresponds roughly to the passing, doubling, and redoubling elements of Contract Bridge.

Skarney Gin Doubles is played and scored the same as you play Skarney Gin with the following exceptions and additional rules.

1. A game terminates at the end of any hand in which a total of 300 or more points is scored by either player.

2. *How and When to Bid.* The bidding begins when each player has been dealt his initial ten-card hand and before either player has drawn a card from the stock. The nondealer makes the first bid, his opponent the second, the nondealer the third if necessary. Following is a description of each of the five possible bids that can be made in Skarney Gin Doubles.

(*a*) The nondealer calls "Pass," and the dealer calls "Pass." The winner of the hand scores the actual penalty point count.

(*b*) The nondealer calls "Pass," the dealer "Double," the nondealer "Pass." The winner of the hand scores double the penalty point count.

(*c*) The nondealer calls "Pass," the dealer "Double," the nondealer "Redouble." The winner of the hand scores quadruple the penalty point count.

(*d*) The nondealer calls "Double," the dealer "Pass." The winner of the hand scores double the penalty point count.

(*e*) The nondealer calls "Double," the dealer "Redouble." The winner of the hand scores quadruple the penalty point count.

3. *How to Score a Bid Hand.* In Skarney Gin Doubles the penalty point score of a pass bid hand remains the same as in regular Skarney Gin, the penalty point score of a double-bid hand is multiplied by two, and the penalty point score of a redouble-bid hand is multiplied by four. *Examples*: (*a*) The winner of a pass hand goes Skarney and catches his opponent with 16 penalty points in his hand. The winner is credited with 16 points plus the 20-point Skarney bonus for a final hand score of 36 points, the same scoring as if he were playing regular Skarney Gin.

(*b*) The winner of a double hand goes Skarney and catches his opponent with 16 penalty points in his hand. The winner is credited with 16 twice, or 32 points, plus the 20-point Skarney bonus for a final hand score of 52 points. (*c*) The winner of a redouble hand goes Skarney and catches his opponent with 16 penalty points in his hand. The winner is credited with 16 four times, or 64 points, plus the 20-point Skarney bonus for a final hand score of 84 points.

The above-described method of calculating the penalty point score of the loser also holds true when a player goes double Skarney. Should a player win the hand with a lesser number of penalty points, only the winning difference in points is doubled, redoubled, or remains the same. The pass, double, or redouble bid affects only the specific hand. It does not have anything at all to do with the score of other hands.

Note: Skarney Gin doubles may be played in all the multiple game and partnership variants described in the following pages.

ROUND-THE-CORNER SKARNEY GIN

This fascinating variation of Skarney Gin is recommended to the nonserious players who like variety and prefer their game to possess more luck and a quicker ending. All the rules governing Skarney Gin apply with the following additional rule:

An ace, in addition to being used in high and low sequences, or poker straights, such as ace–two–three, or ace–king–queen, can also be used to go round the corner, such as king–ace–two; or two–ace–king. These round-the-corner sequence and poker-straight melds may be extended of course. *Examples:* (*a*) king–ace–two–three; (*b*) queen–king–ace two–three; (*c*) two–ace–king–queen–jack; (*d*) three–two–ace–king–queen–jack–ten, and so on.

SKARNEY GIN CAPTAINS

This is a variation of Skarney Gin for three players, borrowed from Backgammon where it is called chouette or "in the box." A plays the first game as captain against B and C; B playing the first hand and continuing to play as long as he wins. But when he loses, C takes his place and continues to play until he loses, when B comes back again, and so on until the game ends. The captain keeps playing to the end of the game, regardless of whether he wins or loses. A single score is kept and totaled at the end of the game. The captain wins or loses the net total from or to each of the opponents. Then B becomes the captain playing against A and C, and so on.

SKARNEY GIN FOR THREE PLAYERS

Skarney Gin, though primarily for two players, makes an enjoyable game for three players. Although three players take part, only two are in play against each other simultaneously, as in captain play.

To determine which two shall start, any player, by consent of the others, shuffles, and the three cut cards. Low man—that man whose exposed card is of lowest rank—sits out the first hand. The other two play a game of Skarney Gin.

The score of the first hand is credited to the winner, and the loser drops out. The winner proceeds to play the next hand against the third man. (Generally the nonplayer keeps the score.) So it goes, loser giving way to nonplayer hand by hand, until one of the three scores 200 points or more.

The winner is paid off in the amount of his credit over each opponent. The player with the second highest score collects from low man. A player scoring a shutout can collect his shutout bonus only from the player who scored zero. For example, A scores 205 points; B, 90; and C, none. A gets credit for a shutout over C but not over B. Value of credits and bonuses is the same as in two-handed Skarney Gin. In three-handed Skarney Gin a player may collect from two players, lose to two players, or win from one and lose to one.

SKARNEY PARTNERSHIP GIN

This is four-handed Skarney Gin. Two players are teamed against the other two. Two games of two-handed Skarney Gin are played simultaneously and the partners enter their score as one. The players cut for partners, holders of the two highest exposed cards being teamed against the holders of the two lowest. All the rules of Skarney Gin apply to this variation. The only variation is in the scoring.

Team scores, not players' scores, are entered. *Example:* (*a*) A and B are partners playing against C and D. A, playing the first hand against his opponent C, wins by 68 points. D, playing against B, wins by 20 points. Team A-B wins the box by 48 points. That is the only score entered on the score sheet. (*b*) As before, A and B are partners against C and D. At the end of the first hand A switches seats with B and plays against D, while B plays against C. At the end of the second hand, A and B shift back to the original positions. This alternation continues with each hand until the game ends.

Note: Due to the great number of cards melded, it is suggested that two tables be used, one for each two contestants. Game is 300 points. Game bonus remains at 200, shutout bonus 200, and all other scoring is as in two-handed Skarney Gin.

SKARNEY GIN STRATEGY

Skarney Gin becomes a considerably more scientific game than regular Gin Rummy, owing to the lack of a discard pile. However, like regular Gin, it is a game of deduction and counterdeduction: (1) You must try to figure out what cards your opponent is holding so that you won't offer him vital cards; (2) you must try to build up your hand for a possible contract meld.

In Skarney Gin, as in most card games of skill and chance, there is a mathematical basis for many correct plays. There are, of course, some probability factors in Skarney Gin which are apparent even to the beginner. It should be obvious that you have a better chance of making a three-card poker straight than a three-card group when you hold a five and six (any suits) than if you hold a pair of sixes. In fact, the odds are 4 to 1 in favor of the poker straight. The reason is there are eight cards (four fours and four sevens) to draw from to make a poker straight and only two sixes to draw from to make a group meld.

At the very beginning of the hand, what is and what is not a safe potential discard is not too important. On the first few rounds any discard with the possible exception of an ace (stop card) is usually accepted. You should not worry at this point because more often than not, your opponent will take it. Therefore, what you should do at the beginning of the hand is to offer potential discards that you wish to get rid of and at the same time concentrate on building up your hand.

While concentrating on building your own hand you should try to keep your opponent in the dark regarding the strength of your hand. An initial meld of three three-card melds is fairly easy to obtain toward the middle of the hand. Even possession of three three-card melds at the beginning of the hand occurs quite frequently in Skarney Gin. But, what to do with such a hand requires some analytical reasoning. Sure, you can go down with your contract meld and put the pressure on your opponent. Great, but what about the one or more cards that will remain in your hand—are they unmatched cards? How about the next potential discard of yours? Is it a part of a matched set or a possible layoff card? Or, is it a useless card to your hand? Do you believe your opponent will take it? All the above factors are vital in playing a good game of Skarney Gin. And such deductions must be studied carefully.

I've seen many a player put down his initial meld after his first pick off the stock—and see his hand grow from two cards to eight or more cards, and his opponent goes Skarney and catches him with a hundred or more points. This upward movement of the number of cards held by a player is caused by his opponent's refusal to accept said player's potential discard, something the player has no control over.

Study your contract meld before putting it down—study it from one angle—then switch your melds around and study it from another angle. You'll be surprised what you'll see that passed unobserved a moment ago. As mentioned earlier, there are more opportunities to lay off on poker straights than group melds. However, don't rule out group melds—they play a vital part in preventing your opponent from getting such cards. The principle of mobility is a general principle in Skarney Gin. To keep your hand fluid at all times and be prepared for most contingencies is of the utmost importance. There can be no definite instruction at this point without ifs, ands, and buts.

In preparing to fulfill your initial meld or in playing for Skarney, try to form as many two-way melds incorporating the same cards in groups and poker straights. For instance, you hold three sixes, three sevens, and three eights. These same three-card groups can and should be switched to three three-card poker straights. It becomes quite a problem to some players when holding 15 or more cards to segregate the melds to their best advantage. The best advice that can be given to achieve this aim is to take your time when sorting out melds in your hand because a simple rearrangement of melds may spell an eventual Skarney for you. In fact, more games are lost by an early improper arrangement of cards in the hand than by all other erroneous plays.

As a rule, it is best to wait several rounds before putting down your contract meld. That is, providing your opponent has not as yet put down his contract meld. If your opponent has fulfilled his contract meld and you have not, by all means get down on the board (if possible) with any kinds of melds you can muster together.

Once your opponent has put down his contract meld, each of your potential discard plays must be thoroughly analyzed. You must be ultra-safe in offering a potential discard. Think twice before offering an ace (stop card) in the later phase of the hand. Study your opponent's and your own melds (if any) very carefully and think twice before playing.

When your opponent's point total is close to game, you must be extra careful about the point total (of melds or unmatched cards or both) in your hand. You must try to "keep under." That means that you must reduce your point total so that, if possible, even if your opponent goes Skarney, you will still prevent your opponent from winning the game. Just being aware of the necessity of keeping under will improve your chances of winning the game by 25 to 33-1/3 percent. Except for expert play, my observation is that every third or fourth final hand of a game is lost because of the avoidable failure to keep under.

It is, I take it, the author's privilege to point out—and the player's privilege to ignore—the fact that there are 15,820,024,220 possible ten-card hands in Skarney Gin. In every game there occurs a certain incidence of useless statistics. I don't expect you to remember how often in how many billion hands your present holding will occur. I shouldn't be surprised if you fail to remember that the odds of the dealer's being dealt one or more three-card melds in his first ten cards is about 15 to 1 in your favor—although remembering that will improve your game. To attempt to tell the player whether to hold possible layoffs in his hand or lay them off seems to be unsound without knowledge of (*a*) the card he holds, (*b*) the melds he sees (if any), (*c*) the cards still alive, and (*d*) the potential discards taken by one's opponent. As to this play, you must use your own judgment—as, in fact, you must learn to do in any hand at Skarney Gin.

20

Scarney Baccarat®

The World's Best Casino Card Game

Scarney Baccarat is the first really new casino banking card game in the past century. This new game, which I invented, combines the principles of the great casino game of Baccarat, Chemin de Fer, Baccarat-Banque, Bank Craps, and Black Jack, plus several entirely new game principles. Scarney Baccarat was first introduced at the Curaçao Hilton Hotel Casino in Curaçao, Netherlands Antilles, and spread rapidly to Nevada, England, Turkey, France, Italy, Yugoslavia, North Africa, and then around the world.

Requirements

1. A regulation Scarney Baccarat table with six betting spaces on its layout.

2. One to seven players, each of whom may bet on one to three hands, depending on the betting spaces available.

3. A card-dealing box called a shoe.

4. Four standard packs of 52 cards each, shuffled together and used as one, a total of 208 cards dealt as a single deck.

5. Two indicator cards. One is used by players to cut the deck and the other indicator card is used to determine the end of the deal.

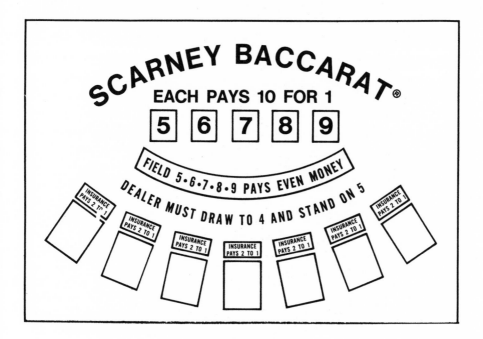

The table layout for the casino game of Scarney Baccarat.

Value of Cards

The ace is the lowest-ranking card and has a point value of 1. Kings, queens, and jacks have a value of 10 each. All other cards have their numerical face value. The deuce is counted as 2, the three is counted as 3, the four is counted as 4, etc. The suits have no value.

Object of the Game

Each player tries to obtain a higher total card count than the dealer by holding a combination of two or three cards totaling 9 or as close as possible to 9, or to a two-digit number ending in 9. *Examples:* 1 + 8 gives point 9; 2 + 5 gives point 7; 3 + 1 gives point 4; and so forth.

When the total of the cards is a two-digit number, only the last digit has any value. *Examples:* 10 + 9 gives point 9; 9 + 3 + 1 gives point 3; 1 + 3 + 10 gives point 4; 6 + 7 + 9 gives point 2; and so forth.

A player, at his proper turn of play and at his own discretion, regardless of the value of his two-card count, may stand or may draw a third card in an attempt to better his card count.

The Shuffle and Cut

The cards are shuffled by the dealer who then hands a player an indicator card and says "Cut please." The player inserts the indicator card into the deck to show where he wants the cards cut.

The dealer cuts the cards at this position, putting the indicator and all the cards above it on the bottom. The indicator goes to the bottom of the packet. The dealer then inserts the second indicator card sixty cards or thereabout from the bottom of the deck and places all the cards into the dealing box face down. The dealer next deals three cards from the shoe and puts them to one side out of play. The shoe is now ready to be dealt by the dealer. When the indicator card inserted by the dealer makes its appearance, and enough cards from below the indicator card have been dealt to complete the round in progress, the deal ends. The dealer must begin a new shuffle and must again repeat the above procedure.

Betting

Before the deal begins, each player must place his bet, in chips, in one of the rectangular betting spaces that are painted on the playing surface; all bets are in full view of the dealer. I repeat, players may place bets on one to three betting spaces providing there are available holes (betting spaces). When a player places bets on more than one betting space at a time, he must play the hand farthest to his right to completion before being permitted to play his next hand or hands.

The Deal

After all players' bets are down, the dealer, starting with the player on his extreme left, begins dealing clockwise. He gives one card face up to each player and one face up to himself. He next deals each player, starting with the player on his extreme left, a second face-up card and one face-down card to himself.

Player's Turn at Play

The player to the dealer's extreme left makes the first play of the hand. He may elect to stay or draw.

1. To stay: Either he is satisfied with his two-card count or he fears that a third and final card may reduce his count. He says "No card," "I have enough," "I stand," or "Good."

2. To draw the third and final card: When a player is not satisfied with his count, he says "Hit me," "Give me a card," makes a beckoning motion by closing his hand, or makes a come-on motion with a finger. The dealer then deals a third and final card from the shoe face up before the player and next to his original two face-up cards. A player is not permitted to draw more than one card. Each dealt hand remains in front of the player or players.

The play moves to the player's left, clockwise, around the table until all players have played out their hands. At this time it becomes the dealer's turn.

The Dealer's Turn at Play

After all the players have played out their hand or hands, the dealer must play his hand and abide by the following rules:

1. He turns up his hole card so that his two cards are exposed.

2. If his count is 5, 6, 7, 8, or 9, the dealer must stay. He is not permitted to draw a third card.

3. If his count is 0, 1, 2, 3, or 4, he must draw a third and final card, after which he must stay. However, if a dealer's three-card count totals zero (0), and is made up of three 10-count cards, he must continue to draw cards until his total count is anything except zero (0). This is called the *Scarney Baccarat* or *Baccarat*. With the above exception, every Scarney Baccarat hand is made up of either two or three cards.

Final Settlement

At the end of his play, the dealer starts with the first active player on his extreme right and moves around the table to the left; he pays off players who have a higher count than his with an amount equal to the bet they placed, and collects the placed bets from players showing a lesser count. If a player and the dealer have the same count, it is stand-off or tie, and no one collects or loses. A total three-card count has the same value as a similar total two-card count. *Example:* A 9-count made with three cards ties a 9-count made with two cards, etc. (The same holds true for a Scarney Baccarat hand comprised of 3, 4, 5, or more cards.)

Splitting Pairs

Any two aces, cards that are identical, regardless of their suits, may be treated as a pair. Also, any two cards each having a count of 10 (totaling zero) may be treated as a pair, such as two tens, two jacks, two queens, two kings, or a combination of any of the two above 10-count cards; such a combination is called baccarat. Each of the above pairs, at the discretion of the player, may be treated as the first card dealt of two separate hands.

A player being dealt two cards forming a pair on the initial round may, if he chooses, separate one from another and treat each card as the first card dealt in two separate hands.

When the pairs are split, the player's original bet is placed on one of these cards and an equal amount must be bet on the other card. The player is then dealt a second and final card face down on the face-up card on his right and then a second and final card face down on the other face-up card. When splitting pairs, at no time is a player permitted to draw a third card on any hand.

Players are not permitted to look at a facedown card until the dealer turns it face up after the deal has been completed.

The Double-Down Bet

A player after being dealt his first two cards (which may be any two cards) may elect to double his original bet before drawing his third card. This is known as a double down or *down for double*. A player at his turn of play, and before calling "down for double" or "double down," must place an amount equal to the original bet on the betting space. The player is then dealt a third and final face-down card on the two face-up cards. The player is not permitted to look at his face-down card until the dealer turns it face up after the deal has been completed.

The Scarney Insurance Bet

If the dealer's face-up card is a 9-count, players (at the dealer's turn of play) may elect to make an insurance bet against a loss or standoff to the dealer's possible two-card 9-count (9 + 10), called *Scarney*. The dealer, before turning his hole card face up, inquires if any player wants *Scarney insurance*. A player who desires insurance places an amount equal to half his present wager towards the center of the table.

After the dealer faces his hole card, and it is a 10-count, he calls "Scarney" and each insurance bettor is paid off at the rate of 2 to 1 for every unit wagered. If the card is not a 10-count, the dealer collects the player's insurance bet and the dealer continues to play out his hand.

The Scarney Baccarat Insurance Bet

After the dealer faces his hole card (at dealer's turn of play) and his initial two dealt cards are both 10-count, players may elect to make the Scarney Baccarat insurance bet. The dealer, before drawing his third card, inquires if any player wants Scarney Baccarat insurance. A player who desires the Scarney Baccarat insurance places an amount equal to half his present wager towards the center of the table.

After the dealer draws his third card, and it is a 10-count, he calls "Scarney Baccarat" and each insurance bettor is paid off at the rate of 2 to 1 for every unit wagered; the dealer continues to play out his hand. If the card is not a 10-count, the dealer collects the players' insurance bets and the hand is played out. If the dealer's third dealt card is a 10-count, a second Scarney Baccarat insurance bet is permitted. Should the dealer's fourth dealt card be a 10-count, a third Scarney Baccarat insurance bet is allowed; and so it goes, insurance bet after insurance bet, until the dealer fails to draw a 10-count card and the hand ends.

The Side Bets

Scarney Baccarat layouts have betting spaces marked 5—6—7—8—9, and above these numbers appears the phrase "Each Pays 10 for 1." Before a new deal begins, the player places his side bet by betting on a specified number or numbers, betting that on the next round of play the dealer's first two dealt cards will total the same count. The dealer pays off such winning bets at odds of 10 for 1. These wagers are also called *propositions*.

John Scarne seen playing Scarney Baccarat at the Hilton Hotel Casino in Curaçao where it was first introduced.

Field Bets

The field bears the numbers 5, 6, 7, 8, 9. When a player puts his bet on the space of the layout marked "Field," he is betting that on the next round of play, the combined total of the dealer's first two dealt cards will be 5, 6, 7, 8, or 9 as shown on the layout. The dealer pays off winning bets at even money. If the dealer's first two dealt cards total 0, 1, 2, 3, 4, the players lose their Field bets.

A dealer's two-card nine count comprised of a 9 and 10 is known as "Scarney." A count of zero with two or three cards is known as "baccarat." A dealer's count of zero with three or more ten-count cards is known as "Scarney Baccarat."

A player is not permitted to double down on a split pair.

Scarney Baccarat Strategy

Before giving a mathematical analysis of the game, I would like to point out that, in Scarney Baccarat, a player cannot bust his hand as in

Black Jack. A player's cards are always in play until the dealer completes his play and the payoff takes place. In Scarney Baccarat the house advantage is the result of the dealer's special play of the game called Scarney Baccarat. In Scarney Baccarat, if the dealer's three-card total is zero (0) and is made up of three 10-count cards, the dealer continues to draw cards until his final count is different from zero. This is the only time a Scarney Baccarat hand is made up of more than three cards. It is not feasible, of course, to figure the exact percentage against individual players because their playing differs so much. Some players will stay on a count of 5 or more; some will draw on 5 and 6; others stay on 4 or more; and there's always the hero who will hit a 7 and an 8. However, since the dealer has no choice as to whether he stays or draws, because the rules predetermine this, he must draw to a count of 4 or less and stay on a count of 5 or more. We can calculate the exact percentage for the house by having a player adhere to the dealer's fixed strategy of drawing to a count of 4 or less and standing on a count of 5 or more and not permitting a player to split pairs or to double down.

If the player adheres to the dealer's fixed strategy, and does not split pairs or double down, the house percentage in which a hand consists of a play of the game which terminates in a win, loss, or tie, is a low 2.44 percent. If a tie is not counted as a trial, then the house advantage is 2.71 percent. In other words, Scarney Baccarat will appear on the average of about once in 37 deals. I must reemphasize one fact you should not forget: The only positive advantage in favor of the bank is the 2.44 percent that it gains through a Scarney Baccarat.

There are several situations which, played properly, give the player an opportunity to cut down this house percentage. Most players handle these situations so inexpertly that, instead of reducing the percentage they are bucking, they add to it. Here are the playing factors which can be utilized to the player's advantage:

1. The player actually knows a little more than the dealer because one of the dealer's two initial cards is dealt face up; this gives the player important information about his possible card count. The rules governing the dealer's play prevent him from making use of similar information about the player's hand, even if the latter's first two cards were dealt face up.

2. Unlike the dealer, the player can stay or draw on any count he wants. At one turn of play he may draw to a count of 3, 4, 5, or more; and at other times he may stand on the same count. In some situations this is advantageous to the player.

3. The player can decide whether or not he wants to double down or split pairs, a strategy denied to the dealer.

4. The player may play one to three hands when there are available betting spaces; the dealer can only play one hand.

5. The player is the one who decides the amount of the bet and can raise or lower it at will within the prescribed betting limits.

6. The player may case the deck. If he can remember the cards previously dealt or exposed, this knowledge will greatly improve his chances of winning.

If you adhere to the strategy that I shall outline for you in the following pages, I promise that you can cut down the house 2.44 percent considerably. The strategy utilizes these factors: The dealer must hit a 4 or less and stand on 5 or more; the knowledge of the dealer's face-up (exposed) card; the player's total count; when it is to your advantage to stand, to draw, to split pairs, and to double down.

Playing according to the table below will assure you that you are fighting an average house advantage of considerably less than 2 percent. However, my strategy does not guarantee that you will win—it simply cuts down the house percentage to its lowest possible level and gives you a much better opportunity to win than any other method of Scarney Baccarat play.

SCARNEY BACCARAT STRATEGY TABLE

Hit-and-Stand Strategy

1. When the dealer's upcard is anything, stand on a count of 6, 7, 8, or 9.

2. When the dealer's upcard is anything, draw to a count of 0, 1, 2, 3, or 4.

3. When the dealer's upcard is 0, 1, 5, 6, 8, or 9, draw to a count of 5.

Splitting Pairs

1. Split threes when the dealer's upcard is 7, 8, or 9.
2. Split fives when the dealer's upcard is 1, 2, 3, 4, or 5.
3. Split sixes when the dealer's upcard is 0, 1, 2, 3, 4, 5, or 6.

4. Split sevens when the dealer's upcard is 0, 1, 2, 3, 4, 5, 6, or 7.

5. Split eights when the dealer's upcard is 7.

Doubling Down

Double down on a count of 4 when the dealer's upcard is 0, 1, 2, 3, or 4.

Double down on a count of 3 when the dealer's upcard is 0, 1, 2, 3, 4, or 5.

Double down on a count of 2 when the dealer's upcard is 0, 1, or 2.

Scarney Insurance Bet

Whenever the dealer shows a nine as his up-card, he will invite you to place an additional wager (called Scarney insurance) equal to half the amount already bet, which will pay you 2 to 1 if the dealer's down-card is a 10-count card, and which you will lose if it is not. In this optional bet, you are thus "insuring" your hand against the possibility of a loss to a dealer Scarney. In order for this bet to be a profitable bet, more than one-third of the undealt cards must be 10-count cards. This is not very often the case, so let's take a look at the usual odds. If the dealer's upcard is a nine, and you have no knowledge of any other cards, the quadruple deck would contain 64 10-count cards.

Suppose you do not look at your own cards, nor do you see any of the other player's cards, prior to taking the insurance. Then the dealer's downcard may be considered drawn at random from the 207 cards that remain unseen. Clearly, 64 of these cards are 10-count and the other 143 are not 10-counts. The odds are 143 to 64 against the dealer having a 10-count in the hole. The payoff is 128 to 64, approximately 7 percent. As a general rule, I don't recommend insurance betting. However, the casual card caser (counter) can use the insurance bet advantageously if he has been keeping track of 10-count cards in previous hands. *Example:* Suppose half the deck (104 cards) has been dealt and the casual card caser recalls that only 12 10-count cards have been dealt. If an insurance bet could be made on the next deal, it would be wise to take insurance because the player has an edge of more than 33 percent over the house on this bet.

Scarney Baccarat Insurance

The house advantage in Scarney insurance also holds true when placing a Scarney Baccarat insurance bet.

Proposition on Side Bets

In addition to the preceding wagers, Scarney Baccarat layouts have spaces marked 5, 6, 7, 8, or 9, and above these numbers appears the phrase, "Each Pays 10 for 1." A bet placed on a 5 means that the player is betting that the dealer, on the next turn of play, will hold a count of 5 with his first two dealt cards. The dealer pays off such winning bets at 10 for 1 and since the correct odds are 9-23/64 to 1, the house enjoys an advantage of 3.46 percent. The same house percentage holds true for the numbers 7 and 9.

When a player places a bet on the 6 (same rules apply as on the 9), he is again paid off at 10 for 1. But since the correct odds on being dealt a count of 6 in the first two cards are 9-43/62 to 1, the house enjoys an advantage of 6.48 percent. The same holds true for number 8.

Field Bet

When a player places a bet on the space of the layout marked "Field" he is betting that the dealer's first two dealt cards on the next round will total a count of 5, 6, 7, 8, or 9. The dealer pays such winning bets at even money. The dealer may be dealt 1,326 different two-card counts of which 632 comprise the field (5, 6, 7, 8, and 9) and 694 comprise the losing numbers (0, 1, 2, 3, and 4). When we subtract 632 winning two-card counts from the 694 losing two-card counts, we find the field bettor has a disadvantage of 62 two-card counts for a dealer's edge of 4.67 percent.

OPTIONAL DEAL RULE FOR SCARNEY BACCARAT

To help protect both casino management and players from being cheated by worn, bent, defaced or marked cards by either house employees or player cheats and to help avoid a conspiracy between both house cheats and player cheats, the following optional deal rule is recommended.

After all players bets are down (field and side bets included) the dealer, starting with the player on his extreme left, begins dealing clockwise dealing one card face up to each player and one face up to himself. He next deals each player starting with the player on his extreme left a second face-up card—but omits dealing himself (the dealer) a second card. After all players have finished playing their hands, the dealer removes (discards) the top card of the card packet and places it in the discard receiver without showing its face value. Next, the dealer deals himself his second face-up card and the standard rules follow. However, if the dealer's first up-card is a nine spot, he must inquire if any player desires a Scarney Insurance bet immediately after players have played their hands and prior to discarding the top card of the card packet.

Glossary of Dice Terms
and Gambler's Argot

ABOVE.   The earnings of a gambling enterprise that are listed in their bookkeeping ledgers.

ACCOMMODATION ARREST.   An arrest of a game operator or employee which has previously been arranged between the police and gamblers to make it appear to the public that the police are doing a good job. Also called STAND-IN ARREST.

ACE.   (1) The one-spot on a die. (2) One dollar. (3) A swell guy.

ACTION.   The betting. "There's plenty of fast action."

ADA FROM DECATUR.   Also EIGHTER FROM DECATUR. The point 8 in Craps.

AFRICAN DOMINOES.   Dice.

AHEAD.   To be winning. "I'm ahead fifty dollars."

ALL OUT.   Pushing the limit to win.

ANGLE.   An idea or method.

AX (There goes the).   Said when the house takes its cut.

BACKER.   The man who finances a game. Same as BANKROLL MAN.

BACK GAME (Backgammon). The strategy of not advancing runners early, but of using them to catch adverse blots when opponent is well advanced.

BACKGAMMON (Backgammon). The winning of a game when the loser has one or more stones on the bar or in the adverse home table.

BACK-LINE ODDS (To lay). A crap player having a bet on the Don't Pass line lays the odds on the point number. (Some casinos pay off this bet at correct odds.)

BACK LINE. See DON'T PASS LINE.

BADGE. A policeman.

BAGGAGE or EXCESS BAGGAGE. (1) A person who cannot pay his own expenses. (2) A person who hangs around the game but does not play. See LUMBER.

BAGGED. Arrested.

BANG UP (To). To close up a house or game.

BANK. (1) The house. (2) The dealer who pays off. Same as banker.

BANK CRAPS. A crap game played on a layout and in which no side bets are allowed, all wagers being made against the house.

BANKER. The dealer who collects and pays off bets for the house.

BANKROLL MAN. The man who finances the game.

BAR (Backgammon). Dividing line between the inner and outer tables.

BAR ON THE FIRST ROLL (The). A bar on one of the crap numbers, either the two-sixes, the two-aces, or the ace-deuce. If the number barred appears on the first roll, it is a stand-off for the wrong bettors and the money rides for a decision on a later roll.

BAR THE FIRST ROLL (To). A hustler's bet in which the first roll is a stand-off for his opponent. A losing decision counts for the hustler's opponent on that roll but he cannot win.

BEEF. A complaint. BEEF (To). To complain.

BEEFER. A consistent complainer.

BEHIND THE SINK. Broke.

BEST OF IT (The). An advantage.

BET. Any wager on the outcome of an event.

BET BOTH WAYS (To). To bet either right or wrong. "The table has two-way action because the players can bet both ways."

BET THE DICE TO WIN (To). To bet that the shooter will pass, to bet right.

BET THE LIMIT.   To bet the maximum amount permitted by the house or game rules.

BEVELS OR BEVELED SHAPES.   Crooked dice having one or more sides slightly rounded rather than flat so that the dice tend to roll off the rounded surface more often than the flat.

BIG DICK.   The point 10 in Craps.

BIG EIGHT.   A space (usually large) on the bank crap layout. A bet placed there indicates that the player is wagering that an 8 will be thrown before a 7.

BIG SIX.   Same as BIG EIGHT except that the player is wagering that a 6 will be thrown before a 7.

BIRD.   A sucker. Also PHEASANT, CHIPPY. See CHUMP.

BITE (The).   A request for a loan. "I put the bite on him for a fin."

BLANKET ROLL.   A controlled shot usually made on a blanket or bed.

BLOOD MONEY.   Money that was hard to get, that one worked hard to earn.

BLOW (To get a).   To be caught cheating.

BLOW (To).   (1) To leave. "I'll have to blow town." (2) To lose. "He blew the bet."

BLOW ONE'S TOP (To).   To become excited, angry, or to fail to realize what one is doing or saying.

BLOW THE WHISTLE (To).   To complain to the cops.

BOARDS.   The raised edge around a crap table against which the dice must be thrown. Also the RAIL.

BONES.   Dice.

BOOK, BOOKIE or BOOKMAKER.   The man who collects and pays off bets for the house. Usually referred to in Open Craps as the book, in Bank Craps as the bank.

BOUNCE SHOT.   A controlled shot in which the dice do not roll.

BOUNCER.   (1) The employee who keeps order in a gambling house and throws out unruly players. (2) A worthless check.

BOX.   The box or bowl in which the stickman keeps the dice on the crap table.

BOX-UP. BOX THEM UP (To).   The stickman mixes the dice and offers them to the player so that he may select another pair.

BOX CARS.   A throw of two-sixes.

BOXMAN.   The houseman who changes money at Bank Craps, giving new and easier to count bills for old ones.

BOX NUMBERS.   Same as OFF NUMBERS. A space on the layout

where each point number appears within a square or box. If the point is 5 and the player wishes to bet that 6 will be thrown before a 7, he puts his money on the box number 6. Usually called Place bets in Bank Craps and Off Numbers in Private Craps. In Open Craps either term is used.

BOYS (The).   Gamblers.

BRASS BUTTONS.   A policeman.

BREAK A GAME (To).   For one or more players to bring the game to a conclusion by winning all or most of the money.

BREAKS.   Good or bad luck depending on the circumstances.

BRICK.   A die that has been cut so that it is not a true cube. Same as FLAT.

BROKE MONEY.   Carfare home, given to the broke player by the house.

BRUSH OFF (To).   (1) To ignore or slight an acquaintance. (2) To get rid of someone. "I gave him a quick brush-off."

BUCK.   A marker used to indicate the point in a house game.

BUCK THE GAME (To).   To bet against the house.

BUCK IT (To).   To repeat a number previously rolled.

BUCK THEM (To).   To continue shooting after one has missed out (permitted only in certain crap games).

BUILD UP (To).   To gain a person's confidence usually in preparation for cheating or borrowing money from him.

BULL.   A detective or policeman.

BUM MOVE.   A suspicious action on the part of a player.

BUM STEER.   Wrong information.

BUNDLE.   A large bankroll.

BURN UP (To).   (1) Said of the dice when they are making many passes. See HOT. (2) Said of a person who is angry.

BUSTERS.   A pair of Tops (Mis-spotted dice). Tops are made in various combinations which make only certain numbers and are called Busters because one combination will bust up another combination.

BUST IN AND OUT (To).   To switch Tops in and out of the game.

BUST-OUT MAN.   A cheat whose specialty is switching crooked dice in and out of the game, usually Tops.

CACKLE (To).   To pretend to shake the dice fairly when they are actually under control.

CANE.   The crap stick used by the stickman to retrieve the dice after the throw.

CAN'T GET TO HIM.   Said of an official or politician who can't be bribed.

CAPPED DICE.   Crooked dice which have been gaffed so that some sides are more resilient than others.

CARPET JOINT.   Plush luxury gambling casino. Also RUG JOINT.

CASE MONEY or CASE DOUGH.   One's last bit of money.

CASE NOTE.   One's last bill.

CASTER.   The shooter in the old two-dice Hazard.

CATALOG MAN.   A person whose superficial knowledge of cheating devices is gained from the supply house catalogs.

CAUGHT UP (He's).   The boys are wise to him. He owes money, can't pay it and has no credit.

CENTER BET.   A wager made between the shooter and faders placed in the center of the playing surface.

CENTURY.   A hundred dollars.

C-NOTE.   A hundred dollar bill.

CHECKER.   A gambling house employee who checks on the luggers to see how many players they bring to the game.

CHEESE-EATER.   A stool-pigeon or informer. Same as FINK.

CHICKEN FEED.   Small change. An insignificant amount of money.

CHILL (To).   To lose interest. "He chilled on me."

CHIP, CHECK.   (1) A token used for betting purposes in place of money. (2) To place chips on a betting layout or to put chips in the pot.

CHIPS (IN THE).   Said of a gambler who has a lot of money.

CHIPPY.   (1) A sucker. (2) An inexperienced player.

CHOPPER.   The cutter in a dice game.

CHUMP.   A sucker. Also, mark, monkey, pheasant, bird, greenie, etc.

CIGAR.   A bawling out.

CLAM UP (To).   To refuse to talk or divulge information.

CLEAN (To).   (1) To rid oneself of any incriminating object. (2) To take all a player's money. "They cleaned him out" or "They took him to the cleaner's."

CLEAN MOVE.   A cleverly executed cheating move.

CLEAR (IN THE).   (1) Free of debt. (2) Innocent of any wrong-doing.

CLIP (To).   To cheat.

COCKED DICE.   Some players do not count the throw and consider it "no dice" if one or more of the cubes come to rest on an irregular surface so that it is difficult to decide which surface is the skyward one. Not recommended. See Rules.

COLD.   Said of dice when they are making more missouts than passes. ICE-COLD. Missing out constantly.

COLD PLAYER.   Player on a losing streak. "He's cold as ice."

COMBINATION.   A syndicate of gamblers.

COME BET.   A bet made after the shooter has come-out on a point, the next roll to be considered to be the same as a come-out roll.

COME-OUT BET.   A bet made on a specific number or on a group of numbers that the number or one of the group will be thrown on the next roll of the dice.

COME-OUT, COME-OUT ROLL (The).   The first throw after a shooter's decision.

COMING OUT!   The stickman's cry that the dice are about to be thrown—a warning to the players to get their bets down.

COMPLIMENTARY PLAY.   A gambling session indulged in by a casino manager in a rival casino or by a bigtime gambler or racketeer as a gesture of friendship toward the casino bosses.

CON ARTIST.   A cheap gambler who tries to borrow money on the strength of a story.

COP (To).   To steal.

COP A SNEAK or COP A MOPE (To).   To depart.

CORKER.   A gambler who is unusual, either good or bad.

COVER (To).   To accept a wager by matching the money either at even money or at odds.

COWBOY.   A reckless or fast gambler.

CRAB.   A losing throw of 2, 3 and sometimes 12 in the two-dice Hazard.

CRAP DEALER.   A crap-table employee who collects and pays off winning and losing bets for the house.

CRAP HUSTLER.   A player who gets the best of it by offering sucker bets.

CRAP.   The numbers 2, 3 and 12.

CRAPS.   (1) The game. (2) The dice.

CRAP OUT.   To roll a 2, 3, or 12 on the first roll.

CREAMPUFF.   A soft-hearted, easy-going person.

CREEP.   An undesirable player or person.

CROSS (The).   A different twist or angle applied to a cheating method so that the cheater is cheated. "Every gaff has its cross."

CROSSROADER.   A card cheat who travels over the country seeking card games in which he can ply his trade.

CRUISING.   Looking for suckers.

CRUMB.   A small-time chiseler.

CRY ACT (The).   Pretending that one always loses—a hustler's habit.

CRY COP or HOLLER COP (To).   To complain to the cops.

CUCUMBER.   A sucker, an especially green one.

CUP.   A leather receptacle in which dice are shaken.

CUT.   (1) A charge taken out by the operator of a game. (2) A share.

CUT-EDGE DICE.   Crooked dice with some edges cut at a 60 degree angle and others at a 45 degree angle. They tend to fall in the direction of the 60 degree cut more often than the 45 degree cut.

CUTER.   Twenty-five cents.

CUTTER.   An operator who charges the shooter when he makes one or more passes and sometimes the wrong player when he refuses to shoot the dice in his turn.

CUT UP JACKPOTS (To).   To talk about previous big winnings, usually with exaggeration.

CUT UP A WIN (To).   To divide the money won.

CUT UP A TOUCH (To).   To divide money obtained by cheating.

DEAD HEAD.   A non-player, the implication being that he is broke.

DEALER.   The bookmaker or banker.

DEAL (To).   To collect from losers and pay off winners. "Sam is dealing the big table tonight."

DEUCE.   (1) Two dollars. (2) The two-spot on a die.

DICE ARE OFF (The).   Said of dice which are not true, either because they are cheap dice or because they are crooked.

DICE DEGENERATE.   Compulsive crap player who can't control his urge to gamble.

DICE MOB.   A group of dice cheats who operate crooked dice games.

DICE PICKER.   A houseman whose job is to pick up the dice that have fallen from the table.

DIMER.   A ten cent piece.

DON'T COME BET.   A bet, the next roll to be considered as a come-out, that the dice will lose.

DON'T PASS LINE.   A space on the layout. Money placed there is a bet that the shooter does not pass.

"DON'T SELL HIM SHORT." Said of a person who has more brains or ability than is immediately apparent.

DOORMAN. Employee who admits players to the gambling room.

DOOR POPS. Mis-spotted dice that make seven or eleven on every roll.

DOUBLE CROSS. To pretend to go along with an honest or dishonest proposition, then do just the opposite.

DOUBLE DEUCE or DEUCES. A doctored die having 2 deuces, the extra deuce taking the place of a 5.

DOUBLE FIVE or FIVES. A doctored die having 2 fives, the extra 5-spot taking the place of the 2-spot.

DOUBLING UP. To double the size of a previous bet on the next wager. Many betting systems are based on this principle.

DRAG DOWN (To). To call back all or part of a wager just won and not let it ride on the next roll.

DROP BOX. A removable, locked cashbox located under a crap table. The money paid by players for chips is dropped into the box through a slot in the table top.

DROWNED (To be). To lose heavily.

DRY. Broke. THE TOWN'S DRIED UP. Most of the players are broke.

DUKE. (1) Hand. (2) (To) DUKE. To hand someone something.

DUMP (SOMEONE) (To). To avoid a former associate.

DUST HIM OFF (To). To flatter a player by telling him how smart he is.

EARBENDER. A talkative person.

EASY MONEY GUY. Anyone who gambles and spends money freely.

EASY WAY. To make a point number (4, 6, 8 or 10) any way but the hard way.

EDGE. An advantage.

EIGHTER FROM DECATUR. The point 8 in Craps.

ELECTRIC DICE. Crooked dice loaded with steel slugs and used over an electric magnet hidden in or under a counter or dice table.

END. A share.

ENGLISH. The simultaneous sliding and spinning action of the dice that is characteristic of most controlled shots.

EVEN-UP. A bet or proposition that is fifty-fifty.

EVEN ROLL. See Blanket Roll.

FADE (To). To cover part or all of the shooter's center bet.

FADER.   A bettor who has made a fading bet.

FADING GAME.   Open Craps.

FARO.   A banking game with cards in which cards drawn from the deck win alternately for the bank and the players.

FAST COMPANY.   Seasoned or smart gamblers.

FAST COUNT.   To short change and conceal it by a rapid count.

FAT.   Said of a person with plenty of money.

FEVER.   The gambling habit.

FIELD.   A space on the layout containing a group of numbers, either 2, 3, 4, 9, 10, 11 and 12; or 2, 3, 5, 9, 10, 11 and 12.

FIELD BET.   A bet that one of the group of numbers on the Field will appear on the next roll.

FILL.   A weight placed in a die. Same as LOAD.

FINGER or PUT THE FINGER ON. To squeal to the police or point out a cheat or crook.

FINGER MAN.   (1) One who points out a gambler to a holdup mob. (2) One who points out an illegal gambling game to the police.

FINIF or FIN.   Five dollars.

FINK.   A stool pigeon or informer.

FIRST FLOP DICE.   Dead Number dice used with the slick cup. Called "First Flop" because they are so heavily loaded that they will bring up the same number each time if properly thrown.

FISH.   (1) A dollar bill. (2) A sucker.

FIX.   Money paid to the police or some other official.

FIX IS IN (The).   The fix has been paid and protection is being received.

FIXER.   A person who has political connections through which he can secure the protection necessary for an illegal enterprise.

FLAG (To).   To call or signal a confederate.

FLAT.   A die that has been cut down so that it is not a true cube. Same as BRICK.

FLAT BET.   A side bet made among players that the dice will or will not win. Similar to Center Bet made between shooter and faders.

FLAT PASSERS.   Crooked dice which have the 6-1 sides cut down on one die and the 3-4 sides cut down on the other so that 4, 5, 9 and 10 appear more often.

FLEABAG.   A cheap hotel.

FLOATING GAME.   A game which is shifted from place to place in order to escape police detection.

FLOATS.   Dice that have been hollowed out so that they are off balance and act as do loaded dice. Called floats because they are so light they almost do float.

FLOORMAN.   The floorwalker in a gambling house. His duties are those of a manager.

FLUSH SPOT DICE.   Dice whose spots are flush with the surface, rather than countersunk, as is customary.

FOLDING MONEY.   (1) Bills. Also the OLD GREEN, the LONG GREEN, SCRATCH.

FOUR BITS. Fifty cents.

FREE BET.   A bet which permits a player who has made a previous bet on the Pass or Don't Pass line to lay or take the correct point odds equal to the amount he has riding on the line.

FREE DOUBLE-ODDS BET.   Same as Free Bet, except that right or wrong bettors with line bets can take or lay double the amount riding on the line. Found in very few casinos.

FREEZE OUT (To).   To force a gambler out of a game.

FRISK (To).   To search a man.

FRISK ROOM.   An anteroom where players are searched immediately after they enter a gambling house.

FROGSKIN.   (1) A dollar bill. (2) Paper money.

FRONT LINE.   Same as Pass Line.

FRONT LINE ODDS.   Taking the odds on the point number. Some casinos permit a player free action on this bet. See Free Bet.

FRONT MAN.   A person, usually without a police record, who is the apparent owner of a gambling operation. "He's fronting for the Cleveland boys."

FRONT-MONEY.   (1) Money that has been won. (2) Money used to make an impression on suckers.

FULL TABLE.   A crowded dice table.

FUZZ.   A policeman or peace officer. Also BRASS BUTTONS, FLATFOOT, BULL.

GAFF.   (1) Any secret cheating device. Same as GIMMICK. (2) The method or device by which dice are altered.

GAG (The).   See the HARD WAY.

GALLOPING DOMINOES.   A pair of dice.

GAMMON.   Loss of a game, when the loser has borne off no stones but has advanced all his stones beyond the adverse home table (Backgammon).

GATE (To). To stop the dice before they have finished rolling, usually when a roll appears suspicious; also done by superstitious gamblers on occasion to change the shooter's luck. Only done in private games.

GEE. A man.

GET BEHIND IT. To back up a crooked gambling move.

GET BEHIND THE STICK (To). For a dealer or stickman to go to work; i.e., to open the game.

GET OUT (To). To regain one's losses.

GET TO (To) (AN OFFICER OR POLITICIAN). To bribe an officer to avoid raids or to obtain a release.

GET YOUR FEET WET. An invitation to a spectator to get into the game.

G. I. MARBLES. Dice.

GIVE HIM A TOWEL. Said about a player who complains too much of his losses.

GIVEN THE DOZENS (To be). (1) To be short-changed.

GIVE (SOMEONE) THE ARM (To). To fail to pay a debt,

GIVE (SOMEONE) THE BUM'S RUSH (To). To evict a player rudely and hurriedly.

GIVE (SOMEONE) THE BUSINESS (To). To harm or cheat someone.

GIVE (SOMEONE) THE GO-BY (To). To ignore.

GIVE (SOMEONE) THE NEEDLE (To). To ride or kid some-one.

GO FOR IT (To). To be taken in by some scheme.

GO FOR THE MONEY. To cheat.

GOOD MAN. (1) A player with a large amount of money. (2) A good cheater.

GOOD THING. A good bet.

GORILLA. A tough guy.

GO SOUTH WITH IT (To). To put money in one's pocket either legitimately or illegitimately.

GRAND or G. One thousand dollars.

GRAVEYARD SHIFT. The early morning shift of a gambling establishment.

G-NOTE. A thousand dollar bill.

GREEK SHOT.   A controlled throw of the dice.

GREENIE.   An inexperienced player.

GRIEF.   Hard luck or trouble.

GRIND.   A slow and hard way of making money. "The hustler's life is a grind."

GRIFTER.   Member of the underworld who lives by his wits.

HANDLE.   The total amount of money that repeatedly changes hands in a betting scheme before it is actually won or lost.

HARD WAY (The).   The numbers 4, 6, 8 or 10 thrown with two duplicate numbers such as two deuces, two threes, etc. Same as The GAG.

HAS A SIGN ON HIS BACK.   Said of a gambler who is widely known as a cheater.

HAY.   Money, chips, dough, sugar, cabbage, lettuce.

HAYSEED, HAYSEEDER.   A farmer, bumpkin, or rube. A chump.

HEAD TO HEAD.   Betting between two players.

HEART.   Nerve. "He has plenty of heart."

HEAT IS ON (The).   The officials have ordered all gambling houses closed and the police are on the alert.

HEAVY.   A bigtime racketeer.

HEEL.   (1) A cheap gambler. (2) Anyone who is no good.

HEELED.   Carrying a gun.

WELL HEELED.   Said of anyone who has a considerable sum of money.

HEIST (To).   To hold up or rob someone by violence.

HEP or HIP.   Smart.

HEP-GEE or HIP-GEE.   A person who is smart (knows a lot) about gambling.

HEPSTER or HIPSTER.   Same as above.

HIGH ROLLER.   Bigtime bettor.

HIPE or HYPE.   Short change.

HIT (To).   To win money.

HITS.   A pair of mis-spotted dice that will not throw seven. They always make or hit the point.

HIT AND RUN (To).   To win quickly and withdraw from the game.

HIT IT (To).   To make the point or number desired.

HIT THE BOARDS.   Term used by the stickman when he requests the shooter to throw the dice against the dice-table rail.

HOLD-OUT ARTIST.   A gambler who, in dividing the amount of money won with his partner or partners, says that his winnings are less than they are and pockets the difference.

HOOKED (To be). To lose money.

HOOK UP (To).   To team up. "They hooked up with the combination."

HORSES.   (Obsolete except in the catalog.) Same as Tops.

HOT.   Said of dice when they are making more passes than miss-outs. RED HOT. Making passes constantly.

HOUSE (The).   The operators of a gambling game.

HUNCH PLAYERS.   Players who know little or nothing about the game on which they are wagering and who bet on impulse.

HUSH MONEY.   A bribe paid to keep someone quiet.

HUSTLER.   A player who gets the best of it by offering sucker bets.

ICE.   The money paid for protection.

ICEMAN.   A front man for either a gambling combine or the politicians and police, who collects the protection money from the gamblers and pays off the police and politicians. Same as BAGMAN.

IN THE CHIPS.   Said of anyone who has a lot of money.

IN THE CLEAR.   Free of debt.

IN THE HANDS OF THE PHILISTINES.   Indebted to loan sharks.

IN THE RED (To be).   (1) To owe money. (2) To be out money.

INSIDE MAN.   An employee in any gambling scheme who handles the bookkeeping or gambling finances.

INSIDE WORK.   Any gaff—loads, for example—placed inside a die or pair of dice.

INSURANCE BET.   Two or more wagers made at a crap table in an attempt to insure one or the other.

IT'S ON THE UP AND UP. IT'S ON THE LEVEL. IT'S ON THE LEGIT. IT'S ON THE SQUARE. IT'S A LEGITIMATE GAME.   Expressions signifying that the game is honest.

JIT.   Five cents.

JONAH (To).   To try to influence the dice with gestures or by talking to them.

JONAH.   One who jonahs.

JUG.   Jail. (In other underworld usage JUG means bank but this is not usual among gamblers.)

JUICE.   Electricity.

JUICE JOINT.   A steer-joint (crooked gambling house) where the table is wired and electric dice are used.

KIBITZER.   A spectator at any game who gives the players unwanted advice.

KICK.   Pocket.

KICKS.   Shoes.

KIDS (The).   Gunmen.

KITE.   (1) A letter (general). (2) A letter or note smuggled out of prison. "He flew a kite out."

KNOCK (To).   To make disparaging remarks.

KNOCKED OFF.   (1) Raided by the police; arrested. (2) murdered.

LADDER MAN.   A Casino employee who sits on an elevated stand overlooking a bank or money-crap or baccarat or chemin-de-fer table and whose duty it is to correct dealer's errors and to spot dice cheats. He occasionally alternates with the box man at the crap table.

LAMSTER, LAMMISTER.   A person who is hiding from the police or from underworld enemies.

LAP (To make a).   To leave the game and go out to get more money.

LARRY.   The player who has the last turn. "He's larry."

LAW, JOHN LAW.   A police officer.

LAY IT (To).   To lay the odds that the dice will lose.

LAY THE ODDS (To).   To bet against the dice (that they lose). The odds are 2 to 1 that a 4 will not appear and the wrong bettor who bets $2 that it will not be thrown is laying the odds. The right bettor who bets $1 that it will be thrown is TAKING THE ODDS.

LAY IT ON THE GREEN.   A phrase used by the houseman to indicate that the house will accept a check offered by a gambler.

LAYOUT.   A diagram with spaces designated for different bets. The players place their money on the spaces to signify what bets they are making.

LEGIT GAME.   An honest game.

LEGIT GUY.   A person who has no underworld connections; this does not necessarily imply that he is an honest man.

LET IT RIDE (To).   To leave the original bet and the money won on the playing surface and wager it again.

LIGHT.   (1) Insufficient amount. (2) Weak. "The P.C. is light."

LIMIT (The). The maximum amount that may be wagered against the house on any one bet.

LINE (The). The Pass Line.

LITTLE JOE. The point 4 in Craps. Also called LITTLE DICK.

LOAD. A weight placed within a die.

LOADS. Loaded dice.

LONG GREEN. Bills (money).

LOOKING FOR ACTION. Said of a gambler who is trying to find a game.

LOOKOUT. Gambling house employee who sees that everything runs smoothly.

LOOSE TABLE. A table that has only a few players around it.

LEFT AND RIGHT (To bet). To bet with the players standing on either side of one.

LUGGER. A person who transports players to the game. Not to be confused with steerer.

LUMBER. (1) A spectator at a dice-game. (2) A player who is out of funds.

LUSH. A drunk.

MAIN. An old term for point number from the English game of Two-Dice Hazard.

MARK. A sucker.

MARKER. (1) An I.O.U. (2) A buck, coin, card, etc., placed on a number space by the stickman to indicate the shooter's point.

MASON. A player who will not part with his money; one who is reluctant to make loans.

MECHANIC. A cheat skilled at dice switching.

MEMPHIS DOMINOES. Dice.

MICHIGAN BANKROLL. A large bankroll consisting mainly of one-dollar bills.

MISS. (1) A missout. (2) (To) MISS or MISS IT. To make a missout.

MISS A PASS. To fail to make a point number. "The shooter missed his pass."

MISSES. Crooked dice that are gaffed to make more missouts than passes.

MISSOUT. A losing decision for the shooter obtained on the come-out when a crap is thrown and after the come-out when a seven is thrown before the point number.

MONICKER.   Underworld nickname.

MONKEY.   A sucker.

MOUSE.   (1) A squealer; one who complains to the police. (2) A timid person.

MOUTHPIECE.   A lawyer.

MOVE.   Sleight of hand.

MUG.   (1) A low character. (2) A sucker.

MURDER.   Hard to beat. "That game's murder."

MUSCLE MAN.   (1) A tough guy or bouncer.

NAILED.   (1) Caught cheating. (2) Arrested.

NATURAL.   A seven or eleven thrown on the come-out roll.

NEW YORK CRAPS.   A form of Bank Craps played mostly in the Eastern states in which the player must pay a 5% charge for betting the box or off numbers.

NINETY DAYS.   The point 9 in Craps.

NO DICE.   A roll that does not count.

NUT.   Overhead or expenses.

NUTMAN.   A hustler.

ODDS.   The ratio of the unfavorable chances to the favorable chances.

OFFICE (The).   A secret signal or sign. Same as WIRE or SIGN.

OFF NUMBERS.   See BOX NUMBERS.

OFF-NUMBER BET.   A bet made at odds that the shooter will or will not throw a specified number other than his point (any of the numbers 4, 5, 6, 8, 9 and 10) before throwing 7.

OKAY.   Protection furnished by politicians enabling gamblers to operate; the "go-ahead" signal.

ONE DOWN.   The stickman's announcement that one die has fallen off the table.

ON THE BAR.   (Backgammon) Awaiting entry, said of a blot that has been hit.

ON THE ERIE (He's).   He's trying to eavesdrop.

ONE BIG ONE.   Gambler's term for $1000.

ONE-NUMBER BET.   A bet that a certain number or group of numbers will or will not be thrown before another number.

ONE ROLL BET.   A bet which is decided on the next roll. Same as a COME-OUT BET.

OPEN CRAPS.   A house game in which side bets among the players are permitted.

OPEN UP (To).   (1) To start a game. (2) To give information.

OUT IN FRONT (To be).   To be ahead money.

OUTSIDE (The).   The players as distinguished from the housemen.

OUTSIDE MAN.   A house employee who works outside the house directing players to the game, transporting them or soliciting business.

OUTSIDE WORK.   Anything done to gaff dice on their surfaces.

OVERLAY.   Said of a player who bets more than his bankroll warrants.

PACK UP.   To stop playing and leave the game.

PAD.   Payroll. "Everybody's on the pad."

PASS.   A winning decision for the shooter obtained on the come-out by throwing a 7 or 11 and on the point by repeating the point.

PASS LINE.   A space on the layout. Money placed there is a bet that the shooter will pass.

PASSERS.   Crooked dice which are so gaffed that they tend to make more passes than fair dice do.

PAYOFF.   (1) The collection of a bet. (2) Any final event.

PAYOFF ODDS.   The odds at which a bet is paid off.

PEG (To).   (1) To place a buck or marker on a number to indicate the point. (2) To place a person in a certain category. "We've got him pegged."

PEPPER.   A sucker who is very green. Same as CUCUMBER.

PERCENTAGE or P. C.   An advantage obtained through offering less than the true odds or by the use of crooked dice or controlled shots.

PERCENTAGE or P. C. DICE.   Dice that give the cheat a percentage in his favor.

PERCENTAGE GAME or P. C. GAME.   A banking game in which a favorable advantage is obtained through offering less than correct odds.

PERCENTAGE TOPS AND BOTTOMS.   A pair of gaffed dice, one of which is mis-spotted. One number, usually the deuce or 5, appears on the die twice.

PERFECTS.   Dice that are true cubes to a tolerance of 1/5,000 of an inch.

PHEASANT.   A sucker or inexperienced player.

PHILADELPHIA LAYOUT.   The first bankcraps layout to give the players an opportunity to bet the dice to win or lose.

PHILISTINES.   Loan sharks.

PHOEBE.   The point 5 in Craps.

PHONY. (1) A person who pretends he is something he isn't. (2) A crooked die.

PIECE. A share of the profits.

PLACE BET. A right point bet at Bank Craps.

PLAY (The). The betting. Same as ACTION.

PK. Psychokinesis. The "mind over matter" effect which Dr. Rhine defines as "The direct influence exerted on a physical system by a *subject* without any known intermediate energy or instrumentation."

POKE. A wallet.

POINT. Any of the numbers 4, 5, 6, 8, 9 or 10 which the shooter throws on the come-out and then tries to repeat before throwing a 7.

POINT BET. A bet at odds that the point will or will not be made.

POLLY. A politician.

POLITICIAN'S JOB. An easy job.

POSING DICK. A gambler who likes to show off.

POUND. Five dollars.

PRIVATE GAME. Any game which has no houseman or banker and in which no charge is extracted for the privilege of playing.

PROPOSITION BET. In private craps any bet not a Point, Off Number or Flat bet.

PULL DOWN (To). See DRAG DOWN.

PUNCHY. Punch-drunk—slow witted or mentally unbalanced.

PUNK. (1) A small time gambler or chiseler. (2) A young man, a novice.

PUT THE BEE ON (To). (Also to PUT THE BITE ON). To borrow.

PUT THE EARS ON (To). To attempt to make a controlled shot.

PUT THE FINGER ON (To). An undercover complaint to the police identifying something or someone as criminal.

PUT THE HORNS ON (To). To give a player bad luck by changing positions at the table, alerting a bet, or using any other superstitious device.

PUT THE PRESSURE ON (To). To exert force or strong persuasion in order to coerce someone.

QUEER. (1) Counterfeit money. (2) (To) QUEER. To upset someone's plans.

RABBIT. (1) A sucker or inexperienced player. (2) A timid person.

RACK. A box to hold chips or checks.

RAP (To). To talk ill of.

RAP. A prison term.

BUM RAP. A prison term served for a crime the convict did not commit.

RAT. An untrustworthy no-good.

READY UP (To). To get anything ready.

REAL DOUGH. A large sum of money.

RENEGE. To refuse to honor a wager or debt; to welch.

RIGHT BETTOR, RIGHT PLAYER, RIGHTIE. A player who bets the dice to pass.

RING IN (To). (1) To introduce crooked dice surreptitiously into a game. (2) To force someone in on another's plans; to "muscle in."

RING IN ONE'S NOSE (To have a). To be losing.

RIP (To). To switch dice, usually Ts.

RIPE. (1) Ready for fleecing. (2) Ready to make a loan. "He's ripe for a touch."

ROCK. A tight-fisted player who refuses to lend money.

ROD. A revolver or pistol.

ROLL (To). (1) To cast the dice. (2) To rob a person while he is drunk or asleep.

ROLLING THE BONES. Shooting Craps.

ROLLING FULL BLOOM. Said of a game that is getting plenty of action.

ROPE (To). To cheat.

ROSCOE. A revolver or pistol.

ROUGH IT UP (To). To bet heavily, thus livening the tempo of the game.

RUBBER. Worthless, said of a check.

RUNNER (Backgammon). A stone in the adverse home table.

RUNNING GAME (Backgammon). The strategy of bringing all stones into the home board as quickly as possible; the period of a game after the two forces have completely passed each other.

RUN STRONG. To operate a game or casino crookedly. "We couldn't pay the nut so we had to run strong."

RUMBLE (To). To get wise to or detect something crooked.

SAWBUCK. Ten dollars; a $10 bill.

SAWDUST JOINT. Unpretentious gambling casino.

SCARNEY BACCARAT. A new banking card game that combines the principles of Baccarat, Chemin-de-Fer, Bank Craps and Black Jack.

SCARNEY BANK CRAPS. A combination of Las Vegas Bank Craps and New York Craps.

SCARNEY DICE.   A set of five specially designed dice. Each die is marked with 1, 3, 4, and 6 spots, plus the word DEAD repeated on two opposite sides.

SCORE (To).   (1) To win at dice. (2) To succeed in any enterprise.

SCORE A BIG TOUCH (To).   To fleece a player for a large amount of money.

SCRAM (To).   To leave.

SCRATCH.   Money, funds; usually paper money.

SEND IT IN (To).   To make big or many wagers, usually against the house.

SETTLERS.   See FIRST FLOP DICE.

SEVEN-ELEVEN.   A bet made for a broke player by another player.

SKARNEY.   A new card game that possesses the bluff of Poker, partnership understanding of Bridge, scoring of Canasta and the flavor of Pinochle.

SKARNEY GIN.   A new two handed rummy type card game that is rapidly replacing regular Gin Rummy as America's favorite two-handed game.

SHAPE.   A die that has been cut down so that it is not a true cube.

SHARK.   A cheater who is skilled at making controlled shots.

SHARP.   Appearing well dressed and contented.

SHIMMY.   Chemin-de-Fer.

SHILLS.   Housemen who pose as players in order to stimulate the play.

SHOOTER.   The player who rolls the dice.

SHORT.   Without much money.

SHORTCAKE (The).   Short change. "I gave him the shortcake."

SHY.   Owing money on a bet.

SHYLOCK.   A loan shark, a usurer.

SHYSTER.   A cheap, unethical lawyer, especially a police-court hanger-on.

SIDE GAME.   A minor banking game in a large casino.

SIGN ON HIS BACK (He has a).   Everybody, even the chumps, know that he's a cheater.

SILVER-TONGUE.   A high-class confidence man. A good talker.

SING (To).   (1) To complain to the police. (2) To squeal or turn stool pigeon.

SINGLE-O.   Working alone.

SIX-ACE FLATS.   A pair of crooked dice (missouts).

SIXTY DAYS.   The point 6 in Craps.

SKINNER.   A cheater.

SLAMBANG.   Fast, plenty of action.

SLAMBANG (To).   To use cheating methods.

SLEEPER.   A wager or part of a wager forgotten by a player.

SLICK CUP or BOX.   A crooked dice cup gaffed by having its inner surface slicked or polished. Used with First Flop Dice.

SLICK DICE.   Crooked dice gaffed so that some sides have a smoother, slipperier finish than others.

SLICKERS.   Professional gamblers.

SLOUGH or SLOUGH UP (To).   To close a game or have it closed.

SLUG.   (1) A dollar. (2) The metallic weight used to load dice.

SMART.   Wise, familiar with gambling.

SMART MONEY.   (1) Money bet by the smart boys. (2) A smart bettor.

SNAKE-EYES.   The throw of two aces.

SNEAK GAME.   A game that operates without an okay.

SOFT.   Anything easy. "He's a soft mark." "It was a soft touch."

SOLID.   Right, good, okay. "He's solid."

SPELL.   A series. HOT SPELL. A series of passes. COLD SPELL. A series of missouts.

SPIN THEM (To).   To attempt to control fair dice thrown from the hand.

SPIT.   A small amount of money.

SPLITTER.   A crooked die which is substituted for one of a pair of crooked dice and changes them from Passers to Missouts or vice versa. It splits up one combination and makes another one.

SPOT.   To detect an irregularity.

SPRING (To).   (1) To pay the check. (2) To get someone released from custody.

SQUARE IT (To).   To amend something or make it right.

SQUARE A BEEF (To).   To satisfy a complaint.

SQUAWKER.   A chronic complainer.

SQUEEZE (The).   (1) The control that operates a cheating device. (2) Pressure or force. "We put the squeeze on him."

STAND.   A high platform on which the lookout sits, usually used only in big games.

STAND-OFF (A).   No decision. Also a 2-ace stand-off means that the wrong bettor does not win when 2 aces appear on the first roll.

STAND-UP GUY.   A person who can be trusted.

STEERER.   The person who locates and brings a sucker in to a steer-joint to be fleeced.

STEER-JOINT.   A crooked gambling house.

STICK.   A crap stick. Also an employee of the house who bets house money and pretends to be a player in order to attract business or stimulate the action. Also known as a shill.

STICKMAN.   A croupier at a dice table.

STIFF.   (1) An unlucky player. (2) A losing number.

STONEWALL JACKSON.   A tightwad.

STORE DICE.   The common garden variety of commercial dice. The term implies that the dice are imperfect.

STORM.   An apparent upset in the law of averages.

STREAK.   A run of good or bad luck.

STRONG ARM (To).   To use force. (A) STRONG ARM. A tough guy.

STUCK (To be).   To be losing.

STUFFED.   Having plenty of money.

SUCKER.   Any inexperienced person.

SUCKER BET.   A bet that supplies the operator or hustler with a high percentage.

SUCTION DICE.   Crooked dice having a concave surface.

SWITCH (To).   To exchange one object for another secretly. See BUST IN, also RIP.

TAKE (The).   The receipts of a gambling house.

TAKE (To).   To accept a bribe.

TAKE or COP A POWDER (To).   To leave.

TAKE IT (To).   To bet the dice to win by taking the odds.

TAKE-OFF CRAPS.   A game in which the cutter charges the shooter when he makes one or more passes and sometimes the wrong bettor when he fails to shoot the dice in his turn.

TAKE THE ODDS (To).   (1) To accept a wrong bet at odds. See LAY THE ODDS.

"TAKE YOUR BEST SHOT."   An expression which indicates that the speaker (a cheater) is allowing other cheaters to use any controlled shot they are capable of throwing.

TAIL (To).   To follow someone secretly.

TAP OUT (To).   To bet one's last bit of money.

TAPPERS.   Opaque loaded dice that contain a shifting load.

TAT (The).   (1) A confidence game in which a mis-spotted die bearing only high numbers is used. (2) Also the die itself.

TELEGRAPH (To).   To betray a cheating move prior to executing it, usually by some unconscious or clumsy movement.

THERE'S WORK DOWN.   An expression signifying that crooked dice are being used.

THEY'RE BURNING UP.   The dice are hot; they are making plenty of passes.

THIN ONE.   A ten-cent piece.

TAKE IT OFF THE TOP (To).   To pay out money from the total on hand before any division of profits is made.

TOP (The).   The officials who supply protection. "The word came down from the Top."

Ts, TOPS, TOPS AND BOTTOMS.   Mis-spotted dice on which some numbers are repeated.

TOUCH (The).   (1) The money obtained by cheating. (2) (To) TOUCH. To ask for money.

TRAP.   (1) A banking game. Term used by operators. (2) A bet that is not what it appears to be.

TRIM (To).   To fleece, gyp, clip, beat, etc.

TRIP DICE.   Crooked dice that are gaffed with edge work.

TUMBLE (To).   To get wise to something crooked. Same as RUMBLE.

TWO ROLL BET.   A bet which is decided within the next two rolls.

TWO NUMBER BET.   A bet that one of a specified two numbers will or will not be thrown before a 7.

UNPAID SHILL.   Casino operator's term for describing a consistent small money bettor.

UP A TREE.   Undecided.

VELVET.   Winnings.

VIGORISH.   A direct charge, usually 3% or 5% of the right money, made by the house.

WALKING ON HIS HEELS.   Dazed or punch drunk.

WAY OFF.   Very imperfect. "The dice are way off."

WEIGHT.   The pace of the game.

WHERE'S BUSTER BROWN?   The office given to the bust-out man to switch in the Tops.

WHIP SHOT.   A controlled dice shot in which the two dice are spun from the hand and strike the table surface with a flat spinning motion so that the controlled numbers are on top when the dice stop.

WIDE OPEN.   Plenty of gambling going on.

WINDOW'S OPEN.   An expression used by cheaters signifying that switching of dice is being done ineptly, and that the alternate die or pair of dice can be seen in the shark's hand.

WIRE (The).   A signal used between gamblers.

WIRE JOINT.   Crooked gambling house where tables are wired for electric dice.

WON'T BITE.   Won't take a chance.

WON'T SPRING.   Won't treat anyone.

WOOD or DEADWOOD.   Hanger-on, non-players, gamblers without money. Same as LUMBER.

WOPPITZER.   A kibitzer with halitosis.

WORK.   (1) Crooked dice. (2) The gaff or method of making dice crooked.

WORST OF IT (The).   A disadvantage.

WRONG BETTOR, WRONG PLAYER, WRONGIE.   A player who bets the dice to lose.

X (The).   Control of all the gambling in town. "The combination has the X on the town."

YARD.   One hundred dollars.

Appendix A

CALCULATING THE AVERAGE NUMBER OF ROLLS NEEDED TO EFFECT A WINNING OR LOSING DECISION

Since the naturals 7 and 11 and the craps 2, 3 and 12 can be made in 12 out of 36 ways, they can, in the long run, be expected to appear 12/36 of the come-out rolls, and 1 roll is required to effect a decision. The average number of rolls needed will, then, be 12/36 of 1 or .333 rolls.

The point 4 will be thrown 3/36 of the come-out throws. Then a 4 or 7 must be thrown to effect a decision. The number of rolls required will be the 3 ways a 4 can be made plus the 6 ways a 7 can be made, a total of 9 ways. The total of 36 ways divided by 9 ways gives 4 rolls. Add the come-out roll and we have a total of 5 rolls needed to effect a decision when 4 is the point. The average number of rolls needed will, then, be 3/36 of 5 or .416 rolls.

The same holds true for the point 10.

The point 5 will be thrown 4/36 of the come-out rolls. Then a 5 or 7 must be thrown to effect a decision which will require 3-6/10 rolls. Add the come-out roll for a total of 4-6/10 rolls needed to effect a decision when 5 is the point. The average number of rolls needed will be 4/36 of 4-6/10 or .511.

The same holds true for the point 9.

The point 6 will be thrown 5/36 of the come-out rolls. Then a 6 or 7 must be thrown to effect a decision which require 3-3/11 rolls. Add the come-out roll for a total of 4-3/11 rolls needed to effect a decision when 6 is the point. The average number of rolls needed will be 5/36 of 4-3/11 or .593.

The same holds true for the point 5.

Adding we have:

Naturals and craps		.333
The point	4	.416
	10	.416
	5	.511
	9	.511
	6	.593
	8	.593
Average number of rolls		3.373

This means that a winning or losing decision will be effected on an average every 3.373 rolls.

Appendix B

METHODS FOR COMPUTING PERCENTAGE ON
TWO-ROLL BETS WITH TWO DICE

Method No 1: Arithmetical

Step 1. Refer first to the Combination and Ways table on page 86 to find out in how many ways the numbers on two dice can combine to form the number or numbers the hustler is asking you to bet on. Suppose, as an example, that he wants to bet that 6 or 8 will not be thrown in two rolls. The table shows that 6 can be made in 5 ways out of 36 and that 8 can also be made in 5 ways out of 36. Together they can be made in 10 ways out of 36. The probability on any one roll that 6 or 8 will be thrown is therefore 10/36. Those numbers can be expected to appear, in the long run, 10/36 of the time.

Next find the probability that these numbers will *not* appear in one roll by subtracting 10/36 from 36/36. In the case of the numbers 6 and 8 this is 36/36 minus 10/36 or 26/36.

Step 2. To find the probabilities that the numbers will not be thrown in more than one roll, we multiply the probabilities for each separate roll. If the probability is, as above, 26/36 on one roll, it will be 26/36 times 26/36 or 676/1296 on two rolls.

485

Step 3. Since 6 or 8 will *not* be thrown on 676 out of 1296 rolls, it *will* appear on 1296 minus 676 or 620 rolls. The wrong bettor who is betting that the numbers will not appear has 676 chances in his favor as against the right bettor's 620 chances. The wrong bettor therefore has an advantage of 56 throws.

Step 4. The percentage is obtained simply by dividing this advantage by the total number of throws, in this case 56 divided by 1296. This gives a percentage in the wrong bettor's favor of 4.320%.

Method No 2: Algebraic

This is exactly the same except that it is expressed more compactly by a formula and can be figured quicker.

The formula is $\text{PERCENTAGE} = \dfrac{N^2 - (C^2 - N^2)}{C^2}$

N = the number of ways the number or numbers *cannot* be made in one roll.

C = the total combinations which, with two dice, is always 36.

Find the number of ways the number or numbers *cannot* be made by referring to the table of Combinations and Ways for the number of ways they can be made and subtract that figure from 36. Example: 6 and 8 can be made 10 ways and cannot be made in 36 minus 10 or 26 ways. N therefore equals 26. Substitute values of C and N in the formula and solve as follows:

$$\frac{26^2 - (36^2 - 26^2)}{36^2} = \frac{676 - (1296 - 676)}{1296} =$$

$$\frac{676 - 620}{1296} = \frac{56}{1296} = 4.320\%$$

Note that whenever the total number of ways the number or numbers cannot be made (N^2) are more than half the total combinations (that is when $N^2 > \dfrac{C^2}{2}$) then the odds are in the *wrong bettor's* favor.

When N^2 is less than half of C^2 the odds are in the *right bettor's* favor.

Appendix C

METHODS FOR COMPUTING PERCENTAGE ON THREE-ROLL BETS WITH TWO DICE

The problem is exactly the same as for Two-Roll bets except that in Step 2 (Method No. 1) the single roll probability that the numbers will not be made is multiplied by itself three times instead of twice. In the example given first 6 or 8 will not appear 26/36 of the time on single rolls and in three rolls will not appear 26/36 times 26/36 times 26/36 or 17,576/46,656 of the time.

Steps 3 and 4 are the same. To get the number of throws on which 6 or 8 will appear, subtract 17,576 from 46,656 for an answer of 29,080. Since the right bettor has 29,080 throws in his favor and the wrong bettor has only 17,576, the right bettor has an advantage of 11,504 throws and this figure divided by the total of 46,656 throws gives an advantage in the right bettor's favor of 24.657%. You will, of course, never hear a hustler offer this bet since he has much the worst of it.

The algebraic formula for computing the percentage on Three-Roll bets is the same as on Two-Roll bets except that the terms are taken to the third instead of the second power.

$$\text{PERCENTAGE} = \frac{N^3 - (C^3 - N^3)}{C^3}$$

Appendix D

TABLES OF ODDS AND PERCENTAGES FOR EASY REFERENCE

ODDS ON ONE ROLL OR COME-OUT BETS

Numbers	Correct Odds	Odds in Terms of $ and ¢ Bets	
Any Pair	35 to 1	$1.75 to .05	$35.00 to $1.00
11	17 to 1	.85 to .05	17.00 to 1.00
Any Crap	8 to 1		
5	8 to 1	.40 to .05	8.00 to 1.00
9	8 to 1		
4	11 to 1	.55 to .05	11.00 to 1.00
10	11 to 1		
6	6 1/5 to 1	.31 to .05	6.20 to 1.00
8	6 1/5 to 1		
Any 7	5 to 1	.25 to .05	5.00 to 1.00
1-2 (3)	17 to 1		
3-4 (7)	17 to 1	.85 to .05	17.00 to 1.00
5-2 (7)	17 to 1		
6-1 (7)	17 to 1		

ODDS AGAINST PASSING ON THE POINTS

The Points	Correct Odds	Odds in $ and ¢ Bets	
4 can be made in 3 ways; 7 in 6 ways	2 to 1	$.20 to .10	$2.00 to $1.00
5 can be made in 4 ways; 7 in 6 ways	3 to 2	.30 to .20	1.50 to 1.00
6 can be made in 5 ways; 7 in 6 ways	6 to 5	.60 to .50	1.20 to 1.00
8 can be made in 5 ways; 7 in 6 ways	6 to 5	.60 to .50	1.20 to 1.00
9 can be made in 4 ways; 7 in 6 ways	3 to 2	.30 to .20	1.50 to 1.00
10 can be made in 3 ways; 7 in 6 ways	2 to 1	.20 to .10	2.00 to 1.00

ODDS AGAINST PASSING THE HARD WAY

The Points	Correct Odds	Odds in $ and ¢	Bets
4 can be made with 2-2 in 1 way	8 to 1	$.40 to .05	$8.00 to $1.00
10 can be made with 5-5 in 1 way	8 to 1	.40 to .05	8.00 to 1.00
6 can be made with 3-3 in 1 way	10 to 1	.50 to .05	10.00 to 1.00
8 can be made with 4-4 in 1 way	10 to 1	.50 to .05	10.00 to 1.00

HARD-WAY BETS

The Bet	Bank Pays	Correct Odds	Bank's Percentage	Bank's P.C. on $5 Bet
4 with 2-2 10 with 5-5	7 to 1	8 to 1	11 1/9%	$ .56+
6 with 3-3* 8 with 4-4*	9 to 1	10 to 1	9 1/11%	.45+
4 with 2-2 10 with 5-5	7 for 1	8 to 1	22 2/9%	1.11+
6 with 3-3 8 with 4-4	9 for 1	10 to 1	18 2/11%	.91+

* Some banks pay only 7 to 1 on the hardway SIX or EIGHT and have an advantage of 27⁳⁄₁₁%, or $1.36 on a $5 wager.

BANK'S PERCENTAGES ON ONE ROLL OR COME-OUT BETS

The Bet	Bank Pays	Correct Odds	Bank's P.C.	Bank's P.C. on $5 Wager
Two Sixes (6-6) Two Aces (1-1)	30 to 1	35 to 1	13 8/9%	$.69*
Eleven (6-5) Three (1-2)	15 to 1	17 to 1	11 1/9%	.56
All Sevens (7)	4 to 1	5 to 1	16 2/3%	.83
Any Crap (2, 3 or 12)	7 to 1	8 to 1	11 1/9%	.56
7 with 3-4 7 with 2-5 7 with 6-1	15 to 1	17 to 1	11 1/9%	.56

The following one roll bets are listed because some smaller banks carry only proposition bets on their layouts and include all possible One-Roll bets.

The Bet	Bank Pays	Correct Odds	Bank's P.C.	Bank's P.C. on $5 Wager
4 in one roll 10 in one roll	9 to 1	11 to 1	16 2/3%	.83
6 in one roll 8 in one roll	5 to 1	6 1/5 to 1	16 2/3%	.83
5 in one roll 9 in one roll	7 to 1	8 to 1	11 1/9%	.56

* The actual figures for the Bank's P.C. on a $5 wager are fractional and have been computed here to the nearest cent.

THE BANK'S P.C. ON BANK CRAP BETS

Bet	P.C. in Bank's Favor	Bank's P.C. on $5 Bet
Win (pass)	1.414%	$.07*
Come	1.414	.07
Lose (don't pass), Bar 6-6 or 1-1	1.402	.07
Don't Come, Bar 6-6 or 1-1	1.402	.07
Lose (don't pass) Bar 1-2	4.385	.22
Don't Come, Bar 1-2	4.385	.22
POINT BETS		
Bank lays 9 to 5 on 4 or 10	6.666	.33
Bank lays 7 to 5 on 5 or 9	4.000	.20
Bank lays 7 to 6 on 6 or 8	1.515	.08
FIELD BETS		
Field (Nos. 2, 3, 4, 9, 10, 11, 12)	11.111	.56
Field (Nos. 2, 3, 4, 9, 10, 11, 12 with double payoff on 2 and 12)	5.263	.26
Field (Nos. 2, 3, 5, 9, 10, 11, 12)	5.555	.27
Big Six	9.090	.45
Big Eight	9.090	.45
TWO WAY BET		
Win (pass) Line plus free point bet to win	.848	.04
Lose (don't pass) plus free point bet to lose	.832	.04

5% and 3% charge P.C. (see Open Craps, p. 157).

----

* The bank's edge on a $5 wager given in cents has in each case (except for the point bet on numbers 5 and 9) a plus fraction which we have omitted.

CORRECT VIGORISH ON THE ODDS WAGERS WHEN THE BOOK PICKS UP THE 5% CHARGE ON RIGHT ACTION AND LETS IT RIDE ON WRONG ACTION

RIGHT BETTOR

Pays 4.761 19/21% or .25¢ on a $5.25 bet on all points

WRONG BETTOR

Pays .813 1/123% or .04¢ on a $5 bet on 4 or 10
Pays 1.290 10/31% or .06¢ on a $5 bet on 5 or 9
Pays 1.818 2/11% or .09¢ on a $5 bet on 6 or 8

CORRECT VIGORISH WHEN THE BOOK PICKS UP THE 5% CHARGE BOTH WAYS

RIGHT BETTOR

Pays 4.761 19/21% or .25¢ on a $5.25 bet on all points

WRONG BETTOR

Pays 2.439 1/41% or .12¢ on a $5 bet on 4 or 10
Pays 3.225 25/31% or .16¢ on a $5 bet on 5 or 9
Pays 4.000% or .20¢ on a $5 bet on 6 or 8

CORRECT VIGORISH WHEN THE BOOK PICKS UP THE 3% CHARGE BOTH WAYS

RIGHT BETTOR

Pays 2.912 64/103% or .15¢ on a $5.15 bet on all points

WRONG BETTOR

Pays 1.477 169/203% or .07¢ on a $5 bet on 4 or 10
Pays 1.960 40/51% or .10¢ on a $5 bet on 5 or 9
Pays 2.439 1/41% or .12¢ on a $5 bet on 6 or 8

SCARNE'S EVEN MONEY PROPOSITION BETS

BET EVEN MONEY THAT the shooter will or will not throw a

4	or	10	before	throwing	7
3	or	9	before	throwing	7
3	or	5	before	throwing	7
2	or	8	before	throwing	7
2	or	6	before	throwing	7
5	or	11	before	throwing	7
6	or	12	before	throwing	7
8	or	12	before	throwing	7
9	or	11	before	throwing	7
		4	before	throwing	10
		5	before	throwing	9
		6	before	throwing	8
2, 3	or	4	before	throwing	7
10, 11	or	12	before	throwing	7

ANY ODD NUMBER before throwing an even number
ANY NUMBER BELOW 7 before throwing any number above 7

Index